D1606048

THE EAST-WEST CENTER—officially known as the Center for Cultural and Technical Interchange Between East and West—is a national educational institution established in Hawaii by the U.S. Congress in 1960 to promote better relations and understanding between the United States and the nations of Asia and the Pacific through cooperative study, training, and research. The Center is administered by a public, nonprofit corporation whose international Board of Governors consists of distinguished scholars, business leaders, and public servants.

Each year more than 1,500 men and women from many nations and cultures participate in Center programs that seek cooperative solutions to problems of mutual consequence to East and West. Working with the Center's multidisciplinary and multicultural staff, participants include visiting scholars and researchers; leaders and professionals from the academic, government, and business communities; and graduate degree students, most of whom are enrolled at the University of Hawaii. For each Center participant from the United States, two participants are sought from the Asian and Pacific area.

Center programs are conducted by institutes addressing problems of communication, culture learning, environment and policy, population, and resource systems. A limited number of "open" grants are available to degree scholars and research fellows whose academic interests are not encompassed by institute programs.

The U.S. Congress provides basic funding for Center programs and a variety of awards to participants. Because of the cooperative nature of Center programs, financial support and cost-sharing are also provided by Asian and Pacific governments, regional agencies, private enterprise and foundations. The Center is on land adjacent to and provided by the University of Hawaii.

East-West Center Books are published by The University Press of Hawaii to further the Center's aims and programs.

MOVING A MOUNTAIN

MOVING A MOUNTAIN
Cultural Change in China

Edited by
Godwin C. Chu
Francis L. K. Hsu

ᚗ *An East-West Center Book*
from the East-West Communication Institute
Published for the East-West Center by
The University Press of Hawaii
Honolulu

Library of Congress Cataloging in Publication Data
Main entry under title:

Moving a mountain.

Papers originally presented at a conference entitled, "Communication and cultural change in China," held in Jan. 1978 at the East-West Center, Honolulu.
    Bibliography: p.
    Includes index.
        1. China—Civilization—1949-   —Congresses.
2. Communication—China—Congresses. 3. Propaganda, Chinese—Congresses. I. Chu, Godwin C., 1927-
II. Hsu, Francis L. K., 1909-   III. East-West Center.
DS724.M67   951.05   79-22037
ISBN 0-8248-0667-0

Contents

Preface vii

I. INTRODUCTION 1

1 Communication and Cultural Change in China:
A Conceptual Framework 2
Godwin C. Chu

II. COMMUNICATION SYSTEM 25

2 China's Mass Communication in Historical Perspective 27
Frederick T. C. Yu

3 The Current Structure and Functions of China's Mass
Media 57
Godwin C. Chu

4 Local Newspapers and Community Change, 1949–1969 76
Lynn T. White III

5 Small Groups and Communication in China:
Ideal Forms and Imperfect Realities 113
Martin King Whyte

6 The People's Commune as a Communication Network
for the Diffusion of Agritechnology 125
Lau Siu-kai

III. POLITICAL CULTURE 151

7 Communication and Political Culture in China 153
Lucian W. Pye

8 The Media Campaign as a Weapon in Political Struggle:
The Dictatorship of the Proletariat and *Water Margin*
Campaigns 179
Merle Goldman

9 Cultural Revolution and Cultural Change 207
Lowell Dittmer

10   Children's Literature and Political Socialization   237
     Parris H. Chang

                  IV. **VALUE CHANGE**   257

11   Traditional Culture in Contemporary China:
     Continuity and Change in Values   259
     Francis L. K. Hsu

12   Value Themes in Short Stories, 1976–1977   280
     Ai-li Chin

13   Peasant Culture and Socialist Culture in China   305
     Vivienne Shue

14   Communication and Value Change in the Chinese
     Program of Sending Urban Youths to the Countryside   341
     Thomas P. Bernstein

15   Communication and Changing Rural Life   363
     William L. Parish

                  V. **CONCLUSIONS**   385

16   The Communication System in China:
     Some Generalizations, Hypotheses, and Questions
     for Research   386
     A. Doak Barnett

17   Changes in Chinese Culture: What Do We Really
     Know?   396
     Francis L. K. Hsu and Godwin C. Chu

     Appendices

        A. Some Observations on Confucian Ideology   419
           Fred C. Hung

        B. Programs of Peking Television Stations   424

     Bibliography   427

     Contributors   437

     Index   441

Preface

In March 1976, several of us—Doak Barnett, Godwin Chu, Francis Hsu, Fred Hung, Daniel Lerner, Stephen Uhalley, and Frederick Yu—gathered for an informal seminar at the East-West Center. We discussed the trends of culture change in China since 1949, and the role of communication in the change process. It was the unanimous opinion of the group that the importance of the issues deserved fuller discussion.

The result was a conference, "Communication and Cultural Change in China," held in January 1978 at the East-West Center. This volume is a product of that conference.

Once the idea of a conference had been decided upon, the task of soliciting the papers fell on Barnett, who spent a year at the East-West Center in 1976–1977 as a Senior Fellow, and on Chu, who took over the logistic duties of conference coordinator. The enthusiastic response we received from scholars in a wide range of disciplines, including anthropology, economics, history, journalism, political science, and sociology, bespoke the vitality of the subject matter.

While social and political changes in China have received much attention among scholars in the field, this is perhaps the first time that these changes have been viewed through the prism of communication in the broad perspective of culture. Our effort, however, is simply a modest beginning. We hope it will be expanded by others who share our concern and interest.

Now a word of caution. This book examines changes in today's China in the context of social and cultural continuity. Despite many changes under communism as an ideology borrowed from the West—from art and literature to communization of land and Anti-Confucius campaigns—the Chinese are, in actuality, building a new political order upon a social and cultural foundation which is intrinsically linked with their own past. Since the visit of Vice

Premier Teng Hsiao-p'ing to the United States, there has been a rush of media and travelers' reports about changes of a different kind—the appearance of social dancing, bobbed hair, sexual laxity, Coca-Cola, and even the occasional Christian service in Peking by visiting American clergy. We remind the reader who is overly impressed by these reports about a few events in the recent past.

In the 1930s, when Generalissimo Chiang Kai-shek was baptized a Methodist, Western missionaries thought Christianization of China was imminent. In the 1950s, especially during the Korean War and McCarthyism, China was seen as inseparable from Soviet Russia. In each case, subsequent events proved the earlier expectations unfounded. Christianity, for example, did not prosper in pre-1949 China, despite the glamor and attraction of Western economic, political, and military power. It is unlikely to make any more headway in the future, however closely some Chinese clergy and their American counterparts work together.

We are not purporting to offer in this volume anything like the whole truth. There is so much that we do not know. We do hope, however, that the findings in the various chapters presented here will be considered in the light of the entire range of evidence, including that from the recent past, before any conclusions are drawn.

It is difficult to acknowledge adequately the generous advice offered by many of our colleagues, whose suggestions and opinions contributed substantially to the planning of this conference. We would like to express our thanks to Doak Barnett, who more than anyone else helped map the outline for the conference, to Ai-li Chin, for her suggestions on organizing this volume and preliminary reading of the papers, and to Wilbur Schramm, who gave encouragement to the initial idea in the fall of 1975 while he was director of the East-West Communication Institute. Jack Lyle, as Schramm's successor, has provided continued support. Fred Hung, chairman of East Asian Studies at the University of Hawaii, was instrumental in making this conference a joint venture of the Center and the University.

A note of appreciation is due our editorial consultant, Victoria Nelson, for her valuable assistance in preparing this manuscript. Funds for the conference and this publication were provided by the East-West Center, with a supplementary grant from the U.S. Office of Education administered through the University of Hawaii.

The views and interpretations, however, are those of the individual contributors and are not necessarily shared by the funding agencies.

As editors, we appreciate the understanding of our wives, Julia Chu and Vera Hsu, for demonstrating once again the traditional Chinese virtue of tolerance during the hectic summer of 1978 when this volume was put together.

GODWIN C. CHU
FRANCIS L. K. HSU

I
INTRODUCTION

Chinese culture, one of the world's oldest and for centuries one of the most stable, is now undergoing extensive changes that affect almost every aspect of Chinese life. These changes are unprecedented because they represent perhaps the first organized attempt in history to induce hundreds of millions of people to unlearn old ways of life and acquire new ones, all within a short span of decades.

Godwin C. Chu, a senior research associate at the East-West Center, offers a conceptual framework for analyzing the *what* and *how* of cultural change in China. He also seeks to explain *why* the Chinese Communist Party leadership has considered it necessary to use communication media as an instrument of cultural change.

1

Communication and Cultural Change in China: A Conceptual Framework

Godwin C. Chu

For nearly three decades, the people of China have been organized into a huge communication network in which they both receive and exchange messages on what new values and beliefs they should adopt in place of the old. The chapters in this volume will address themselves to the following questions:

1. What various processes of communication—the mass media, small groups, and interpersonal and organizational channels —has the Chinese Communist Party been using for the purpose of cultural change?
2. What new values, beliefs, and behavioral standards are being transmitted through the various communication channels to the Chinese people?
3. What is the extent of the traditional culture's influence on cultural continuity and resistance to change?
4. What are the effects of communication on behavioral conformity in the political arena and more lasting changes in social relations, values, and beliefs?

We hope that this collection of studies, even with the limited data available, will begin to illuminate the extent and process of cultural change in China.

We shall begin the discussion by presenting one hypothesis.

Chinese culture is now undergoing changes that touch every individual and every aspect of Chinese life. The Chinese are being urged to move out of the shadows of their ancestors and to pledge their loyalty to a new collectivity. The age-old custom of noninvolvement in extrakinship affairs is being eroded by a new norm of activism. Instead of following the Confucian ethic of interpersonal harmony, the people of China are being taught to accept conflict as a way of life and social progress. Innovation and national self-reliance are being espoused to edge out traditional conservatism.

A major mechanism of change in China is communication, the fundamental social process by which information is shared, sentiments are expressed, and human relations are maintained. Through communication, human groups maintain surveillance of their environment, coordinate and achieve their societal goals, and transmit the cultural heritage to the younger generation.[1] Thus communication functions as the basic cord of human interaction and reflects the substance of social life. In this sense, communication *is* culture. Sapir made this very point when he said that "every cultural pattern and every single act of social behavior involve communication in either an explicit or implicit sense."[2] Culture, even including artifacts and technology, finds its expression and becomes manifest through the symbolic behavior that is communication. Both perception and interaction, the crucial elements of communication, take place within the confines of culture and at the same time become its concrete embodiment.

The experience in China in the last three decades, however, seems to reach beyond this affinity between communication and culture. There, communication is more than a reflection of culture; it has been used as an active catalyst for cultural change. The idea that communication can be employed as a means of molding a new culture is not totally novel. If communication is the major coordinating and controlling apparatus of society, as the British sociologist Herbert Spencer suggested a century ago,[3] then it could conceivably be used either for maintaining the status quo or for setting a new cultural direction. However, while several historical figures have made attempts to introduce a new way of life by communication,[4] the experience of China deserves special scrutiny because it is a case in which the resources of the state have been vigorously mobilized to propagate new cultural patterns. Every conceivable communication channel in China—the Party's organizational hierarchy, the mass media, and small local groups—has been employed to carry the new messages, the new societal goals, and the new revolutionary values to the Chinese masses.

A Proposed Paradigm

Some elements of Chinese culture are undergoing changes and other elements demonstrate continuity. How do we look for clues that will help us organize our observations and make sense out of our data? We begin by examining patterns of behavior, viewing the other elements of culture as either instruments and products of behavior, such as artifacts and goods, or cognitive correlates of behavior, such as ideas and values.[5]

At this point, the question of cultural *diversity* versus *uniformity* needs to be briefly noted.[6] Individual differences in behavior and cognition exist among members of any cultural group, since no two persons are exactly alike. We assume, however, that despite the range of individual diversities, it would be possible and useful to identify elements of uniformity that are common to most members of a particular cultural group. It is this uniformity within a range of diversities that we are seeking as a basis of understanding the Chinese culture. Cultural change then refers to the process or trend by which part of the cultural uniformity takes on new forms.

With this distinction in mind, we propose to start our analysis of behavioral patterns with a hypothetical prototype, an approximate representative of the majority members of the cultural group. We shall refer to this hypothetical individual as the self, who is part of a configuration of diverse but related roles. In the self's realm of behavioral interactions, we can identify three broad *cultural elements:*

- Significant others, individuals in the self's social environment with whom he constantly interacts in various kinds of relations
- Materials and objects in the self's physical environment which he relies on for his survival and which, through the extent of technology, support and hence mediate his social relations (with the significant others)
- Ideas (including ideology and religious beliefs)—both cognitive and evaluative—which influence the way the self perceives his social and physical environments, and set priorities for his decision making in his social relations and in the manipulation of materials and objects in his physical environment

The relations involving the self, significant others, materials and objects, and ideas are graphically represented in the proposed paradigm (see Figure 1–1). Our behavior is predicated by our social relations, that is, relations with the various significant others in our

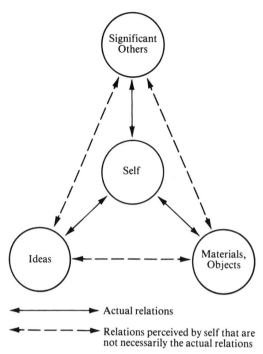

FIGURE 1-1. Paradigm of cultural components.

social environment, by our access to and search for materials and objects which we consider necessary for our survival, and by the values, beliefs, and behavioral standards which we hold. In the China of today, for instance, how a person behaves depends on his relations with the Party cadres and others who have the responsibility to supervise him, on the availability of material resources to which he may have access, and on the degree to which he has either accepted the new ideology or still holds on to the traditional values. For this hypothetical individual, ''culture'' is the unique manner of these relations, organized and integrated into a system in which he functions. The affinity between culture and communication lies in the fact that these relations are maintained and organized through communication.

The relations between the self and the three other cultural elements are direct and reciprocal.[7] These actual relations (represented by solid lines in the paradigm) are very much affected by the perceived relations (represented by dotted lines). The social relations between the self and significant others will depend, in part, on the self's perception as to whether the significant others are endorsing the prevalent cultural ideas which the self is expected to follow. Likewise, these social relations will depend on whether the self sees the significant others as cooperating in his pursuit of materials (i.e., significant others will aid his activities), or competitive (i.e., significant others are seeking the same objectives as the self), or antagonistic (i.e., significant others are opposed to his activities).

Concerning the relation between the self and ideas, the self often has to assess how his social relations might be affected, before he follows or rejects these ideas. Also, it is through significant others, whether by direct or indirect communication, that the self acquires his ideas in the first place and modifies some of his ideas later. In other words, communication with significant others plays a key role both in the process of enculturation and the process of cultural change.

The perceived relation between ideas and materials-objects can be important to the self's own relations with the materials-objects. That is, the self's pursuit of material objectives will depend on whether this goal is considered to be ideologically appropriate.

This paradigm does not assume that relations between the self and the other cultural elements are of equal importance. In reality, the links have different weights depending on the nature of a particular culture. In general, it is through social relations that the relevance of the two other cultural elements—ideas and materials-objects—becomes manifest. In the process of social relations, ideas are affirmed or rejected. And through these same relations, materials are processed and distributed for the maintenance of individual selves as well as the group. This perspective puts communication explicitly in the center of cultural processes, and suggests a clue to analyzing the dynamics of cultural change.

Process of Cultural Change

We can examine cultural change either descriptively or analytically. To study cultural change descriptively we need to add a time dimension to our paradigm. In China, for instance, we can describe these relations as they existed before 1949, and compare them with what they are today. Such a comparative study will show what aspects of Chinese culture have changed in the course of thirty years, both in the content and the pattern into which the cultural elements are organized. This is the *what* of cultural change. A number of the chapters in this volume present data to illuminate these two aspects.

To understand cultural change analytically, however, we need to know more than what has changed. We must examine the process by which the change has come about, thus answering the question of *how*. Having done this, we may then be in a position to speculate about the question *why*—that is, why changes have taken place in a particular manner in some aspects of the Chinese culture but not in others.

In discussing the process of cultural change, our premise is that a cultural system is generally in a state of transient equilibrium, in which the various relations involving the self, significant others, materials and objects, and ideas maintain a delicate level of symbiosis. A culture is said to be undergoing change when some or all of these relations are changing. This happens when (and because) some of the cultural elements have had new input. A cultural system is conceptualized as a moving rather than a static entity, although the pace of change varies.

We assume that the predominant patterns of social relations are highly resistant to change. Whether they are anchored in the self or oriented toward significant others, such as the primary group, these patterns tend to maintain their course unless changes occur outside their boundaries—either in the relations with materials and objects, for instance, due to innovations in technology, or in the sphere of ideas, initiated by ideological novelty of which the human mind is uniquely capable. In other words, we are suggesting that the initial impetus in cultural change will come either from new technology or new ideology, with its eventual impact on the relations between the self and significant others.

Regardless of the source of impetus, the course of change will not be smooth; it necessitates difficult adjustments. It is our contention that the way a culture responds to the forces of change will depend on (1) the impetus of change, whether it is originating from technology or ideology, and (2) the predominant cultural ethos that exists before a culture encounters the impetus of change. In short, we assume that certain cultures will respond more readily to changes that are technological in nature. When new technologies are introduced that change the self's relations with materials and objects, accommodating changes will eventually take place in social relations as well as in ideas. Other cultures, however, will tend to resist technological changes and will require fundamental changes in ideology before changes in social relations can become stabilized.

It is our hypothesis that in order to understand the process of cultural change—whether and how a culture responds to technological or ideological changes—we must examine the nature of relations between the self and significant others, because these constitute the fundamental web of human existence. These social relations, as reflections of the cultural ethos, hold the key to the dynamics of cultural change.

Role and Affect Relations

In any human group, relations will be varied. An attempt to identify the predominant features of these relations in a cultural group runs the risk of oversimplification. Such labels as "traditional" and "modern," for instance, carry a possible value judgment. To bring meaning and order to our diverse observational data, however, we need a conceptual framework. We begin by examining the basic nature of social relations.

Two broad categories come to mind. In any group there are various tasks that must be performed to contribute to the material subsistence and survival of its members, either directly or indirectly. Beyond task performance, any group must also maintain other relations that contribute to group cohesion and fulfill the affiliative needs of its members.

Various concepts have been proposed to distinguish these two broad categories of relations. Talcott Parsons speaks of instrumental versus expressive action orientations. George Homans refers to external and internal systems. Robert Bales has analyzed task performance and integrative functions of interactions.[8] For our purpose of understanding the process of cultural change, we prefer two concepts proposed by Francis Hsu, not only because they seem to distinguish most closely between these two categories of relations, but also because they suggest a way to examine both cultural change and persistence. These concepts are "role" and "affect."[9]

Role refers to relations that arise out of task performance or exchange of goods and services. Role relations are defined by rights and obligations that are specific to the task or exchange situation. They are characterized more than anything else by instrumentality. These relations are means to specific ends and ideally should not be affected by change of role performers. Occupational role relations are an example: a new staff technician should perform the same task and presumably carry on the same relations with his colleagues as did his predecessor. We assume that because role relations are task oriented, materials and objects are highly important to the continuation of such relations because they are essential to the task. Materials and objects are important also because they are usually the ends to which the role relations are the means. Technological changes can affect role relations because they can change the material basis of the task performance and at the same time bring about a redistribution of the material reward.

Affect refers to relations that are personal in nature and maintained primarily for their intrinsic, affiliative qualities. They are characterized more by feelings and emotions than by instrumentality. Relations of this nature are primarily an end in themselves, even though they can be and sometimes are pursued for the purpose of promoting other ends. Affect relations also involve rights and obligations, but these tend to be diffuse rather than specific to any task or exchange situation.

The term "affect" does not need to imply romantic involvement.[10] Many forms of relations are anchored in different shades of intrinsic attachment in which romance plays no part at all. The five *t'ung* (same) relations in the traditional Chinese culture are a good example. *T'ung tsung* refers to relations with individuals bearing the same surname, thus originating from the same ancestors "five hundred years ago," as the Chinese used to say. *T'ung tsu* refers to relations between individuals belonging to the same kinship network, which can be either direct or remote. *T'ung hsiang* refers to relations between individuals from the same native "place," which can be a rural district, a county, or a province. *T'ung hsüeh* refers to relations between individuals who went to the same school, or studied under the same master, not necessarily at the same time. *T'ung shih* refers to relations between individuals who had the same career affiliation, for instance, by once serving in the same government department. The last two *t'ung* relations had only a simulated kinship basis.[11]

Each of the *t'ung* relations carried its own kind of attachment which was meant to be permanent and binding. The rights and obligations may be less demanding in some instances than in others—something the Chinese who grew up in the old culture knew well.

Nevertheless, they were supposed to be lasting and mutual regardless of the specific role situations. For example, if someone wanted a favor of a *t'ung hsiang* that was appropriate to ask and that the other party was capable of giving, the latter was supposed to oblige even though his role should not permit it. Later, when the *t'ung hsiang* himself should need a favor, he would expect the same kind of accommodation from one of his *t'ung hsiang* who might be in a position to help.

Affect relations of this nature are specific to individuals but diffuse in their content of rights and obligations. Role relations, on the other hand, involve rights and obligations specific to the roles regardless of the role performers.

We prefer the role-affect distinction, rather than, say, Parsons' instrumental-expressive action orientation, because affect relations can be both expressive *and* instrumental. Although instrumentality is not the primary basis of affect relations, it can derive from the relatively lasting bond characterized by some form of affect. Furthermore, affect relations develop out of circumstances over which the individual has little control. For instance, one simply happened to be born in the same county, or happened to have the same surname. Even with *t'ung hsüeh* and *t'ung shih,* the relations were seldom consciously developed in the first place. All this illustrates that affect relations tend to be less flexible and more permanent than role relations, and thus less amenable to change.

Few relations are characterized exclusively by role or affect, though most relations are weighted primarily toward one or the other. Also, although both role and affect relations exist in all cultures, we assume that different cultures can be distinguished by the degree to which either role or affect is predominant.

Our hypothesis is that a culture with a predominant mode of role relations will respond more readily to technological changes, while a culture with a predominant mode of affect relations will respond less readily to technological changes. In the latter case, changes in ideology are necessary to alter social relations.

We have already noted that materials are essential components of role relations, both as a means to carry on the relations and as part of the reward. In a culture where role relations predominate, in which the social relations are largely based on relations involving materials, the element of ideology will generally be supportive of the material aspect of social life. When new technologies emerge that require new relations between the self and significant others, changes can be expected to take place in the ideology to accommodate the social relational changes. It seems that most Western cultures, which are sometimes characterized as "modern," evidence these tendencies in varying degrees. By and large, cultural change in the Western world has followed the initiation of technological innovation, accompanied by changes in social relations and by emergence of supportive values and beliefs.[12]

Affect relations carry various kinds of feelings and include expressions of care and concern. But these are the overt manifestations of affect, not the source that defines the expression of affect. That source, we submit, lies in that cultural element referred to as *ideas*.[13] The five *t'ung* relations in traditional Chinese culture illustrate this point. What types of feelings distinguished which kinds of *t'ung* relations, with what range of diffuse rights and obligations—these distinctions were all defined by the cultural ideas then current in China. This point can be further illustrated by the relations between husband and wife. While these relations contain elements of universal commonality in all cultures, the specific forms of affect that exist between a couple and the permanence of affect vary greatly according to the predominant ideas in a culture. We shall not discuss the divergent displays of affect but shall merely note the varied degrees of permanence. In traditional China, for instance, there was a popular saying regarding the wife's commitment to the husband: "When married to a rooster, follow the rooster; when married to a dog, follow the dog." That is, no matter what happens, stay with the husband.

In a culture in which social relations are permeated with affect defined in terms of traditional ideas, we would expect the relations between the self and materials-objects to carry relatively less weight. In a culture of this kind, the people would pay only secondary attention to the pursuit of material development.[14] Internal technological innovations would have relatively little chance to develop, while external technology would meet with resistance. Cultural change, if it occurred, would not likely be the result of technological change alone but would have to penetrate, in one way or another, the social relations between the self and significant others. The pace of cultural change would be slow and the process of adjustment would be difficult, because it would take time for the tradition oriented affect to be modified.

We have discussed this at length to illustrate that in a culture where role is the predominant mode, relations between the self and materials-objects will be accentuated while relations between the self and ideas will be relatively weak and readily changeable. In a culture where affect is the predominant mode, relations between the self and ideas will be relatively strong and stable while relations between the self and materials and objects will be less important. These observations are proposed as a hypothesis to conceptualize the process of cultural change in general, and to help us understand *how* and *why* Chinese culture in particular has followed its dual course of persistence and change.

Cultural Change in Traditional China

One way to understand a culture is to analyze the relative importance of role and affect relations and the degree to which they are compartmentalized or intertwined. Traditional Chinese culture was one in which role relations tended to be submerged under affect relations. The five *t'ung* relations we have discussed provide an example. Chinese bureaucracy, which should ideally be a structure of role relations, was in fact an intricate and delicately linked network of these *t'ung* ties. One had to be connected with part of the network to move around and get things done. If no such ties existed, the parties involved would seek to establish some basis of affinity through an "eight-line" *(pa hang shu)* letter of introduction from somebody already in the network. It was only after an affect oriented, personal relationship had been established that one would proceed to interact on a role basis and perform the necessary tasks. The same *t'ung* relations permeated private business.

Related to its strong affect orientation, traditional Chinese culture had another salient feature. This was its rigid social hierarchy. In the three cardinal relations *(san kang),* the ruler, the father, and the husband were superior, while the subject, the son, and the wife were subordinate. The same patterns held for teachers and students, masters and servants. Even among brothers and friends, younger ones were expected to defer to those senior in age. The Chinese were so conscious of hierarchical relations that when placed in a situation of unclear status definition they would seek to establish a hierarchy. For instance, it was a well-known custom for a man to address a new acquaintance as *lao hsiung* (older brother), and refer to himself as *hsiao ti* (younger brother). Indeed, few relations functioned entirely on an equal basis.

A cultural ethos of submission to authority underlay hierarchical relations.[15] What is important to realize is that submission to authority in China was not merely based on roles but was accented by affect and supported by traditional ideas. This can be illustrated by a Chinese saying: "[If someone was] once my teacher even for a day, [he will be] like my father for the rest of my life." That is, affection and respect will carry on, even after the student has attained a high position later in his career.

The whole thrust of traditional Chinese culture—the submerging of role relations in affect relations, the rigid social hierarchy, and the core value of submission to authority—contributed to the relative stability and endurance of Chinese society for centuries.[16] These cultural traits are rooted in traditionally defined affect as the basis of relations between the self and significant others. Because of these affect-oriented, tradition-based social relations, the Chinese society was able to withstand the many changes of dynasties, including a number established by foreign conquerors, and to maintain its general social organization over approximately twenty-two centuries since the days of Shih Huang Ti of the Ch'in Dynasty (221-209 B.C.).

Accompanying the slow pace of cultural change was China's neglect of technological development, which is understandable in the light of the secondary emphasis it placed on the relations between the self and materials. There was no scarcity of indigenous inventions in China. But most of them were simply buried in personal archives and ignored.[17] Those that gained broad circulation and adoption tended to be the kind that would improve transportation or working efficiency without requiring major changes in the social organization that would upset affect-oriented relations.[18]

This preoccupation with maintaining traditional social relations is most vividly illustrated by China's response to Western technology in the nineteenth century. China was stunned by the armored steamboats and powerful firearms of the European powers, who were considered to be uncultured barbarians. The brutal force of reality, however, made it obvious that China must adopt the alien technology to survive, but the efficient use of machines would require a type of organization that was role oriented and impersonal. This would mean seriously twisting or even abandoning the traditional, affect-oriented relations which had been dear to the Chinese. Despite all discussion of grafting Western technology onto the base of Chinese culture, the various efforts proved to be futile because a role oriented organization could not be built on an affect dominated foundation. One extreme response to this exercise in futility was the Boxer Rebellion. Frustrated by repeated setbacks, a sufficient number of Chinese leaders were blind enough to engage in an ideological fantasy in which the Boxers were relied upon to use their magic *kung fu* to overwhelm the Western artillery fire.

This dilemma posed by the tension between a strong desire to maintain affect oriented relations and the need for survival through technological development due to foreign encroachment could be said to characterize the stagnant Chinese culture from the Republic Revolution of 1911–1912 to the time the Communist Party took power in 1949.

Process of Change since 1949

Unlike its predecessors, the Chinese Communist leadership had no nostalgic concern about maintaining the old, affect oriented relations of traditional Chinese culture. Soon after Mao Tse-tung had entered Peking, he initiated a sweeping, nationwide land reform program based on the Party's previous experience in the border areas around Yenan. The land reform, undertaken between 1950 and 1952, changed economic relations by redistributing arable land from landlords to tenants. The social significance of the land reform, however, was meant to reach beyond the economic sector, because the peasants were organized through various communication strategies to take part in denouncing and deposing the landlords. Before the mass trials of landlords began, the peasants were called together by the Party's work teams to engage in "spit bitter water" sessions to arouse their emotional antagonism against the landlords. At the mass trials, the landlords were required to confess their wrongdoings in front of the entire village gathering.[19]

The purpose of these mass movements, in which the peasants were asked to participate, was quite separate from the redistribution of wealth. Rather, these movements were intended to destroy the affect oriented, hierarchical relations in the Chinese villages, in which landlords were deferred to by peasants both with awe and affection. What the Party wanted to remove was not just the economic influence of the landlords but also, perhaps more importantly, the traditional patterns of relations the vast rural Chinese population had been accustomed to. The humiliation of the landlord class was the first step toward establishing a new set of role relations in the villages according to the ideals of Communism.

It did not take the Party leadership long to realize, perhaps as a surprise, that the old social relations, with all their implications manifested in the five *t'ung* linkages, were difficult to erase. These relations had been part of Chinese culture for so long that most people brought up in that culture, including many members of the Party, were susceptible to it. Affect dominated relations, heavy reliance on personal connections to get things done, whether legally or not, and practices of favoritism and even undisguised corruption soon eroded the Party's rank and file.[20] The Party found it necessary to initiate self-cleansing campaigns, known as *San-fan* (Three-Anti) and *Wu-fan* (Five-Anti) in 1951 and 1952. In the rural countryside, there was a similar lapse back to the old way of life. Many Party cadres at the village level took advantage of the institutional vacuum created by the removal of the landlords and established themselves, in effect, as the new landlord class. The Party responded by launching a Rural Rectification campaign in 1953 to arrest this trend.[21]

In all these campaigns, the Party relied on the communication strategy of "criticism and self-criticism" to extinguish the undesirable tendencies that characterized the old affect dominated relations, and to establish the new behavioral roles of an ideal Communist Party member. It was around that time that the Party leadership became aware of an unexpected degree of ignorance about Communist ideology among many members.[22] Judging from the many ideological indoctrination campaigns waged afterwards, it was quite likely that Mao and some of his top advisers soon became convinced that they would have to lay a cognitive foundation of new ideology before new social relations could become firmly established. In terms of our conceptual framework, it meant that the Party would have to change the relations between the self and ideas before they could shift the relations between the self and significant others.

These events in the early days of the People's Republic may explain, at least in part, why Mao seems to have departed from the philosophy of Marx regarding the process of social transformation. According to Marx, economic relations, particularly control over the means of production, determine social relations. Consciousness —that is, ideology—is not ignored but is regarded as a mediating factor between economic and social relations. If Marx was right, then ideological indoctrination would not be necessary because, following the establishment of new economic relations, new social relations and new consciousness would emerge.

What Marx probably failed to realize—something which Mao in his native insight seemed to understand from the beginning—is the possibility that the Marxist theory is not culture free but culture bound. Whether the Marxist predictions would come true, would depend on the preexisting cultural foundation upon which the new economic and social relations were to be built. In a culture with a general ethos founded on role relations, in which man-material relations assume primary importance, changes in economic relations may foster changes in social relations and, eventually, changes in ideas and values in the desired direction. But in a culture such as the Chinese, in which affect based human relations assumed primary importance, merely changing the economic relations would probably not bring about the ideal goal of a Communist system. The experience in the early 1950s showed that even the power of the state could not twist social relations in China.

Because the old social relations contained strong elements of affect rooted in traditional ideas, a consciously organized effort had to be made not only to destroy the old affect, as in the land reform, but also to inculcate new values and beliefs. In other words, the economic structural change introduced by the Party in the 1950s cannot be assumed to have preceded the desired change in social relations and the emergence of new values, as Marx seems to suggest. Rather, the new social relations must have been actively initiated and reinforced by the deliberate introduction of new values and beliefs. This is the approach the Party has followed.[23]

The massive Chinese effort, in which the entire population has been expected to take part in a rigorous ideological learning experience, appears to be unparalleled anywhere else in the world. Chinese history tells us why such a rigorous and wideranging ideological approach would be necessary. Throughout its history, China has been exposed to various kinds of alien influence. The more notable were the Northern Kingdoms (386–581 A.D.) following the Han Dynasty, the Five Barbarian Dynasties (907–960 A.D.), the Mongols (Yüan Dynasty), and the Manchus (Ch'ing Dynasty). These alien conquerors, who were militarily strong, were somehow fused into Chinese culture. Unless a new ideological base is developed, the new economic and social relations which the Party has established may sooner or later be absorbed into China's traditional cultural mainstream.

The secret of this assimilative capacity seems to lie in Confucian ideology. The social philosophy of Confucius (551–479 B.C.) had relatively little influence during his own time. In fact, Mencius (390–305 B.C.) noted that during his time the Confucian philosophy was a minority ideology, merely one of the "hundred schools" that contended for the attention of the kings and rulers. The philosophies of Yang Chu and Mo Ti, for instance, had far greater influence among the intellectuals, while the Legalists were favored by the ruling elite. It was some four centuries after Confucius, during the reign of Emperor Wu of the Han Dynasty, that the Confucian ideology was salvaged from obscurity and elevated to a position of unchallenged ideological supremacy. (See Fred C. Hung's succinct discussion of Confucianism in Appendix A.)

The person who helped establish the lasting influence of Confucius was Tung Chung-shu (179–105 B.C.), a scholar personally selected by Emperor Wu to build an ideological foundation for his empire. Tung argued that the diversity of ideologies was a major factor contributing to political instability during the period of the Warring States. Emperor Shih Huang Ti of the Ch'in Dynasty, who unified China during his brief reign (221–209 B.C.), recognized this diversifying influence. But he followed a negative approach by ordering the burning of all books of classics, and burying alive upwards of 460 dissenting scholars. That was an ineffective measure. The Ch'in Dynasty, which was meant to last ten thousand generations, collapsed three years after the founding emperor died. Tung convinced Emperor Wu that his empire would be secure if it was built on a unifying ideological base that would lend support to the political and economic systems.

The ideology Tung advocated was a concocted version of the Confucian philosophy, couched in the somewhat mystic notions of *yin* and *yang* and the five elements of the universe.[24] The important historical fact is that, by preaching harmonious interpersonal relations in an inflexible social network in which authority was highly respected and in which each person kept his or her place, this ideology held the Chinese society together for some two thousand years, until the onslaught of Western influence. The enormous importance of ideology to Chinese culture did not seem to be unobserved by Mao, who was well versed in Chinese history.

The process of cultural change pursued by post-1949 Chinese authorities can be broadly identified in three stages. Each of these blends into the others, and all are still going on in some form. The primary emphasis of change, however, had progressed from the early prelude through the first major stage, to what seems to be the second major stage, up to the time Mao died. They are as follows:

1. *Prelude:* primarily change of self-material relations, exemplified in the Land Reform, the Five-Anti movement, and the Public-Private Joint Management program, with secondary attention to change of social relations.
2. *First major stage:* more concerted effort at changing the social relations, as in the Three-Anti movement, the Anti-Rightist movement, and the Socialist Education movement; these movements also contained some elements of ideological indoctrination.
3. *Second major stage:* still more concentrated attention on change of self-idea relations, as in Thought Reform, the Cultural Revolution, the May Seventh school program, and the *hsia-hsiang* (sent-down) movement.

In every stage of the change process, in every campaign, communication has been used extensively to impress upon the Chinese people the need for a new way of life and a new set of ideologies. The Chinese, young and old, are constantly reminded about the right way to behave and the right thought to entertain.

Events in China since 1949 suggest that a political group *can* introduce a new socioeconomic system without waiting for fundamental changes to take place in pertinent values and beliefs. In China's case, however, after the new socioeconomic system was introduced, efforts had to be made, through intensive communication campaigns, to facilitate the internalization of new values and beliefs in order to remove the ideological base of the old affect oriented relations and to secure a cognitive foundation for the new role oriented relations. While the initial measures taken by the Party authorities in the 1950s and early 1960s were largely addressed to the new relations involving the self, significant others, and materials (see Figure 1-2), the continuous ideological campaigns, particularly since the Cultural Revolution, have been directed more at establishing firm connections between the new ideas on the one hand, and the self, significant others, and materials on the other (see Figure 1-3).

The manner in which communication has been used by the Party

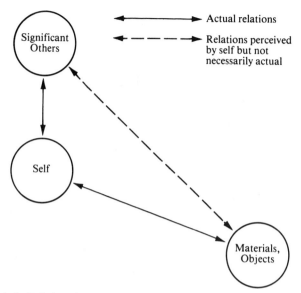

FIGURE 1-2. Relations between self, significant others, and materials.

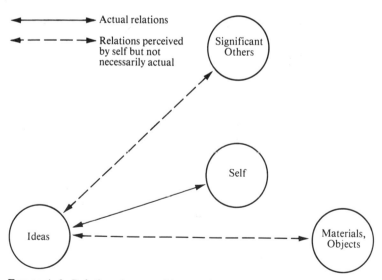

FIGURE 1-3. Relations between ideas and self, significant others, and materials.

leadership reflects in part the Chinese Communist theory of psychology, particularly with regard to the role of perception in human behavior.[25] This theory, perhaps following the thinking of Mao, assumes that the mass of people, if left alone, will not necessarily develop the desirable consciousness according to the Communist doctrine, because their eyes may not see "objective reality." In other words, objective reality is very much a perceptual reality, and it is the Party's role to provide the ideal context in which the ideologically sound elements of reality will be correctly recognized. Only in this way will the right kind of consciousness develop among the mass of people. It is in this perspective that we can begin to understand the many campaigns and movements in which all kinds of media are employed to deliver the Party's messages, so that only the correct perceptions regarding relations among significant others, ideas, and materials (the dotted lines in our paradigm) will prevail. These correct perceptions, in Mao's thinking, are essential to the learning of new values and beliefs, that is, the establishing of new relations between the self and ideas, which in turn will help secure the new relations between the self on the one hand and the significant others and materials–objects on the other hand (the solid lines in Figure 1-1). In short, *correct perception* holds the key to a new Chinese culture.

Several elements are relied on to facilitate this correct perception. First, the new values and beliefs are often presented in concrete terms through clearly understandable behavioral models rather than in obscure theories. Second, the messages reach a large multitude, even though with varying degrees of intensity. Heroes and heroines, as behavioral models, are chosen from among the common people so that there can be a broad basis of identification to aid acceptance of the messages. A continued vigil is observed to keep out competing messages lest the perceptual reality be contaminated.

Other measures have been taken to ensure *behavioral enactments* of the new ideas and to provide various kinds of *reinforcement*. In China, the people do not merely receive the new messages passively but are encouraged to be personally involved by publicly rehearsing and actively transmitting them, as a way of behavioral commitment. Emotional arousals—love for the people and hatred of the oppressors—are extensively employed to activate a process of catharsis and weaken the old basis of affect in social relations. To increase popular acceptance, interpersonal communication in small groups *(hsiao-tsu)* is constantly mobilized to apply group pressure and provide social reward.

How is current Chinese communication organized and how does it function? What is the impact of this massive effort on certain selected areas of Chinese culture? In what ways have the communication campaigns been effective in introducing new values and beliefs? What are some of the reasons why the effects have at times been less than expected? The chapters in this volume, by addressing themselves to these questions, will allow us to make some inferences about the nature of the emerging new Chinese culture and will help us assess the role communication has played in cultural change in China.

NOTES

I wish to acknowledge the critical comments and suggestions for revisions by a number of colleagues, particularly A. Doak Barnett, Ai-li Chin, Lowell Dittmer, Francis L. K. Hsu, William Parish, William Skinner, and Martin Whyte.

1. Harold D. Lasswell, "The Structure and Function of Communication in Society," in Lyman Bryson, ed., *The Communication of Ideas* (New York: Institute for Religious and Social Studies, 1948); also in Wilbur Schramm, ed., *Mass Communications* (Urbana: University of Illinois Press, 1960), pp. 117-130.

2. Edward Sapir, "Communication," in *Encyclopedia of the Social Sciences,* vol. 4 (New York: Macmillan, 1931), p.78.

3. Herbert Spencer, *Principles of Sociology,* vol. 1 (London: Williams and Norgate, 1876), pp. 437-442.

4. Two prominent examples come to mind: Confucius and Jesus. Each in his own way believed that human beings can be changed by communication.

5. For definitions of culture, see, for instance, Bronislaw Malinowski, "Culture," in *Encyclopedia of the Social Sciences,* vol. 4 (New York: Macmillan, 1931), pp. 621-646; Edward Sapir, *Selected Writings of Edward Sapir in Language, Culture, and Personality,* ed. D. G. Mandelbaum (Berkeley: University of California Press, 1949); and particularly A. K. Kroeber and Clyde Kluckhohn, *Culture, A Critical Review of Concepts and Definitions* (New York: Vintage Books, 1963), p. 357.

6. For a discussion of cultural diversity versus uniformity, see Anthony F. C. Wallace, *Culture and Personality* (New York: Random House, 1961).

7. A parallel between the elements in the proposed paradigm of culture and some of the familiar concepts in the literature may be noted. The complex network of directional relations between self and significant others which one constructs from the observation of a concrete group of individuals has been termed *social organization* by Raymond Firth. The general principle on which the forms of such relations depend, and which one abstracts from concrete observations, may be called the *social*

structure. See Firth, *Elements of Social Organization* (London: C. A. Watts, 1951). The commonality of shared ideas—knowledge, values, and beliefs, which Kroeber and Kluckhohn consider to be the essential core of culture—can be treated in this paradigm as the *cognitive foundation* of the social structure. It is part of our broader concept of culture. The distribution of and access to materials constitute the *economic foundation* of the social structure. Together, these three elements—social structure, cognitive foundation, and economic foundation—form the contours of culture. They are held together through communication and could conceivably change if the patterns and content of communication should change.

8. Talcott Parsons, *The Social System* (New York: The Free Press, 1951); George Homans, *The Human Group* (New York: Harcourt, Brace & Co., 1950); Robert F. Bales, "Task Roles and Social Roles in Problem-Solving Groups," in Eleanor E. Maccoby, Theodore M. Newcomb, and Eugene L. Hartley, eds., *Readings in Social Psychology* (New York: Holt, Rinehart and Winston, 1958), pp. 437–447.

9. See Francis L. K. Hsu, "Psychosocial Homeostasis and *Jen:* Conceptual Tools for Advancing Psychological Anthropology," *American Anthropologist* 73(1971): 23–44.

10. See Francis L. K. Hsu, "Eros, Affect and *Pao,*" in Francis L. K. Hsu, ed., *Kinship and Culture* (Chicago: Aldine, 1971).

11. Another strong tie of a rather peculiar nature, one that applied only to the literati of the past, was known as *t'ung nien.* This refers to individuals who passed a state examination during the same year, even though they had never met each other before. The lasting nature of these *t'ung* relations was indicated by the fact that they applied not only to the individuals directly involved but to their sons as well, under different simulated kinship terms. It is interesting to note that a comrade is called *t'ung chih* in China.

12. For a discussion of innovation as a cause of cultural change, see H. G. Barnett, *Innovation: The Basis of Cultural Change* (New York: McGraw-Hill, 1953).

13. Clyde Kluckhohn, for instance, speaks of affect-laden customs or traditions. See Kluckhohn, "Values and Value Orientations in the Theory of Action," in Talcott Parsons and Edward A. Shils, eds., *Toward a General Theory of Action* (New York: Harper & Row, 1962), p. 390.

14. This does not imply that people in such a culture do not enjoy material well-being. Our assumption is that in such a culture the development of material aspects of life receives relatively less attention. This is in contrast to a culture with role-dominated relations, which seem to be characterized with a "mastery-over-nature" orientation, as conceptualized by Florence Kluckhohn. See "Dominant and Variant Value Orientations," in Florence Kluckhohn and Fred L. Strodtbeck, *Variations in Value Orientations* (Evanston, Ill.: Row, Peterson and Co., 1961), pp. 1–48. In our paradigm no assumption is made about whether the self-material relations in Chinese culture are characterized by "subjugation-to-nature" or "harmony-with-nature" orientations, as discussed by Kluckhohn.

15. For a discussion of the Chinese cultural trait of submission to authority, see Francis L. K. Hsu, *Under the Ancestors' Shadow* (Stanford, Calif.: Stanford University Press, 1971). Skinner and Winckler are of the opinion that compliance is still the main characteristic in the interaction between the peasantry and the Party. See G. William Skinner and Edwin A. Winckler, "Compliance Succession in Rural

Communist China: A Cyclical Theory," in Amitai Etzioni, ed., *A Sociological Reader on Complex Organizations,* 2nd ed. (New York: Holt, Rinehart and Winston, 1969), pp. 410–438.

16. This does not mean that Chinese society did not change in the past. For a succinct discussion of some of the social and economic changes in Chinese history, see Mark Elvin, *The Pattern of the Chinese Past* (Stanford, Calif.: Stanford University Press, 1973). We are referring here to the enduring nature of Chinese society, which stayed intact until the advent of European colonial influence, whereas the Roman Empire and those prior to it had all eventually collapsed.

17. For some of the truly innovative ideas, see Joseph Needham, *Chinese Science* (London: Pilot Press, 1945); and Needham, *Chinese Science: Exploration of an Ancient Tradition,* ed. Shigeru Nakayama and Nathan Sivin (Cambridge, Mass.: M.I.T. Press, 1973).

18. For a discussion of some of China's technological development in the past, see Elvin, *The Pattern of the Chinese Past.* Nothing, however, was on the order of the new technologies that brought about the industrial revolution and major social organizational changes in Europe. Elvin has noted that China had attained a high level of economic development by about 1100, but the pace of technological advance slowed down after about 1350. Elvin has proposed his hypothesis of the high-level equilibrium trap to explain this phenomenon; see Elvin, pp. 298–315. For an alternative explanation employing the role versus affect distinction, see Francis L. K. Hsu, *American and Chinese: Reflections on Two Cultures and Their People,* 2nd ed. (New York: Doubleday & Company, 1970).

19. For an analysis of the social significance of the land reform and the roles of communication in that movement, see Godwin C. Chu, "Communication, Social Structural Change, and Capital Formation in People's Republic of China," paper 9, East-West Communication Institute, East-West Center, Honolulu, Hawaii, 1974.

20. The interim confusion in rural China due to the institutional vacuum following the removal of the landlord class has been analyzed in Godwin C. Chu, "Group Communication and Development in Mainland China—The Functions of Social Pressure," in Wilbur Schramm and Daniel Lerner, eds., *Communication and Change: The Last Ten Years—and the Next* (Honolulu: The University Press of Hawaii, 1976), pp. 119–133.

21. For an analysis of *San-fan, Wu-fan,* and the Rural Rectification campaign, see Godwin C. Chu, *Radical Change through Communication in Mao's China* (Honolulu, Hawaii: The University Press of Hawaii, 1977), chap. 3, "Communication and Political Socialization of Cadres," pp. 61–87.

22. For instance, in a survey conducted in 1951 of 109 Party members in four villages in Shansi Province, it was found that nobody had any idea how the goal of Communism was to be reached. *Shansi Jihpao* [Shansi Daily], August 22, 1951.

23. Martin K. Whyte has noted two conceptions in the current literature regarding the process of social change in China. One theory, stemming from Marxist theory with Maoist modifications, regards most traditional customs as the negative legacy of the class oppression inherent in China's feudal landlord system. Establishing socialism would eliminate the social basis of the old customs, but changes in social relationships, attitudes and customs would not be immediate. Ideological campaigns can accelerate the process of change by persuading the peasants to abandon outmoded customs. A competing theory claims that the traditional customs hold so

much cultural meaning and provide such harmony, security, and satisfaction that Chinese peasants continue to cherish them today. According to this view, the peasants will not make the desired changes unless forced to do so. The repeated campaigns staged by the government are aimed at coercing the peasants to abandon traditional ways. See Whyte, "Rural Marriage Customs," in *Problems of Communism* 26 (July-August, 1977):41–55.

The position taken in this Introduction does not impute either a persuasive or a coercive nature to the communication campaigns. It simply asserts that because of the affect oriented relations between the self and significant others and the strong support by traditional values, changing economic relations will not necessarily bring about changes in social relations and cultural ideas. Rather, an organized communication effort is necessary to provide a new cognitive foundation for a new type of role oriented social relations.

24. Tung Chung-shu capsulized the philosophy of Confucius into three cardinal relations *(san kang)* and five basic behavioral standards *(wu ch'ang)*. The three cardinal relations were those between ruler and subjects, between father and son, and between husband and wife. The five basic behavioral standards were humanity *(jen)*, righteousness *(yi)*, propriety *(li)*, knowledge *(chih)*, and faithfulness *(hsin)*. Tung then tried to strengthen the social validity of Confucian philosophy by anchoring it on the ancient mythology of *yin* and *yang,* and the five elements of the universe: wood, metal, water, fire, and earth. The ruler, the father, and the husband belonged to the *yang,* the superior, while the subjects, the son, and the wife belonged to the *yin,* the subordinate. Each of the five behavioral standards was supposed to have an inherent basis in the five elements: humanity in wood, righteousness in metal, propriety in water, knowledge in fire, and faithfulness in earth. While these correlations were neither intuitively clear nor systematically explained, they acquired, once endorsed by Emperor Wu, a sort of prima facie validity because of their mystic simplicity, and became readily accepted by the Chinese people. These ideas have had a lasting influence on Chinese culture. For a brief presentation of Tung Chung-shu's philosophy, see Richard Vuylsteke, "Tung Chung-shu: A Philosophical Case for Rights in Chinese Philosophy," in Richard Vuylsteke, ed., *Law and Society* (Honolulu: East-West Culture Learning Institute, East-West Center, 1977), pp. 303–313.

25. For a detailed analysis of psychological research in the People's Republic of China, see Robert and Ai-li Chin, *Psychological Research in Communist China: 1949-1966* (Cambridge, Mass.: M.I.T. Press, 1969).

II

COMMUNICATION SYSTEM

Understanding China's communication system is the first step toward assessing the role of communication in the process of cultural change there. Over the last half century, the Chinese Communist Party has developed one of the world's most extensive and best coordinated communication systems, despite the relatively low level of technology at its disposal. Much of the philosophy of communication, the use of criticism and self-criticism as a means of ideological reform, and the manipulation of communication in the Party's struggle for power and eventual military victory over the Nationalists—these and other strategies were developed in the tortuous growth of the Party since the 1920s. Throughout this period the influence of Mao Tse-tung has been predominant. Frederick T. C. Yu, professor of journalism at Columbia University, graphically catches the key points in the evolution of China's communication system.

How the mass media in China is currently organized to fulfill certain major functions is the topic of the chapter by Godwin C. Chu. Out of the major tasks assigned by the Party to the mass media, Chu identifies four functions: mobilization of the population for socialist reconstruction, information dissemination in support of mass mobilization, political power struggle, and ideological reform as part of cultural change in what Mao called "combatting the wicked wind." The important components of China's media include central newspapers, provincial and local newspapers, news bulletins in the communes, radio and television, and wall posters.

Lynn T. White III, associate professor of political science at Princeton University, delves into an area relatively unknown to the outside world—provincial and local newspapers as a major input for community change in China. Using materials largely from the late 1950s, before the flow of publications to Hong Kong slowed to a trickle, White illustrates some of the problems local newspapers encountered in selecting and presenting revolutionary messages to their audience. Even in a system as firmly coordinated as China's, however, total control of local newspapers was difficult to maintain because of the uneven conditions under which local newspapermen worked. As a result, local newspapers could at times strike a dissonant note in a chorus of near unanimity and concordance.

A key feature in China's communication system is the local small group, known as *hsiao-tsu*. While the vital role of personal contact as a linkage with the mass media has long been recognized by communication scholars and practitioners in the West, it remained for the Chinese to place interpersonal communication in the context of close supervision. How these small groups are organized and supervised, how they meet for various purposes, including criticism and self-criticism, and the effectiveness and limitations of this social mechanism are succinctly analyzed by Martin King Whyte, associate professor of sociology at the University of Michigan.

China's communication system relies heavily on formal organizational channels as well. One such channel at the grassroots level that is likely to play an increasingly prominent role in China's future is the dissemination network for agricultural technology in the communes. Using data collected during field trips to Kwangtung, Lau Siu-kai analyzes the organizational features of this communication network and discusses both its many strengths and some of its structural shortcomings. Dr. Lau, a lecturer in sociology at the Chinese University of Hong Kong, is a member of the University's Social Research Centre, which has been doing field research in Kwangtung during the last two years.

2

China's Mass Communication in Historical Perspective

Frederick T. C. Yu

To trace the evolution of the Chinese Communist communication system is easy in theory, difficult in practice.

Theoretically, to understand the history of a country's communication system is to study the development of its mass media. This normal—indeed typical—approach of Western communication researchers does not fit the case of China. We need to change the lens through which we examine Peking's communication system. Peking's concept of communication is not limited to the mass media and does not depend heavily on modern technology; it utilizes, shrewdly and systematically, such simple channels as hand-written *tatzupao* or "big character posters," blackboards, wall newspapers, streetcorner shows, storytellers, *hsüeh-hsi* or study meetings; it includes formal channels of education and every form of "criticism," "struggle," and "reform." The Chinese Communists have in a sense transformed all forms of communication into "mass media." To understand the historical background of this communication system is, in fact, to study virtually all feasible vehicles of human expression and every means of influencing attitudes and behavior.

This system is both an instrument and an outcome of the Chinese Communist Revolution. It is shaped by Chinese Communist politics and policies, by the personalities who control it, and by the problems with which the Party is confronted. In theory, anyone who tries to get a general picture of the history of Peking's communication system must have a clear understanding of the interaction of all these forces. This means not only a review of the growth of Chinese Communism but also an examination of some of the most involved and intriguing ideological clashes and power struggles within the Party during the last fifty-six years. One quails before such a task. Yet the effort must be made.

We will examine the development of the Chinese communication system in five successive historical periods.

The First Period, 1921–1927

The official birthdate of the Chinese Communist Party is July 1, 1921. At the Party's First Congress, which opened in the French Concession in Shanghai and continued on a boat on South Lake in Chekiang, three officials were elected to take care of "secretarial, organizational and propaganda work." Ch'en Tu-hsiu became the secretary; Li Ta was put in charge of propaganda; and Chang Kuo-t'ao, in charge of organization.[1]

The First Congress, according to Chang Kuo-t'ao, concentrated on "practical problems" and had only enough time to "touch upon" such things as a "Party newspaper to carry on propaganda work." But the Congress did discuss "the task of Party organs to propagate Marxism among the masses of workers through such means as publication of popular reading material."[2] The Party at this time had no communication system to speak of; many of its members were politically inexperienced and ideologically confused. Mao was not yet a leading figure in the Party. The moving spirits were Ch'en Tu-hsiu, Li Ta-chao, and others who had no practical revolutionary experience and whose greatest influence was on other intellectuals.

The Party's propaganda work gained momentum under P'eng Shu-shih, director of the Party's propaganda department, in 1924. He was, according to Chang Kuo-t'ao, "responsible for directing propaganda work within the Party, including popular propaganda, political propaganda, and cultural and educational activities for Party members." But the supervision of Party newspapers seemed to be in other hands. One detects already some jostling for power among the Party's chief propaganda figures during this period. Chang wrote:

> The editing of Party publications *Hsiang-tao Chou-pao* [Guide Weekly]—the main significance of which, the CC [Central Committee] felt, was to guide political guidance—was entrusted to Tsai Ho-sen and Chu Ch'iu-pai, with editorial policy being decided by the CC. Such work was not subject to interference from the Department of Propaganda.[3]

The present *People's Daily* had its roots during the early period. It was, according to an official Peking source, "the *Guide* in the

Period of the First Revolutionary Civil War (1924-27)."[4] Another important publication during this period was *Hsiang-chiang P'inglun (Hsiang River Review)*, one of the magazines published and edited by Mao. Still another was Ch'en Tu-hsiu's *Hsin Ching-nien (New Youth)*.

It is difficult to evaluate Mao's contributions to the development of the Chinese Communist communication system during this period. For obvious and understandable reasons, his role tends to be exaggerated by his official biographers. Already an experienced organizer when he joined the Party in 1921, he formed a number of organizations, including the Hsin Min Study Group in 1917 while he was a student at a normal school in his native Hunan. His work was primarily propaganda and agitation at this time, and many of his methods of revolutionary communication became common practice in later periods—wall newspapers, mass demonstrations, union work, discussion groups, night schools or literacy classes for workers and peasants, "youth corps," and many others.[5]

Perhaps as a result of circumstances rather than choice, Mao spent more time during this period on practical insurrectional politics than on theoretical study of Marxism-Leninism. He worked more closely with peasants, workers, and students of his own background than with the intellectual elite. He developed a practical approach to political and ideological problems.

In March 1927, Mao published his now widely publicized article "Report on the Investigation of the Peasants' Movement in Hunan." He had much to say about propaganda in this piece. He urged, for instance, the establishment of "peasants' associations" as "the means of engaging in political propaganda." He wrote:

To use those simple slogans, pictures and speeches for political propaganda is like sending every one of the peasants to a political school. The success is big and great. . . . In places where peasants associations are set up, such mass meetings have popularized quite effectively our political propaganda and mobilized into action whole villages. We should in the future make use of all opportunities to enrich the content of the simple slogans and to make their meaning better understood gradually.[6]

Many of the methods of "attacking the landlords politically" described in this article were used later in the Land Reform movement of the early years of the People's Republic of China, and some were used against the "capitalist roaders" during the Cultural Revolution. One such treatment was the "high hats parade":

> The villains and bullies were each given a paper-made high hat on which their crimes were given. They were led with a rope with large groups of people around them. Gongs were sounded and flags were raised high in order to attract public attention. Such punishment frightened the villains and bullies most.[7]

The Second Period, 1928–1935

From 1928 to 1934, strong military pressure from Chiang Kai-shek's "extermination campaigns" forced Mao and his comrades to retreat to Kiangsi, where they established the Kiangsi Soviet. They had become "armed revolutionaries" and now had a base of operation.

The problem of ideological indoctrination began to attract Mao's attention very early in this period. Many of the tactics he used later had their initial tryout during these years. In 1928, shortly after the founding of the Red Army, Mao wrote an article on "The Battle of Chingkanshan" in which he (1) emphasized "political education" and demanded "class consciousness" for all officers and soldiers of the Red Army; (2) talked about the need for purge in the Party, which he called *hsi-tang* or "washing the Party" rather than *ssu-hsiang kai-tsao* or "ideological remolding" (a term he used later); and (3) called attention to symptoms of "dangerous and erroneous thoughts" operating against the Party.

A year later, in 1929, Mao was able to sort out these existing "erroneous thoughts and ideas" within the Party and to suggest some remedial measures in his article "Regarding the Correction of Erroneous Ideas in the Party." His diagnosis:

> The various incorrect ideas within the Party in the Red Fourth Army were caused by the fact that people with peasant and petty bourgeois backgrounds have formed the absolute majority of the Party's fundamental organization and that the leading authorities of the Party have failed to engage in a resolute struggle against such erroneous ideas and to offer the Party members an adequate education and indoctrination.[8]

Here Mao singled out criticism as one of the best tools for destroying "petty bourgeois individualism" and "subjectivism." The method of *ssu-hsiang tou-cheng* or "ideological struggle" was already his prescription at this time.

These early writings of Mao must not mislead one into believing that Mao alone was doing all the planning for the Party's propaganda. During this period, he did not even have full control of the Party, sharing it instead with Li Li-san, Chu Ch'iu-pai, Chen Shao-yü (Wang Ming), Ch'in Pang-hsien (Po Ku), and Chang Kuo-t'ao. These leaders, in spite of their political differences, were all experts on insurrectional politics and veterans in propaganda work. Li was known for his work in labor organization and his style or fashion of propaganda in urban areas. Chen Shao-yü and Ch'in Pang-hsien, both leaders of the "Moscow-returned students' clique," approached propaganda with a different orientation.

The First All-China Congress of Soviets established the Chinese Soviet Republic in Juichin in Kiangsi on November 7, 1931, with Mao Tse-tung as chairman. A month later, on December 11, the first organ of the Chinese Soviet Republic was launched. It was *Hung-se Chung-hua (Red China),* which was first published as a weekly and later on a three-day basis. The newspaper was available in all Soviet areas and reported a circulation of 50,000 in 1934.

Another important Communist publication during this period was *Tou-cheng (Struggle),* which was launched in 1933 as a merger of two official newspapers in the Soviet area, the *Shih-hua (Plain Talk)* and *Tang-ti Chien-she (Party Construction).* This became the official organ of the Central Bureau of the Soviet Areas of the Chinese Communist Party.

A third important publication during this period was *Hung Hsin (Red Star),* which was launched in 1933 as the official mouthpiece of the General Political Department of the Red Army in the Chinese Soviet Republic in Kiangsi. It lasted until 1934, shortly before the Chinese Communists started their Long March from the Kiangsi Soviet bases, where they reportedly published thirty-four newspapers during the 1930s.[9]

The history of the present New China News Agency also dates from this period. It was organized by Mao in 1929 as a department within the Red China Newspaper Agency *(Hung-se Chung-hua Pao-she)* in Juichin in the Kiangsi Soviet, and it accompanied the Communist forces on the Long March in 1934 to Yenan. According to a recent *People's Daily* story, which traces the origin of the agency to April 1937, the New China News Agency sent national and international news dispatches to Mao's cave office in Yenan every evening.[10]

There is no doubt that the famous Long March taught the

Chinese Communists some valuable lessons in propaganda and indoctrination. Mao, who hailed the March as "a manifesto, a propaganda-agitation corps, and a seeding-machine," explains its "significance" in this way:

> The Long March is a manifesto. It has proclaimed to the world that the Red Army is an army of heroes, while the imperialists and their running dogs, Chiang Kai-shek and his like, are impotent. It has proclaimed their utter failure to encircle, pursue, obstruct and intercept us. The Long March is a propaganda force. It has announced to some 200 million people in eleven provinces that the road of the Red Army is their only road to liberation. Without the Long March, how could the broad masses have learned so quickly about the existence of the great truth which the Red Army embodies? The Long March is also a seeding-machine. In the eleven provinces it has sown many seeds which will sprout, leaf, blossom, and bear fruit, and will yield a harvest in the future.[11]

The Third Period, 1936–1949

During this period of fourteen turbulent years—from the end of the Long March in 1935 to the Communist takeover in 1949—the Party fought full-scale propaganda war on three fronts: the Communist-controlled ("red" or "liberated") area, the Kuomintang-controlled ("white") area, and the Japanese-controlled or guerrilla area. This was a period when the Party made a concerted effort to win the support of the Chinese populace and discredit the Kuomintang government. During this process, the Party itself underwent some very important and intricate ideological changes. What the Party did and learned about propaganda, agitation, and indoctrination during this period has inevitably influenced the subsequent development of mass communication in the People's Republic of China.

It was not long after Mao led his ragged Red Army into Shensi that he took over the leadership of the Party. But that does not mean that he faced no competition or challenge in the Party, which was still in many ways Moscow oriented. Mao was determined to consolidate and strengthen the control of the organization and ideology of the Party. He warned against "erroneous ideas in the Party" and complained frequently about the "low level of understanding of Marxism-Leninism" among Party members. But he urged the Party to pay serious attention to the problem of intelligentsia and bourgeoisie, whom he distrusted but needed.

In 1939, Mao wrote: "The organization of revolutionary forces and the accomplishment of revolutionary tasks cannot succeed without the participation of the intelligentsia."[12] He accepted the need for the participation of the bourgeoisie in the Chinese Communist revolution; he attacked those who opposed its participation as the "Trotskyite approach" or "closed-door-ism." To him, the Party's "alliance" with the bourgeoisie was "precisely a bridge that has to be crossed on our way to socialism."[13]

Mao was determined to cross this bridge safely and he relied on the weapon of "ideological struggle" to do so. Eventually, he became the chief architect of a series of programs for ideological rectification and thought reform to eradicate bourgeois ideologies and practices within the Party. The main method for such surgical operations in the ideological field turned out to be criticism and self-criticism. The Maoist solution to the problem of the "low level of class consciousness" and the "low level of understanding of Marxism-Leninism" was a rigorous program of *hsüeh-hsi* or "study,"[14] which was proposed in 1938. Interestingly, Mao used two Confucian expressions to introduce two slogans for this movement: "to learn without satiety" and "to teach without weariness."

In 1939, *Kung Ch'an Tang (Communist)*, a special Party journal, was introduced to guide the study of Party members and cadres. This was followed by another journal, *Chung-kuo Kung-jen (Chinese Workers)*, intended to appeal to the working class. A few other Party leaders joined Mao in publishing some writings on the importance of ideological training of Party members. One was Liu Shao-ch'i, who in 1939 wrote the article "On the Training of a Communist Party Member."

In 1942 came the famous *Cheng Feng* or "Ideological Remolding" campaign. This was the first major ideological rectification campaign of the Party. It was launched officially on February 1, 1942, when Mao delivered the speech "Rectify the Party's Style in Work." Eight days later, Mao followed with an article entitled "Opposing the Party 'Eight-Legged Essay.' " Three months later, Mao delivered his "Talk at the Yenan Forum on Art and Literature," which was from then on to guide the Party's work in art and literature, and propaganda work as a whole.

Lu Ting-i, who headed the Party's propaganda department until he was ousted during the Cultural Revolution, described the method used in the *Cheng Feng* movement as "the most effective that is proven by history":

> This is a method of study that requires a thorough grasp of several fundamental Marxist-Leninist documents. These documents are used as a basis for one to investigate his own thoughts, to engage in criticism and self-criticism, to analyze the correct and erroneous elements in his own thoughts, to study their composition, to discover the reasons, environment, and sources of their growth and development, to work out the practical methods of correcting the mistakes and to write down one's conclusions of study.[15]

Students of China are familiar with such famous cases in the *Cheng Feng* movement as those of Wang Shih-wei[16] and Ting Ling.[17] But this was an ideological remolding campaign which involved the entire Party. Newspapers, magazines, wall posters, and all other possible forms of persuasive communication were mobilized.

It is a common view of students of China that Mao's real objective in launching the *Cheng Feng* movement was sinification of Marxism-Leninism, and that the movement was a trial not merely of the "fragile and wicked petty bourgeois mentality" but of the political theories held by such foes as Li Li-san, Ch'en Shao-yü, and Ch'in Pang-hsien. It serves no useful purpose to speculate on the relationship between the movement and power struggle within the Party. But it is significant that during this period Mao made some serious attempts to consolidate and strengthen the control of the Party both organizationally and ideologically, to fight against incompatible ideologies, and to experiment with various methods of thought reform.

To some Western communication researchers, this discussion of ideological remolding of intellectuals and the problem of the bourgeoisie may seem out of place in a historical essay on the development of propaganda and communication in China. It is instructive to recall that even in 1957, many years after the *Cheng Feng* campaign and numerous thought reform movements, the ideological problem of the intelligentsia and the bourgeoisie continued to be Mao's main concern when he addressed the Party's National Conference on Propaganda Work. This was one of Mao's major policy speeches on propaganda. He made eight points in this speech, six of which addressed the issues of intellectuals, bourgeoisie, and ideology. Mao warned:

In our country bourgeois and petty-bourgeois ideology and anti-Marxist ideologies will persist for a long time. Basically, the socialist system has been established in our country. While we have won basic victory in transforming the ownership of the means of production, we are even farther from complete victory on the political and ideological fronts. In the ideological field, the question of who will win out, the proletariat or the bourgeoisie, has not yet been really settled. We still have to wage a protracted struggle against bourgeois and petty-bourgeois ideology. It is wrong not to understand this and to give up ideological struggle.[18]

Anyone who has followed the development of events in China after the fall of the Gang of Four realizes how and why this issue is not only still alive but indeed critical.

If one were to take seriously the Chinese Communist claim that every member of the Party is expected to be a propagandist, the growth of the Chinese Communist army of propagandists during this period was phenomenal. There was a meteoric increase in Party membership, indicative of widening support among the Chinese. In 1937, at the beginning of the Sino-Japanese War, the Party had approximately 40,000 members. The membership grew to 1,211,128 in 1945 and reached 4,500,000 in 1949.[19]

It was during this period that Mao developed the policy of "mass line"—that the target and the timing of the Party's program depends on whether the masses are sufficiently mobilized and educated through propaganda and indoctrination "to demand action voluntarily," and on whether the action serves the purpose of the Party. The communist formula for the operation of the mass line is that "the policy and methods of work of the Party must originate from the masses and go back to the masses." A cynical interpretation of the formula would be that the Communists merely try to make the ideas of the Party sound as if they were ideas of the people. It is more useful, however, to suggest that they attempt to transform the sentiments of the masses into an idea that, on one hand, seemingly expresses a public will and, on the other, qualifies the purposes of the Party.

Mao explained the formula this way in 1943:

In all practical work of our Party, correct leadership can only be developed on the principle of "from the masses, to the masses." This means summing up [i.e., coordinating and systematizing after careful study] the views of the masses [i.e., views scattered and unsystematic], then taking the resulting ideas back to the masses, explaining and popularizing them until the masses embrace the ideas as their own, stand up for them and translate them into action by way of testing their correctness. Then it is necessary once more to sum up the views of the masses, and once again take the resulting ideas back to the masses so that the masses give them their whole-hearted support . . . And so on, over and over again, so that each time these ideas emerge with greater correctness and become more vital and meaningful. That is what the Marxist theory of knowledge teaches us.[20]

Mao made use of a talk he gave to the editorial staff of the *Shansi-Suiyuan Daily* to hammer hard on the policy of mass line.

Our papers talk about the mass line every day, yet frequently the mass line is not carried out in the work of the newspaper office itself. For instance, misprints often crop up in the papers simply because their elimination has not been tackled as a serious job. If we apply the method of mass line, then when misprints appear, we should assemble the entire staff of the paper to discuss nothing but this matter, tell them clearly what the mistakes are, explain why they occur and how they can be gotten rid of and ask everyone to give the matter serious attention. After this has been done three times, or five times, such mistakes can certainly be overcome. This is true of small matters, and of big matters.[21]

In a directive which Mao drafted in 1948 on behalf of the Party's Central Committee on the tasks of land reform and Party, Mao even went into such details as methods of conducting a cadre's conference. He carefully spelled out step by step the procedures which the cadres should follow to make a conference successful, such as studying the Party's directives, reviewing the major issues in order to guide the discussion during the conference, and preparing a detailed report afterwards.[22]

We now turn to the development of the Party's formal media of mass communication during this period.

The official organ of the Party during the early part of this period was *Hsin Chung-hua Pao (New China Daily)*, which was established in Yenan on January 29, 1941. It was published until May 5, 1941. The following day, the paper became *Chieh-fang Jihpao (Liberation Daily)*. This paper was published until the spring of 1949, when Yenan was occupied by the Kuomintang forces under Hu Tsung-nan.

The *Liberation Daily* was first under the direction of Chin Pang-hsien, one of the "Russian-returned students," who was also in charge of the New China News Agency. The deputy editor was Ai Szu-chi, who became chief editor in May 1944.

Another important publication of the Party during this period was *Chieh-fang (Liberation),* a weekly. It was started in 1937 and published until 1941.

The predecessor of the current *People's Daily* in Peking was a two-page newspaper bearing the same name which started in 1946 in Hantan, Hopeh. It was the official mouthpiece of the Chin-Chi-Lu-Yü Pien-ch'ü government (Shansi-Hopeh-Shantung-Honan Border Region) until 1948.

In 1948, the victorious Chinese Communists combined the Shansi-Hopeh-Shantung-Honan (Chin-Chi-Lu-Yü), the Shansi-Chahar-Hopeh (Chin-Ch'a-Chi) and the Shansi-Suiyuan (Chin-Sui) Border Regions into one single North China Base under the North China Bureau of the Chinese Communist Party. This reorganization was followed by the amalgamation of the original *People's Daily* and the Kalgan *Chin-Ch'a-Chi Jihpao (Shansi-Chahar-Hopeh Daily).* The result was the present *People's Daily,* which was first published in Shih-chia-chuang in 1948 and moved to Peking in 1949. This is the official organ of the Central Committee of the Chinese Communist Party.

During the eight years of the Sino-Japanese war, the Party published a number of papers in "border regions" under very trying conditions. According to Chi Wu, a Chinese Communist writer, in the Shansi-Chahar-Shantung-Honan (Chin-Ch'a-Lu-Yü) Border Region alone, for instance, more than thirty printing plants were burned down by the Japanese.[23]

Among the leading papers published in this border region during this period were *Kang-chan Jihpao (War of Resistance Daily), Wei-ho Jihpao (Wei-ho Daily), Lu-hsi Jihpao (Lu-hsi Daily),* which later became *Chin-Chi-Yu Jihpao (Shansi-Hopeh-Honan Daily), Chi-nan Jihpao (South Shansi Daily), Tai-yüeh Jihpao (Tai-yüeh Daily),* and *Chung-kuo-jen Pao (Chinese Daily).*

The most popular forms and methods of social education and organization during this time were character-recognition classes (literacy classes), winter schools, people's schools, people's blackboards, newspaper-reading groups, people's revolutionary rooms (used as recreation rooms), and various kinds of rural theater groups.[24]

The so-called Kuomintang-Communist coalition during the Sino-Japanese War permitted the Party to publish several editions of the *Hsin-hua Jihpao (New China Daily News)* in several cities in Kuomintang territory during this period. It was the responsibility of *Hsin-hua Jihpao* in Chungking to speak for the Party, attack the Kuomintang, and win over the masses. The paper was under the direction of Chou En-lai, who was in charge of the Party's liaison office in Chungking. The chief editor was Pan Tzu-nien.

Development of the Chinese Communist broadcast system also had its beginning during this period. In 1940, according to a recent report prepared by the Theory Group of the Central Broadcasting Bureau, a Committee of Broadcasting was organized and chaired by Chou En-lai in Yenan to make plans for the establishment of a broadcasting station. Within that same year, a group of radio workers recruited from all over the country had converted an old automobile engine into a generator with an odd assortment of rebuilt or handmade parts and had built the Yenan Hsin Hua broadcasting station.

Mao, according to this report, made a personal contribution to the station.

> In the summer of 1941, the Yenan station finally, after exploring all sorts of possibilities, managed to get hold of an old manual gramophone. But there were no records. When Chairman Mao heard about this, he turned over to the station more than 20 records of his own.[25]

The Chinese Communists made immediate use of their broadcasting station. In May 1941, according to this same story, Chairman Mao, in a directive drafted for the Party's Central Committee, "asked all liberated areas to receive regularly Yenan's broadcasts."

There is no doubt that the Party relied heavily on this channel during this period to keep in touch with liberated areas and, more importantly, with its guerrilla units and armed forces. Radio at this time was not a principal instrument of the Party to indoctrinate and organize the masses in Red areas, although it was to become a major tool of propaganda almost immediately after 1949. In the Red areas, radio transmission and receiving facilities were few and inadequate. Nor did the Party make much significant use of radio to mobilize public opinion in Kuomintang-controlled areas. In these areas, radio quickly became a mass medium in big cities, for the medium was under the tight control of the Nationalists.

It was in the field of art and literature that the Chinese Communists fought some of their hardest battles and scored some of their greatest victories. In his "Talk at the Yenan Forum on Art and Literature," Mao spoke about the Chinese Communist Party's operations on two fronts: "the civilians' front and the soldiers' front, i.e., the cultural front and the military front." He talked about the Party's need for "a cultural army which is absolutely indispensable for uniting ourselves and defeating the enemy." And he traced the roots of this cultural army to the days before the Chinese Communist Party was founded. "Since the May 4 Movement of 1919," Mao said, "this cultural army has taken shape in China and has helped the Chinese revolution in gradually reducing the domain and weakening the influence of China's feudal culture and her comprador culture which is adapted to imperialist aggression."[26] Yenan's problem in 1942, as Mao put it, was how to "fit art and literature properly into the revolutionary machine as one of its component parts, to make them a powerful weapon for uniting and educating the people and for attacking and annihilating the enemy, and to help the people to fight the enemy with one heart and one mind."[27] How this problem was handled by the Chinese Communist Party is a long and involved story by itself. But developments and problems in this vast area of communication in China since 1949 have been heavily conditioned by the development of this cultural army from 1921 to 1949 and, most importantly, by what it did and learned in "the Period of the 1930s."

In pre-1949 days, the Party had, roughly speaking, two main groups of cultural workers in the field of art and literature. One, led by Mao and his followers, operated in the countryside and participated in the building of big revolutionary base areas, first in the Kiangsi Soviet from 1929 to 1934 and later in the border regions from 1935 to 1949. The other lived and worked in urban centers in Kuomintang-controlled or "white" areas among intellectuals and had little direct contact with peasants and soldiers. One could perhaps add a third group which was attached to the Communist armed forces as "cultural workers corps," which grew rapidly during the five to ten years before the Communist takeover of the Chinese mainland. It is not possible in this historical essay to discuss, even briefly, the differences and conflicts between those who handled propaganda work among peasants, workers, and soldiers and those who worked mainly with the intelligentsia.[28] But we should at least call attention to the fact that these conflicts, which Mao tried to resolve in his Yenan talk more than three decades ago, are by no means settled, and that they have acquired some new significance in the shaping of the communication system in China today.

One of the popular Chinese Communist themes during this period was to push forward the revolutionary movement in art and literature and to get closer to the masses by making use of traditional forms or media in art and literature which the largely illiterate populace could understand and appreciate. Popular drama, for instance, was very effectively used to disseminate information and propagate ideological lessons. In retrospect, it was in the border regions and revolutionary base areas that the Maoist style in mass politics and mass culture conceived in Kiangsi grew to maturity. Central to this style is the doctrine that art and literature must serve the interests of workers, peasants, and soldiers, and that all programs in art and literature after 1949 must necessarily be developed to complement this style.

The Fourth Period, 1949–1966

The new government faced the task of mobilizing the population for national reconstruction after nearly a generation of war. The people had to be informed of the national goals, including programs of collectivization, and their support had to be enlisted. It did not take the Party very long after 1949 to develop a crude but remarkably effective system of mass communication which brought more people into direct close contact with the central government than ever before in Chinese history. While much has happened to the Party and to this system during the past twenty-eight years, many important characteristics of the system remain unchanged. It continues to be pervasive and penetrating, successfully integrating all oral, informal, casual, and traditional means of communication with the more conventional channels and methods of mass propaganda and indoctrination. It has always been controlled by an elite group in the Party—whether a clique of "capitalist roaders" or the Gang of Four. There have been changes —in its control, its content, and even in some of its components —but these changes seem to be more results of Party policies and developments within the Party rather than isolated changes in the system of communication.

We can raise two kinds of questions to organize our inquiry into the development of China's communication system since 1949. One is: *When did the Party do what with or about its communication system and why?* To answer the question is to focus attention on the Party's policies and practices in propaganda, its organizational and operational principles and problems, functions of the major components, and chronological stages of development of this system. It was this type of question students of communication, including this writer, asked during the early years of the People's Republic of China.[29]

We can now probe into the background of the communication system and ask: *Who controlled what and made what use of the communication system to say or do what and with what impact?* This would help us concentrate on three important aspects of the development of the system:

1. *Men:* Who controlled what parts of the system? And who challenged the control?
2. *Media:* What media or channels were controlled and used for what purposes?
3. *Messages:* What was the substance or content of the struggle?

Our task of answering these questions is made easier by political events in China during the last ten years. During the Cultural Revolution, when Mao decided to have it out with his political foes and tell all, we had our first inside, though necessarily distorted, view of China's communication system under the control of Liu Shao-ch'i from 1949 to 1966. It was during these turbulent years that we read Chiang Ch'ing's condemnation of "the heinous crimes in which the former Peking Municipal Party Committee, the former Propaganda Department of the Party Central Committee and the former Ministry of Culture ganged up against the Party" and Yao Wen-yüan's denunciation of "the former Propaganda Department of the Central Committee of the Chinese Communist Party" as "the court of the Demon King, where the counterrevolutionary revisionists had seized power."[30] Almost immediately after the downfall of the Gang of Four in 1976, we began to get Peking's official version of how the Gang seized all means of communication and used them to serve its "black line."

The temptation is to treat the evolution of China's communication system since 1949 as no more than a seesaw fight over an instrument of power in power struggles. Such an approach, though suggestive, oversimplifies an extremely complex development. One may get somewhat nearer to a balanced view by taking into account (1) the basics of Chinese Communism, on which the development of the communication system is based and around which personal and political struggles on one hand and ideological and cultural clashes on the other relate in very complex ways, and (2) the political conditions under which this communication system has grown and taken form.

What has set Chinese Communism somewhat apart from other systems or forms of communism in the world is the thought of Mao Tse-tung as applied Marxism-Leninism, which shapes the course of development of the Chinese Communist society and necessarily influences every policy and activity of the Party.

A master key to understanding the role of Mao Tse-tung's thought in the development of China's communication system is the Maoist dictum that "thought determines action," and that "politics should take command" over everything in the country. The idea is that, if people can be made to think "correctly," they will naturally act "correctly." In this respect, the Maoists have gone somewhat beyond the Marxist dogma which maintains that changes in a society are determined by its political and economic systems. They choose to believe that attitudes, opinions, ideas, and thoughts must first be revolutionized in order to build a solid foundation for the planned political, economic, social, and cultural changes. Very clearly, Mao had this in mind when he declared, shortly after the Communist takeover of the Chinese mainland, that the method of persuasion was to be used among the people "on a nationwide and full scale." His aim, as he expressed it earlier in his article "On People's Democratic Dictatorship," was for the Chinese people to

> educate and remould themselves . . . shake off the influence of domestic and foreign reactionaries . . . rid themselves of the bad habits and ideas acquired in the old society, not allow themselves to be led astray by the reactionaries, and continue to advance—to advance towards a socialist and communist society.[31]

This important dogma was put into practice in the form of a nationwide *hsüeh-hsi,* or study movement, immediately after the establishment of the People's Republic of China in 1949.

The man who led the *hsüeh-hsi* movement during the early years of the People's Republic was Ai Ssu-ch'i. The major content of the mass study movement was class struggle and production. There were four kinds of study: (1) the study of theories of social development, (2) the study of history, (3) the study of revolutionary policies, and (4) the study of work or occupation.[32] The main forms of study were: reading of assigned documents, small group discussion, criticism and self-criticism, and preparation of one's ideological conclusions. *Hsüeh-hsi* was always closely integrated with other mass movements in the country: land reform, Resist-America Aid-Korea, suppression of counterrevolutionaries, and so on. By 1952, when the Executive Committee of the People's Political Consultative Council in its thirty-fourth session passed the "Resolution Concerning the Development of the Ideological Reform Study Movement of People of all Circles," the mass study movement had already become a formalized institution in the country.

It is instructive to recall that while Mao Tse-tung's thought was hailed by Liu Shao-ch'i as "the highest expression of the intellect and the highest theoretical attainment of the Chinese people,"[33] it did not occupy nearly as important a place in the early study movement as it did later after the fall of Liu.

An important book during the early mass study movement was Ai Ssu-ch'i's *Ta-chung Che-hsüeh (Popular Philosophy),* which he wrote in 1936 and revised in 1947. It was written in simple Chinese and used common anecdotes, old sayings, and familiar jokes. The main purpose of the book was to popularize Marxism and Leninism rather than to introduce any new idea or philosophy.

The Party guided the mass study movement with two magazines: the *Hsüeh Hsi (Study)* magazine, which first came out in Shanghai in 1949 as a monthly and six months later as a fortnightly, appearing simultaneously in China's major cities, and *Hsüeh Hsi Ch'u-chi-pan (Study Primer).* The former was edited for the use of the intellectual and educated class; the latter mainly for people of little education.

It is significant to note that publication of the popular and powerful *Hsüeh Hsi* magazine was temporarily suspended in 1952. The April 10, 1952, issue of the magazine carried an article signed by the entire editorial board, which stated:

> After an initial review of previous *Hsüeh Hsi* issues, we gain a feeling that . . . there have been many articles characterized by bluffing and emptiness and lacking concrete analysis of concrete problems.

. . . Some articles on the question of the bourgeoisie committed the mistake of one-sidedness. . . . The work done by *Hsüeh Hsi* magazine has great shortcomings and shows great mistakes. . . . The Editorial Board is now conducting a thorough check-up and will inform our readers of the results of the check-up.

Apparently, Ai Ssu-ch'i, the chief technician of the *Hsüeh-Hsi* movement, got himself into some serious ideological trouble during the Three-Anti movement. About a month before the suspension of the *Hsüeh Hsi* magazine, the March 15, 1952, issue of the magazine carried an article in which Ai painfully criticized himself for failing to see clearly the basic reactionary nature of the bourgeois class. Very little has been heard from or about Ai since he published this article of apology or confession about twenty-five years ago.[34]

By this time, the Party had made enough use of its system of persuasive and coercive communications to begin to streamline its agitation-indoctrination-propaganda work. The key link in the system at this time was *People's Daily,* through which the Department of Propaganda operated and to which all publications in the nation turned for guidance and direction. This authority of *People's Daily* was shared with *Hung Ch'i (Red Flag)* when it was published in 1959. Still later, for political and other reasons, the *Chieh Fang Chün Pao (Liberation Army Daily)* joined the two for a trinity of power in propaganda.

What was published in *People's Daily* was reprinted or quoted in Party newspapers at different levels and in other publications. Its reports were carried by the Central People's Broadcasting Station in Peking, which transmitted them to stations in the provinces and other cities or regions, and these stations in turn sent the word further down through the radio broadcasting network, which made the message available to listeners either in collective listening meetings or in blackboard or wall newspapers. Eventually, the messages were printed as pamphlets that were made available for study groups. In transmitting a message from Peking, the local newspapers, magazines, radio stations, and all other media of communication were expected to "integrate" the message with the local situation to set the stage for agitation work in whatever mass movement or tasks were prescribed by the Party at the moment.

The Department of Propaganda during this period guided, directed, and supervised the nationwide agitation-propaganda activities. But, strictly speaking, it was not an operational organization, although it had a wide range of responsibilities and a vast variety of activities. It did not own or control the Party newspapers, which came under the jurisdiction of the Party Press Commission of the Party's Central Committee. It did not operate radio stations or make films, since these activities, in appearance at least, came under the government. The department, during these years at least, remained in the background in supervision and control.

A major influence in the Department of Propaganda during this period was Chou Yang, its deputy director and minister of culture. Chou Yang was later harshly criticized by the Maoists during the Cultural Revolution. He seemed to be at the top of the hate list of Yao Wen-yüan, one of the Gang of Four who served as Chiang Ch'ing's communication czar until their downfall. Yao wrote a 66-page article entitled "On the Counter-revolutionary Double-dealer Chou Yang."

Chou Yang was accused of deceiving Mao and sabotaging some of Mao's major projects on the ideological front: the criticism of the film *Life of Wu Hsün* in 1951; the "struggle" against Yu Ping-po's *Studies of "Dream of the Red Chamber"* in 1954; the "struggle against the counter-revolutionary Hu Feng clique" in 1955; and the attack on the "bourgeois Rightists" in 1957. The list of Chou Yang's crimes was indeed long, including the serious charge of opposing Chairman Mao and Mao Tse-tung's thought. Here are a few examples:

- At the forum on creative work in literature and art in February 1959, Chou Yang attacked the Great Leap Forward and praised the "international standard" of art set by modern revisionism.
- In March 1961, Chou Yang went to Fukien to vilify Mao Tse-tung's thought, saying: "Mao Tse-tung's Thought is a red thread, but laid on too thick it ceases to be red thread and turns into a piece of red cloth."[35]
- At the forum on literary and art work held in June 1961, Chou Yang warned that radio and television should not always be propagating support for Chairman Mao.

Yao called Chou Yang the "ring leader" of a "black line" in literature and art. This "black line," Yao wrote, "included Hu Feng, Feng Hsüeh-feng, Ting Ling, Ai Ching, Chin Chao-yang, Lin Mohan, T'ien Han, Hsia Yen, Yang Han-sheng, Chi Yen-ming, Ch'en

Huang-mei, Shao Ch'uan-lin and the rest." Many Maoist critics traced Chou Yang's "crimes" to the period of the 1930s. Included in these accusations were also other "old Party members" and "old left-wingers" who all became prominent during the 1930s and occupied key communication positions until the Cultural Revolution.

Some readers may question the usefulness of such data. Yao's denunciations of Chou Yang, especially when translated into English, sound odd to Western ears. But they hold historical interest and offer far more insight into what was involved in this important area of communication than does any analysis of Chou's writing.

We note an important style of Chinese Communist communication as well as a treacherously difficult problem for Western researchers who deal with Chinese Communist polemics. The Chinese Communist leaders apparently use mass media to transmit very important political messages to one another in such a way that the outside world does not understand or even notice. For instance, when volume 5 of the *Selected Works of Mao Tse-tung* was published, *Red Flag* carried an introduction to the volume.[36] We now know from this introduction:

- The article "Take Mutual Aid and Co-operation in Agriculture as a Major Task," published in 1951, was Mao's criticism of Liu Shao-ch'i's opposition to the policy on agricultural cooperatives.
- The article "Refute Right Deviation Views that Depart from the General Line," published in 1953, was another criticism of Liu Shao-ch'i's ideological mistakes.
- The article "Combat Bourgeois Ideas in the Party," published in 1953, was intended as a criticism of Po I-po.

Before we leave this eighteen-year period from 1949 to 1966, we should note two important contributions which Mao made to the development of the communication system during this period. One was an action taken to keep the cadres better informed of news about the outside world. This concerned the publication of *Ts'an-k'ao Hsiao-hsi* or *Reference Information*. The Party decided to increase the circulation of this publication from 2,000 to 400,000 in 1957, apparently on Mao's recommendation.

In his "Talks at a Conference of Secretaries of Provincial, Municipal and Autonomous Region Party Committees," in January 1957, Mao said:

We have now decided to increase the circulation of *Reference Information* from 2,000 to 400,000 so that it can be read by people both inside and outside the Party. This is a case of a Communist Party publishing a newspaper for imperialism, as it even carries reactionary statements vilifying us. Why should we do this? The purpose is to put poisonous weeds and what is non-Marxist and anti-Marxist before our comrades, before the masses and the democratic personages, so that they can be tempered. Don't seal these things up, otherwise it will be dangerous. In this respect our approach is different from that of the Soviet Union. Why is vaccination necessary? A virus is artificially introduced into a man's body to wage "germ warfare" against him in order to bring about immunity. The publication of *Reference Information* and other negative teaching material is "vaccination" to increase the political immunity of the cadres and the masses.[37]

The other Maoist contribution was the *tatzupao* or "big character posters." This unusually powerful means of propaganda had been developed and promoted, though not invented, by Mao. There is, of course, nothing new about the use of posters for propaganda purposes. But to use them as a medium of mass communication is innovative and perhaps even Maoist.

Tatzupao were used on a dramatically large scale during the Hundred Flower and Anti-Rightist movements in the 1950s. Mao had this to say about *tatzupao* at a conference for cadres on July 9, 1957, in Shanghai:

The big-character poster is a fine thing and I think it will be handed down to future generations. The *Confucian Analects,* the *Five Classics,* the *Thirteen Classics* and the *Twenty-Four Dynastic Histories* have all been handed down to us. Won't the big-character poster be handed down to posterity? I think it will. Will it be used in the future when rectification is unfolded, in factories for instance? I think it is a good idea to use it, the more the better. Like language, it has no class nature. Our vernacular has no class nature. We all speak in the vernacular and so does Chiang Kai-shek. We no longer speak literary Chinese exemplified by sayings like—"Great pleasure is derived from learning and constantly reviewing what has been learned" and "Welcoming friends from afar gives one great delight." The vernacular is used by the proletariat and also by the bourgeoise. The big-character poster can be used by the bourgeoisie as well as by the proletariat. We believe that the majority of the people are on the side of the proletariat. Therefore, the big-character poster as an instrument favors the proletariat, not the bourgeoisie.[38]

During the same time, Mao had occasion to write an article discussing "The Situation in the Summer of 1957"; he brought up the matter of *tatzupao* again and said: "Big-character posters, forums and debates are three excellent forms for revealing and overcoming contradictions and helping people make progress in institutions of higher education, in departments and organizations at the central, the provincial, and municipal, the prefectural and the county levels and in large urban enterprises."[39]

The Fifth Period, 1966–1976

This was a period of intense and almost continual power struggle, in which the mass media played essential roles. At the Tenth Plenum of the Eighth Central Committee of the Party in 1962, Mao observed: "In order to overthrow a political regime, it is always necessary to prepare public opinion and carry out work in the ideological field in advance. This is true of the revolutionary class; it is also true of the counter-revolutionary class."[40] Four years later, this observation of Mao became the battle cry of his rebels in the Cultural Revolution. Day in and day out, this Mao statement was quoted in speeches, cited in editorials, and even chanted in songs.[41]

The purpose of the revolution, as the Maoists put it, is "to settle the question of 'who will win' in the ideological field between the proletariat and the bourgeoisie."[42] But one very specific purpose, as a *Red Flag* article states it, is "to establish the ascendancy of Mao Tse-tung's Thought."[43]

There is no need to summarize here, even briefly, how the Maoists seized control of the communication system and waged a full-scale propaganda war that stands unique in both the history of communism and the history of communication. Many parts of this story are well known to students of China, and some parts are too complicated to be told briefly. But it may be useful to consider (1) the ascendancy of the thought of Mao Tse-tung, and (2) some changes in the communication system.

To trace the ascendancy of the thought of Mao Tse-tung is to understand how cautiously, systematically, and shrewdly Mao fought this important battle on the ideological front. He directed particular attention to consolidating ideological control over the Party and the nation. When he emerged as the victor on the mainland in 1949, his thought had already been given a place of honor in the Constitution of the Party. He did not rush to the printing press in 1949 to have his writings published as required readings. As a matter of fact, the twelve books prescribed by the Party as "required readings" for cadres did not include a single book or article by Mao.[44] During those early days of the People's Republic of China, Mao appeared as a humble but advanced student of Marxism-Leninism-Stalinism. He was careful to refer to his views as "the thought of Mao Tse-tung" instead of Maoism, a term he never used. In 1953, in a speech called "Combat Bourgeois Ideas in the Party," he reminded his comrades of a set of regulations that were adopted at the Second Plenary Session of the Seventh Central Committee. One of the regulations was "a ban on placing Chinese comrades on a par with Marx, Engels, Lenin or Stalin." "Our relationship to them," Mao said, "is one of pupils to teachers and that is how it should be. Observance of these regulations is true modesty.[45] But Mao was, of course, very careful to see to it that the phrase "the greatness of Marxism, Engelsism, Leninism, Stalinism and the thought of Mao Tse-tung" was on the lips of all people of China.

It was not until 1952 that the first national mass movement to study Mao Tse-tung's *On Contradiction* took place. In 1956 came the national movement to study the *Selected Works of Mao Tse-tung*. The following year, a movement to study Mao's *On the Internal Contradictions among People* was organized. This was followed in 1958 by another mass movement to study the *Selected Works of Mao Tse-tung*. It is significant to note that, up to this point, the movements were organized to study the "works" or "writings" of Mao Tse-tung rather than "the Thought of Mao Tse-tung," as it became known in later years. In spite of Mao's difficulties with his top colleagues in the Party, the prestige of his "Thought" continued to escalate. But its height was not reached until the Cultural Revolution. The Communiqué of the Eleventh Plenary Session of the Eighth Central Committee, which was adopted on August 12, 1966, put it this way:

> Comrade Mao Tse-tung is the greatest Marxist-Leninist of our era. Comrade Mao Tse-tung has inherited, defended, and developed Marxism-Leninism with genius, creatively and in an all-round way, and has raised Marxism-Leninism to a new stage. Mao Tse-tung's Thought is Marxism-Leninism of the era in which imperialism is heading for total collapse and socialism is advancing to world-wide victory. It is the guiding principle for all the work of our Party and country. The plenary session holds that Comrade Lin Piao's call on

the People's Liberation Army to launch a mass movement in the army to study Comrade Mao Tse-tung's works has set a brilliant example for the whole Party and the whole nation. The most reliable and fundamental guarantee against revisionism and the restoration of capitalism, and for victory of our socialist and communist cause, is to arm the masses of workers, peasants, soldiers, revolutionary intellectuals and cadres with Mao Tse-tung's Thought and to promote the revolutionizing of people's ideology.[46]

Between January 1, 1966, and November 30, 1968, according to a story in *Peking Review,* Peking issued 150 million *sets* of the *Selected Works of Mao Tse-tung* in Han, Mongol, Tibetan, Uighur, Kazakh, and Korean; 140 million copies of *Selected Readings of Mao Tse-tung;* and 740 million copies of *Quotations of Mao Tse-tung.*[47]

Mao's writings, according to Maoists during the Cultural Revolution, did not fare very well under Liu Shao-ch'i's regime. One of the many "crimes" of Chou Yang, then minister of culture, was to sabotage the publication of Mao's writings. Yao Fa-kuei, director of the Bureau of Publication of the Ministry of Culture, had this criticism of Chou Yang in 1966:

> In recent years, at the high tide of studying Chairman Mao's Writings, many soldiers, peasants and workers wrote us letters to say that they found it difficult to buy Chairman Mao's writings. . . . Who were responsible for not printing enough copies of Chairman Mao's books? Chou Yang and his black gang who controlled the Ministry of Culture. . .

> In 1962, Chairman Mao's Writings constituted only 0.57% of the books published in the country. During that year, the reprinting of *Dream of the Red Chamber* and *Romance of the Three Kingdoms* consumed as much as 7,500 tons of paper. But only 70 tons of paper was used for the printing of Chairman Mao's writing.[48]

It was during the Cultural Revolution that all quotations of Mao Tse-tung were printed in boldface type. This was not just a typographical device to make the quotations stand out. It seemed to be a special sign of honor reserved for the Chairman.

Very clearly, it was during the Cultural Revolution that "Mao's Thought" advanced to the status of an unchallengeable dogma and became the ultimate symbol of legitimacy in the Party. The *People's Daily, Red Flag,* and *Liberation Army Daily* said simply in a joint editorial on October 1, 1967: "The history of the past eighteen years fully proves that only Mao Tse-tung's Thought can save China."

As for changes in the communication system, there was the biggest shakeup ever in the Party's propaganda organization and an almost complete change in leadership in the Department of Propaganda and Ministry of Culture.

New propagandists emerged. During the early period of the Cultural Revolution, these were the Red Guards. In 1968, the power of the Red Guards began to decline. Their exit in late 1968 was as quiet as their appearance was dramatic in 1966. On October 31, 1968 at the close of the Twelfth Plenum of the Central Committee which officially ousted Liu Shao-ch'i, the communiqué did not include a single reference to Red Guards. Instead, a new corps of propagandists or revolutionary cadre was created. In a special directive, Mao announced the formation of the "Worker's Mao Tse-tung"'s Thought Propaganda Team," who were to be stationed "permanently" in schools and colleges. The formula for the composition of the propaganda team was called "three-in-one union" (workers, soldiers, and revolutionary activists in schools, under the leadership of the working class).

One detects few changes in the functions of the Department of Propaganda and Ministry of Culture during this period. But there are reasons to believe that during the mid-1970s some new groups gained special power. After the fall of the Gang of Four, the "Big Criticism Group" at Peking University and Tsinghua University was identified as the "chief secret liaison point" for all the gang's "plots and activities."[49] This group, during the last three years before the fall of the Gang, reportedly "manufactured" as many as 219 important articles and actually published 181 pieces—some under the pen name of Liang Hsiao.

There were no new propaganda publications. For a while, Red Guard newspapers were among the most important weapons of the Cultural Revolution. But they did not last long.

Significant changes in the communication system during this period seemed to be more in substance than in structure and more in the field of art and literature than in conventional mass media. If one were to put side by side two copies of the Peking *People's Daily*—one published, say, in 1974 and one in 1964—there would be no striking change in appearance. But if one were to examine the content of pieces about problems in history, art, and literature, some differences would emerge.

It is a common criticism of Chiang Ch'ing and her followers that their control of the field of art and literature was so tight that all creative impulses were stunted. This is not a difficult case to document, and the Chinese Communist press since the fall of the Gang of Four has been flooded with stories testifying to this "suffocating" influence over the field of art and literature. It is true that Chiang Ch'ing and her followers had much to say not only about what the content in art and literature should be but also about how this content should be handled. For instance, there was the so-called high-great-complete principle in the creation of main characters in drama—that is, the writer should start with a "high" point in the life of the hero or heroine, emphasize the "great" wisdom of the characters (so great as to be godlike), and deal with the "complete" or "whole" success of the characters.[50]

There were innovations in form and style in both art and literature. Chiang Ch'ing's introduction of piano to Peking opera immediately comes to mind. There is enough evidence to suggest that Chiang Ch'ing and her followers made rather vigorous use of the traditional media of art and literature for political purposes and in so doing made these media more important than before.

The Future: The Post-Mao Era

Instead of making prophecies, we would like to close this chapter by describing a few recent Chinese scenes without interpretation.

Compare two issues of *Red Flag,* randomly chosen: one published in 1976, shortly after the arrest of the Gang of Four, and one in 1977. The 1976 issue (no. 12) started with four full pages of quotations of Mao Tse-tung in big boldface type. That had been the practice of the magazine for some time after the Cultural Revolution. The first quotation, on the front page, was Chairman Mao's handwritten note to Hua Kuo-feng stating that with Hua in charge he would have no worry. The third quotation was a criticism of Chiang Ch'ing.

The 1977 issue (no. 5) carried *no* quotations of Mao. An article, written by the commentator for the *People's Daily, Red Flag,* and *Liberation Army Daily* and entitled "The Black Gang of Old and New Counter-Revolutionaries," asks this question: "Who are Wang Hung-wen, Chang Ch'un-ch'iao, Chiang Ch'ing and Yao

Wen-yüan?"[51] The answer, after more than six months of investigation: "Chang Ch'un-ch'iao was a Kuomintang agent." "Chiang Ch'ing was a traitor and political swindler." "Yao Wen-yüan was a class enemy." "Wang Hung-wen was a new-born capitalist." A few brief explanations: "Chang Ch'un-Ch'iao came with a family background of officials and landlords and became a Kuomintang secret agent during the 1930s when he was a middle school student in Tsinan." "Chiang Ch'ing, also with a landlord family background, started her counterrevolutionary political career in the 1930s." "Yao Wen-yüan's father, Yao Pang-tse, betrayed the Party in 1934 when he was released from jail and later served as a secret agent in cultural affairs for the Kuomintang." "Wang Hung-wen, although coming from a proletarian background and having experience in the armed forces and as a worker, did not behave properly in the armed forces and in the factories."

The October 1, 1977, issue of the *People's Daily* celebrated the anniversary of the People's Republic. The paper published a list of some eight hundred dignitaries who participated in the ceremonies of the celebration. The list starts on the front page and goes on to page 3. The name immediately before the last: Chou Yang, the minister of culture purged in the Cultural Revolution.

NOTES

1. Chang Kuo-t'ao, *Autobiography*, vol. 1, *The Rise of the Chinese Communist Party, 1921–1927* (Lawrence, Kansas: The University of Kansas Press, 1971), p. 151.

2. Ibid., p. 151.

3. Ibid., p. 408.

4. *People's China* (Peking), January 16, 1954, p. 12.

5. See Lee Jui, *Mao Tse-tung T'ung-chih Ti Ch'u-chi K'e-ming Huo-tung* [Comrade Mao Tse-tung's Early Revolutionary Activities] (Peking: Chin Nien Chu Pan She, 1959).

6. *Mao Tse-tung Hsüan-chi* [Selected Works of Mao Tse tung], vol. 1 (Peking: Jenmin Chu Pan She, 1953), pp. 36–37.

7. Ibid., pp. 25–27.

8. "Regarding the Correction of Erroneous Ideas in the Party," in *Mao Tse-tung Hsüan-chi*, vol. 1, p. 87.

9. Franklin W. Houn, *To Change a Nation* (Glencoe, Ill.: The Free Press, 1961), p. 27.

10. *Jenmin Jihpao* [People's Daily], September 20, 1977.

11. "On Tactics of Fighting Japanese Imperialism," in *Mao Tse-tung Hsüan-chi,* vol. 1, p. 145.

12. Mao Tse-tung, "On Intelligentsia and Students," in Chieh Fang She, ed.,

Chih-shih Fen-tzu Yü Chiao-yü Wen-ti [Intelligentsia and Educational Problems] (Canton: Hsin Hua Shu Tien, 1949), p. 6.

13. "Strive to Win over Millions upon Millions of the Masses to the Anti-Japanese National United Front," in *Mao Tse-tung Hsüan-chi,* vol. 1, p. 267.

14. "The Role of the Chinese Communist Party in the National War," in *Selected Works of Mao Tse-tung,* vol. 2 (London: Lawrence and Wishart, 1954), pp. 214–216.

15. Lu Ting-i, "Fifteenth Anniversary of the Ideological Remolding Movement," in *Hsin Hua Pan Yueh K'an* [New China Fortnightly], no. 7, 1957, p. 52. The article was published originally in *People's Daily,* March 5, 1957.

16. Wang Shih-wei, a Communist writer, was denounced as a typical representative of "bourgeois individualism and liberalism," which the Party was determined to eradicate. The immediate cause for the vehement campaign against him were two short essays—*Tsa Wen* [Miscellaneous Essays] and *Yeh Pai-ho-hua* [The Wild Lily] —in which he had some harsh criticism of the Party.

17. Ting Ling, a woman novelist, wrote in 1942 an essay entitled "Some Thoughts on Women's Day" in the Yenan *Liberation Daily.* It was singled out as an attempt to attack "the entire social system of the liberated areas." Her short story "In the Hospital" was similarly denounced.

18. "Speech at the Chinese Communist Party's National Conference on Propaganda Work," in *Selected Works of Mao Tse-tung,* vol. 5 (Peking: Foreign Languages Press, 1977), p. 434.

19. Franz Schurmann, *Ideology and Organization in Communist China* (Berkeley: University of California Press, 1966), p. 129.

20. *Selected Works of Mao Tse-tung,* vol. 4 (London: Lawrence and Wishart, 1954), p. 113. This quotation is from a resolution on methods of leadership drafted by Mao on behalf of the Central Committee of the Communist Party. The resolution was passed in July 1943 by the Party Politburo. The Chinese text is available in *Cheng Feng Wen-hsüan* [Documents of the Party's Ideological Remolding Movement] (Hong Kong: Hsin Min Chu Ch'u Pan She, 1949), pp. 139–144.

21. "A Talk to the Editorial Staff of the *Shansi-Suiyuan Daily,"* in *Mao Tse-tung Selected Works,* vol. 5 (New York: International Publishers), pp. 241–245.

22. "The Work of Land Reform and of Party Consolidation in 1948," ibid., pp. 253–259.

23. Chi Wu, *I Ke-ming Ken-chü-ti Ti Ch'eng-chang* [The Development of a Revolutionary Base] (Peking: Jenmin Chu Pan She, 1957), pp. 213–214.

24. Ibid., p. 227.

25. *People's Daily,* September 15, 1977.

26. *Selected Works of Mao Tse-tung,* vol. 4 (London: Lawrence and Wishart, 1954), p. 63.

27. Ibid., p. 64.

28. For a thoughtful analysis of these differences and conflicts, see Merle Goldman, *Literary Dissent in Communist China* (Cambridge, Mass.: Harvard University Press, 1967).

29. See, for instance, his *Mass Persuasion in Communist China* (New York: Praeger, 1964); "Communications and Politics in Communist China," in Lucian W. Pye, ed., *Communications and Political Development* (Princeton, N.J.: Princeton University Press, 1963), pp. 259–297; "Campaigns, Communications, and

Development in Communist China," in Daniel Lerner and Wilbur Schramm, eds., *Communication and Change in the Developing Countries* (Honolulu: East-West Center Press, 1967), pp. 195–215; and "Persuasive Communications during the Cultural Revolution," *Gazette* (International Journal for Mass Communication Studies) 14 (1970): 73–87 and 137–148.

30. Yao Wen-yüan, "On the Counter-Revolutionary Double-Dealer Chou Yang," *Chinese Literature* (Peking), no. 3, 1967, p. 24.

31. *Selected Works of Mao Tse-tung,* vol. 4 (Peking: Foreign Languages Press, 1969), p. 418.

32. Ai Ssu-ch'i, "The Question of Study," *Ta Kung Pao* (Shanghai), April 9, 1950.

33. Liu Shao-ch'i, *On the Party* (Peking: Foreign Languages Press, 1950), p. 34.

34. He was heard briefly in 1956 when he participated in a forum organized by the Institute of Philosophical Research of the Academy of Sciences to discuss "the nature of the contradictions between the national bourgeoisie and the working class." *Kwang-ming Jihpao* [Kwangming Daily] (Peking), October 24, 1956.

35. Yao Wen-yüan, "On the Counter-Revolutionary Double-Dealer Chou Yang," p. 49.

36. *Hung Ch'i* [Red Flag], no. 5, 1977, pp. 21–42.

37. *Selected Works of Mao Tse-tung,* vol. 5 (Peking: Foreign Languages Press, 1977), pp. 369–370.

38. Ibid., p. 464.

39. Ibid., p. 481.

40. *People's Daily,* February 16, 1967.

41. The February 9, 1967, issue of the *People's Daily* devoted its entire fourth page to nine songs with quotations of Mao Tse-tung as lyrics. The title of the first song: "To overthrow a political regime it is always necessary to manufacture *[tsao cheng]* public opinion first."

42. *Peking Review,* no. 25, June 17, 1977.

43. "A Great Revolution to Achieve the Ascendancy of Mao Tse-tung's Thought," Editorial, *Red Flag,* no. 15, 1967. *Long Live Victory of the Great Cultural Revolution under the Dictatorship of the Proletariat—In Celebration of the 18th Anniversary of the Founding of the People's Republic of China* (Peking: Foreign Languages Press, 1968), pp. 28–29.

44. The twelve books are: *The Communist Manifesto,* by Marx and Engels; *The Ideology and Methodology of Marx and Engels,* compiled by the Liberation Press; *Socialism, Utopian and Scientific,* by Engels; *The State and Revolution,* by Lenin; *Left-Wing Communism, an Infantile Disorder,* by Lenin; *Foundations of Leninism,* by Stalin; *Lenin and Stalin on China,* compiled by the Liberation Press; *Short Course of the History of the Communist Party of the Soviet Union,* edited by the Central Committee of the CPSU.; *Political Economy,* by Leontiev; *The History of the Social Development,* compiled by the Liberation Press; *Lenin and Stalin on the Socialistic Economy* (two volumes), compiled by the Liberation Press: and *Imperialism, the Highest Stage of Capitalism,* by Lenin. See *People's China* (Peking), September 16, 1950, p. 25.

45. *Selected Works of Mao Tse-tung,* vol. 5 (Peking: Foreign Languages Press, 1977), p. 111.

46. *Survey of China Mainland Press,* no. 3762, August 17, 1966.

47. *Peking Review,* no. 2, January 10, 1969, p. 3.

48. *Wu-tsan Chieh-chi Wen-hua Ta-ke-ming Chih-liao-hsüan* [Collections of Reference Materials on Proletarian Cultural Revolution], vol. 2 (Hong Kong: San Lien Shu Tien, 1966), pp. 188–189,

49. *People's Daily,* July 13, 1977.

50. *People's Daily,* July 1, 1977.

51. *Red Flag,* no. 5, 1977, pp. 74–78.

3

The Current Structure and Functions of China's Mass Media

Godwin C. Chu

The importance of communication to building a Communist China was spelled out by the late Chairman Mao Tse-tung in a talk in 1943: "We should go to the masses and learn from them, synthesize their experience into better, articulated principles of methods, then do propaganda among the masses, and call upon them to put these principles and methods into practice so as to solve their problems and help them achieve liberation and happiness."[1] This strategy of organizing and mobilizing the people by communication has been followed since the Yenan days. By initiating a two-way communication, the Party leadership expects to learn from the masses and then reorganize their experiences into new programs of socialist reconstruction. China's mass media have played essential roles in this respect.

A related function of the Chinese media is to provide information that can support mass mobilization. Mao had this to say to the editorial staff of the *Shansi-Suiyuan Daily* in 1948:

> Our policy must be made known not only to the leaders and to the cadres but also to the broad masses. Questions concerning policy should as a rule be given publicity in the Party papers or periodicals. . . . Once the masses know the truth and have a common aim, they will work together with one heart. . . . The role and power of the newspapers consists in their ability to bring the Party program, the Party line, the Party's general and specific policies, its tasks and methods of work before the masses in the quickest and most extensive way.[2]

Over the last three decades, another function has become prominent. This is the use of the media as an instrument of political power struggle, a function which has been expanding with the growth of the Party but which has come to the fore more strikingly since the Cultural Revolution.

A fourth function of China's media, one that relates closely to cultural change, is what Mao called "combatting the wicked wind." It was during the Anti-Rightist movement of 1957, in the wake of the Hundred Flowers movement, that the primary objective of the media shifted from one of mobilizing for reconstruction to one of stressing the correct thinking of the people, particularly the intellectuals. There was concern that the objective of national mobilization would be seriously impaired unless the undesirable thinking was weeded out. Foreseeing such a shift, Mao came back to this theme again and again in a major policy speech in January, 1957: "By a wicked wind, we mean to say that these are not individual mistakes, but have become a general trend. Therefore we must strike it down. The way to strike it down is by reasoning. If we have persuasive power, we can knock down this wicked wind. If we don't have persuasive power, and only say nasty things, this wicked wind will keep blowing and growing."[3]

The current structure and content of China's mass media can be understood in the perspectives of these four functions: mobilization, information, power struggle, and ideological reform. The relative importance of each function has fluctuated somewhat during the last thirty years in response to the prevailing political, economic, and ideological climates. Except in the early 1950s, when the Party was able to operate with a moderate degree of unity in the first few years of the new regime, China's mass media have been inseparably involved in the internal contentions for power. This has been evident both before and after the death of Mao.

Mass mobilization for reconstruction has tended to occupy greater attention in the media when the power struggle moves toward a visible outcome and there are practical tasks to be performed. This trend can be detected during and after the Great Leap Forward, then again in the few years when Chou En-lai was picking up the pieces from the Cultural Revolution before the Chiang Ch'ing group mounted its Anti-Confucius and Anti-Lin Piao campaign, and now in the aftermath of the Gang of Four.

Providing information about Party policy, something Mao emphasized on the eve of the Communist victory, has been a function only when the media play a supportive role in either mobilization or political campaigns. The Chinese are generally told what is happening in their country when such information serves other official purposes.

The role of mass media as an instrument of ideological reform and cultural change has been emphasized since the Cultural Revolution, particularly in the few years before the death of Mao when Chiang Ch'ing was promoting her "newborn things." While there are subtle indications that the new government under Hua Kuofeng and Teng Hsiao-p'ing is less interested, at least for the time being, in this function of the media, we should not conclude that ideological reform has been abandoned. It may someday be revived should the need ever arise again—for instance, if the current trend toward material improvement should begin to threaten the very foundation of the Chinese Communist system.

To carry out these functions, the Party leadership has developed an extensive mass communication system in which the various media —the New China News Agency (Hsinhua), the *People's Daily,* the Party magazine *Red Flag,* the provincial newspapers, radio, and television—deliver essentially the same official messages. (See the chapter by Merle Goldman for analysis of policy debates in the mass media.) They are supervised by the Department of Propaganda under the Party's Central Committee and, for the provincial media, through the Party's provincial committees. In practice, the operation of these media reflects a brand of investigative reporting with a one-sided perspective. *Red Flag* explained it this way: ". . . guided by Chairman Mao's proletarian revolutionary thinking and the various policies and directives, we must go to the masses, and carry out serious and not perfunctory investigation and research. We must grasp model materials that can point to the correct direction of a movement. Then we must use accurate, clear and vivid language to write our reports on the objective reality."[4]

This objective reality is not what is or has happened. Rather, it is the final outcome of a long and involved process by which "the rich materials we [Chinese media personnel] obtain from our senses are screened by a careful thought process, which retains the essence and leave out the unimportant, keeping the truth and eliminating the falsehood." It is meant to be a "penetrating, accurate and complete representation of objectivity" that has progressed from sensory perception to a kind of "rational perception."[5] It is a reality seen through the Party's ideological lens rather than through the uncultivated eye of the individual. The whole approach suggests a philosophy that control of information input can structure the individual's perception, which in turn can influence his values, beliefs, and behavior.

In the following pages, we briefly discuss China's major communication media.

People's Daily

The most important official newspaper in China is the *People's Daily (Jenmin Jihpao)*, voice of the Chinese Communist Party. Operated under the close supervision of the Department of Propaganda, the *People's Daily* has a large circulation, estimated in 1974 to be approximately 3.4 million copies.[6] It reaches all the agricultural production teams, some 740,000 of them, and all schools, factories, and government offices in the cities. The total number of readers reached by this official newspaper is much greater than its circulation figure would indicate because of the existence of newspaper reading groups. In each group a student or someone else reads the stories from the *People's Daily* to his illiterate neighbors. The Party's supervision over the *People's Daily* is such that major editorials have to be cleared with the highest authorities. The editorial on National Day in 1972, for instance, was approved by Chou En-lai himself.[7] All news stories, domestic and international, reflect the official stance.

The *People's Daily* appears in six full-size pages. Page 1 is for important news, mostly domestic (e.g., production campaigns), and for editorials, which appear not every day but only when important issues call for official enunciation. Pages 2 and 3 carry other domestic news and features. When there is a political campaign, such as the one criticizing Lin Piao and Confucius, long articles of criticisms are published on these two pages to signify the current ideological thinking. Letters to editors, published occasionally, appear mostly on page 3 and sometimes on page 2. Another column is called "Life of the Party," in which Party members write about their own experience in improving their ideological rectitude. The achievements of model workers, such as Iron Man Wang Ching-hsi of the Tach'ing Oilfield, and of model units, such as the Tachai Brigade, are publicized for the whole country to emulate. Sometimes a particular model is given front page coverage, such as the Hsiao Chin Chuang Brigade outside Tientsin during the days of Chiang Ch'ing. Page 4 is usually for domestic news of a more routine nature, as well as literary and art news. Sometimes this page is reserved exclusively for pictures celebrating an important domestic event, such as the inauguration of Chairman Hua Kuo-feng. Occasionally revolutionary poems and songs are reproduced. Pages 5 and 6 display foreign news. The weekly programs of

Peking Television are printed on one of these two pages, although not regularly. So are announcements of revolutionary operas and other entertainments.

All foreign news stories originate from the official New China News Agency, which has correspondents in major capitals of the world. Important domestic news stories are also released by the agency. The *People's Daily* has correspondents all over the country to cover local features. Occasionally, an article from a provincial newspaper is reprinted if it is considered worthy of national attention, but no other news sources are used. Like all other newspapers in China, the *People's Daily* carries no advertising. The post office handles subscriptions and delivers the newspaper.

Provincial and Local Newspapers

Other than the *People's Daily,* there are some 350 provincial and local newspapers in various provinces and municipalities. They publish four pages a day. The *Wen Hui Pao* (Wen Hui Report) in metropolitan Shanghai, probably one of the largest, has a circulation of 900,000 copies. Other better-known local papers include the *Kuangchow* (Canton) *Daily* and *Nan Fang* (Southern) *Daily,* both published in Canton, and the *Shensi Daily* in Sian, which distributes 320,000 copies daily.[8] Unlike the *People's Daily,* which is distributed overseas as well as in China, provincial and local newspapers are not available to readers outside the country.

The reason, according to Edward Murray of the *Detroit Free Press,* who visited China in 1972, was the nature of the local news the provincial papers contain. Murray had this to say: "These newspapers, we learned from interviews, not only print local news. But they are so close to the people that news has to be factual, which is to say, sometimes they present a much more negative picture than China wants to project to the outside world."[9] We have recently obtained from Hong Kong one copy of the *Kuangchow Daily* and one copy of the *Nan Fang Daily,* both dated June 1975. Except for three brief commentaries and a few provincial news items, however, these two newspapers are highly similar in content to the *People's Daily.*[10]

Three brief commentaries in the *Nan Fang Daily* were selected from among those displayed in the Revolutionary Criticism Column and Blackboard Paper of Tatung Brigade in Kwangtung. They were prefaced with this editor's note:

In the Revolutionary Criticism Column and the Blackboard Paper of Tatung Brigade there are often published brief commentaries that have a fighting spirit. Employing the teaching of Marx and Lenin and the Thought of Mao Tse-tung as their weapons, and in coordination with a realistic class struggle, these commentaries criticize various undesirable trends, rotten people and rotten behavior, in order to attack the class enemy and educate the people. We have selected three as follows. [11]

The first commentary criticized the resurgence of superstition among the peasants. The second condemned the selfish behavior of one commune member. This person, and others as well, had planted cucumbers and vegetables on a strip of land on the top of the commune's reservoir dike. When told that this practice would encourage the growth of capitalism, all of them cooperated and dug up what they had planted. But this particular commune member carried away some thirty loads of topsoil from the dike because he said he had put in chemical fertilizer. His behavior was denounced.

The third commentary was the most critical of all. It gave a rather candid account of how some members in the commune were interested in nothing but their private plots. Whenever they got together, before or after work, or after supper, they talked all the time about what vegetables to plant for the most profit, and where to sell them for the best prices. Some of them went to work on their private plots even when they should have been working for the commune. As a result, the commune's production suffered. This practice, said the commentary, must be stopped.

Interesting as these commentaries are, it must be pointed out that they did not reveal anything substantial which the *People's Daily* has not criticized from time to time. What they did contain, which is usually not found in the *People's Daily,* were factual details of the misdeeds.

Reference Information

China also has a special newspaper that is becoming more widely known to the outside world in recent years. This is *Reference Information (Ts'an-k'ao Hsiao-hsi).* First published in the early 1950s by the New China News Agency as an internal news bulletin for high-level Party cadres, *Reference Information* expanded its circulation in 1957 from some 2,000 to more than 400,000 following a major decision by Chairman Mao.[12] The latest estimate puts the total circulation of this tabloid-size newspaper at 6 million copies, larger than the circulation of the *People's Daily*.[13] It now appears daily, usually in four pages. It contains news from around the world, both favorable and unfavorable to China, which does not appear in other newspapers in the country. Its circulation is not limited to Party members; anyone who has a cadre position can subscribe. Although the subscriber is not supposed to share this publication with nonsubscribers, including the spouse and members of the family, this rule is apparently not rigidly enforced. Accounts by former residents of China indicate that *Reference Information* is perhaps the most popular newspaper in China.

The function of *Reference Information,* according to Mao, is to provide a dose of inoculation so that the Chinese will not be totally unprepared for the realities of the world outside.

Apparently following this policy, *Reference Information,* for instance, reported on the defection of a Chinese Communist jet pilot, Lt. Liu Ch'eng-ssu, in a MIG-15 in March 1962.[14] It would be misleading, however, to assume that this publication carries anything secret about internal political affairs in China. An examination of the issue of October 9, 1972, made available to this writer by a friend, reveals that the contents of *Reference Information* are mostly reprints, without interpretation, of news and commentaries from foreign news agencies and newspapers.[15] Even though this particular issue contained nothing unfavorable to China, the news stories and commentaries it carried do present a much broader variety than those of the *People's Daily* and the provincial newspapers. The amount of international news in *Reference Information* seems to be much more than what is generally found in an average American metropolitan newspaper.

Commune Newspapers

A kind of grassroots newspaper that serves the production brigades and production teams in the communes has appeared in China since the Cultural Revolution. Sometimes called the war bulletin *(chan pao),* this is a mimeographed information sheet edited and produced by peasants in the brigade. Called *tu* (muddy) correspondents, because they have mud on their feet and calluses on their hands, they have been compared to the barefoot doctors. The Huang Lou Commune near Shanghai provided an example of how these correspondents operate.[16] In that commune there were some one hundred and fifty peasant correspondents in 1968.

Because they work on farms, "muddy" correspondents understand the problems of peasants in a way that urban reporters cannot. Most of them are sons and daughters of poor and lower-middle peasants. They usually have no training other than elementary or junior high school. More important than professional training, however, is loyalty to the Party and to Chairman Mao. A peasant correspondent must first of all be a capable and diligent worker, thus having the respect of other peasants; the ability to write well is of secondary importance.

Wen Hui Pao (Wen Hui Report) of Shanghai has reported on the style and content of the commune-level news bulletins.[17] One night a peasant correspondent at Huang Lou Commune heard over the Central People's Broadcasting Station an article from the *People's Daily* on the barefoot doctor system. Although it was already past 10 p.m., she called together the poor and lower-middle peasants in her production team to discuss the article. Afterwards, she wrote an article expressing their support to be broadcast over the commune's line-broadcasting station the following day.

In another case, several commune members were carrying topsoil for their private plots during the commune's working hours. One peasant correspondent learned about it and got someone to write a letter. He then published the letter in the production brigade's news bulletin, with an editor's note. This story was later broadcast on the commune station.

Another commune member was preparing to give a big birthday feast to celebrate the "longevity" of his grandmother according to old Chinese traditions. When a peasant correspondent learned about it, he did not write an article of criticism but instead organized the poor and lower-middle peasants of the production team to talk to this person. They finally convinced him to give up the feast and the birthday celebration.

In general, the peasant correspondents act as opinion leaders in the village, using the news bulletin to disseminate information from the national mass media and to correct what are considered to be undesirable behavioral patterns.

Tatzupao

Tatzupao, an age-old Chinese medium of communication, has now developed into a major component in China's media system. The

Chinese have traditionally used wall posters for public announce-ments, such as the emperor's edicts, and for airing private griev-ances.[18] The Chinese Communists began to make effective use of this form of information dissemination as early as the Yenan days, perhaps because of the widespread use of posters in collective farms and factories in Soviet Russia shortly after the Russian revolu-tion.[19] Those were the days when the Chinese Communists were eager to follow the Russian model.

It was during the Hundred Flowers movement and the subse-quent Anti-Rightist movement that the *tatzupao* took on a new function. It became a powerful instrument of criticism and counterattack. When the Party invited Chinese intellectuals to voice their complaints in the spring of 1957, many in Peking, Shanghai, and other big cities posted lengthy criticisms. These, however, cannot compare in magnitude and vehemency with the organized *tatzupao* campaign mounted by the Party in the summer of that year to refute the rightist intellectuals.[20]

By that time, *tatzupao* had already been recognized as an effec-tive means of mobilizing the masses for political participation. It was not until the Cultural Revolution, however, when for months China was literally covered with millions of posters voicing all kinds of contentions, that *tatzupao* became widely known to the world outside. The Cultural Revolution has firmly established *tat-zupao* as a major social institution in China.

The ingenious way in which the big character posters were used by the Maoist group in 1966–1967 to disrupt the channels of com-munication of the Liu Shao-ch'i group, to create an atmosphere of confusion and a sense of impending change, and to lend a basis of legitimacy to the power struggle has already been analyzed.[21] After the Maoist group came back to power, a halt was put to the *tat-zupao* rampage. Once the Chinese got a taste of what this simple form of communication could do, however, a need grew for its continued application. In fact, since the 1975 constitution, the *tat-zupao* has been recognized as a legitimate means of expression for the common people.[22]

From what we know, the ordinary people in China can put up *tatzupao* to make a complaint about the wrongdoing of lower-level cadres, or to air grievances of a minor nature. However, they must first submit the posters to the responsible local unit for approval.[23] It would be misleading to think that anybody in China can put up a *tatzupao* any time he likes.

Because of its rather surprising effects in the Cultural Revolution, the *tatzupao* has earned a permanent role in the process of China's political struggle. Opposing sides have often used the same strategy of attacking opponents in posters that are either anonymous or attributed to the study groups of some obscure units. This has been the practice both before the death of Chairman Mao, when the Chiang Ch'ing group was engaged in a power contest with Teng Hsiao-p'ing, and since the purge of the Gang of Four, as different factions jostle for authority in the new government.

Political posters of this nature often appear at odd moments in unexpected places, perhaps as a way to avoid premature confrontation. This practice, however, has made it possible for genuine critics to take advantage of the *tatzupao* as an uncensored means of attacking government policies. They can do this with temporary immunity because the local authorities are often not sure whether such attacks are part of an organized power struggle involving top-level contenders. They would thus hesitate to take punitive actions before the lines were clearly drawn.

This happened to a lengthy *tatzupao* posted in Canton in 1974 by three young intellectuals which severely criticized the Maoist policies of the Party and demanded more freedom and democracy. For days, the poster signed by Li I-che remained intact for thousands of local residents to peruse. Once the municipal authorities made sure that there was no powerful faction behind it, it was torn down. Handwritten copies of this *tatzupao* have made their way to Hong Kong, and were subsequently published by a Hong Kong periodical.[24]

Radio Broadcasting

Radio broadcasting in Communist China has come a long way from the small, antiquated transmitter which Chou En-lai brought back to Yenan from Moscow in 1940.[25] Today, nearly four decades later, radio broadcasting in China reaches all cities, more than 92 percent of the agricultural production teams (villages), and some 70 percent of the peasant homes.[26]

The development of radio broadcasting in the 1950s and the 1960s has been discussed by Frederick Yu and Alan Liu.[27] Since those days, the organizational channels for radio broadcasting have remained the same. The Central People's Broadcasting Station in Peking directs and coordinates all radio broadcasting in the provinces and large municipalities. The primary language on radio is Mandarin, but other dialects such as Cantonese, Fukien, and Hakka are used for regional broadcasts. The Central People's Broadcasting Station operates two channels, CPBS I and CPBS II, which broadcast essentially the same programs but at different hours.

The provincial and municipal stations relay a large portion of the central broadcasts and add programs of a regional nature, primarily news events in the provinces and criticisms of local deviances. Provincial broadcasts are further relayed to the counties and, subsequently, to the communes, production brigades, production teams, and individual peasant homes. Wired broadcasting is used extensively at the local level. In China, practically all places for public gatherings have installed loudspeakers, which apparently are turned on from early in the morning till closing time. By latest estimates, there were some 106,000,000 loudspeakers in China in 1975, averaging about one for every eight Chinese, young and old. The corresponding number in 1964 was 6,000,000.[28]

The radio program content is closely supervised by the Central Broadcasting Bureau, which maintains regional offices in the provinces. The bureau has four divisions: administration, technology, radio broadcasting, and television. Operating under the Office of the Premier, the bureau is not involved in actual program production but assumes the responsibility of technological improvement, personnel training, and program supervision. Major policy decisions, however, are handled by the Department of Propaganda, not by the Central Broadcasting Bureau.

A typical domestic radio broadcast begins at 4:00 a.m. for CPBS I (5:00 a.m. for CPBS II) with a brief preview of the programs for the day. There are news broadcasts, as many as ten times a day, and ideological commentaries and criticisms. There are special programs for children, for intellectual youth sent to the villages, for workers, for commune members, and for the People's Liberation Army. Special programs are featured on agricultural technology, sanitation, and physical exercise. Music, drama, art and literature, and the selected works of Marx, Lenin, and Mao Tse-tung make up the rest of the programming. The station goes off the air for about an hour in the afternoon and resumes broadcasting before 4:00 p.m. Signoff for the day comes at 1:35 a.m. for CPBS I and at 11:30 p.m. for CPBS II.

Other than relaying the central and provincial broadcasting programs, local stations at the county and commune levels carry programs of their own:[29]

1. Broadcasting of criticism sessions: The Shanghai Broadcasting Station, for instance, broadcast the sessions of criticism of antirevolutionary thinking held at the Shanghai Diesel Engine Factory in 1970.

2. Broadcast of meetings: When cadres from the counties and communes in a region meet to discuss a major problem, the meeting is sometimes broadcast live for the local audience.

3. Experience of pioneer models: The experience of model units is sometimes broadcast as a special educational program. The experiences of Tachai Brigade and Tach'ing Oilfield have been widely publicized on the radio is this manner.

4. Mobilization for production: Communes have used wired broadcasting to organize production campaigns.

Television

Television broadcasting in black and white started in Peking on September 2, 1958. Color television broadcasting is now available, but color sets are few. There are currently 37 television broadcasting stations and 120 relay stations in the country, including those in Sinkiang and Tibet.[30] In 1958, there were about 10,000 television sets in Peking. The current total has been estimated at 1,000,000 sets in the whole country.[31] Television broadcasting is centrally controlled in Peking. The Peking Television Station, which produces most programs, operates under the supervision of the Central Broadcasting Bureau. The provincial stations transmit the programs from Peking and sometimes produce programs of their own. Local programming may increase in future.

The government is planning to expand television reception. The immediate target was to reach 2,000,000 sets by 1978 so that each production brigade would have one receiving set. All factories, schools, and hospitals with more than 100 individuals would also have at least one set by the end of 1978. Eventually cable will be used to send the signals to peasant homes.[32]

Television sets in China are domestically assembled. Most sets are 9 inches, in black and white, and priced at approximately US$130. A 12-inch black and white set is sold at US$250. Sets with larger screens, 14 and 16 inches, are available, but relatively few.

Reports from China in 1975 suggest that the television set factory at Shaoshan, Hunan, was capable of producing 19-inch color sets.[33] The Peking Television Station broadcasts on two channels, channel 2 and channel 8. Both channels begin their evening broadcasts at 7:00 p.m. and sign off at 10:00 p.m. In addition, channel 2 has three morning broadcasts a week, on Tuesday, Thursday, and Sunday, from 10:00 a.m. to noon. Channel 8 has a morning broadcast only on Sunday, from 9:00 a.m. to 11:00 a.m. The evening broadcasts on both channels begin with half an hour of domestic and international news, followed by a variety of programs that are highly similar in content to the radio broadcasts.[34] There are programs on science and technology, health and sanitation, art and literature, sports and, above all, the experiences of model units whose achievements are dramatized. Almost every day there is something for children—songs, dances, and stories—to instill a revolutionary spirit in young minds. Several times a week, feature films are shown, usually after 8:00 p.m. They are generally about the unusual feats of revolutionary heroes, such as Lei Feng, a Liberation Army martyr, model communes and factories, or sent-down youths whose self-sacrificing behavior deserves praise.

The Chinese have made ingenious use of popular, traditional forms of performing art on television. For instance, *hsiang sheng* (the traditional Chinese comic duet) has been used to present a program called "Learn from Iron Man Wang Ching-hsi," an exemplary tale of a model worker at the Tach'ing Oilfield. As far as we can tell, no regular programs on television teach the works of Marx, Lenin, and Mao. (See appendix B for a listing of one week of programs on Peking Television in August 1977.)

Trends—Past and Future

One of the primary functions of China's media is to help change the behavioral patterns and ideological orientations of the Chinese people away from the confines of the past toward the new ideals of the proletariat. To achieve this objective, the media have been used to criticize, in periodical campaigns and routine reminders, the "wicked winds" mentioned previously. At the same time, in big headlines and accentuated accounts, the media feature new behavioral models and ideological commitments to teach the values of altruistic service and loyalty to the collectivity. These spell out dos and don'ts for the people of China. Any information or ideas that are contrary to the Party's ideals, whether they originate from within or without, are kept out lest the minds of the people be contaminated.

How well have the Chinese accepted this mode of communication? What has been the response of the people to this form of ideological education? No clear answers are yet available, for there are no Gallup polls in China. We may gain a circumstantial index of the impact from the way the media content is perceived by the audience. The *Takung Pao (Takung Report),* a Hong Kong newspaper that generally reflects Peking's official thinking, recently revealed some noteworthy insights.[35] Quoting an editorial in the *Liberation Army Daily* of November 14, 1977, the report said that most Chinese newspapers during the reign of the Gang of Four were filled with empty words. "In a news item of thousands of words, from the beginning to the end you could not find a single concrete example." Furthermore, said the *Takung Pao,* quoting another editorial in the *Liberation Army Daily* from the middle of October 1977, the Gang of Four created a new "eight-legged" *(pa ku)* style of fabrication: "They used false speech, fabricated events, made false reports, created false models, publicized false experiences, wrote false history, and even falsified the sayings of our revolutionary teacher," so that the credibility of China's newspapers and publications was impaired.

Another trend prevalent during that period, noted the *Takung Pao,* was wooden-headed copying. Newspapers all over the country were forced to reprint articles composed by the Gang's writers. "You take a thousand newspapers, they all have the same front page. You take a thousand publications, they all have the same tone." The Chinese have even concocted a popular saying: "Small newspapers copy big newspapers; big newspapers follow Liang Hsiao" *(Hsiao pao ch'ao ta pao, ta pao ch'ao Liang Hsiao).*[36] "During those days," said the *Takung Pao,* "when people read a newspaper, they only looked at the headlines. When people read a book, they only looked at the cover. Newspapers and publications were not well received by the mass of people."

The *Takung Pao* cited three letters to the editor published in Peking's *Kuangming Daily* on December 3, 1977, to point out that the practice of reprinting approved articles has not abated even though the Gang of Four has been toppled. One letter said that many professional publications were still reprinting political articles and documents from official newspapers on a massive scale, making themselves almost archives of documents.

Thus, according to the *Takung Pao,* a movement is currently afoot to reform China's newspapers and to restore the spirit which Chairman Mao encouraged during the Yenan days.

While it is too early to assess the results of this reform, an examination of the *People's Daily* issues in the spring of 1978 reveals some changes as well as continuities. The most apparent change has to do with quotations from Chairman Mao. Before his death, the upper right corner of the front page was exclusively reserved for a daily display of his sayings, always framed in a box. This box has been appearing less and less frequently since his death. When it does appear, more often than not it features a quotation from Chairman Hua. In the days when Chiang Ch'ing was in power, articles in the *People's Daily* were accentuated by quotations from Mao, set in bold type. This custom is no longer practiced, although the late Chairman is still mentioned in news articles now and then.

The makeup of the official newspaper appears to be more lively than before, with a more liberal use of pictures, sometimes in color, as during the Fifth People's Congress in March 1978, or when Chairman Hua visited the Miyun Reservoir in December 1977 to help shovel mud.[37] Pictures of Chairman Mao are now printed in black and white.

There are more articles on science and technology, a reflection of the new policy. Reports on science and technology customarily begin with an acknowledgment of the leadership of Chairman Hua and the Party's Central Committee, and make a routine condemnation of the Gang of Four. As in the past, there are seasonal reports on campaigns of spring planting and industrial production, and the slogan *ta-kan k'uai-shang* (do big tasks fast and upward) is still frequently referred to as the cardinal principle. There seems to be more concern about practical problems, such as how to streamline the accounting system, or how to develop commune enterprises.[38] Somewhat more attention is given to details in the news stories.

Now as well as in the past, long ideological treatises occupy much space, sometimes a full page. The differences in content and style from the past, if any, is difficult to detect, except that the target of criticism is now the Gang. The rationale and the terminology, however, remain much the same. An example is a full-page article called "A Criticism of the Pragmatic Philosophy of Lin Piao and the Gang of Four," in April 1978.[39] Aside from the incongruity of associating the Gang with a pragmatic philosophy, this article could have been written in its current tenor before October 1976.

Undoubtedly, a trend toward pragmatism has begun to emerge in China's media, rather slowly and often imperceptibly. How far this trend will develop remains to be seen.

NOTES

1. Mao Tse-tung, "Get Organized!" *Selected Works of Mao Tse-tung,* vol. 3 (Peking: Foreign Languages Press, 1966), p. 158.

2. Mao Tse-tung, "A Talk to the Editorial Staff of the *Shansi-Suiyuan Daily,"* *Selected Works of Mao Tse-tung,* vol. 3 (Peking: Foreign Languages Press, 1969), p. 241.

3. Mao Tse-tung, "Talks at the Meeting of Party Secretaries of Provincial Level," *Selected Works of Mao Tse-tung,* vol. 5 (Peking: People's Publishing Press, 1977), p. 350.

4. Chiang Hung, "Strengthen the Ideological Development of the News Reporting Groups," *Red Flag,* no. 2, 1971, p. 10.

5. Ibid., p. 11.

6. Richard Dudman, "Headlines and Deadlines: Chinese Style," *Nieman Reports* (Spring and Summer 1977): 19–21.

7. Wilbur E. Elston, "In China, Newspapers Serve the Party," in *China Today* (Detroit: *Detroit News,* 1972), p. 52.

8. J. Edward Murray, "How China's Press Handles News," in *4000 Miles Across China* (Detroit: *Detroit Free Press,* 1972), p. 23.

9. Ibid.

10. The *Canton Daily* (June 12, 1975) had two stories on the front page: a telephone-broadcasting meeting among factory workers and cadres in the province to study the instructions from Chairman Mao on promoting industrial production; the visit by the president of Zambia to China. Page 2 carried an editorial supporting Chairman Mao's latest instructions and three more stories about the visit of the president of Zambia. Page 3 had three provincial news items: a feature story on ideological education for students, and two brevities. Page 4 carried mostly foreign news from the New China News Agency.

The *Nan Fang Daily* (June 13, 1975) displayed on its front page a picture of Chairman Mao greeting the president of Zambia. There was a story on how the Canton Railway Station set a record of freight transportation during the first half of the year. In another announcement, Marshal Chu Teh and Premier Chou En-lai sent a message on the Phillippine Independence Day. Page 2 carried two stories about model peasants and three brief commentaries we shall discuss. Page 3 had four stories about revolutionary operas. Page 4 had mostly foreign news from New China News Agency dispatches, in addition to reproduced posters about the first Chinese National Games.

11. *Nan Fang Jihpao* [Southern Daily], June 13, 1975.

12. Mao Tse-tung, "Talks at the Meeting of Party Secretaries of Provincial

Level," *Selected Works,* vol. 5 (Peking: People's Publishing Press, 1977), p. 349. The immunizing function of what Mao called "negative materials" was discussed recently in the official press. See Hsiao Kui, "Negative Materials and Smallpox Vaccine," *People's Daily,* August 14, 1977.

13. Emmett Dedmon, *China Journal* (Chicago: Rand McNally, 1973), p. 140. Also Chang Kuo-hsin, "World News Read Only by China's Selected Few," *IPI* [International Press Institute] *Report* 25 (February 1976): 1-2.

14. "A Journalist and His Paper," in Francis Harper, ed., *Out of China: A Collection of Interviews with Refugees from China* (Hong Kong: Dragonfly Books, 1964), pp. 222-225.

15. On Page 1, the major story was ABC's commentary on Deputy Foreign Minister Chiao Kuan-hua's address at the United Nations. Another leading story summarized a feature from *Tokyo Shimbun* on American and Russian reactions to the reduction of tension in Asia. A report in *Yumiori Shimbun* on normalization of relations with China and on Japan's territorial claims with Soviet Russia was also reproduced. The other three pages carried news, all from foreign sources, about: a visit by a Polish Delegation to France and the signing of an economic pact between the two countries, Brezhnev's impending visit to the United States, the conclusion of a visit to Russia by the Malaysian prime minister, Egyptian Prime Minister Sadat's interview on the Lebanon incident, Yemen's criticism of Sadat, a statement by the Indian defense minister on India's military deployment in the Himalayan region, a story in the *Washington Daily News* on China's relations with Latin America, and a train accident in Mexico. Interestingly, this particular issue carried four items on page 4 about scientific development in the United States and Soviet Russia.

16. "Peasant Correspondents of Huang Lou Commune," *Wen Hui Pao* [Wen Hui Report], December 24, 1968.

17. Ibid.

18. For a brief discussion of the traditional use of posters in China, see Godwin C. Chu, *"Tatzepao,"* in *Radical Change through Communication in Mao's China* (Honolulu: The University Press of Hawaii, 1977), pp. 232-238; also Barry M. Broman, *"Tatzepao:* Medium of Conflict in China's Cultural Revolution," *Journalism Quarterly* 46 (Spring 1969): 100.

19. See David Jim-tat Poon, *"Tatzepao:* Its History and Significance as a Communication Medium," in Godwin C. Chu, ed., *Popular Media in China: Shaping New Cultural Patterns,* (Honolulu: The University Press of Hawaii, 1978), pp. 184-221.

20. See Godwin C. Chu, "Communication and Conflict Resolution," in *Radical Change,* pp. 215-252.

21. See Broman, *"Tatzepao";* also Godwin C. Chu, Philip H. Cheng, and Leonard Chu, *The Roles of Tatzepao in the Cultural Revolution* (Carbondale, Ill.: Southern Illinois University, 1972).

22. "Constitution of the People's Republic of China," article no. 13, *People's Daily,* January 20, 1975.

23. See Poon, *"Tatzepao."*

24. The *tatzupao,* signed by Li I-che, was posted in a public street in Canton in November 1974 and was addressed to Chairman Mao and the Fourth National People's Congress. Its preface and text, about 23,000 words long, were later carried in full in *Ming Pao Monthly* (Hong Kong) 10 (December 1975): 53-60. Li I-che, in

reality, was three persons: *Li* Cheng-tien, a 1966 graduate from the Canton Art Institute, Chen *I*-yang, and Huang Hsi-*che,* both offspring of Party cadres. All active Red Guards during the Cultural Revolution, they criticized the Party for what they considered to be major shortcomings of the Chinese Communist system. For a brief summary of their criticisms, see "Lee's *Tatzepao:* To Mao with Dissent," *The Asian Messenger,* Spring 1976, p. 27.

25. Hu Shou-heng, "A Current Analysis of Broadcasting and Television in Communist China," in *Pao Hsüeh* [Studies of Journalism] 5 (June 1977): 121–122.

26. *Peking Review* 18 (1975): 30.

27. See Frederick T. C. Yu, *Mass Persuasion in Communist China* (New York: Praeger, 1964); and Alan P. L. Liu, *Communications and National Integration in Communist China* (Berkeley: University of California Press, 1971).

28. Ming Ch'en, "Broadcasting Network in Rural China Since the Cultural Revolution," *Ming Pao Monthly,* no. 121, 1976, pp. 93–100.

29. Ibid.

30. Huai Yu, "Television Broadcasting in Communist China," in *Studies on Chinese Communism* (March 15, 1977): 73–78.

31. Ibid., p. 75.

32. Ibid.

33. Leonard Chu, "Television Broadcasting in China," *Ming Pao* [Ming Report] (Hong Kong), April 26, 1977.

34. We shall briefly describe one newscast, on August 14, 1977, from Peking Television Station. The program started with a preview of the news items for the evening. The first, lasting seven minutes, was a report on recent developments in Wenchou, Chekiang Province. Factory workers and peasants were shown to be raising their hands to denounce the Gang of Four and working hard to rebuild Wenchou from the destruction suffered under the Gang of Four's reign. The female announcer, who did not appear, emphasized that the people of Wenchou were carrying on the reconstruction following the instructions of the late Chairman Mao. The camera showed an ironworks, a china factory, and an embroidery shop. Men and women were shown busy at work, much like those pictured in *China Reconstructs,* an official Chinese pictorial for overseas distribution. Next was brief (one and a half minutes) coverage of a salt field near Canton, where production had gone up. For the next three and a half minutes, Vice Premier Li Hsien-nien was shown greeting the prime minister from Sao Tome. Pictured were the handshaking at the Peking airport, the reception line showing each of the dignitaries present, and the dinner party, at which Li was shown making a speech; a female voice narrated. After that, Vice Premier Chi Teng-k'ui bid his welcome to a visiting group from Japan, with handshaking and a reception line.

The domestic portion of the newscast was concluded by a 6-minute report on the resurrection of a Hopeh vernacular stage show, "A Commonplace Post," which had been killed by the Gang of Four. The report began with a criticism of the Gang of Four and then proceeded to show how the actors and actresses were rehearsing for their new performance. It was a story about a young worker who did not like to carry human manure but wanted to be a truck driver in the city. His Party secretary, an old worker, eventually convinced him that he could make a contribution to the revolution even in his commonplace post as a manure collector.

International news (10 minutes) began with the introduction of the Japanese edition of volume 5 of Chairman Mao's selected works in Japan. Japanese visitors were shown buying the book at a trade fair. This was followed by a brief report on the West African economic conference in the capital of Togo, and exchange of visits by presidents and premiers in Africa and Latin America. The international news for that day included a horsemanship event in Europe and an international track meet. These events occurred in July. The weather in Peking ended the news program.

While it would be difficult to generalize from the news program of one day, several characteristics may be noted. No one talks on television in the entire news program. Everything is voiced over by the female announcer, who remains anonymous and does not appear during the program. Timeliness seems to be of no particular consequence, as most of the domestic events reported that day took place during the previous month. The leading news item, on Wenchou, was not about a particular event. None of the news reports presented any details. There were no commercials.

35. The following is based upon Chai Chi, "Newspapers in China Are Undergoing a Major Reform," *Takung Pao* (Hong Kong), December 7, 1977.

36. Liang Hsiao, apparently a pseudonym, is pronounced the same way as "two schools" in Chinese. It is generally assumed that "Liang Hsiao" referred to the team of theoretical writers from Peking University and Tsing Hua University that wrote important articles for Chiang Ch'ing and her followers prior to the death of Chairman Mao.

37. "Courageous and Capable Leader, Chairman Hua Kuo-feng, Joins Manual Labor at Miyun Reservoir," *People's Daily,* December 2, 1977.

38. For instance, see "Resolutely Support the Accountant Who Dares to Uphold a Sound Financial System" and "Commune Enterprises Need Big Development," *People's Daily,* April 4, 1978.

39. "A Criticism of the Pragmatic Philosophy of Lin Piao and the Gang of Four," *People's Daily,* April 3, 1978.

4

Local Newspapers
and Community Change,
1949–1969

Lynn T. White III

Modern philosophers tell us that man is essentially a symbol maker.[1] The habit of assigning significance to otherwise meaningless events gives the human species no end of pretensions, but it also allows us to achieve a degree of mutual cooperation even more complex than that among the ants or the bees. Anything social can be discussed as communication. Indeed, in a sense communication is culture.

Thus any subject in contemporary Chinese culture—the rate of industrial investment, the view of art, the military posture, or changes in any of these—would be fair game for discussion here. A study of mass communication in China, even of just one medium such as newspapers, should help to describe the whole process of community change. In fact, many Chinese social topics have already been treated from a communication perspective.[2]

The present chapter reverts to an old-hat definition of communication. It is about newspapers, not about all the formal and informal media that together contribute to community change. Such a focus may lose the breadth of the more general approach, but research on the Chinese government's self-conscious use of newspapers may provide some insight about the broad functions of media in a developing state under strong rule. How effective (or ineffective) are newspapers in the task of spreading official enthusiasms? Are local newspapers read differently from national ones? A study of these specific aspects of Chinese journalism can help us understand the impact of mass communication on the modern Chinese process of community change.

This chapter is organized according to three formal aspects of communication: message formulation, message sending, and message reception. They will be analyzed separately, in that order.

The first aspect has to do with content. In a country as large and complex as China, the sources even of official media easily become disunited. Chinese newspapers often report (usually with vituperative emphasis) that policy factions have existed in the Communist Party, and that they have published inconsistent norms, incoherent signals. Some of the most effective journalistic writers, especially in the 1950s, have not even been Communists. The Party controlled their careers but was unwilling to neglect the large readerships which their somewhat unofficial styles served; so as a group, they had some minor leverage. Coherence in the source of public messages has nonetheless remained a basic Communist goal. The techniques for attaining unity, and the major problems in doing so, are the first topic of study.

After a signal has been determined, the next step is to send it. Governmental top-to-bottom messages are the ones on which we have most data. A study of signal sending becomes largely an analysis of the postal system, because in China almost all newspapers are distributed through the post office. Ordinary circuit characteristics, such as the volume and speed of communication flows, become the main objects of study. China's poverty and size impose evident difficulties for maintaining the strength and clarity of messages, as they are transferred over space with time delays. Coherence of the mechanism to solve these problems, and the conditions under which they are solved or not, is the second aspect of our examination.

Third and finally, messages are received. At least, that is the intention of the senders. Techniques that encourage people actually to read newspapers, rather than to ignore them, have been numerous in the People's Republic of China. Many efforts have been made, with more or less success at various times, to increase literacy, increase the credibility that readers accord print materials, make newspaper articles more interesting, and above all assure that readers will put in their minds and convey to their friends the content of the approved press.

One disconcerting conclusion from the evidence that follows is that Western researchers of China have ordinarily been reading newspapers that most Chinese find less interesting, less credible, and generally less worthwhile than other materials, which have wider circulations. The *People's Daily,* for example, emerges as the most important source of information for almost nobody in China. Cadres read limited-circulation (but very large-audience) periodicals, which are more informative. Peasants and workers read local newspapers, which are more interesting. They all receive important signals from nonprint sources. Occasional efforts to change this situation, by sharply altering the content of either the *People's Daily* or of the local and functional papers, have proven unsuccessful. Over the long term, however, regional Chinese media undoubtedly help to integrate the national community. Pre–Cultural Revolution local newspapers, which this chapter emphasizes, were the predecessors of county and commune bulletins *(t'ung-hsün)* that now dominate the regional print media of the era of Hua Kuo-feng. All three aspects of the communication process are deeply influenced by local forces. This process nonetheless is leading to a China that will be bound together ever more tightly as time passes, even though it is not yet so closely integrated as most publications about it suggest.

The sources for this study should be mentioned, because they are identical with its subject. The footnotes refer mostly to local Chinese newspapers that are available at the Union Research Institute, 9 College Road, Hong Kong, whence they may be obtained on microfilm.

Determining Signals

China is the country where newspapers were invented, and the first journalism there was just as official as the present variety. The *Ti Pao,* a summary of proceedings at the Han court, was the world's first newspaper. Chapter 2 of this volume, by Frederick Yu, summarizes the historical roots of contemporary Chinese journalism.

Newspaper content depends largely on the nature of the publisher, and four types of ownership can be distinguished in the People's Republic: (1) by the Communist Party at any of its many levels; (2) by mass organizations, such as "democratic parties"; (3) by state or collective institutions, such as military jurisdictions, offices, hospitals, agricultural collectives, or factories; and (4) by newspaper publishers or staff (although this last type of ownership became joint "state-private" in the mid-1950s). In principle, Party propaganda departments in each regional jurisdiction are supposed to oversee all nonmilitary papers within their areas. Especially since the Anti-Rightist Campaign of 1957, they have done this strictly, within some limits imposed by their expectations concerning how well various kinds of messages may be received. For this reason, theme and content distinctions among newspapers in the People's

Republic can most cogently be made on the basis of the functional and geographic readerships they serve.

In mid-1955, seventeen "national" newspapers were officially listed.[3] Some regional newspapers not on this list, such as the *Liberation Daily* of the East China Party Bureau or the *Southern Daily* of the South China Party Bureau, are clearly more important than certain "national" papers published by Peking ministries.[4] Province-level units, such as Szechuan or Shanghai, can also publish newspapers in each of the ownership categories. Still lower in the geographical hierarchy, many "special districts" (*chuan-ch'ü,* or equivalent "regions," "autonomous districts," or "municipalities") have established official organs for their Party committees, and may also publish other kinds of local serials. In the late 1950s, at least five hundred such newspapers existed.[5] At still lower levels, it is likely that at least two thousand counties (*hsien,* or equivalent "banners" and "towns") also had newspapers. Below that, collectives, public institutions such as factories and communes, and many other organizations could and did establish printed newspapers, mimeographed newspapers, and "blackboard newspapers."

Regulating the content of these publications has been a major job of the Party's propaganda departments, which are themselves diverse at many levels. The degree of content uniformity in these media has depended largely on the degree to which official viewpoints are controversial among people who can write well. Some government aims, especially those associated with the modernization of the economy and of certain traditional attitudes, are also fully shared by most non-Party writers. For example, Canton's *Southern Daily* frequently carried articles emphasizing the importance of natural science, and associating it with atheism, in the mid-1950s.[6] Even the *West Kwangtung Peasants' Report (Yüeh-hsi Nung-min Pao)* had writers in Tsamkong to dwell on this theme: "This newspaper has told the peasants that 'gods and spirits' *[shen kuei]* and 'fate' *[t'ien ming]* are all fake. Anybody who is sick must call a doctor. If there is a natural disaster, we must rely on our own strength, organize ourselves under the leadership of the Party, and walk the road of mutual aid and cooperation."[7] Non-Communist newspapermen have also generally agreed with the Party on economic development. When the *Inner Mongolia Daily* wanted more articles on handicrafts and technical subjects,[8] there was no shortage of writers to do the job.

Other issues are more sensitive and controversial. Especially in campaign periods, and for reprinting Peking-approved texts in Party organs at lower levels, controls for content orthodoxy have been strict. When reports from the New China News Agency are printed in newspapers, they may not be excerpted or changed in any way. Under each article draft, the number of characters is noted; and according to an ex-journalist, "it is a serious mistake if a newspaper or magazine prints one character more or less."[9]

There are two kinds of journalism in the People's Republic for which the procedures to establish signal coherence are less rigorous than for centrally approved articles. In both of these, the main form of guidance is indirect: namely, long-term career controls over newspapermen and relevant Party committee members.

First, there are locally written articles that are published in local newspapers, especially at the county level and below. Variety, and some signal incoherence, is allowed in the local papers to induce people to read them.

Second, there are limited-circulation periodicals that translate foreign news sources. These inform the large cadre community which rules New China. The main limited-circulation serial is *Reference Information (Ts'an-k'ao Hsiao-hsi)*, mentioned in chapters 2 and 3.[10]

A more detailed serial, with similar contents, is *Reference Material (Ts'an-k'ao Tzu-liao)*, whose circulation is far more restricted. This periodical is more voluminous, but cadres whose work does not concern foreign affairs do not generally see it; unlike *Reference Information*, it is really an elite medium. In *Reference Material*, even the headlines are translated and are not interpretive.

The other main type of less official journalism—locally written articles printed in local newspapers—covers a wide variety of social topics. It is not a free press, because of indirect controls over writers' and sponsors' careers, but the style and content are not so rigid as in the *People's Daily*. Above all, the combined circulation of such journals dwarfs that of *Reference Information*, not to mention any other national paper. An example, in a relatively large jurisdiction, is the *Yang-ch'eng Wan-pao (Canton Evening News)*. At the time of its founding, this paper was officially assigned to a constituency different from that of the local main Party organ, the *Southern Daily*. "The main readers of *Yang-ch'eng Wan-pao* will be intellectuals, office employees, and residents of the city. In content and style, it will have its own character. This newspaper will mainly report international affairs, cultural life, and news closely connected with the people of the city."[11] Thus a non-Party paper of this type was defined by its readership rather than its ownership.

The most important source of signal incoherence in Chinese local newspapers arises from the fact that they are supposed simultaneously to praise progress and to raise criticisms. They must describe exemplary models, but they also must give credible reports. These norms are in conflict. Sometimes one of them has been emphasized; sometimes the other. Never has either been completely foresworn. The problems inherent in this dualism are evident in the following, from a "construction worker":

Once there was a journalist of a certain newspaper who asked me, "What newsworthy situations do you have at present?" I spoke to him for a long time about problems in our construction work which needed to be solved. And I said, "Comrade journalist, please give us some help." But this journalist impatiently answered, in a disappointed tone, "These are all work problems. I want to know about the new climate *[ch'i-hsiang]* here. Please talk about the new climate at this construction site!" I said, "New climate? I am very sorry, but I can't see any sign of it. Wait until we have solved these problems; then you can come again, looking for a new climate." After this, the journalist didn't come again.[12]

Conflicts between journalists and officials affect the content of the news as surely in the People's Republic as in the United States. Almost everywhere, investigative reporting is a check on bureaucrats and can be used by higher levels to keep lower functionaries in line. As early as April 1950, the Central Committee of the Party encouraged this function by resolving:

It is very important to induce the masses to criticize the shortcomings in our work, and to educate Party members, especially Party cadres, to carry out self-criticism. Because now the civil war on the mainland is over, and our Party is already the leading political power, arrogant attitudes can easily arise. We will be poisoned by bureaucracy and prevented from accomplishing the task of building New China, if we cannot exercise criticism and self-criticism in an open and timely way. . . . This must be done with respect to all mistakes and shortcomings in our work, at all public occasions, and especially in the newspapers and periodicals.[13]

Sometimes high Communist leaders have almost assigned criticism quotas to newspapers, as if this were an economic function. For example, the Chekiang provincial Party organ once complained that criticism was not being carried out sufficiently: "From May 18 to November 11 [1954], the *Chekiang Flax Worker [Che Ma Kung-jen]* published only fifteen articles of criticism, and during the month September 15 to October 16, the *Production Express [Sheng-ch'an K'uai-pao]* of the Chekiang Third Silk Factory did not publish a single criticism article."[14] The effect of this observation, on foremen in the relevant factories, can easily be imagined.

Party members and nonmembers both affect the content of newspapers. As a Changsha paper put it, "Leading Party comrades from all levels must personally write editorials and articles."[15] When a nonparty schoolteacher in Shanghai asked *Liberation Daily* editors whether nonmembers might write articles for columns entitled "Party Life" *(tang ti sheng-huo),* the response was a resounding yes.[16] Nonetheless, the distinction between members and nonmembers affects the information-gathering process. When a reporter from the New China News Agency and a reporter from the *News Daily (Hsin-wen Jihpao)* went together to the Shanghai Municipal Commerce Bureau, they had different receptions. The New China News Agency man was assumed by bureau officials to be a Party member. The one from the ex-bourgeois paper was assumed to be a nonmember. The reporters together asked to see some materials. These documents were shown to the New China News Agency man only after the *News Daily* correspondent had left. The bureau cadres said, "It was not convenient for us to let you see these things just a minute ago, because the other reporter is not a Party member."[17] In fact, neither of these correspondents belonged to the Party.

Sometimes the animosity of Party cadres toward newspapermen was frankly expressed. In 1956, one of them is quoted as having said, "Journalists are really disgusting, just like flies."[18] The quasi-liberal climate of 1956–1957 brought a flood of publication about conflicts between journalists and officials, and especially about the means that bureaucrats use to keep newspaper investigators in the dark. The *Fushun Daily* explained that the Party committee of nearby Tahuofang Reservoir had decreed that "each criticism article must be 100 percent true, the result of thorough investigation and solicitation of opinions from many sides. Articles which want to criticize cadres at the levels of section chief, Party branch secretary, or assistant engineer or above, must first ask for the Party committee's opinion. To criticize organizations, ask first for the higher-level organization's opinion."[19] Attempts to restrict criticism have undoubtedly been more successful at other times than they were during the Hundred Flowers, when this incident occurred.

In the spring of 1957, a *cause célèbre* for journalists was the case of Tso Yeh, assistant to the minister of agriculture. News photographers complained that "he always stands in front of the cameras." When he was asked to "step aside a little," he reportedly "scolded the journalists," saying, "What! Are you important, or me? If you push me around once more, you all go out!"[20] The *Workers' Daily* published a special article contrasting the "consideration and help" given to journalists by Premier Chou En-lai with the different attitude evinced by Assistant Tso Yeh.[21] The *Wen Hui Pao* (Wen Hui Report) also published an editorial on this subject entitled "Respect the New Journalists."[22]

At a meeting with journalists called by Shanghai Party Secretary K'o Ch'ing-shih that spring, "the newspapermen put forward examples of organs that restricted journalists, holding back articles and paying no attention to newspapermen. . . . Some organs regard journalists as always troublesome." One reporter urged the *Liberation Daily* "to develop a democratic work style." Another said that the *Hsin-min Pao* (Hsin-min Report) editors should "not fear poisonous weeds but should energetically seek the blooming of fresh flowers."[23]

Journalists were among the few intellectuals who received any minor lasting benefit from the Hundred Flowers movement after its conclusion—and only because high Party officials retained an interest in investigations of lower bureaucrats. In the two weeks before the axe fell on the "democratic parties" in June 1957, various provinces decreed rules to protect some reportorial rights. In Hopei, the provincial committee decried Party cadres who "feared that journalists would criticize their shortcomings" and "exercised news blackouts." The committee announced that "leading cadres must personally receive journalists, if possible, and answer their questions" upon the presentation of press cards *(chi-che cheng)*.[24] The Shanghai Party Committee resolved that "every organ should allow journalists with press cards to do reporting if they are from local newspapers, from the Shanghai People's Broadcasting Station, or from the local branch of the New China News Agency."[25] The fact that the Anti-Rightist campaign had already begun by early July did not prevent Hupei officials from issuing a practically identical statement, prohibiting "trivial regulations for secrecy."[26]

The officials had some victories, too. In late August, at the depths of the Anti-Rightist campaign, some correspondents of the *Liaoning Daily,* the *Shenyang Daily,* and the Shenyang branch of *China Youth Report* were all criticized. After the Tso Yeh case had made a splash in Peking and Shanghai, it was alleged that some "correspondents even regarded proper regulations and rational restrictions as 'brutal interference' and 'obstruction.'" Officials claimed that reporters "cannot understand the actual difficulties of the departments in which they want to interview, and they are not happy when they meet with any kind of inconvenience." One of the reporters, making a self-criticism, said, "I stressed the 'rights' of journalists too much. I became dissatisfied with the established regulations of the departments concerned, so that when the *Wenhui Report* and the rightists provoked the whole press world to attack the Party, I wrote an article which was not true to the facts."[27]

The Great Leap Forward strengthened local-level control of the content of local newspapers. In some areas, such as Inner Mongolia, the provincial Party committee mandated that all "organs, big and medium factories and mines, and universities at the county level and above must appoint a local news secretary *[hsin-wen mishu]* to manage correspondence and to provide the press with articles."[28] In 1958, both the New China News Agency and the *People's Daily* "transferred the leadership" of all their branches outside Peking to provincial Party committees.[29] This localization of control over newspaper content was extended even further in Anhwei, where newspapers sent the job of writing some editorials to lower-level Party committees.[30]

The Anti-Rightist campaign depleted the supply of journalists who were trusted by the Party; but the Great Leap Forward, less than a year later, increased the Party's need for writers who could effectively propagate the ideals of that mass campaign. Two approaches to this problem were made: First, many newspapermen (most who avoided being sent during the Anti-Rightist campaign to "reform through labor") were enrolled in new "journalistic workers' night universities," for more political education.[31] Second, people with other jobs were trained in new "spare-time journalism schools." These schools were attached to newspapers that were short of staff, such as the *Pengpu Daily* in Anhwei. The *Sian Daily* in Shensi had a school that enrolled four hundred people, mostly cadres.[32] In Heilungkiang, a special course of this sort was set up to train press photographers.

Many bureaucrats could use this extra education in writing for their ordinary, official work. For this reason, an administrative district in Hopei prevailed on the *Hantan Daily* to supplement its journalism school with a special three-month course, to teach cadres how to write government reports.[33] The most impressive change in Great Leap journalism, in fact, lay in efforts to create new "writing small groups" *(hsieh-tso hsiao-tsu)* in many nonpublishing institutions.

After the Leap was under way, spare-time journalists became very numerous. At one point, the *Lüta Daily* boasted "more than 3,000 correspondents."[34] The *Hsinmin Report* of Shanghai had more than 1,000, but only "200 often keep in contact with us."[35] The fortnightly *Coal Industry (Mei-t'an kung-yeh),* published by a ministry in Peking, had 75 "correspondence groups," 923 part-time reporters, and 33 "worker-commentators" at the K'aip'ing mines alone. In the first quarter of 1959, they produced 150 articles.[36]

By the middle of that year, the *Peking Evening News (Pei-ching Wan-pao)* was gathering 60 percent of its articles "from outside," and the situation at other important local papers, such as Shanghai's *Hsinmin Evening News* and the *Canton Evening News,* was similar.[37] The *Hailun Daily* further decentralized its work by creating thirty-three county-level "small editorial boards."[38]

Nonjournalistic professions did not participate in such activities equally. The *Wenhui Report* received frequent articles from nonstaff, and "many of the writers are intellectuals, of whom half were teachers."[39] Publication has often been a benefit to academic careers.

The means for hiring outside correspondents were simple. When the *Teachers' Report* needed three hundred more of them, it advertised that an applicant should send three sample articles, plus name, Party affiliation, occupation, address, and military service unit or "name of directly leading unit."[40] Undoubtedly, a connection with a journal would be useful for any ambitious cadre. Shantung's *Masses Daily (Ta-chung Jihpao)* in early 1959 was receiving ten thousand articles per month from six thousand spare-time correspondents. Since the staff of this newspaper numbered only forty, the portion of their time spent sifting and editing, rather than writing, must have been high. In the fourth quarter of 1958, professionals on the *Southern Daily* staff wrote about three quarters of the articles printed; but by the first quarter of the next year, that portion was halved. "A target was put forward that the correspondents' articles should be 70 percent, and those of the journalists should be 30 percent."[41]

Plagiarism became a problem, because scattered correspondents had local career incentives to submit any publishable article, regardless of its provenance. Often editors did not catch plagiarized manuscripts before printing them. In a single year, the *Teachers' Report* published no fewer than four such pieces. These were later exposed, "because our readers' eyes are sharp." [42] One such essay was translated, without acknowledgment, from a Russian periodical; only the names had been appropriately sinicized. Another was slightly revised from a 1929 primary school textbook.

Along with the quick increase of manuscript materials in 1958, writers' per-word manuscript fees *(kao-fei)* were reduced sharply —usually by half.[43] In the true spirit of the Great Leap, the orders for this wage deflation were published by local Party committees.

The importance of the two years from mid-1957 to mid-1959 for the reformation of the Chinese press cannot be overestimated. Not only were newspaper practices changed in the many ways indicated. In addition, local branches of the All-China Journalists' Association were established widely.[44] The magazine *News Front (Hsinwen Chan-hsien)* also began to appear in late 1957, and it played a crucial role in propagating, as models, local newspapers that effectively spread the ideals of the Leap. *News Front* was at the center of efforts to persuade journalists that they should undertake "five roles" in society: "organizing, propelling, encouraging, instigating, and criticizing."[45]

When bad weather and rural distribution problems combined to threaten the Party's political base after the Leap, *News Front* printed model article after model article, from Honan, Hupei, Liaoning, Hopei, Kiangsi, Kweichow and elsewhere, showing newspapermen how they might persuade readers to "uphold the absolute leadership of the Party."[46] Slogans proliferated. The *Hei-*

lungkiang Daily resolved to "fight well the four reporting battles" (which dealt with news on the Eighth Party Plenum, on 'increasing production and practicing economy,' on the Tenth Anniversary of the Republic, and on the 'superiority of the people's communes').[47] The *Szechwan Daily* averred that "we must strongly reflect the growing and dauntless spirit of the cadres and masses in their struggle against natural calamities, and must criticize the right-deviationist sentiments of surrendering in the face of difficulties and being pessimistic."[48] The *Kwangsi Daily* organized a competition (the awards were not material) among correspondents, who raced to write "the most timely report of new successes on all fronts."[49] The *Honan Daily,* in just three weeks, published 13 editorials, 169 news stories, 43 feature articles, 27 columns, and 11 "special pages" *(chuan-yeh)*—all to show what a good idea the communes had been.[50]

By 1960, for political reasons, some newspapers were merged. Shanghai's *News Daily,* which had been very successful during the Leap, was combined with the *Liberation Daily* in 1960, "in order to concentrate our strength" and "to reflect better the socialist construction and the continuing Leap Forward."[51] In January, the *Kuang-chou Jihpao (Canton Daily)* was similarly absorbed by the *Yang-ch'eng Wanpao (Canton Evening News),* which then came under the authority of the municipal Party committee.[52] In this period of shortage, even more than before it, the dominant slogan held that "the whole Party must run newspapers." In particular, first Party secretaries at various levels were charged with the job of paying personal attention to all the media within their jurisdictions.[53] This became the pattern for the next few years of slow recovery.

By 1964, as the economic depression was ending, in many local jurisdictions "there appeared a tendency of lavishly publishing small newspapers." For example, in the town of Pakhoi on the Gulf of Tonkin, there was a rash of "occupational small newspapers" *(yeh-wu hsing hsiao-pao).*[54] In Pakhoi, the *Tsamkong Daily (Chan-chiang Jihpao)* was usually available, as was the *Southern Daily* from Canton. Nonetheless in 1964, there quickly appeared a local *Kung-yeh K'uai-pao* (Industrial Express), a *Chiao-yü T'ung-hsün* (Education Bulletin), a *Yü-yeh T'ung-pao* (Fishing Informer), a *Pei-hai Wei-sheng Hsiao-hsi* (Pakhoi Public Health Information), a quarterly *Pei-hai Wei-sheng Chien-hsün* (Pakhoi

Public Health Summary), and a journal called *Chung-yi* (Chinese Medicine) from the local hospital. The Women's and Children's Clinic and the Pakhoi Public Health Education Clinic both published "gazettes." The tendency of Chinese organizations to diversify their functions, which Franz Schurmann calls "gigantism," means that they easily establish new journals. Leap localization combined with rising prosperity in the mid-1960s to cause an explosion in the number of "occupational small newspapers."

The Cultural Revolution only furthered this process. Every faction and splinter, and every coalition of them, put out its own tabloid. Evanescent journals rose and fell with great speed, and there were many temporary closures in major newspapers; Ting Wang has already published a book-length compendium on that subject.[55]

In general, the army took responsibility for publishing needed local newspapers that were organs of now-paralyzed Party committees. For example, in Canton from March 13, 1967, the *Southern Daily* was under the control of a military commission.[56] In the autumn of the next year, revolutionary committees in cities such as Nanchang and Wuhan called meetings of press workers to restore more authority to civilians,[57] and "Mao Tse-tung Thought Propaganda Teams" entered newspaper publishing offices in greater numbers.[58]

By the end of the decade, more permanency, and by the same token more control of message signals, had been reestablished in the Chinese press. For example, in Canton only four daily papers were on sale publicly in 1969, although inside the walls of relevant institutions there were "worker papers," "Red Guard papers," and "peasant papers" *(kung tai pao, hung tai pao, nung tai pao).*[59] The hope of attaining complete unanimity in the press of such a complex society had only been partially successful, even after many campaigns and social struggles. This essentially stable, controlled, patriotic, but not fully unified press remains the general standard today.

Sending Signals

Newspaper sales and distribution in China are responsibilities of the post office. This enormous institution stands between higher-level Party committees, which are supposed to print proper doctrine, and lower-level Party committees, which are supposed to assure that it is read. A more reliable recipe for minor bureaucratic conflicts, on a continuous and cumulatively massive scale in so large a country, cannot be imagined.

Especially in the 1950s, the newspaper distribution system was typified by unevenness in both time and space. During major political campaigns, pressure from higher Party officials on the Ministry of Posts and Telecommunications was great. Some low Party officials also needed the papers to perform their assigned campaign tasks, so that circulation totals rose and fell along with campaigns. For example, subscriptions in factories of many urban papers increased during the Five-Anti movement of 1952, but during the next year, the subscriptions subsided along with the mass movement. In a Tientsin garment factory by early 1953, "over the past few months" the number of subscribed copies of the *Tientsin Daily* went down from twenty-three to ten, the *Tientsin Worker's Daily* was reduced from eighty-eight to one, the *People's Daily* went from two to nil, the *Peking Worker's Daily* from five to two, and the *China Youth Report* from seventy-seven to twenty-seven. Over the same time period, the number of workers in that factory almost doubled.[60]

The same pattern was repeated a few years later, during the "transition to socialism." When this movement began, "the cadres paid much attention to it" in the Tientsin Road Department Store of Dairen. Subscriptions in the store rose to 100 newspapers. "This enthusiasm lasted three months, but afterward the subscriptions went down. In November they were reduced to eleven, and by December to six. In January and February of the next year, only one newspaper subscription was held, and from March on, there were none at all."[61]

Imbalance in the spatial distribution of newspapers was an even greater obstacle to thorough communications. In 1952, the *Honan Masses* was distributed in 4,000 copies to Mi County; but in Nanyang County, its circulation was only 5—even though Nanyang Town is important enough to be the seat of a special district.[62] There was only one *Honan Daily* for each 6,400 peasants in the province. Under these circumstances, the top leadership realized that a scattered bureaucracy such as the post office would need major spurring, before the problems could be alleviated. The *Southern Daily* complained: "The main reason for the backwardness of circulation work in the countryside is that . . . work in the post office is not done well. . . . In the districts and townships, many Party and government cadres wrongly regard circulation work as solely the duty of the post office."[63] One solution was to set up thousands of "voluntary rural post stations *[yi-wu hsiang-yu chan].*"[64] More than 80,000 were established by the end of 1955. Continued unevenness was evident in the fact that half of these were in Hopei Province, surrounding Peking.

Apparently the greatest obstacle to the extension of the message-transferring network in China was political. Although some low-level rural cadres could further their careers by using newspapers in campaigns, this group was probably a minority of cadres. During most times, newspaper communications from higher authorities diminished the independence and authority of established local leaders. There was thus some cadre resistance to newspaper distribution. From Nanning, the *Kwangsi Daily* stated the problem frankly:

> The supply and marketing cooperatives are closely linked with the peasants in life and production, and they should handle some of the work of the post office. But many of their leading comrades think there is little to be gained from setting up distribution agencies. That is why they are not enthusiastic about it. . . . Many are not at ease *[pu an-hsin]* with distribution work; they feel it has no future and is troublesome. . . . They do not help deliver the newspapers on time. They use copies which are held back for pillows and for wrapping paper.[65]

Also, some higher officials were especially charged with increasing the numbers of newspaper subscriptions. They benefited whenever total circulation figures in their jurisdictions grew—and less surely, when a quota of papers was distributed widely to people who would actually read them. Gross circulation figures were easier to check than were distribution or willingness to encourage reading. The main career incentives for bureaucrats were oriented toward circulation numbers.

Publications thus accumulated, in stacks, at offices. It was reported from Ts'ao County, Shantung:

> There are many newspapers and magazines here that nobody ever reads. . . . Why does this cooperative subscribe to so many papers? It is because the personnel of the Ts'ao County Post Office only care about circulation figures and use forceable methods. For example, an employee of the Post Office was not satisfied with the number of

newspapers purchased by this cooperative; so he unreasonably criticized cadres for having rightist conservative ideas![66]

The Chefoo branch of the New China Bookstore, which was supposed to distribute rural booklets published by newspapers, reported: "We have a great overstock. . . . The circulation figures have
been subjectively decided, without any reference to the actual situation."[67]

Local newspaper staffs grew furious with post offices which did
not deliver copies that had been printed, addressed, and sent. In
1956, when a county in Yünnan established its *Hsiang-yün Hsiao-
pao* (Hsiang-yün Briefer), "the post office only distributed two
hundred copies, and this was not even one-tenth of the first issue's
circulation. . . . By the time the third issue was published, nine cooperatives were still reading the first one. The circulation work of
the Hsiang-yün County Post Office must be improved."[68] A cadre,
who ordinarily read his *Chinghai Daily* on a wall in a Muslim area
county seat, for several days running returned in vain to the
newspaper-posting board. He found each time that the copy had
not been changed; so he went to the county post office to inquire
why. At the office, "I was shocked when I saw 5,000 papers lying
there." The postmaster calmly assured him that the postmen were
very busy, and that they would deliver the papers when they got
around to it.[69]

In Shensi, a reader with well-honed sarcasm explained: "In the
past, we received our newspapers from Sian after only seven or
eight days." He was used to this. "But now we receive them after
twelve or thirteen days. It would be nice if we could receive them
earlier rather than later." The *Shensi Daily,* of course, was only too
happy to print his complaint.[70]

The patience of another reader, at Chin County's Tiger Mountain District Central Primary School, was apparently less great:
"Because the *Lü-ta Jihpao* is a daily, readers in this town should
see it every day. But the newspapers, which are delivered from the
Sanshihlipao Post Office Branch, have in fact become 'weekly
newspapers.' "[71] A subscriber in Sinkiang said that "reading a
newspaper is like studying history," because some of his issues
were arriving nearly a month late if they arrived at all.[72] A *Fukien
Daily* subscriber averred that, by the time he received his newspapers, they had become "historical relics *[li-shih wen-wu].*"[73]

Post offices often delivered subscriptions that had not been ordered. When a Dairen reader subscribed to *Wen-yi Hsüeh-hsi* (Literature and Arts), he actually received a *China Youth Report*.[74] When a Hantan reader complained to a postman for giving him a *Hopei Daily*, rather than the *Takung Report* for which he had paid, the postman replied, "You read this newspaper, instead! No matter which it is, they are all the same."[75]

By 1957, officials in Peking were so concerned by the ineffectiveness of efforts to change this situation that they cut back on the waste by declaring that there was a shortage of newsprint; 10.2 percent less paper was allotted for serials in 1957 than in 1956.[76] Exclusively local papers were not affected by this rule, and they continued to prosper. New subscriptions to some of the more famous papers, however, became temporarily unavailable.[77]

Some of the circulation problems that emerged in the tumultuous years of 1957–1958 resulted simply from the quick rate of change at that time. The post office was unable to keep up with stable production and pricing schedules; but when, as in 1958, periodicals were merged, abolished, created, and repriced like topsy the burden only became heavier. No amount of "hoping that the Post Office will make a Great Leap Forward"[78] actually achieved that result.

Increasingly, mid-level Party committees took on the job themselves. In Hunan, a provincewide telephone conference was held in September 1958, to plan for the regional circulation of all newspapers and magazines.[79] At that time, monthly newspaper subscriptions in Hunan stood at 1,620,000. Of these, only 23,383 (about 1 percent) were to the *People's Daily;* another 176,078 (11 percent) were attributable to the *New Hunan Report;* and the remaining 88 percent were taken up by a multitude of small newspapers. The provincial post office averred that the *People's Daily* circulation might be raised to 50,000; but even if this plan had succeeded totally, the Central Committee's organ would still have comprised only 3 percent of Hunan's newspapers.

For comparison, some calculations with Roderick McFarquhar's 1972 figures, gathered on a visit to China, indicate that throughout the country as a whole, about 36 million copies of newspapers were printed daily. Of these, about 9 percent were copies of the *People's Daily,* nearly half of them in Peking itself. An additional 17 percent of the total was attributable to *Reference Information.* The remaining three quarters were mostly local papers of various sorts, the main sources of domestic news.[80]

The fact that newspaper reading is disproportionately an urban phenomenon in China was of more concern, during the Great Leap Forward, than the fact that the central Party organ did not go to a broader readership. In Kiangsi, Party cadres prevailed on the post office to invest in motorcycles, so that papers might be delivered more readily to rural areas.[81] In Chengtu, the *Szechwan Daily* founded some "voluntary retail selling groups," one of which included the chief editor; and apparently in this way, it temporarily shamed the local post office leaders to become deliverymen, too.[82] When the *Changchow Daily* in Kiangsu tried to do the same thing, however, its group of cadre-salesmen managed to sell only seven hundred papers in three days—a record that suggests less than total enthusiasm, on their part, for this kind of work.[83] Kirin authorities attempted to bypass and supplement the postal system entirely by establishing a network of "newspaper retail sales departments," "sales booths," "distribution vehicles," "committee-run retail sales points," and ordinary newspaper salespersons.[84]

In some provinces, during 1958 and 1959 at least, these efforts bore fruit temporarily. Anhwei, for example, had more than a thousand press cadres, all told, by mid-1959. Each county in that province had its own newspaper, and more than half of these had been established during the Great Leap Forward. The circulation of the *Anhwei Daily,* only 80,000 in 1957, had doubled by 1959.[85] Similarly, in Canton the 1957 circulation of the *Canton Evening Post* had been 75,000; but after it was merged with the *Canton Daily* in 1959, its circulation went up to 170,000, and later in the year even to 270,000. The *Post* quickly became the most popular paper in South China—although it was not allowed to retain that distinction for long.[86]

The sequel, when the effects of the economic depression became obvious, was equally dramatic. By 1960, circulations had already dropped; and by 1962, the *Canton Evening Post,* to continue the example, was reportedly selling well below twenty thousand copies, less than one twelfth of its earlier level.[87] Just before this, in late 1959, a National Publications Distribution Work Conference had been held in Peking.[88] Awards were established for "outstanding distribution stations *[yu-hsiu fa-hsing chan],*" and plans were made for the recruitment of students and cadres to keep up the subscription numbers.[89] But during the early 1960s, almost nothing was published about newspaper circulation work, because the news was apparently all bad. Leap levels were clearly not maintained.

By the spring of 1963, when the economic recovery was under

way, the emergence of many new local papers made distribution less of a problem than it had previously been. Control of newspaper content was correspondingly a greater problem. At that time, 98 percent of the production teams in the Canton suburb of Hua-hsien were subscribing to at least one peasant newspaper,[90] but this area is atypical. At Loch'ienpo, Ch'engmai County, in the middle of Hainan Island, the whole town subscribed only to a single copy of the *Hainan Daily*.[91] For 300 inhabitants, including "many intellectual youths" who had apparently been sent there from Canton, this circulation was low. A third Kwangtung example, over a larger area, indicates the same basic conclusion: In Szu-p'ing Commune, Kaochou County, which may be a reasonably typical place despite its proximity to the railhead at Maoming, the 18 production brigades and 558 production teams together subscribed to 1,300 copies by 1965. But there was only one postman in the whole commune. He did not deliver newspapers below the production brigade level. The Commune Party Committee decided to use local "social forces" (*she-hui li-liang;* i.e., ambitious and corvée labor) to do the job. Thirty-two "red scarf postal redistribution stations *[hung-ling-chin hsin-pao hsiao-chuan chan]*" were ordered into existence—one in each of the commune's thirty-two primary schools.[92]

The postal infrastructure was clearly insufficient for the task of distributing newspapers all over China, and the Cultural Revolution did not basically change that situation. Progress has been made since 1949 in adding some strength to the capacity of China's communications infrastructure, but the national economy allows few spare resources for that project. No one must imagine that all the ideals of the Central Committee can be immediately and fully transferred to every citizen of the People's Republic. Sufficient credit must be given to the extent of the network-building task that still remains.

Receiving Signals

After newspapers arrive in the hands of their subscribers, they do nothing to change culture unless they are read. Dull media are not effective for community change or any other purpose; people do not pay attention to them. In order to strengthen China's communications network, the leaders of the country are aware that it is not only necessary to increase the transfer capacity of media. It is also necessary to ensure that the system inspires credence among the people. Since there are so many different Chinese people, that is quite a task.

Pye has pointed out that "a modern communications system involves two stages or levels. The first is that of the highly organized, explicitly structured mass media, and the second is that of the informal opinion leaders who communicate on a face-to-face basis, much as communicators did in traditional systems."[93] Many practices in the People's Republic, as Schurmann says, imply as strong a belief in the efficacy of "human organization" as in "technical organization" for modern purposes.[94] The informal, human aspects are important because the basis of a culture is not simply "utilitarian" and role-oriented, but contains affect as well as role relations.[95] The main Communist Chinese method of attempting to link the modern daily press with personal communications is, characteristically, a state policy: the establishment of "newspaper reading groups."

Even before 1949, Party cadres in base areas and political commissars in army units often convened meetings to explain current affairs. The idea that this habit should be spread over the population of all China was more notable for its ambition than its feasibility. Nonetheless, the cadres set to work; and by 1951, over 60,000 newspaper reading groups had been reported, involving nearly 700,000 people.[96] A typical group of this sort thus included about eleven participants. The whole movement involved less than one fifth of 1 percent of China's population.

Even the great majority of Party members did not participate in newspaper reading groups, as these statistics show. The establishment of reading groups, and the willpower to convene them regularly, were both dependent on political campaigns. Like most other journalistic phenomena of the early 1950s, these organizations were urban at first. When the Five-Anti campaign was launched in 1952 to reform business practices, 38,000 groups were set up for nearly 700,000 people in Shansi.[97] (This was the province of warlord Yen Hsi-shan, where attempts to make modern enthusiast groups were not new with the Communists.) The average size of the Shansi conclaves was 70 percent larger than the average reading groups throughout the whole country just a year earlier. If everyone came to the meetings, and if in many cases twenty people were present, the experience for the participants must have strongly resembled a lecture.

Enthusiasm for the groups was hard to maintain. The *Fukien Daily* reported that even among cadres in the provincial government's finance and trade bureau, "only about half of the employees paid attention to reading newspapers."[98] Another report, from an urban hospital, said that more than half of the staff did not bother to read any newspaper: "It is not because they are busy with work, but mainly because they neglect politics. During their spare time, they read textbooks, bourgeois literature, American novels, magazines, the Bible, decadent and reactionary works, or else they spend their time eating and drinking, or listening to records."[99] Because of other preoccupations among the people, the cadres' only feasible means of engaging mass interest in the newspapers was to sponsor campaigns and link the content of journalism with them. Political movements were confidentially described in "internal notices *[nei-pu t'ung-pao]*." These were small booklets, published periodically by major newspapers for their staffs, coordinating propaganda on themes that might relate to the lives of the readers.[100] Even when this was done, the newspaper groups did not usually sustain themselves well over time.

One minor difficulty was that subscription fees, and sometimes money for lamp oil or electricity, were in many cases divided equally among group members. A *Yangtze Daily* reader complained: "We each had to give .15 *yüan* for the subscription fee, but at most times we could not see the newspaper. The instructor read it only at group meetings; at other times, it was 'in his care.' "[101]

Another, more important, problem lay in the reported tendency of the meetings to be boring. As a reading-group member in Foochow once put it, "The newspaper reader *(tu-pao yüan)* has no experience. He only reads word after word, article after article, and the listeners doze off."[102] This "grave tendency to formalism," as a Kansu paper chose to describe it, made reading groups very difficult to run.[103]

One solution was to organize periodic meetings of the official "newspaper readers," so that they could study relevant articles and learn how to present the material in a lively way.[104] Temporary nurseries could also be set up for newspaper groups in residential units, such as the Foochow one mentioned earlier, where "most of the members were housewives." Increasingly, the costs of urban reading groups' subscriptions were borne from enterprise or office "operating expenses," as the *Hengyang News* reported.[105] In urban areas, where enterprises could generally afford the cost without any trouble, individual subscriptions delivered to employees' homes were increasingly paid out of company funds.[106]

In rural areas, these techniques did not work very well. A report from Lungyen, in the *West Fukien Daily,* suggested that an old quasi-*literatus* gentleman would be good as a "newspaper reader,"[107] and the *South Szechwan Report* from Luchow said that upper primary school graduates could also perform this function.[108] But adult peasants apparently did not have much time or will to participate in these groups. As a rural Inner Mongolian Party branch secretary put it, "We will be criticized if we don't perform production work well; but failing to lead a newspaper reading group won't mean a thing."[109] In his township, all seven newspaper groups ceased to meet during the busy farming season. Similarly, in Kwangsi, it was reported that a reading group that studied the local *Yung-ning* (County) *Farmer's News (Yung-ning Nung-min Pao)* could find time to meet only during the slack agricultural season.[110] The *Hopei Daily* at one point reported, "In some cooperatives, the newspaper reading groups exist only in name. . . . In these places, newspapers are seldom read."[111]

Even in suburban areas close to large cities, "the great majority of the peasants never look at newspapers or magazines."[112] A 1960 report from Shantung gives statistics from which it can be deduced that only one newspaper reading group existed for every five hundred persons in that populous province.[113] Even if all those groups really met and were fully attended, the coverage was nonetheless minimal.

Blackboard newspapers *(hei-pan pao)* generally proved to be a more effective way of encouraging signal reception at low levels. This is a traditional medium. For centuries, government offices in East Asia have posted decrees on public boards. Popular familiarity with this medium, the fact that acquisition of knowledge from it is less likely to be mixed with requests for personal commitments than in meetings, the brevity of the blackboard reports, their availability for perusal at any time, the emphasis on very local and interesting material—each of these factors probably contributed to the notice boards' apparent effectiveness for communicating factual knowledge.[114]

In the mid-1950s, a visiting group of overseas Chinese saw blackboard newspapers in all kinds of institutions: "factories, schools, government offices, agricultural production cooperatives, hospitals, sanitoriums, jails, workers' clubs, everywhere."[115] Sometimes these newspapers were used as ordinary official bulletin boards *(t'ung-kao p'ai)*. Usually the articles were less imperative than suggestive of actions which local officials wanted. In a factory, when one workshop voted to challenge another for a production award, it issued a "declaration of war" in the blackboard newspaper. If the work efficiency of a unit went down, a critical article might well appear on the blackboard. On the blackboard newspaper of Peking's New China News Agency itself, the tourists read an article signed by "a little reporter," which criticized the higher-ups for sending only "big journalists" to accompany foreign visitors, never "small journalists."[116]

Sometimes the blackboard newspapers persisted over many years; sometimes they fell into disuse. In 1964, four villages in Anhwei celebrated the twelfth anniversary of their joint *Production Mobilization Report (Sheng-ch'an Ku-tung Pao)*. By that time this board had chalked up 300 issues and was apparently a fortnightly.[117] In the same year, Shansi's Juich'eng County reported 3,800 blackboard newspapers, more than one per village. Ideally, the "editorial small group" was supposed to write a new issue each week, including both national and international news. But a visitor to parts of rural Shansi observed that in practice "many blackboard newspapers were blank. In some others, the content had not been changed for a long time. . . . It is certainly not easy for a country as big as ours to have everyone read a newspaper."[118] Considering the size of the problem, this medium seems nonetheless to have encouraged signal reception more effectively than most other means.

The tradeoff for the local readership is some unorthodox content. A reporter from Shanghai described this kind of situation:

Recently, I went to a factory on business. When I entered the gate, I saw a blackboard newspaper, and its location was not badly chosen. But when I looked at it, I saw to my astonishment four big characters: Welcome the Spring Festival! *[Huan-tu ch'un-chieh!]* When I read the content of the articles, it turned out to be generalized propaganda for the Lunar New Year. Some workers, with whom I talked about this, said, "The blackboard newspaper of our trade union is a newspaper for special occasions. Each year, it comes out five times, on January 1, the Lunar New Year festival, May 1, July 1, and National Day." It was clear that this blackboard newspaper often "took a rest."[119]

Another specialized, and politically safer, way to attract readers was the use of functional newspapers. The most important type was published for peasants. Rural editions *(nung-min pan* or *nungts'un pan)* of major newspapers such as the *Southern Daily* were common.[120] Occupational organs were also established for many other kinds of work. Cantonese boat people, for example, were served by the *Kwangtung Fishermen's Report.*[121] The *Militia Report* served Shensi's militia organization, whose older members had fought long in the civil war.[122] Overseas Chinese in Fukien were served by an *Overseas and Native Place Report.*[123] Szechwan in the mid-1950s had six administrative-district newspapers designed mainly for peasants, plus another designed mainly for workers in salt mines, still another for Tibetans in the mountainous west, and thirty-six other major factory and mine newspapers.[124] Even popular entertainers had a local paper in Kwangtung, entitled *Club (Chü-lo-pu).* It supplied performance and song materials and gave pointers on how to establish cultural centers in rural areas.[125]

Although the cumulative circulation of the local and functional organs certainly vouches for their popularity, three more things about them must be said: First, their political viability always depended on general campaigns. Second, their content was often different from that in centralist newspapers. The *Hang County Report* of Chekiang, for most of one month in 1955, contained not a single article about international or even national affairs; its interest was purely local.[126] Third, the relative popularity of the local papers did not entirely solve Peking's problem of trying to expand the national communications system, because these newspapers were based on smaller communities and interests.

In 1955 in a Kwangtung township that governed a population of 3,800 in sixty-six cooperatives, only a single newspaper was on subscription at the township seat.[127] Most Chinese, like most citizens of any large nation, are not immensely interested in international affairs. They often find national directions to be of less immediate interest than local events. This fact is a constant puzzlement to elites in large countries.

Thus far, we have discussed institutional means of trying to catch the masses' attention, such as reading groups and blackboard newspapers. But the substantive content of media is more important than institutions, for causing people to read. A few imaginative Communist leaders have long been aware of their comrades' tendency to dull verbiage, of which the classic genre is the printed conference speech. As early as 1950, the *New Hunan Report* assured its readers:

> We have recently checked the news on conferences that is published in our paper, and we have discovered that there are serious shortcomings. First, the quantity of such reporting is very large. In October of last year alone, there were sixteen reports on conferences in Hunan. Together they would occupy six full pages. . . . If we let so much reporting, which lacks lively content, take up so much space, then news about actual life and production cannot be published, and this will reduce the role of the newspaper.[128]

Some Party leaders perceived that few people want to read lists of the tasks of organizations, lists of the names of representatives, lists of the names of leaders of standing committees, reports of opening ceremonies, speeches from long-winded authorities, reports of closing ceremonies, and so forth.

Even the cadres themselves, whose livelihoods and careers were involved in this process, sometimes lost patience with it. A Kwangtung Party secretary, at the end of a very long speech, claimed, "The first lesson of the revolution is to train your rear ends. . . . If you don't understand, listen anyhow."[129] He was criticized by cadres for this arrogance.

Mid-level functionaries' interest in foreign matters, for instance, is demonstrably low. In 1952, a survey was conducted among eighty-six cadres of the Peking Municipal Government, which is not a peripheral organization in China, to see how much they knew about international affairs. When they were asked to list the democratic people's republics in Eastern Europe, 35 percent "could not answer at all," and only 7 percent answered correctly and fully. Cadres as high as group heads and deputy section heads included Indonesia and Japan in the list. Members of the Peking Party propaganda department thought that India, the Netherlands, and Sweden were Eastern European democratic people's republics. A further survey of 7,772 employees of the city government determined that 16 percent "seldom or never" read newspapers, 59 percent "only read headlines and articles of interest," and 25 percent read "often and earnestly."[130]

If newspapers had this much difficulty directing the attention of cadres to large issues, their task among the population as a whole was indeed major. To some extent, reform of news presentation and more attractive pages helped. The *Tsingtao Daily* and the *Peking Daily* in the mid-1950s promised their readers shorter and more informative articles.[131] Brief headlines were also an official policy, hard to implement in the face of Germanic-Marxist tendencies toward lengthy officialese. After the *People's Daily* printed a sixty-one-character dull headline, it had to publish a letter excoriating such practices and claiming, "This headline was too long and required too much energy to read."[132]

Problems of credibility were even more basic than problems of format. During the Hundred Flowers era, a flood of letters criticized inconsistencies and inaccuracies in previously published articles. After the *Ch'inghai Daily* printed a headline saying that a local hero had "killed a fierce tiger barehanded," it also published a letter pointing out that the hero in fact had used a weapon.[133] Later in the same paper, there was a story full of statistics from which several absurdities could be calculated—for example, that the average family size in a certain village was 170 persons.[134] When the *People's Daily* published an egregious report that a certain mining district had "thousands of trucks," a reader from the area respectfully submitted that it had fifty.[135] After discovering eighty mistakes in a three-week period, ranging from wrong characters to factual misinformation, the *People's Daily* editors promised to strengthen "checking work *[chien-ch'a kung-tso].*"[136]

Some hopeful fabrication may possibly be inherent in the goals of revolutionary cadres and journalists, and may arguably be inherent in the business of long-term modernization in a country of China's size and poverty. Nonetheless, the tendency "only to talk about quantity and not about quality, only to talk about number and speed *[to, k'uai]* and not about excellence and economy *[hao, sheng],* only to report the bright side and not the dark side"[137] sometimes led to misrepresentations that were conscious. An ambitious journalist named Huang Chih-ch'ao was criticized for two such articles, about progress in the Argun Banner of Heilungkiang. He reported in a national newspaper, the *Kwangming Daily,* that 90 percent of the Argun peasant households had joined agricultural cooperatives, when in fact only 2 percent had done so. He said that the local government was building new houses in hunting areas, when "in fact not one house was built." He claimed that winter schools had "basically eliminated illiteracy; but this was also not consonant with the facts." "Although in the past our banner set up a winter school which on two occasions held training classes to eliminate illiteracy, only a minority participated." Huang said that 20,000 square *li* of land were still virgin forest, but "this figure is not true." His critics, writing a letter to the editor, did not mince words: "We think that the writer's fabrication and exaggeration of facts cannot be separated from his view of newspapers and of the purpose of writing articles. . . . When he received a fee from your newspaper for his first article, he told a comrade here, 'This is a good bargain,' meaning that 'You can make money and also make a good name in this way.' "[138]

High Communist officials apparently realized the connection between local newspapers and solving the problems of credibility and liveliness that bedeviled the national organs. Mao Tse-tung himself had edited the *Hsiang River Review* from Changsha in 1919, and his prowess in local journalism at that time has received much praise.[139] In the mid-1950s, the *People's Daily* itself resolved to "print excerpts from local newspapers."[140] Provincial newspapers such as the *Kiangsi Youth Report* promised to carry "fewer instructions and more short articles about rural areas."[141] Even the local *New Kweichow Daily* was encouraged to publish verbatim, from still more local sources, a column entitled "Factory Blackboard Report."[142] When by 1958 it was announced that Pishan County in Szechwan had 113 local mimeographed papers, this trend was praised in Peking: "If the articles are about local persons and local happenings, the masses like to read them."[143]

The Hundred Flowers movement, despite all its deception of Chinese liberals, articulated the parallel interests shared by them and by some high Party leaders, who were aware of the political inefficacy of dull newspapers. Mao Tse-tung might well have agreed with a journalist who, at one of the blooming sessions, said that the central press could not play any role as a " 'listener,' but could only play the role of a 'mouthpiece.' "[144] A former editor of the *Chekiang Daily* said that his newspaper had "become a notice board full of directives."[145] A former publisher of the *Southern Daily* complained that "from the first line of the front page to the last paragraph of the last page, it was all theory, nothing but theory upon theory," and this was ineffective for any purpose.[146]

The Anti-Rightist movement nonetheless encouraged "the idea

that news work is dangerous."[147] Indeed, the circulation of the most important "democratic party" newspaper, the *Kwangming Daily,* plummeted so much in the Anti-Rightist months that its editor went as far as Kansu to drum up business, and to debunk "the old impression about the *Kwangming Daily,* which still causes too few people to read this socialist newspaper, so that there are not many subscribers."[148]

The 1957 emphasis on the advantages of noncentralist styles continued strongly into the Great Leap Forward. As late as mid-1959, local papers—and particularly evening papers—had extremely large circulations, because they "did not stress giving direct guidance, but gave only indirect guidance," and strove to write about events that were "story-like *[yu ku-shih hsing].*"[149] In Shanghai, the *New People's Evening News* completely gave up writing editorials; it substituted less directive columns, generically called articles of "miscellaneous feelings *[tsa-kan].*"

At the end of the decade, central newspapers were scheduled to arrive in only 50 percent of China's provinces on the day of publication. Province-level newspapers were scheduled to arrive in about 70 percent of the local counties on the same day. But county-level newspapers arrived at over 80 percent of the communes on the publication date.[150] Whether or not these quick-delivery plans were actually maintained, it is clear that one of the attractions of local papers is that they tend to be more up to date than papers from higher levels.

Mao Tse-tung, visiting Nanning, pointed out that "provincial newspapers play a great role in organizing, encouraging, instigating, criticizing, and propelling the work of the provinces and of the whole people."[151] Despite this authority, the early Cultural Revolution was in some ways antilocalist in journalism. Critics of the *Canton Daily,* for example, castigated its policy of "having strong local characteristics." This was only "a camouflage to hide the counter-revolutionary faces" of the editors.[152] Liu Shao-ch'i himself was criticized for having asked, "Bourgeois newspapers let their reports become interesting; so why can't we make more interesting news?"[153] He was excoriated for having told journalists, "The first thing in your work is to be truthful. Don't add salt and pepper on purpose. Don't use colored spectacles."[154]

Nonetheless, provincial newspapers such as the *Wen Hui Report* were clearly influential during the Cultural Revolution. They obviously could not reproduce the official line from Peking, when several conflicting official lines were emanating from that direction. Some Red Guard tabloids had high technical and professional quality,[155] and the spread of journalistic skills at this time may have had a lasting effect. Even the campaign exaggerations, which the Cultural Revolution certainly encouraged, may later have led some cadres to favor more veracity in reporting, by way of contrast. As a frustrated reader in Canton calculated, on a hot summer day in the late 1960s: "It is better to buy a popsicle than to buy a factional newspaper that only fabricates information."[156]

Conclusion: Patterns of Community Change

Determining messages, sending messages, and receiving messages are the main analytic categories organizing this chapter. The final topic, however, is community change. It is one, not three; and it is more dynamic over long time periods than are the processes which apply to any single message. The three communication functions relate to the changing rate of community modernization in specifiable and general ways. An effort to construct a model of these relations is presented as a mathematical annex to this chapter.

Several conclusions should be emphasized from the data. First, the capacity of the Chinese state's communication system is large only in the sense that China is large; it is small on a per capita basis. Claims from other economic sectors on scarce resources have prevented it from expanding quickly. Second, there is some distortion in this communication network. There is no reasonable hope that complex or specific messages, concocted at the top of China's hierarchy, always reach common citizens in exactly the same form they took at Peking. For that reason, the most astute Chinese leaders, especially Mao Tse-tung, have habitually couched their policy pronouncements as general, anecdotal, exemplary, suggestive parables, rather than as complex or purely documentary orders.[157] Third, a great deal of background noise exists in this system. It mainly takes the form of nonnational signals which are received in terms of localist interests.

All of these difficulties become important only because the Communist government, more than any previous Chinese regime, is trying to mobilize its citizens. These problems would not arise, and would not be reported, if there were not an intense, progressive attempt to unify the country in a single efficient communications network. Failures measure the effort as well as the context.[158] Small Chinese communities are slowly but surely giving way to the larger Chinese nation state. The focus of identification for individual citizens is changing gradually. This change affects every aspect of culture—and it affects personalities—in that huge country.

NOTES

1. For example, Susanne K. Langer, *Philosophy in a New Key: A Study in the Symbolism of Reason, Rite, and Art* (New York: Penguin, 1942).

2. See especially the recent book by Godwin C. Chu, *Radical Change through Communication in Mao's China* (Honolulu: The University Press of Hawaii, 1977). Previous explorations include Franklin Houn, *To Change a Nation* (New York: The Free Press of Glencoe, 1961); Frederick T. C. Yu, *Mass Persuasion in Communist China* (New York: Praeger, 1964); and Alan P. L. Liu, *Communications and National Integration in Communist China* (Berkeley: University of California Press, 1971). On a closely allied subject: Merle Goldman, *Literary Dissent in Communist China* (Cambridge, Mass.: Harvard University Press, 1967).

3. *Kuang-ming Jihpao* [Kwangming Daily], Peking, May 20, 1955. *Union Research Service* 78 (February 4, 1975):8–10 reports the post office subscription lists for 1973 (Peking) and 1975 (Canton). These lists, and especially the increase of subscribable items between them, indicate that the number of national papers fluctuated sharply from time to time.

4. An example of the latter sort is the *Chien-k'ang Pao* [Health Report], published by the Ministry of Public Health in Peking.

5. *Fei-ch'ing Yen-chiu Yüeh-k'an* [Studies in Communism], Taipei, April 10, 1969.

6. *Nan-fang Jihpao* [Southern Daily], Canton, April 1, 1959.

7. Quoted in *Hsüeh-hsi* [Study], Peking, May 2, 1959.

8. *Nei Meng-ku Jihpao* [Inner Mongolia Daily], Huhehot, May 12 and 13, 1957.

9. Quoted from ex–New China News Agency journalist Chi Kuei-lin, *Chin-jih Ta-lu* [Today's Mainland], Taipei, May 16, 1961.

10. This journal is printed in a larger number of copies daily than *any* other periodical in China, including even those whose circulations are not limited. It began long ago in Yenan. About 1951, it was circulated among county-level cadres in the countryside and among section-level *(k'u-chi)* cadres in cities. By 1954, the circulation was extended; and in 1957 *Reference Information* was available to nineteenth-grade cadres, military commanders of platoon rank, political commissars of squad level, many factory, trade union and enterprise cadres, university professors, Party and Youth League committee members, and some teachers and students even in middle and primary schools. By 1971, after the number of daily copies of *Reference Information* had been doubled, reportedly at the personal behest of Premier Chou En-lai, any cadre or teacher could take out a personal subscription for 1.50 *yüan* per quarter. This foreign news serial, which sometimes prints articles from abroad about China, has probably been read more than the *People's Daily* (especially since that Central Committee organ sells far less than local newspapers in all parts of China ex-

cept Peking). The headlines and selection of articles in *Reference Information* are interpretive, but the texts are unadorned translations, whose content has not been subject to any further Party approval. Knowledge of the content of this serial was practically unlimited in circulation.

Interview with Mr. Hsu Hung-wen, who helped greatly to provide information for this paper. See also Henry G. Schwartz, "The *Ts'an-k'ao Hsiao-hsi:* How Well Informed Are Chinese Officials about the Outside World?" *China Quarterly* 27 (July 8, 1966):54–83, and *Today's Mainland,* January 1, 1964. The author, walking down a street in Shanghai in February 1976, was startled to see a man, obviously a cadre, standing at a door reading a copy of *Reference Information* openly. The cadre saw the foreigner's curiosity but was nonchalant about being seen in public with this supposedly confidential document.

11. *Southern Daily,* September 28, 1957. This description of the *Yang-ch'eng Wan-pao* is particularly interesting because it appeared in a Party organ in the depths of the Anti-Rightist campaign.

12. *Jenmin Jihpao* [People's Daily], Peking, October 22, 1954.

13. Quoted in *Hsin-hua Jihpao* [New China Daily], Chungking, March 1, 1953.

14. *Che-chiang Jihpao* [Chekiang Daily], Hangchow, February 5, 1955.

15. *Ch'ang-sha Jihpao* [Changsha Daily], July 1, 1956.

16. *Chieh-fang Jihpao* [Liberation Daily], Shanghai, February 8, 1957.

17. *T'ien-wen-t'ai Pao* [Observatory Report], Hong Kong, June 20, 1957.

18. *Kung-shang Jihpao* [Industrial and Commercial Daily], Shanghai, May 20, 1957.

19. *Fu-shun Jihpao* [Fushun Daily], February 20, 1957.

20. *Kwangming Daily,* May 11, 1957.

21. *Kung-jen Jihpao* [Workers' Daily], Peking, May 9, 1957.

22. *Wen Hui Pao* [Wenhui Report], Shanghai, May 8, 1957.

23. *Wenhui Report,* April 18, 1957.

24. *Ho-pei Jihpao* [Hopei Daily], Tientsin, June 12, 1957.

25. *Wenhui Report,* May 10, 1957.

26. *Ch'ang-chiang Jihpao* [Yangtze Daily], Wuhan, July 7, 1957.

27. *Shen-yang Jihpao* [Shenyang Daily], August 23, 1957.

28. *Inner Mongolia Daily,* July 13, 1958.

29. *People's Daily,* June 16, 1960.

30. Ibid., another article.

31. *Wenhui Report,* March 17, 1958.

32. *Hsin-wen Chan-hsien* [News Battlefront], February 9 and May 24, 1959.

33. Ibid., June 24, 1959.

34. Ibid., April 29, 1959.

35. Ibid., June 9, 1959. A "correspondence group" *(t'ung-hsün tsu),* of five members who contributed eight or nine articles monthly, is noted in Hopei's *T'ienmen Pao* [T'ienmen Report], May 1, 1957.

36. *Mei-t'an Kung-yeh* [Coal Industry], April 19, 1959.

37. *News Battlefront,* June 9, 1959.

38. Ibid., June 24, 1959.

39. *Chung-kuo Hsin-wen* [China News], Canton, September 30, 1963.

40. *Chiao-shih Pao* [Teachers' Report], Peking, January 7, 1958.

41. *News Battlefront,* January 24 on Shantung, and May 24 on Kwangtung, 1959.

42. *Teachers' Report,* October 15, 1957.

43. *Liao-ning Jihpao* [Liaoning Daily], Mukden, October 10, 1958; *Kwangming Daily,* October 3, 1958; and *Wenhui Report,* September 21, 1958.

44. *Hsin-wen Jihpao* [News Daily] states that the Shanghai branch was established on March 16, 1968. *An-hui Jihpao* [Anhwei Daily], Hofei, June 29, 1958, indicates that that province's branch was established on June 23. The Kiangsu branch was not established until November; and the Tsinghai and Honan branches, not until February of the next year, according to *News Battlefront,* January 9, February 9 and 24, 1959.

45. *News Battlefront,* March 24, 1959.

46. Ibid., January 9, February 9, April 29, August 9, November 23, and December 24, 1959, respectively.

47. Ibid., September 9, 1959.

48. Ibid., August 23, 1959.

49. Ibid., September 9, 1959.

50. Ibid.

51. *People's Daily,* May 26, 1960.

52. *P'i T'ao Chan-pao* [Criticize T'ao Chu War Report], published by Peking Red Guards in Canton, March 24, 1967.

53. *People's Daily,* June 6, 1960.

54. *Southern Daily,* October 12, 1964.

55. Ting Wang, ed., *Chung-kuo ta-lu hsin-wen-chieh wen-hua ta ko-ming tzu-liao yin-pien* [A Compilation of Press Articles on Peking's News Policy during the Cultural Revolution] (Hong Kong: Chinese University of Hong Kong, 1973).

56. *Hsing-tao Jihpao* [Singtao Daily], Hong Kong, January 23, 1968.

57. Hupei People's Radio, October 8, 1968, and Kiangsi People's Radio, October 18, 1968. (Radio transcripts at URI).

58. Shanghai People's Radio, October 13 and 23, 1968.

59. *Singtao Daily,* July 8, 1969.

60. *T'ien-chin Jihpao* [Tientsin Daily], February 1, 1953.

61. *Lü-ta Jihpao* [Lüta Daily], April 23, 1956.

62. *People's Daily,* October 9, 1952.

63. *Southern Daily,* April 16, 1965.

64. *Chung-kuo Ch'ing-nien Pao* [China Youth News], Shanghai, November 17, 1955.

65. *Kuang-hsi Jihpao* [Kwangsi Daily], Nanning, June 5, 1955.

66. *People's Daily,* June 17, 1956.

67. Ibid.

68. *Yün-nan Jihpao* [Yünnan Daily], Kunming, June 15, 1956. A similar report appeared on August 29.

69. *Ch'inghai Jihpao* [Tsinghai Daily], Sining, October 11, 1956.

70. *Shan-hsi Jihpao* [Shensi Daily], Sian, July 4, 1956.

71. *Lüta Daily,* April 6, 1956.

72. *China Youth News,* November 13, 1956.

73. *Fu-chien Jihpao* [Fukien Daily], Foochow, June 21, 1955. Newspaper staffs across the country were scandalized by the post office's slowness. They printed far more sarcasm on this subject than there is space to dwell on here. Most of it was in the form of letters to editors. A chronological sampler, over a relatively short period

only, might include: *Southern Daily,* July 18, 1955; *Ch'ung-ch'ing Jihpao* [Chung-king Daily], July 20, 1956; *Ha-erh-pin Jihpao* [Harbin Daily], August 3, 1956; *Kuang-chou Jihpao* [Canton Daily], August 4, 1956; *Kung-jen Sheng-huo Pao* [Worker's Life News], Shanghai, August 19, 1956; *Liaoning Daily,* September 2, 1956; *Hsin-hua Jihpao* [New China Daily], Nanking, October 13, 1956; *Chi-lin Jihpao* [Kirin Daily], December 1, 1956; and the *Ch'ün-chung Pao* [Masses' Report], Chengteh, Hopei, December 23, 1956.

74. *Lüta Daily,* April 6, 1956.

75. *Ta-kung Pao* [Takung Report], Tientsin, May 24, 1956.

76. *Takung Report,* Peking, May 22, 1957.

77. *Pei-ching Jihpao* [Peking Daily], April 3, 1957.

78. *Fukien Daily,* April 22, 1958; an article title. Descriptions of 1958 "circulation work plans," "circulation propaganda months," and other subscription changes can be found in *Pao-t'ou Jihpao* [Paotou Daily], August 14; *Ta-chung Pao* [Masses' News], Suiteh, Shensi, January 23; *Yen-an Pao* [Yenan News], April 23; *Yünnan Daily,* July 26 and August 9; *Chungking Daily,* June 2; and *Tsinghai Daily,* May 18, all 1958.

79. *Hsin Hu-nan Pao* [New Hunan Report], Changsha, September 25, 1958.

80. MacFarquhar's figures are: 30 million dailies (possibly including some weeklies, etc.), plus 6 million *Ts'an-k'ao Hsiao-hsi.* Of the 3.4 million *People's Daily,* 1.5 million are printed in Peking. See Roderick MacFarquhar, "A Visit to the Chinese Press," *China Quarterly* 53 (January-March 1973):148.

81. *Chiang-hsi Jihpao* [Kiangsi Daily], Nanchang, April 1, 1958.

82. *Szu-ch'uan Jihpao* [Szechwan Daily], Chengtu, March 28 and April 19, 1958.

83. *Ch'ang-chou Jihpao* [Changchou Daily], March 3, 1958.

84. *Chi-lin Jihpao* [Kirin Daily], October 21, 1957.

85. *News Battlefront,* April 9, 1959.

86. *Today's Mainland,* September 25, 1963.

87. *Shih-pao* [The Times], Hong Kong, October 13, 1960, and August 6, 1962.

88. *Takung Report,* Peking, December 2, 1959.

89. *Kwangming Daily,* December 18, 1959.

90. *Southern Daily,* April 25, 1963.

91. Ibid., December 18, 1964.

92. *Yang-ch'eng Wan-pao* [Canton Evening News], October 13, 1965.

93. Lucian W. Pye, *Aspects of Political Development* (Boston: Little, Brown, 1966), pp. 157–158.

94. Franz Schurmann, *Ideology and Organization in Communist China* (Berkeley: University of California Press, 1966).

95. Godwin C. Chu, "Communication and Cultural Change in China: A Proposed Conceptual Framework," chapter 1 in this volume.

96. *People's Daily,* August 15, 1951.

97. Ibid., August 4, 1952.

98. *Fukien Daily,* May 29, 1952.

99. *People's Daily,* April 19, 1952.

100. *Tzu-lien T'ung-hsün She* [Tzulien Press Service], Hong Kong, June 7, 1955.

101. *Yangtze Daily,* June 16, 1958.

102. *Fukien Daily,* May 26, 1958.

103. *Kan-su Jihpao* [Kansu Daily], Lanchow, January 9, 1955.

104. A Shansi experience of this sort is described in *People's Daily,* January 20, 1955.

105. *Heng-yang Hsin-wen* [Hengyang News], August 21, 1956.

106. *News Daily,* September 14, 1956.

107. *Min-hsi Jihpao* [West Fukien Daily], Lungyen, April 13, 1958.

108. *Ch'uan-nan pao* [South Szechwan Report], Luchow, April 13, 1958.

109. *Inner Mongolia Daily,* October 1, 1956.

110. *Kwangsi Daily,* Nanning, June 5, 1955. A similar report is in the *Tsinghai Daily,* Sining, March 19, 1958.

111. *Hopei Daily,* March 19, 1957.

112. *Yangtze Daily,* December 17, 1955, an article about the suburbs of Wuhan.

113. *China Youth News,* January 15, 1960.

114. The author's senior-year roommate in college, Ma Yeh-hsiang, had previously been editor of a blackboard newspaper in a Shanghai middle school. Some notions are induced from conversations with him.

115. *Nan-yang Shang-pao* [South Seas Commerce Report], Singapore, January 1, 1957.

116. Ibid. This was, of course, during the Hundred Flowers period.

117. *People's Daily,* March 3, 1964.

118. Ibid., March 9, 1964.

119. *Hsin-min Wan-pao* [People's Reform Evening News], Shanghai, April 23, 1964.

120. See *Southern Daily,* January 31, 1963.

121. *Kuang-tung Yü-pao* [Kwangtung Fishermen's Report]; see *Kuang-tung Nung-min Pao* [Kwangtung Farmers' Report], Canton, January 9, 1959.

122. *Min-ping pao* [Militia Report], described in *Hsi-an Jihpao* [Sian Daily], October 30, 1958.

123. *Ch'iao-hsiang Pao* [Overseas Chinese Report], Foochow, October 7, 1956.

124. *People's Daily,* January 17, 1955.

125. *Chung-shan Nung-min Pao* [Chungshan County Farmer's Report], Kwangtung, April 7, 1956.

126. *Hang-hsien Pao* [Hanghsien Report], described in *Chekiang Daily,* July 17, 1955.

127. *Southern Daily,* April 16, 1955.

128. *People's Daily,* June 21, 1950.

129. Ma Chün's frank words are recorded in Ezra F. Vogel, *Canton under Communism: Programs and Politics in a Provincial Capital, 1949-1968* (Cambridge, Mass.: Harvard University Press, 1969), p. 60.

130. *People's Daily,* July 18, 1952. One man, Premier Chou En-lai, apparently deserves much credit for trying to change this situation in subsequent years, through his constant support of *Reference Information.* The thirteen municipal bureaus in the larger survey together subscribed to 1,286 newspapers.

131. *Ch'ing-tao Jihpao* [Tsingtao Daily], September 11, 1956, and *Peking Daily,* September 4, 1956.

132. *People's Daily,* June 13, 1959.

133. *Tsinghai Daily,* Sining, August 15, and October 4, 1956.

134. Ibid., October 11 and November 2, 1956.

135. *People's Daily,* August 17 and 31, 1956. Another example, involving the ca-

pacity of a workers' club, was misreported on October 23 and corrected on November 28.

136. Ibid., August 11, 1956.

137. Ibid., March 14, 1956.

138. *Kwangming Daily,* February 19, 1955.

139. The review's name in romanization: *Hsiang-chiang P'ing-lun.* See *China News,* July 23, 1956, and *News Battlefront,* May 9, 1959. The latter publication, in this issue and on May 24 and July 24, published detailed descriptions of early leftist journals, including *Lao-tung chieh, Lao-tung yin, Jen sheng, Lao-tung che, Kung-ch'an-tang, Hsin she-hui, T'ien-hsiang, Jen-tao yüeh-k'an, Hsien-ch'ü,* and *Chung-kuo jen.* Not only did China invent newspapers; she also invented illegal newspapers, which were first called *hsiao-pao* during the Sung.

140. *People's Daily,* October 26, 1956.

141. *China Youth News,* April 13, 1956.

142. This *Kung-ch'ang Hei-pan Pao* column appeared in the *Hsin Ch'ien Jihpao* [New Kweichow Daily] and was reported in *People's Daily,* June 3, 1955.

143. *People's Daily,* July 19, 1958.

144. *Kwangming Daily,* May 19, 1957.

145. *People's Daily,* August 8, 1957.

146. *Studies in Communism,* April 10, 1969.

147. *Hsin-wen kung-tso wei-hsien lun* [Journalism work entails risk]. Hupei People's Radio, September 8, 1969.

148. *Kansu Daily,* May 10, 1958.

149. *News Battlefront,* June 9, 1959. At this time, some evening paper circulations were: *Hsin-min Wan-pao* [Hsin-min Evening News], 230,000; *Hsin-min Pao* [People's Renovation News], 90,000; *Yang-ch'eng Wan-pao* [Canton Evening News], 170,000; *Pei-ching Wan-pao* [Peking Evening News], 150,000.

150. *Takung Report,* December 2, 1959. The *Yüeh-hsi Nung-min Pao* [West Kwangtung Report], Tsamkong, August 15, 1955, implied a much slower delivery schedule. See also *Kansu Daily,* May 17, 1958. The *Chekiang Daily,* September 15, 1958, has data showing that the Hangchow provincial paper maintained its fivefold lead in circulation over the *People's Daily* in Chekiang between April and September—even though the circulations of both doubled in this Leap period.

151. *People's Daily,* November 26, 1958.

152. *Southern Daily,* January 23, 1969.

153. *Hung-se Hsüan-ch'uan Pao* [Red Propaganda Report], Peking, May 10, 1967.

154. *Wen-hsüeh Chan-pao* [Literature War Report], Peking, April 28, 1967.

155. *South China Morning Post,* Hong Kong, September 8, 1968.

156. *Singtao Daily,* January 1, 1968. The quotation refers to the *Southern Daily,* and the critic was a member of the East Wind faction of Red Guards then attacking it.

157. On norm specificity and Chinese politics, see Lynn T. White, "Shanghai's Polity in Cultural Revolution," in John W. Lewis, ed., *The City in Communist China* (Stanford, Calif.: Stanford University Press, 1971), esp. pp. 357–370. Also, Michel C. Oksenberg, "China's Politics and the Public Health Issue," in John Z. Bowers and Elizabeth F. Purcell, eds., *Medicine and Society in China* (New York: Josiah Macy, Jr. Foundation, 1974), pp. 128–161. Mao's famous blast at the "Ur-

ban Public Health Ministry of the Privileged" is a good example of his circumspect willingness to trade specificity for cogency in making public pronouncements; and this tendency to compromise is reflected in the capabilities and incapabilities of the Chinese communication system.

158. It should be mentioned that prospects for creating such an intense communication system in China after the country's economic prosperity increases are bright on the basis of what other Chinese have done *outside* the People's Republic. On this subject, see the excellent book by Chang Kuo-hsing (Chang Kuo-Sin), *Chung-wen pao-chih kai-kuan* [A Survey of the Chinese Language Daily Press] (Hong Kong: Kuo-chi Hsin-wen Hsieh-hui, 1968).

Mathematical Annex on Community Change

Each of the three signal processes discussed in chapter 4 can be loosely associated with a particular pattern of community change. These patterns could be represented, and then combined, by drawing curves on graphs; but the simplest way to present them is to use equations. Also, it is interesting to search for formulas containing a list of variables (here, they will be called m, p, a, and f) that are sufficient to generate and combine the influences of the three signal processes on total community change. In a graphic or verbal presentation, there would be no way to show that any such list is exhaustive, although none of the modes of presentation in this paper would require exact means to operationalize the variables. The order of discussion in the annex (sending, receiving, formulating) is slightly altered from the order in the rest of the chapter.

Signal-sending capacities tend to change in an increasing, perhaps roughly linear, fashion. Modernization of the post office network surely progresses that way, largely because truck and railroad transport do so. Many causes of this kind of growth can be traced to technological innovations. There is no sure way to predict the appearance of such inventions, and the speed of their social application may also be difficult to know in advance. Over the next several years, however, it is probable that more extensive use of radio will enhance the government's communicative efficiency in reaching more Chinese people. If c were the number of "communicators" added to the state-oriented "community" (of size capital C) in any small time period t, and if m were assumed to be a constant representing a rate of "modernization" (and if we assume no knowledge of whether technological impulses within t will increase or lessen to make m rise or fall), then we might define that $c_t = m$. The cumulative function, for C beginning at $t = 0$ and then proceeding on, would be

$$C_t = C_0 + mt.$$

Signal-receiving processes, however, may loosely tend to change in a way that would be better represented by a bell-shaped curve than by a roughly steady line. Their rate of change may follow an exponential pattern, first accelerating and then decaying. Surely literacy is like that. The number of new literates added, during any short time period, must largely depend on the total number of current literates at that time who can act as teachers. But in the future, when the number of literates begins to approach the size of the total population, the rate of new additions to "community" on account of this cause should decline. (This always assumes that "community" is defined in a peculiarly official way, and that literates actually read the state newspapers.) Certain other community-related factors, such as the spread of the "common" Mandarin dialect of Chinese, may affect c similarly. Poisson or Gaussian equations are often used to represent this shape, but the simplest formula is:

$$c = t\, e^{-(t-p)^2}$$

where e is the transcendental constant (about 2.72) and p is the value of t at which c "peaks." The cumulative function for C, which could be graphed by a "lazy S" curve, is then a matter for integration. This can be found in the equation:

$$C_t = C_0 + mt + \int_0^t te^{-(t-p)^2} dt$$

Signal formulation may tend to change in yet a third way. Especially for China, the land of Long Marches, Great Leaps Forward, and Cultural Revolutions, the smooth linear and exponential descriptions just given may suggest more patience about progress than is real. China is now the world's foremost platform for huge political campaigns, and they affect message determination by first purging mediamen and then rehabilitating them, by first mandating strict orthodoxy in newspaper content and then encouraging relaxation. These movements also affect signal-reception processes, although their influence on signal concocting is greater. It is no new idea that these changes move like sine waves. Let the severity (amplitude) of campaigns by measured by a and their frequency by f. If sinoidal affects on c were combined with the exponential ones mentioned above, then

$$c = te^{-(t-p)^2} + a \sin ft.$$

Because the last term in this equation would be negative at some values of t, this way of stating the case would allow both a general pattern of community expansion and also the possibility of contraction at some times. Finally, if we assume that linear innovation-induced growth, exponential community-size-induced growth, and sinoidal campaign-induced growth can be analyzed independently, then

$$C_t = C_0 + mt + \int_0^t te^{-(t-p)^2} dt + a/f \cos ft$$

Any of the last three terms in this equation could be used more than once, if different values of m, p, or a and f were found to be needed for analytically separable kinds of modern changes, exponential changes, or cycles.

These forms obviously go beyond questions concerning newspapers. They are not culturally specific to China. They would be difficult to operationalize. The main point is that research on the specific efficiencies of China's communication system can be related to the task of trying to find out how the Chinese community as a whole changes.

5

Small Groups and Communication in China: Ideal Forms and Imperfect Realities

Martin King Whyte

A number of observers have commented on the distinctiveness of the small group *(hsiao-tsu)* and the important role this institution plays in communications within China.[1] I wish to consider here the strengths and shortcomings of the network of *hsiao-tsu,* both in theory and practice.

Briefly, individuals in many different organizational settings in China—such as schools, offices, factories, urban neighborhoods, military units, forced labor camps—are organized on a regular basis into *hsiao-tsu,* which commonly have about eight to fifteen members.[2] *Hsiao-tsu* are formed on the basis of existing organizational boundaries—classrooms and rows, platoons and squads, and so forth. Each group has a head, and occasionally other designated leaders as well, such as a vice head or recorder. Individuals generally carry out the normal activities of their organization—work, study, and so on—in these *hsiao-tsu,* but the latter are also convened for extracurricular activities I have called "political rituals." Members meet to study and discuss political documents assigned by the group head (who in turn is generally directed by the Party branch secretary and propaganda officer of the organization), and they engage in criticism and self-criticism. In the latter "ritual," each member of the group is expected to compare his or her attitudes and behavior critically with the ideals expressed in the study materials or other leadership proclamations. Each member also submits to criticism or commendation from other members of the group. The group head reports to the leadership the views expressed in these meetings, and the latter, in turn, closely supervises the selection of *hsiao-tsu* leaders. The frequency of *hsiao-tsu* meetings varies from organization to organization and over time. In some cases there is one meeting a week, in others three a week, and during a political campaign there may be daily meetings, with ordinary activities suspended in favor of these mass ruminations. Not all political study meetings in *hsiao-tsu* are accompanied by mutual criticism, and sometimes the groups meet for other purposes, as, for example, professional study in an office, or mutual academic help in school.

The *hsiao-tsu* network and "rituals" are an organizational innovation of the Chinese Communists, although they have some precedent in both Chinese and Soviet experience. From traditional China come such elements as the view that the government is obliged to provide moral instruction to the population and the notion of using semiofficial groupings of the ordinary population, embodying a mutual responsibility principle, to supplement the official political hierarchy. From the Soviet Union comes the form of the political rituals themselves, designed originally to mold members of the Bolshevik Party into a cohesive and disciplined unit. From the decades of guerrilla warfare in China come the tactics for communicating to and organizing the ordinary population that came to be called the "mass line." The combination of all of these elements into the *hsiao-tsu* network and ritualized performance of criticism seems to have occurred by trial and error in the Red Army and to have been gradually applied to many other sectors of the population before and after 1949. This network is one element that makes Chinese social organization today quite different from that prevailing in either traditional China or in the Soviet Union.

Hsiao-tsu play a number of important roles in the Chinese political system,[3] and three of these relate to communications. First, they are a vital part of the system of *downward* communication used to get the government's message across to the population. Even without considering the *hsiao-tsu* network, China has an impressive downward communication system for a developing country. Centralized control over the mass media, a national network of wired and wireless radio communication, the hierarchical information transmission channels in the Party, the Youth League and various mass associations, and many other devices make it possible to get the government's message communicated to distant corners of the Chinese realm. But the *hsiao-tsu* network adds effectiveness to this information flow. Illiterates can be effectively reached, since a *hsiao-tsu* needs only one literate member to be able to translate printed matter into group discussion. Then, as communications from higher authorities are discussed in a *hsiao-tsu,* the group head has the responsibility for making the ideas expressed more concrete and applying them to the local situation. Group members are expected to discover how abstract ideas about combatting Confucianism or the influence of the Gang of Four are relevant to their task of producing steel or studying physics. If satisfactorily done, the level of public comprehension of the government's goals should be heightened. Finally, the *hsiao-tsu* makes for active, rather than passive, reception of communications. The ideal is that all members of the group should state their understanding of the message in their own words and give their reaction to it, so that higher authorities can be sure that the message is getting across. In general, then, the *hsiao-tsu* network provides a regular verbal mechanism for reinforcing communications coming down through the official media.

The second role of *hsiao-tsu* in communication involves public commitment and persuasion. Individuals are supposed not only to become aware of and understand the government's goals, but to commit themselves publicly to carrying them out and to come to accept these goals as right and proper. In part, this is expected to happen through the rhetorical skills of the group head and the "activists" in the group. They are expected to notice reluctant and unconvinced members and to make them the targets for their efforts to explain and justify official policy. Ideally, the emphasis should be on persuasion and not on commands and threats, but the threat of subjecting "backward elements" to group criticism can produce an atmosphere that one scholar has termed "coercive persuasion."[4] The Chinese Communists make use of an important social-psychological principle here. In any society, individuals have their attitudes shaped in powerful ways by the views expressed by members of the primary groups in which they live—friends, fellow workers, neighbors, kin, and so forth. By controlling the interaction process in the group, mutual criticism rituals aim to ensure that group members all pressure one another to support official norms. Each member is dependent upon group acceptance for preservation of his or her self-esteem, and will react with alarm to any group criticism initiated by departure from official norms. If properly organized, this should provide a powerful force for attitude change.[5] Thus the *hsiao-tsu* network aims to coopt and control primary group ties and communication within organizations and to carry out much of the task of mass persuasion.

The third role of the small group network concerns *upward* communication. This occurs through the regular reports of the *hsiao-tsu* heads to their Party supervisors. They are expected to relay upward what the initial reactions of group members to study materials were, what confusions arose, and the level of approval that subsequently developed. As part of the official mass line leadership style —"from the masses, to the masses"—this information is supposed to give authorities the means to take mass reactions into account in planning future policies and how these should be communicated. In theory, this provides a national network capable of continued monitoring of mass attitudes.

Hsiao-tsu have an important negative role to play in communication as well. The network is designed to inhibit horizontal communication other than what takes place within the group structure. Individuals belong to one *hsiao-tsu* (except Party and Youth League members, who meet in *hsiao-tsu* of these organizations as well as the ordinary *hsiao-tsu*). There is no regular mechanism for communication across groups.[6] Norms exist which discourage discussing group and organizational activities with outsiders. The effectiveness of the groups in communication depends on their ability to minimize extraneous and uncontrolled horizontal communications reaching group members.

In spite of this problem, however, such a system of mass communication should in theory be unusually effective. Messages from Peking or lower centers of authority can be disseminated rapidly throughout the country, and they can be communicated verbally in terms comprehensible to a poorly educated audience. Group interaction can be controlled so that dissident views have no chance to be heard or to influence members, and social pressure can be mobilized to persuade members to change their attitudes and support new policies enthusiastically. The feedback aspect also allows authorities to monitor how official messages are being received. This system is supposed to depend primarily on Chinese skills in manipulating human relationships, rather than on force, commands, or material incentives. Whether viewed as the communicator's dream or a totalitarian nightmare, this seems like a very powerful system, one made possible by the strong and effective political infrastructure that the Chinese Communists have built.

In practice, however, a number of problems make this system somewhat less effective than it seems. I will discuss several of these problems and consider how they apply to the three distinct communication roles just outlined.

First, inherent conflicts exist among the roles *hsiao-tsu* are supposed to perform. The major thrust of *hsiao-tsu* operations is to communicate new goals and ideals and persuade the masses to accept them. Basic-level cadres and *hsiao-tsu* heads are under a great deal of pressure to show a high degree of support for new goals and programs. In this situation, individuals who express reservations or objections are likely to be criticized harshly and perhaps even given a negative label—"backward element," "rightist sympathizer," and so forth. Since, as Chinese media remind us, "the masses' eyes are bright," they understand where the emphasis lies and are not likely to stick their necks out by voicing their doubts. The result is often that group members carefully search for cues about what public statements are required of them and make them, no matter what their private views and reservations are. Such sessions can become a charade that group members feel they must engage in.

Higher authorities are not unaware of the fact that mass opinions may not be fully and faithfully conveyed in *hsiao-tsu* meetings, and they make periodic efforts to stimulate more upward communication. Individuals are encouraged to "go against the tide." Party statutes are rewritten to allow complaints to be forwarded over the heads of one's own local Party leaders to higher levels. Periodic rectification campaigns and the writing of wall posters are designed to draw out concealed grievances. Such needed special efforts seem to testify that the natural tendency of *hsiao-tsu* operations is to report upward fairly automatic approval of policies and programs.

Furthermore, the special efforts are themselves highly coordinated so that they suit the desires of higher authorities. Individuals who "go against the tide" on their own take on substantial risks.[7]

The result is that in most circumstances the upward communication role of *hsiao-tsu* is undermined. It is possible for pleasant messages to continue to flow upward while serious feelings of grievance are accumulating below, creating the potential for social conflict if political controls are relaxed, as has occurred at a number of points over the years, particularly in the last decade. Whether Chinese authorities have effective alternative mechanisms for monitoring public attitudes on a regular basis—perhaps through informants serving the public security system—remains an open question.

Another set of problems in *hsiao-tsu* operations is that the network is not effectively established everywhere, and that even where it is established, it does not monopolize persuasive communications. The most important gap involves the largest part of the Chinese population—the peasantry.[8] *Hsiao-tsu* are predominantly an urban phenomenon. Peasants are organized into communes which are divided into production brigades and production teams. But teams are not usually subdivided into *hsiao-tsu* that meet on a regular basis for political study and mutual criticism. Political meetings, when they occur, are generally held with the entire team (such as a unit of 30 to 40 households, or 150 or more people), usually with the team head or other cadre speaking to a fairly passive audience. In Kwangtung Province, at least, most production teams do not even have a regular schedule of political study meetings as in urban organizations. Team cadres convene such meetings on an ad hoc basis when there is an important political directive or communication to announce, and this may be only once a month or so.

At various points in time the authorities have tried to introduce a more rigorous political study system in the countryside. For instance, in the wake of the Cultural Revolution, many localities chose a new team officer, a "political commander," to be assisted by study advisers *(fu-tao yüan)* directed to organize peasants for regular political study. In a few localities, these individuals tried to organize individual peasant families into "family Mao Tse-tung's Thought study classes," usually with youths taking the lead in introducing political concepts to their elders.[9] These more rigorous political study routines did not last for long, however, and today and in most other periods the rural political communication system has been considerably looser.

Still, this less rigorous organization does not mean that downward communication does not reach Chinese peasants fairly effectively. At least for Kwangtung, our research indicates that peasants have a fairly high level of awareness of current official goals, political slogans, and media jargon. But without a rigorous small group network, this awareness can be a passive or even hostile one, since control over interactions and village social pressure is generally not very tight.

This weakening of the political communication system in the countryside is not without a beneficial side. It increases the potential for meaningful upward communication. Peasants are freer to grumble about policies and programs they do not like than are urbanites, and team and brigade cadres are more likely to have the vigor of their enforcement of official policies tempered by their reading of public opinion. [10] Thus the government may not be able to exert such effective social pressure in support of its ideas, but may be able to get a fairly accurate idea through normal bureaucratic channels of the effects of its policies on rural public opinion.

Chinese villages are not the only setting where social ties and interactions are not effectively captured by the small group network. The problem of uncontrolled ties and communications affects all organizational settings to some extent (although perhaps least so the army and forced labor camps). The main problem is that people have important ties outside their group, and in many cases these are their most salient personal ties. Such ties obviously include families and kin, as well as friends, former schoolmates, neighbors, and even other acquaintances within their organization.

Chinese organizations are quite "inclusive" compared with their counterparts in the West or the Soviet Union, in the sense that individuals spend much time within their confines and in outside activities monitored by organizational authorities. For example, a worker may spend all day working in his factory, have several hours in the evening occupied by political study or group recreation organized by the factory, and then return to spend the night in a dormitory run by that unit. But this is relative and not total inclusiveness. The worker has some opportunities for informal and unsupervised exchanges with friends in the factory during the day; he has a good deal of political privacy at home with his family; and he has many opportunities to see old friends and schoolmates during his leisure time. These other contacts need not consist of whispered counterrevolutionary statements for the persuasive effectiveness of the small group experience to be undermined.

The impact of small group criticism depends on the individual feeling that he or she is isolated among others who are withdrawing their valued approval. If that individual has other, more important ties that provide sympathy and support not dependent upon uttering the proper political phrases, he or she will be somewhat immune to the group's pressure. These alternative ties need not be with "outsiders." The effect of the group sessions is obviously weakened more dramatically if two members of the same group confide to each other later in private that their public comments were a sham, although obviously some risk is involved in such confidences.

We have tried to indicate that the negative role of the small group network in excluding extraneous or contrary messages is not fully effective. Most individuals have important social ties not captured by the group network that can undermine the role of group rituals in persuasion.

In a more complex sense, the *hsiao-tsu* system is also less than totally inclusive. One conception of the communication process might be that individuals respond to persuasive messages coming to them from their environment. If all of the communicatons reaching an individual sing the same tune, then they should be persuasive. If they offer conflicting views, then none will be as persuasive, for the individual will be able to compare and weigh each, based on their logic, the nature of the source, and so forth.

In reality, the connection between communication and the process of attitude change is more complex than this conception allows. Individuals have past histories and life experiences, they are involved in sets of social obligations and power relationships, and they live in social structures that provide them with a framework for calculating costs and benefits. Any new communication is weighed not only against competing messages, but against a complex set of memories, obligations, opportunities, and so forth. If official communications call for changes that are seen as unrewarding in the local structure in which the individual lives, they may be ignored or complied with grudgingly, without influencing the individual's attitudes favorably.

The Chinese have in a sense tried to construct a social system that would conform to the prescriptions for a better society put forth by B. F. Skinner.[11] In that system, each individual is surrounded by influences all working in uniformity to reward "good" behavior, although in the Chinese case negative sanctions, particularly mutual criticism, also receive heavy emphasis.[12] However, the Chinese case also neatly illustrates the difficulty of fulfilling the Skinnerian scheme. Even in a highly organized and controlled society, it has proved very difficult to screen out all extraneous social ties and communication. As a result, active rumor networks and a somewhat autonomous public opinion coexist with controlled *hsiao-tsu* communication.

Another set of problems in *hsiao-tsu* operations involves the fact that the groups and organizations involved may not be as salient in the lives of members as our original discussion assumes. For persuasion to be successful, group members must feel that the organization is important to them, and must value the ties with other group members and desire to win their approval. But in many settings it is difficult to assure these things. The most obvious example is the forced labor camp. *Hsiao-tsu* members are in the camp against their wills, they are assigned to groups on bases other than compatibility (or even because of incompatibility), and they are unlikely to view group pressure as constructive criticism from valued colleagues.

Urban neighborhood *hsiao-tsu* are also affected by the problem of low salience. Many individuals living in a neighborhood are not subject to local residents' committee and *hsiao-tsu* supervision because they work or go to school and are organized into *hsiao-tsu* in outside units. This leaves mostly the retired, disabled, and unemployed to be supervised. The families living in a particular neighborhood may not have much in common to serve as a basis for group solidarity and may not feel that these groups are a very important part of their lives. With the exception of former housewives employed in street workshops and other enterprises, the individuals brought together in residential *hsiao-tsu* meetings do not generally share other activities and interests outside of these meetings.[13]

Authorities recognize some of these problems of salience and solidarity, and sometimes organize separate political study groups for unemployed youths and occasionally also for the retired. Still, the greater salience of ties to family, friends, and others is likely to weaken the effect of social pressure from these groups.

The entire *hsiao-tsu* network depends upon effective leadership at various levels. The critical role of the *hsiao-tsu* head and local Party supervision should be clear from our opening discussion. If the head is not respected by the members, is not skilled at relating to them, does not understand the documents that are to be studied, or is not able to translate their abstract formulas into local concerns and problems, then the group sessions are likely to degenerate into an empty and tedious routine. Cursorily going through the motions is probably the most common "deviation" from ideal *hsiao-tsu* operations. If serious enough, ineffective leadership may affect not only the persuasion role of the group, but the downward communication role as well.

Leadership problems can also occur at higher levels in the system. Up to now, we have assumed that official messages come down the hierarchy to *hsiao-tsu* at the bottom in a coherent fashion, giving a uniform view of official policy. But recent history in China has not always fit this image. Erratic shifts in official line have been the rule rather than the exception. Factional cleavages at various levels in the hierarchy have been clearly visible, with different groups trying to gain control of various parts of the communications system and sending out competing messages in their efforts to mobilize mass followings.[14]

These phenomena can undermine all three of the *hsiao-tsu* communication roles. Groups and their leaders and supervisors may become confused and not know what goals and standards should be stressed, leading to timidity and anxiety. Cracks in the leadership structure may lead to cynicism and a desire to avoid any but minimal commitment by those at the bottom. Or competing factions and exhortations may provide leeway for those below with axes to grind to choose up sides and struggle to undercut their local rivals, a phenomenon seen all too often in the last few years. The leadership is likely to receive contradictory information coming upward on what mass attitudes are, providing various factions with the conviction that the masses *really* favor them over their rivals. Whatever the local response, without forceful and uniform direction from above, the effectiveness of the *hsiao-tsu* communication system is diminished, and the potential for maneuver and conflict at the bottom is enhanced.

I have posed here some of the types of problems that may make actual *hsiao-tsu* operations somewhat different from how they should work "in theory." Upward communication, it has been argued, is not very effectively carried out wherever the group system is well organized. Perhaps this observation may be seen as confirmation of the inverse relationship posited by David Apter between coercion and information in political systems.[15] Persuasion is carried out fairly effectively in some settings, but not very well in many others (see Whyte, 1974, for more detail on this point).

Downward communication, however, can be effectively carried out even when the other two roles are not. Less is required for effective downward communication. The national political hierarchy has to be operating effectively, messages have to be fairly uniform and readily interpretable, *hsiao-tsu* heads have to be literate, motivated, and capable of conveying the messages in terms members can understand and appreciate, and group members have to be willing to attend regularly and pay some attention. These conditions seem to be fulfilled fairly well at most times and places (including in the countryside), and thus it is usually possible for the government to get its goals and ideas communicated fairly uniformly and rapidly throughout the realm.

In summary, even taking into account the problems discussed, we have the distinctive features of *hsiao-tsu*—active discussion, statements of comprehension in terms of local conditions, and required public pledges of approval—that create a system of downward communication which should be the envy of communicators elsewhere. The *hsiao-tsu* network seems to play an effective role in keeping most of the population aware of the government's changing views and objectives.

Awareness, however, is not necessarily acceptance, not to mention enthusiasm. By keeping the potential problems of the *hsiao-tsu* system and its several communication roles in mind, we should be in a position to understand how a government able to mobilize mass declarations of support for one set of policies is able to shift policies rapidly and mobilize new mass declarations. We should also be closer to understanding how a population which observers describe as dedicated and content at one moment can produce hostile and angry mobs and violent confrontations with authority the next. We should also be aided in recognizing that the gap between publicly expressed views and private opinions is smaller in some groups and organizational settings and larger in others. The Chinese system of communication must be judged as one of the most sophisticated and effective in the world, but we should keep in mind that there is more to this system than meets the eye.

NOTES

1. See, for example, Alan P. L. Liu, *Communications and National Integration in Communist China* (Berkeley: University of California Press, 1971); Godwin C. Chu, "Group Communication and Development in Mainland China—the Functions of Social Pressure," in W. Schramm and D. Lerner, ed., *Communication and Change: The Last Ten Years—and the Next* (Honolulu: The University Press of Hawaii, 1976) pp. 119–133; and Kenneth Lamott, "The Maoist Solution to the Energy Crisis," *Human Behavior* 6 (1977):8.

2. For detailed treatment of many of the issues here, see Martin King Whyte, *Small Groups and Political Rituals in China* (Berkeley: University of California Press, 1974).

3. Roles not discussed here include behavior control, detection of deviance, and fostering of leadership skills. See the discussion in Whyte, *Small Groups and Political Rituals,* chap. 2, pp. 7–17.

4. Edgar H. Schein, *Coercive Persuasion* (New York: W. W. Norton, 1961).

5. For some relevant Western research on this point, see Whyte, *Small Groups and Political Rituals,* chap. 2, pp. 7–17.

6. There are occasional exceptions to this generalization; for instance, when several *hsiao-tsu* convene a joint meeting to deal with a problem common to all, or when group heads exchange experiences on how best to organize group sessions.

7. Several examples of the harsh treatment of insufficiently cautious "tide challengers" are given in "In Defense of Truth," *Peking Review* 28 (July 8, 1977): 15–17, 20.

8. I will not consider here the situation in national minority regions, where it is possible that the *hsiao-tsu* system may be poorly developed.

9. For more details on these developments, see Whyte, *Small Groups and Political Rituals,* chap. 7, pp. 135–166.

10. For a fuller development of these points, see William L. Parish, Jr., and Martin King Whyte, *Village and Family in Contemporary China* (Chicago: University of Chicago Press, in press).

11. See especially B. F. Skinner, *Beyond Freedom and Dignity* (New York: Alfred A. Knopf, 1971).

12. One other critical difference between Skinner's ideas and those of the Chinese, besides the latter's greater emphasis on negative sanctions, is that Skinner is not concerned with internal thought patterns, motivation, and will. He sees the human mind as a black box which produces behavior in response to present and past patterns of rewards and punishment. The Chinese, of course, do not accept these tenets of behaviorism, and are intensely concerned with human attitudes and motivations, and how these can be changed.

13. For more systematic discussions of this topic, see Martin King Whyte, "Change and Continuity in China: The Case of Rural Marriage," *Problems of Communism* 26, no. 4 (1977):41–55, and Parish and Whyte, *Village and Family in Contemporary China.*

14. For the period 1973–1976, this situation of different factions controlling different parts of the communications system is now openly discussed. See, for example, "A Mouthpiece of the Gang," *Peking Review* 29 (July 15, 1977):26, 31–32.

15. David Apter, *The Politics of Modernization* (Chicago: University of Chicago Press, 1965).

6

The People's Commune as a Communication Network for the Diffusion of Agritechnology

Lau Siu-kai

Technological change in agriculture in China can be divided into two parts: the creation of technological innovations, and their diffusion. Both are forms of cultural change, as they involve an addition to the stock of knowledge in society and a reorganization of man's conception of nature and society as well as of the individual's relationship with others. Technological change, therefore, requires not only a rearrangement of the physical layout in the production process but also a transformation of social values, norms, and institutions. As technological change is generated by invention (whether indigenously created or borrowed from outside), its key determining factor is diffusion, a process of communication. The communication structure of a society, in patterning its forms of information transmission and social interaction, critically conditions the extent and speed of diffusion of innovations.

The people's commune can be understood as a planned organizational device to foster development in rural China. The kind of development envisioned by the Chinese planners is multifaceted; it is nothing less than the total transformation of rural society and the personality of the rural people. In this chapter, I focus on the relationship between the people's commune and technological change in the agricultural sector. The major argument is that, at least in an ideal sense, the structural characteristics of the commune engender a particular type of communication system that is conducive to the diffusion of agricultural technology.

The People's Commune as an Organization for Change

The people's commune in China is an organization for change with the explicit goal of structuring individual and group behavior in rural society. It is a mobilization system capable of emancipating human resources (including man's physical labor, his desires, emotions, loyalties, identifications, orientations, beliefs, etc.) and material resources (capital, land, production tools, etc.) from traditional utilization for deployment in more efficient and innovative production modes.[1]

The people's commune manifests a certain amount of *centralization* of power and collective coercion. On the other hand, because the commune is intended to foster change and to transform itself in accordance with the demands of the changing situation, it should have a certain degree of flexibility.[2] The level of centralization cannot be overly high.[3] The coexistence of centralization and *decentralization* of power is thus the first major structural characteristic of the commune.[4] These two principles signify that power and decision-making prerogatives will be divided among the three levels of the commune organization according to the issues and functions concerned. In the words of the Chinese, this combination is called "democratic centralism," its major features being "centralization on the basis of democracy, and democracy under the direction of centralization. [Democratic centralism] realizes the unity of democracy and centralization, and the unity of freedom and discipline; hence it is an important component of the Marxist-Leninist line of Party building, and it consolidates the unitary leadership pattern in all organizations."[5]

As a second important structural feature, the behavioral implications of democratic centralism at the commune level are the *involvement of a majority of the members* (excluding those individuals classified as bad elements) in the decision-making process, and the solicitation of suggestions from the members by cadres at different administrative levels. Once a decision has been made, it will automatically assume a compelling nature and it is the responsibility of each individual to abide by it.

The third structural characteristic of the commune is its *low level of formalization*. Formalized rules and regulations, as well as sanctions stipulated for their violations, are rare. Except for a set of rough guidelines, individual commune members are left with a broad scope for individual interpretation of proper conduct, though social and political controls no doubt serve as constraining factors. Nonetheless, as inferred from our conversations with the cadres in the communes we have visited, and from officially published materials, the Chinese peasants seem to have the endemic tendency to drift away from the line of approved conduct and to indulge in tilling of private plots, overfrequenting towns and theaters, and so on. To correct deviant behavior, oftentimes the cadres have to rely on persuasive techniques, most probably based on personal relationship; seldom are appeals to formal rules made to rectify the conditions.

A fourth structural feature is a *low level of stratification.* The people's commune is characterized by a relatively egalitarian distribution of political power, social status, and economic rewards, though absolute equality is impossible. Conversely, a high level of stratification is considered detrimental to the commune's goals of planned change and self-transformation. Individuals and groups in possession of greater power, higher status, and larger economic rewards will be resistant to change lest their vested interests be affected; and a high level of stratification would lead to greater social distance between upper and lower strata, which would in turn hamper social interaction between them.[6]

Openness is a fifth structural feature of the commune. Administratively, the commune serves as the intermediary between the state, primarily represented by the *hsien* (county), and society, thus subjecting society to political, ideological, and economic control and manipulation by the state. In many areas—education, health care, family planning, and so on—the commune is an integral part of a large, complex national network. Through these multiple networks, the commune engages in intensive exchanges with other organizations at equivalent and higher levels.

In a structural arrangement such as the commune, a complicated communication system is both the key to effective functioning as well as its logical derivative. The communication system in the commune is an open one, as it is a part of a national network of communication. Within the commune, intensive communicative activities are maintained both vertically and horizontally as a result of power decentralization, democratic centralism, low stratification, and low formalization. Both the mass media and interpersonal communication channels are of equal importance. The mere size of the commune organization certainly necessitates the installation of a mass media network. The more intimate interpersonal relationships resulting from the shortening of social distance among people, however, stimulate a large volume of interpersonal communication and render the mechanism of interpersonal influence a viable means to effect personal and social change. In the case of diffusion of agritechnology, both the mass media and the interpersonal channels of communication play crucial roles. The mass media channels are primarily effective in the propagation of technological information, especially that of exogenous origin. Interpersonal channels are critical in adoption of technological innovations.

Organizations for Technological Innovations in Chinese Agriculture

One of the core tasks of the commune since their establishment in 1958 is the development of agriculture. From 1961 on, technological innovation for agricultural development has been increasingly emphasized. Despite interruptions from the Cultural Revolution, rural China has witnessed a gradual technological improvement in agriculture. Since the downfall of the Gang of Four in late 1976, there has been even more emphasis on agricultural innovation.

For technological innovation in agriculture, the openness of the commune organization can be illustrated by the four-tiered network of agricultural science *(ssu-chi nung-k'o wang)*. At the *hsien* (county) level and at each of the levels of the commune (the commune, the production brigade, and the production team), scientific research and technical units are set up to perform agricultural experimentation and diffusion of innovations.[7] Each year, the units at higher levels devise research and action plans, which are then discussed by people at the lower levels. After the plans have been agreed on, they are implemented by all units in the network. Periodic progress reports are submitted to higher-level units for evaluation.

In one of the communes we visited—the Huan Ch'eng commune in the county of Hsin Hui—there was a three-tiered agricultural research network, which was linked to the Bureau of Agricultural Research *(Nung-k'o Chü)* located in the county seat. (When the county research unit is included, it will be called the four-tiered network.) Most of the information on advanced agricultural technology was procured by the commune through the bureau, which functioned to collect scientific information from national institutions. In the three-tiered network, there was an Agricultural Research Institute *(Nung-k'o So)* operated by the commune, with about seventy employees. About 70 *mou* of arable land had been furnished by the commune for agricultural research. Financial expenses each year for the institute varied between 8,000 and 10,000 *yüan (jen-min pi).* The institute imported new knowledge and technology from the outside (particularly through the *hsien*) for use in the commune. The institute, however, had to study the new technology to determine its utility and feasibility within the natural and social conditions of the commune before disseminating it.

The main activities of the institute included large field experimentation of seed species and the provision of fine-breed seeds to the production brigades and teams, small field experimentation of seed species to test the suitability of imported fine-breed seeds to local soil and climatic conditions; plant protection, such as using a black-light lamp to measure the regularities of insect damage, providing assistance and instruction to the insect extermination work of the brigades and production teams, and conducting insecticide and pesticide tests; experiments on fertilizers, such as determining the ideal methods of fertilizer application and the usefulness of imported chemical fertilizer to the commune. Training sessions were organized periodically by the institute for agricultural technicians in the brigades, the teams, and other communes. The institute was also responsible for sending agricultural technicians of the commune to the *hsien,* the provincial capital, and other places for advanced training.

For the sake of agricultural innovation, the Huan Ch'eng commune had also set up an Agricultural Technology Diffusion Station *(nung-yeh chi-shu t'ui-kuang chan),* which was run by five people. Close liaison was maintained between the diffusion station and the Agricultural Research Institute. These five people were to visit the production brigades and teams in the commune to teach innovative production techniques. The commune would often organize diffusion activities for the peasants, such as demonstration sessions *(hsien-ch'ang hui),* visits to experimental fields and observation of the results obtained, meetings among the peasants where experiences were discussed, the setting up of "models" to inspire emulation, and the dispatching of peasants to visit advanced units outside the commune.

A scientific research group *(k'o-hsüeh shih-yen tsu)* existed in each production brigade of the Huan Ch'eng commune, staffed by three to nine persons. The research group in the Tien Lu brigade, which we visited, had six full-time employees. Its major duty was to ascertain the applicability of new techniques originating from other communes, brigades, and elsewhere. Those techniques deemed useful would be propagated within the brigade.

In the small group for scientific application *(k'o-hsüeh hsiao-tsu)*, set up by the production teams themselves, equipment and facilities were even cruder.[8] These small groups were usually run by around three persons, and their main functions were to cultivate fine-breed seeds for the production teams, and to provide instructions for the peasants. Because of their close relationships with the peasants, the small group members were of critical significance in the diffusion of agritechnology.

Conditions found in the Ta Li commune (Nan Hai County, Kwangtung Province), another commune we visited, were similar.

The four-tiered agricultural research network is at the present moment an institutionalized phenomenon in rural China (Figure 6-1).[9] Through the network, the people's commune can systematically introduce new agricultural techniques from the outside, rely on outside units to train its own technical personnel, and obtain from outside the necessary resources for developmental purposes.[10] At

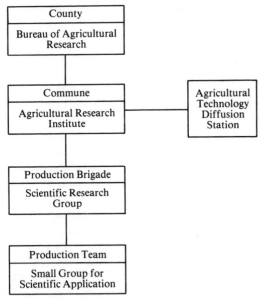

FIGURE 6-1. Four-tiered communication network for diffusion of agritechnology.

the same time, the people's commune itself, if it is relatively advanced technologically, can assist other units (particularly neighboring communes) in the training of technical personnel.[11] Hence, in view of the relationship between the commune and its environment, the four-tiered network constitutes a technical communication network that links up the commune with the outside world.

The agricultural research units at the three levels within the commune itself are fabricated into a communication network for the exchange of technical information. This internal technical communication system has played a key role in the diffusion of new agritechnology throughout the commune. Innovative technical information is transmitted both vertically (especially the diffusion of new techniques and production experiences originated from the outside) and horizontally (the exchange of information between units at the same level) by means of this communication network. Simultaneously, practical problems faced by lower-level units in the process of application of new techniques, and new solutions designed in handling these problems, can also be transmitted to the outside through this communication network.

Organizational Characteristics of the Three-Tiered Network

The three-tiered network of agricultural science can be conceptualized as a suborganization within the commune. The three-tiered research network structurally resembles the commune organization as a whole. It is an open organization. Its power structure is marked by a relatively high level of decentralization, coupled with centralization of decision making on some issues. The gradation of authority between upper and lower levels is based on technological competence and administrative responsibilities. Power difference between different levels, however, only signifies the power to guide and direct, not absolute control. The duties of the research units at various levels do not differ much, except for their scale of operation. All the research units at the three levels are involved in experimentation and diffusion, as the following passage illustrates:

> In the past, experimentation and diffusion constituted two systems in the Hua county of Kwangtung. The county's Agricultural Science Institute only worked on experimentation, at the expense of diffusion, while the Technology Diffusion Station concentrated on diffusion, without involving itself in experimentation. It therefore did not have first-hand information obtained from actual practice. This disjunc-

tion resulted in impractical experimentation and blind diffusion. The four-tiered agricultural research network was established after taking into consideration lessons from past experience. Now there are research units at all levels. The technical cadres of the county's Agricultural Bureau, the communes' agricultural research institutes, and other research units in the commune, working with the peasant technicians in the communes, the brigades, and the teams, are able to make use of these bases to engage in experimentation and diffusion simultaneously, thus forging close connections between them. The technical personnel of both the county and the communes, aside from conducting experiments in their respective research units, are also assigned to stay with the production teams for a period of time to give demonstration sessions and to diffuse advanced techniques.[12]

On the other hand, the agricultural research units at various levels are also under the leadership of the administrative organization and the Party organization at the corresponding levels. Because of the existence of dual leadership, the extent of centralization of power at the top of the agricultural science network is minimized.

The democratic-centralistic decision-making pattern within the three-tiered network reflects clearly its high level of power decentralization. In Huan T'ai County in Shantung, for instance, four measures have been implemented to strengthen the planning and management of scientific experimental work in the communes:

1. The formulation of research plans starts from the bottom, and goes to the top. First, the scientific research groups of the production brigades propose their research projects. After extensively soliciting opinions and suggestions from peasant commune members, these proposals are then submitted to the Party branches in the production brigades for permission, and finally recorded in the communes concerned. After studying the research plans of the brigades, the research units in the county and the communes arrive at important research problems deemed of general interest, and these become the research projects of the communes and the county.

2. After the commune has finalized its research plan, division of labor among the brigades' research groups is designed so as to maximize their effectiveness. These groups meet before the autumn planting, spring planting, and summer planting of each year to summarize results and plan for the future. For those important research tasks, the county and the communes organize several co-

operative teams, each of which comprises several research groups. During the process of implementation, activities such as result investigation, evaluation, mutual learning, and reciprocal visitations are also organized.
3. In-the-field technical files are set up, consisting primarily of observation records in connection with the implementation of research projects in the field.
4. After an experiment, each research group prepares a summary report. Meetings to summarize results and disseminate research findings are convened periodically by both the county and the communes.[13]

From this evidence we see a low level of formalization in the three-tiered network. Regulations are strictly stipulated and enforced, but they are neither voluminous nor all encompassing. In most cases, the duties of the agricultural technical personnel are determined after extensive discussions and after due consideration has been given to unique local conditions. Regulations in the three-tiered network only delineate a broad range of behavioral standards, and there is enough flexibility in the formulation of concrete action plans. This inherent flexibility in the network is conducive to the generation and diffusion of agritechnologies.

The level of stratification in the three-tiered network is also quite low. The most important underlying factor is the relative homogeneity in the socioeconomic background of the technicians, as well as in their social status and the economic rewards received. The commune, the production brigades, and the production teams will only "select those commune members with correct upbringing, high political consciousness, enthusiastic attitude toward manual labor, and keen interest in agricultural research to be members in the research groups."[14] In the places we visited—the Hung Wei orchard in Kai P'ing County, the Huan Ch'eng commune, and the Ta Li commune—the technicians in their research units were primarily poor, lower-middle peasants. The incomes of the technicians at different levels were approximately equal, and they were more or less equivalent to the incomes of the commune members.[15]

This phenomenon of reward leveling is common. According to a verbal description by Mr. Me, secretary of the revolutionary committee of the Chang Sha commune (Kai P'ing County, Kwangtung), the staff members of the commune's Scientific Management Station *(k'o-hsueh kuang-li chan)*, the production brigades' agricultural science teams, and the production teams' science and technology small groups all received work points. The number of work points they earned did not differ too much from the average work points earned in the commune as a whole. The leveling of economic rewards between the technical personnel and other peasants tends to narrow the social distance between them. This promotes social interaction between technicians and ordinary peasants, and more intensive communicative activities between them are instrumental to the transmission of new information on agritechnology and its diffusion.

From a communication point of view, the structural characteristics of the three-tiered agricultural research network generate a communication network where intensive exchange and transmission of scientific technology can take place. The vitality of this communication network in the dissemination of scientific information can be deduced from the exemplary case of Huan T'ai County, Shantung. This county suffered from a deficiency of technical specialists, which seriously hampered scientific experimentation and the timely resolution of problems both in production and in the diffusion of agritechnology. To cope with this obstacle, one of the communes, the Tang Shan commune, divided itself into four sections, which together constituted a communication network for the exchange of experimental and scientific information. The agricultural technological station of the commune was in charge of coordinating the activities in the communication network. This communication network in turn coordinated the research activities of the experimental teams of the brigades. Finally, the brigades' teams were responsible for supervising the scientific experimental group of the production teams.[16]

The technological communication network embedded in the system also makes it possible for the three-tiered research organization to engage in self-expansion. By self-expansion, I mean that the communication network tends to increase the number of technicians in the commune through mutual learning and on-the-job training. It thus enlarges the number of persons playing the role of "change agent." This tendency plays a significant role in the diffusion of advanced agritechnology.

Informal Channels of Communication in the Commune

The three-tiered agricultural research network is a potent communication mechanism for the diffusion of agritechnology. Nevertheless, in itself this network constitutes only the formal communication channels, which do not account for all the communicative activities within the commune. As a matter of fact, the structural characteristics of the commune organization, in particular its low formalization and relatively high decentralization of power, are conducive to the proliferation of informal channels of communication.

As a sociopolitical organization superimposed from above, the commune inevitably comes into conflict with the traditional features of social structure which have existed for centuries in rural China, and which, having not yet been totally displaced, are still viable. Traditionally, Chinese rural society was a sociopolitical organization with families, clans, and villages as the basic constituent units, integrated by the gentry and official groups.[17] This traditional social organization possessed its own characteristic power structure, value system, behavioral norms, reward distribution patterns, criteria for status assignment, channels for interpersonal communication, and forms of social relationships. Generally speaking, the village in traditional China was an organization for stability with strong change-resisting tendencies. The people's commune, as a formally constructed organization for change, has to destroy, limit, or modify the traditional organizational principles to counteract its detrimental influence, or, better still, to transform its effect to make it serve the new organization. Otherwise, the individuals in the commune will be faced with two sets of normative and behavioral demands ensuing from two conflicting organizational formats, and the incongruent personal and structural consequences arising from this stressful situation will hamper the process of rural development in China.

The conflict between the formal organization of the commune and the traditional village social organization can be described as the simultaneous existence of two sets of communication channels, differing in both the patterns of communication and the messages transmitted. The structural characteristics of the commune encourage every commune member to participate in the communication process on a more or less egalitarian basis, and vertical (in both directions) and horizontal channels of communication are provided to facilitate popular participation. Change and innovation constitute the main communication content of this formal network. In the informal communication network, on the other hand, initiators of communication were limited to traditional authority figures such as the elderly and the gentry. Message transmission was usually one-sided, ideological in content, and change resistant in orientation.

The people's commune, an imposed form of social organization in rural China, has brought about a weakening of the traditional social organization, whose staunch supporters have largely lost their bases of power and status. Nonetheless, it cannot be denied that traditional influences are still present. They are particularly strong in the province of Kwangtung, with its traditional clan organizations still very much a social determinant of behavior. In a booklet published by the People's Press in Kwangtung, the author, Shao Ching-wen, has the following to report:

> In some places, the recalcitrant landlords, rich peasants, reactionaries, bad and rightist elements who had not yet been completely reformed had made use of the conflicts between clans and lineages on matters of controversy such as land, forestry, and water to sow seeds of discord. They instigated clan strifes between villages and between production teams. They deliberately aimed at disintegrating the coalition of the poor and the lower-middle peasants, and at paralyzing the "grasp revolution, promote production" movement. When they saw the poor and the lower-middle peasants in neighboring production teams working on land reclamation and irrigation projects, they would talk nonsense about the disruption of the *"feng shui"* [geomancy], with the vicious motives of fostering disharmony among these peasants and stirring up armed fights among them. In these ways the class enemies were to employ clan-ism to wreck our Learn from Tachai movement and to obstruct our socialist reconstruction endeavors.
>
> In some places, the recalcitrant landlords, rich peasants, reactionaries, bad and rightist elements had, through kinship relationships, drawn cadres and the mass to their side and incited them to concentrate on individual prosperity, thus blowing up the evil wind of capitalism. They advocated "dividing up and completely eating up" *(fen-kuang ch'ih-chin)*. They agitated for "contract work and contract production" *(pao-kung pao-chan)*. They promulgated the freedom to plant and the freedom to buy and sell. In a variety of ways they conspired to undermine and weaken the collective socialist economy. . . .
>
> In some places, the recalcitrant landlords, rich peasants, reactionaries, bad and rightist elements had, through kinship connections, used the methods of "forcing in" *(ta-chin lai)* and "pulling out" *(la-chu-ch'u)* to usurp local leadership, engage in lunatic revenge, and

persecute the poor and the lower-middle peasants. Some of these bad guys managed to disguise themselves and made use of kinship relationships to deceive the cadres and the mass. Some of these bad guys, by means of throwing feasts and sending gifts, coopted cadres with the same family names and had them corrupted, and, in the process, controlled the actual power in the production brigades or production teams.[18]

From conversations with the leading cadres in both the Huang Ch'eng and Ta Li communes, we have more or less arrived at the conclusion that there were conflicts between the commune and the traditional social organization, though not of serious proportion. In diffusion of agritechnology, it is still true that resistance to new production techniques is primarily transmitted through the traditional, informal communication channels. Many of the elderly peasants are still very skeptical of agricultural innovations, either out of superstitious beliefs or because of their anxiety about the possibility of further reducing their living standards if the innovations were to fail. However, one of the most important reasons for this resistance to innovations encountered in rural China is the preference of many peasants for immediate consumption as against collective savings. This phenomenon can be readily seen in the controversy over agricultural mechanization within the communes. Given the low standard of living of the peasants at the present moment, it is understandable that they would opt for a higher ratio of consumption over savings.

To speed up the diffusion of agritechnology, resistance to innovations, largely activated through the informal communication channels, has to be overcome. As the structural characteristics of the people's commune facilitate communicative activities on an informal, interpersonal basis, the influence of the "resistance leaders" can be very much enhanced. Acceptance of new agritechnology is contingent upon communication with the peasants. As the information on new agritechnology is initially communicated through the three-tiered agricultural research network, its effective diffusion requires the linkage of this formal communication network with the informal, interpersonal network, which may not necessarily be favorable to the adoption of innovations.

The social relationships among the individuals in both communication networks are the crucial factor. Each individual can be considered to be participating in both networks, though the relative extent of participation may differ. Therefore, in analyzing the diffusion of agritechnology in the commune, the patterns of social relationships between the people working in the three-tiered agricultural research network (themselves already closely connected through the formal channels) and the people in the informal network are the key social phenomena to be studied. Moreover, in penetrating the informal communication network, the agricultural research network is facilitated by its relationships with other formal networks of communication in the commune organization, especially the commune administration and the Party. As these formal networks have their own particular relationships with and influence on the informal network, their incorporation into the diffusion process means that, theoretically, the people's commune relies on the combined effort of several formal communication networks, with the agricultural research network as the key component and the other networks playing different supportive roles.

Role Integration and the Linkage between Formal and Informal Channels of Communication

To translate this theory into practice, the concept of *role integration* becomes important. "Role" is defined as "a set of norms and expectations applied to the incumbent of a particular position";[19] thus, role integration defines a situation where several roles are closely coordinated. There are two major means whereby role integration is created by the commune organization to promote the diffusion of agritechnology.

Intrapersonal role integration. This form of role integration results from the performance of several diffusion-related roles by one single individual. For example, an agricultural technician can be a cadre at the same time, hence playing the roles of both change agent[20] and decision maker. He may also be a member of the Communist Party, assuming more or less the role of legitimizer. If he happens to be an elderly peasant, who is able to command respect in the traditional social organization and who can exert influence on other peasants through the informal communication channels, he can simultaneously take on the role of opinion leader. Lastly, he also most probably participates in production chores, thus carrying the adopter role.

Naturally, this example represents only an ideal case of intrapersonal role integration. In reality, the concentration of *all* the diffusion related roles in a single individual is rare, since the inevitable consequence is to create powerful authority figures in rural society, and this the Chinese leaders would try to avoid. However, there are numerous cases where an individual plays several diffusion-related roles at the same time. For instance, the research technicians in the Hung Wei orchard of Kai P'ing Country are cadres and workers at the same time. In the case of Huan T'ai County of Shantung, we have cadres playing the role of change agent as well.

Turning to other examples of intrapersonal role integration, there are numerous instances of common peasants, primarily "adopters" of innovation, also participating in scientific experimentation, thus playing at the same time the role of change agent. The active promotion of the mass movement of scientific research by the communes is aimed at involving the common peasants in the technique generation process. In this way, the technological level of the average peasant will be upgraded, and they will be more capable of understanding the viewpoints and the work of the technicians.

Other examples can also be cited, though detailed descriptions are not necessary: the assumption of both roles, change agent and adopter, by the educated youth dispatched to the countryside, the simultaneous playing of the roles of change agent and legitimizer by the elderly peasants, the promotion of qualified technicians to the ranks of cadre and Party member, and so on.

The occurrence of intrapersonal role integration serves to reflect two social phenomena in the people's commune. First, because of the tendency for technicians to assume other social roles, the commune can be conceptualized as a "fused organization" in which the suborganizational boundaries become blurred. Intrapersonal role integration not only speeds up the diffusion of agritechnology; it also increases the degree of homophily among peasants. Second, because of the prevalence of intrapersonal integration, specific roles are not monopolized by a minority of the people. Therefore, there is a multitude of change agents, opinion leaders, legitimizers, and decision makers. Linkages and interactions among these roles increase geometrically, thus injecting a large measure of flexibility into the commune organization that is beneficial to diffusion of agritechnology.

Interpersonal role integration. This signifies the shortness of social distance between different role incumbents and the dense communication networks among them. The structural features of the commune organization, in shortening social distance and allowing for a large amount of interaction between different role incumbents at different authority levels, will naturally lead to interpersonal role integration. In particular, the commune's low level of stratification reinforces the high degree of homophily among the commune members, facilitating communicative activities among role incumbents. Furthermore, in view of the high levels of compatibility, empathy, and credibility among commune members, the reception of technicians by the peasants will be improved. This trustful attitude of the peasants toward the technicians is critical to the diffusion process.

There are close relationships between the technicians and the cadres who play the role of decision makers. At the same time, a portion of the cadres are also Party members themselves. Therefore, the relationship between the technicians and those who play the role of legitimizer or opinion leader is also intimate. In general, there are some cadres in the communes who are primarily responsible for the implementation of agricultural research and the diffusion of agritechnology. In these cases, the relationships between technicians and cadres will be greatly strengthened.

The role of the technicians as change agents and the role of the common peasants as adopters are closely connected through a series of social measures. Aside from such diffusion devices as blackboards, radio broadcasts, wall posters, and other mass media, the major channel of communication between the technicians and the peasants is the interpersonal one, marked by face-to-face interaction. The most illustrative cases of interpersonal communication are "heart talk" with the peasants, taking the peasants to the model fields, setting up discussion with the peasants at the experimental fields, assisting the peasants in the conducting of agricultural experiments, initiating learning movements among the peasants, and so on.

Nevertheless, the most significant example of interpersonal role integration is the organization of ad hoc task groups so that different role incumbents can be assembled to resolve problems in unison. The main purpose of these task groups, usually small in size, is to intensify communication between roles, and to achieve simultaneously the goals of experimentation, demonstration, and diffusion, thus shortening the time needed for diffusion. The Chinese usually call this strategy of task group formation the "three-in-one" technique *(san-chieh-ho)*. As with other small group techniques, the intention here is to create enough interpersonal pressure to promote the acceptance of new agritechnology. In the words of Godwin Chu:

> What is uniquely Chinese is the way communication has been used to form new groups; it is not merely an instrument of political surveillance and control as it is in Russia. Rather, the Chinese have used the groups to generate social pressure and apply it to the restructuring of economic, cultural, and family relations—indeed, to every process of a changing social system.
>
> By instituting the new Chinese groups, the party has created an effective agent for the state that can (1) carry out the development programs, (2) exercise social control over the group members, and (3) provide a mechanism for conflict resolution and group integration at the grassroots level.[21]

The groups created in connection with the diffusion of innovation are largely temporary in duration. These task groups are formed in reaction to certain problems. A certain individual may shift quite frequently, from one such task group to another, as a result of which he will be able to meet with people from various socioeconomic backgrounds. Besides solving the specific problems at hand, this shifting of membership also operates to enlarge the person's interpersonal communication network and develop understanding among the commune members. Even though the strategy is labeled "three-in-one," most of the time more than three roles are involved, and the roles selected for the task groups are situationally contingent. For example, it can refer to the "three-in-one" coalition of the cadres, the elderly peasants, the educated youth, and the technicians.[22] It can also refer to the alliance among the cadres, the educated youth, and the elderly peasants,[23] to the alliance among the cadres, the elderly peasants, and the carpenters,[24] or to the alliance among the poor and lower-middle peasants, the teachers, and the students.[25] Nonetheless, for the purpose of diffusion of agritechnology, the most typical form is the task group consisting of cadres, technicians, and peasants.

The structural content of the alliance of cadres, technicians, and the masses also has political connotations, which somehow reflect the nature of the commune organization:

> . . . that the cadres, through participation in agricultural research, are capable of acquiring the technology of production is a contribu-

tory factor to the assumption of leadership on the part of the Party over agricultural science and technology, as well as over agricultural production. The alliance with the cadres and the masses on the part of the agricultural technicians would facilitate the demolition of their bourgeois tendencies of knowledge monopolization, and hence would narrow the three differences in China, and would enable the intelligentsia to walk on the path leading to both redness and expertness.[26]

The combined effect of all of this is to level differences, or to increase homophily among the commune members.

From the communication point of view, both intrapersonal and interpersonal role integration, and particularly the latter, are structural mechanisms to establish linkages between the formal and informal channels of communication, and direct manifestations of the meshing of the formal commune organization and the traditional social organization. They are essential in overcoming resistance to innovation coming from the peasants, especially the elderly ones. In intrapersonal role integration, the elderly peasants who might be superstitious and conservative are exposed to a variety of other experiences and outlooks so that their adamant negative attitude toward new things can be diluted. As they might also be the opinion leaders in the rural society, their changed attitudes will be transmitted through the traditional channels of communication to other peasants who are under their social and ideological influence.

Interpersonal role integration, in contrast, is the explicit measure whereby the formal commune organization establishes direct linkages with the traditional social organization and informal communication network. The major purpose is to incorporate the traditional, informal communication channels into the formal communication system, so that the content of the messages can be determined or at least influenced by the formal channels. One of the most important means of doing this is to enlist the elderly peasants into the three-in-one task groups. In terms of age, these task groups usually show a combination of elderly, middle-aged, and young. In terms of social-psychological functions, the task group members may specialize in the function of evaluation, the function of affectivity, or the function of cognition. In each task group, the role requirements are delicately balanced so that not only is the diffusion of agritechnology enhanced, but other political, social, and ideological goals can be achieved at the same time.

Conclusion

The "Chinese model" of diffusion of agritechnology we have presented is more or less an ideal type. Many questions are still unanswered: How far is the ideal type realized in actuality? In various localities, how is the ideal type modified to adapt to local conditions? What are the dynamic social-psychological processes involved in the actual application of the ideal type?

Moreover, even considered as an ideal type, the Chinese model of diffusion of agritechnology is not impeccable. Without being exhaustive, some of its shortcomings can be listed:

1. Because of the need to ascertain the applicability of a specific item of agritechnology to the local situation, it usually takes a long time before a decision is made to have that item diffused. In this experimentation peiod, many peasants and technicians, at different levels of organization, are involved. Aside from the educational and persuasive effects which can be produced, this means that the commune cannot capitalize immediately on the most advanced techniques of production. After this lengthy period of experimentation, however, the process of diffusion will normally be a rapid one and the innovations, once adopted, will not be immediately abandoned afterwards.

2. The varying resource endowments among production teams, brigades, and communes will mean that they have different capacities to adopt innovations. The communication networks in rural society have managed to provide a largely even flow of scientific information to these constitutent units and, in the process, have raised the aspirations for innovations among the peasantry. Different capacities to adopt innovations will, sooner or later, lead to social and economic inequities not only within the commune but among the communes as well. This tendency toward inequity is at odds with the planned direction of change envisioned by the Chinese authorities. Up to now, the problem of inequity has remained insignificant, and the Chinese can still afford to pay little attention to it. As the problem grows in magnitude, however, its detrimental implications for Chinese society can become serious.

3. In forging a linkage between the formal and informal communication channels, the planners have the manifest intention of exploiting the informal channels for the purpose of diffusion of agritechnology. The success of this mechanism is not certain, how-

ever. Ideas against change can likewise be transmitted from the informal channels to the formal channels. As a matter of fact, official publications in China have, on many occasions, referred to the "corruption" of the cadres and Party members by traditional elements through informal means. As it is not unusual for the cadres and the Party members to share the same lineage and surname with most of peasants in the production teams, it is natural for them to identify with their fellow clansmen. Moreover, the lack of geographical and social mobility of most of the grassroots-level cadres and Party members forces them to realize that if they are to have harmonious social relationships with their fellow villagers, they should try as far as possible to cater to their needs from time to time. Consequently, innovations will sometimes be withdrawn from diffusion voluntarily by the technicians, cadres, and Party members. Thus, to ensure the dominance of messages issued from the formal channels over those coming from the informal channels, external control over the technicians, cadres, and Party members has to be exerted to dilute their loyalties to their fellow villagers and clansmen. During periods of political campaigns and power struggle at the center, such control over rural society will be slackened and in many places the diffusion of innovations will slow down.

4. The integration of the three-tiered network of agricultural research with other suborganizations in the commune means, on one hand, that the resources from other suborganizations will be pooled to bolster the endeavor of the three-tiered network and, on the other hand, that the network will suffer if its own resources are transferred to other suborganizations to support their activities. A typical example of the latter case can be seen most clearly in times of political movements, as, for instance, during the Cultural Revolution and its aftermath, when political activities became everyone's major preoccupation. Recently, in the political struggle involving the Gang of Four, research activities of the technicians in some communes of Kwangtung have been put to a stop.[27]

At any rate, the Chinese model of diffusion of agritechnology, judged against current practices in many developing countries in the world, seems to be a successful one. Its effectiveness depends in large measure on an internal communication system which links up the formal and informal channels in the commune. However, as the adoption of this model will necessitate drastic structural change in any adopting country, wholesale transference is out of the question. Instead, alternative communication structures might be devised, and these await further study and experimentation.

NOTES

This study is a part of the Commune Study Project of the Social Research Centre, The Chinese University of Hong Kong. I am grateful to the Lingnan Foundation for funding the project. A large portion of the field data discussed in the paper was collected during a field trip to China in December 1976, in which a number of sociologists from the Social Research Centre took part. For about two weeks, we visited factories, communes, production brigades and teams, peasant families, and cities. Our research interests, however, were focused upon two communes: the Huan Ch'eng commune in the county of Hsin Hui, and the Ta Li commune in the county of Nan Hai, both in the province of Kwangtung. An earlier draft of the research report, in Chinese, was completed in March 1977, and it has been thoroughly scrutinized and commented on by other members of the project. During his stay in Hong Kong in August 1977, Godwin Chu also read through the Chinese version and recommended some constructive guidelines for the revision of the paper. These have subsequently been incorporated into the English version of the paper, which is presented as this chapter. I would like to extend my gratitude to S. L. Wong, the leader and mentor of the Commune Study Project, Godwin Chu, C. K. Yang, and all my colleagues in the project for their invaluable assistance and support throughout the preparation of this paper.

1. For a detailed treatment of the concept of "social mobilization," see Karl W. Deutsch, "Social Mobilization and Political Development," *American Political Science Review* 55(1961):493–514. For the application of this concept to the political realm, see J. P. Nettl, *Political Mobilization: A Sociological Analysis of Methods and Concepts* (London: Faber and Faber, 1967).

2. The historically and situationally contingent character of the people's commune has been extensively elaborated in Chinese publications. As the compiling group *(pien-hsieh-tsu)* of the *Cheng-chih ching-chi hsüeh chiang-hua (She-hui chu-i pu-fen),* [A Talk on Political Economy (Section on Socialism)], for instance, put it, "At present, the institution of 'three levels of ownership with production as the foundation' found in the agricultural people's communes, for most areas in the country, is compatible with the level of productivity in the rural sectors. However, with the popularization and promotion of the movement to build Ta Chai–type counties, with the development of large-scale socialist agricultural enterprises, and, in particular, with the expansion of the economies at the commune and production brigade levels, as well as the heightening of the peasant mass's communist consciousness, the present ownership system, which has the production team as the basic accounting unit, will, as conditions become available, gradually shift to an ownership system which has the production brigade, or even the commune, as the basic accounting unit. All these steps will then furnish the prerequisites for the transition from the collective ownership pattern to the public ownership pattern, as well as from socialism to communism, in the distant future" (Peking: People's Press, 1976, p. 61). See also the Theoretical Group of the Poor and Lower-Middle Peasants of Yang-kang Brigade, Hsin-chiao Commune, Yu-lin County, and the Writing and

Editing Group on the Socialist Collective Ownership System of Yu-lin District, comp., *She-hui chu-i chi-ti so-yu-chih* [Socialist Collective Ownership System] (Kwangsi: People's Press, 1976), pp. 24–41; and Su Hsing, *Chung-kuo nung-yeh ti she-hui chu-i tao-lu* [The Socialist Road of Chinese Agriculture] (Peking: People's Press, 1976), pp. 99–106.

3. Many sociologists have argued that there is an inverse relationship between centralization of power and authority and the possibility of social change in organizations, particularly complex organizations. For a succinct summarization of the literature, see Gerald Zaltman et al., *Innovations and Organizations* (New York: John Wiley & Sons, 1973), pp. 161–162. See also Jerald Hage and Michael Aiken, *Social Change in Complex Organizations* (New York: Random House, 1970), pp. 38–39.

4. Compatibility of centralization and decentralization of power is a core problem in the theoretical system of Chinese communism. It arises out of the need to resolve a practical problem in connection with the socialist reconstruction process: how to achieve centralized and coordinated unitary leadership functions during the process of planned social change without paralyzing effects on the initiative of the localities and the masses? To this, Mao Tse-tung has the following answer: "To resolve this contradiction, our attention should now be focused on how to enlarge the powers of the local authorities to some extent, give them greater independence and let them do more, all on the premise that the unified leadership of the central authorities is to be strengthened; this will be advantageous to our task of building a powerful socialist country" ("On the Ten Major Relationships," in *Selected Works of Mao Tse-tung,* vol. 5 [Peking: Foreign Languages Press, 1977], p. 292). Franz Schurmann also has commented on the problem; see his *Ideology and Organization in Communist China,* 2nd ed. (Berkeley: University of California Press, 1968), pp. 86–87.

5. The Writing Group of the Committee of the Textiles Bureau in Shanghai, *Chia-chiang tang ti i-yuan-hua* [Strengthen the Unified Leadership of the Party] (Shanghai: People's Press, 1974), p. 47.

6. Hage and Aiken, *Social Change,* pp. 45–46.

7. According to a news release by the New China New Agency from Peking on October 7, 1977, more than half of the counties, communes, production brigades, and production teams had already set up their own agricultural research units. About 14 million persons were involved in research activities, and around 40 million *mou* of arable land have been assigned to research purposes. The news release also reported that since 1973, more than 600 research products had been obtained through the joint efforts of agronomists and the masses.

8. We have not visited any experimental small groups belonging to the production teams. Based on the impression gathered from the laboratory of the Hung Wei orchard of Kai P'ing County, however, we may be able to infer their organization. The laboratory of the Hung Wei orchard, which specialized in the production of mandarin oranges, was located in a small hut built with red bricks. The major equipment of the laboratory was the microscope, the constant-temperature box, and three *mou* of experimental land. Five persons were in charge of the laboratory, and all of them were at the same time ordinary orchard workers. Their major duties were to develop research projects with the masses, assist in drawing scientific conclusions from the experiments, and guide the productive activities of the orchard.

9. The Editorial and Selecting Subgroup for Village Books, comp., *Ch'un-chung hsin nung-yeh k'o-hsueh shih-yen huo-tung hsüan-chi* [Selected Readings on the

Agricultural Scientific Experimentation Activities of the Masses] (Peking: Agricultural Press, 1976).

10. The Agricultural Science Institute in Hua County of Kwangtung, for example, had an affiliated technical school, which, working in close cooperation with the institute, periodically provided training for the agricultural technicians of the communes and the brigades. The institute would also, according to the needs of agricultural production as well as the diffusion of agritechnology, establish short-term training sessions on specific techniques, or convene meetings where exchanges of scientific information could be made (see ibid., p. 10). Other examples can be found in Bureau of Farm Machine Industry of the Ministry of Agriculture and Forestry, comp., *Nung-yeh ti ken-pen ch'u-lu tsai yu chi-hsieh-hua* [The Fundamental Outlet for Agriculture Lies in Mechanization], vol. 2 (Peking: Agricultural Press, 1976), pp. 9–10; Party Committee of Hsin-shou County in Hupeh, *Hsin-shou nung-yeh chi-hsieh-hua* [Agricultural Mechanization in Hsin-shou] (Peking: Agricultural Press, 1974), pp. 73–74. The Hsin Hui Agricultural Machinery Factory, which we visited, also had extensive connections with the communes, brigades, and teams in the county. There was an experimental group in the factory consisting of six to seven mechanical technicians, whose major job assignments involved demonstrating the uses of agricultural machinery to the peasants, repairing the machines currently in use, and training technicians for the communes and their constituent units. For a large part of the year, these technicians were not stationed in the factory but traveled around the county, carrying with them the two or three tractors used for demonstration purposes. This factory had, in addition, set up training courses the purpose of which was to offer short-term, on-the-job training to the machine operators and repairmen sent to the factory by the communes and brigades in the county. On the average, each such course would take about two to three months to complete. At the time of our visit, around seventy trainees were under training there.

On many occasions, technical schools and colleges outside the communes are the means for the introduction of new agritechnology into the rural areas. In the academic year 1974, the students of the Chao-yang Nung-hsüeh Yüan in Chao Yang County of Liaoning Province had rendered assistance to the surrounding rural areas in the formation of 72 scientific research teams, the completion of more than 200 training sessions, the training of more than 3,000 peasant technicians, the opening, with the help of the poor and lower-middle peasants, of more than 7,400 *mou* of experimental fields and fields for the breeding of seeds, the grafting of 530,000 trees, the shearing of 157,700 fruit trees, and the treatment of more than 26,000 sick domestic animals. See Bureau for Science and Education of the Ministry of Agriculture and Forestry, comp,, *Chao-yang nung-hsuch-yuan tsai tou-cheng chung chien-chin* [The Chao-yang Agricultural School Marches Forward Amidst Struggle] (Peking: Agricultural Press, 1976), p. 85.

11. If a people's commune has developed innovations in agritechnology, it can have them disseminated through its communicative connections with other communes, counties, and higher-level units. The diffusion of the method to produce microbial products in Hsikou Commune of Shansi Province is a case in point. As described by Mary Altendorf et al.: "We asked a little about the history of the project at Hsikou and found that the school originally took on the project as part of a larger effort to make scientific education serve production. They first heard of the process when the Southeast Shansi District had a meeting at which someone from

the Ch'angchih school spoke about making bacterial fertilizer. To learn the process they sent two people to Ch'angchih (the largest city in southeast Shansi) to attend lectures and practice techniques for four or five days. Since mastering the art, Hsikou has in turn taught bacterial fertilizer making to people from about twenty other communes. Similar processes of face-to-face contact and exchange appear to be exceedingly important in the transmission and popularization of science in China. Because such exchange generates little or no printed material, western observers, who tend to believe that all scientific communication of any note eventually reaches print, are likely to overlook what appears to be a vast network of informal scientific exchange in the Chinese countryside." See their *China: Science Walks on Two Legs* (New York: Avon Books, 1974), pp. 47–48.

12. See Revolutionary Committee of Hua County, Kwangtung, "Some Reflections on the Utilization of the County's Agricultural Research Institute as the Center to Establish the Four-tiered Agricultural Research Network," in *Chün-chung-hsin nung-yeh k'o-hsueh shih-yen huo-tung hsüan-chi* [Selected Readings on the Agricultural Scientific Experimentation Activities of the Masses], p. 6.

13. See "With the Struggle between Lines as the Key Link, Penetratingly Promote Agricultural Scientific Experimentation Activities among the Masses," ibid., pp. 20–22.

14. Ibid., p. 18.

15. Ibid., pp. 11–12.

16. Ibid., p. 20.

17. See Lau Siu-kai, "Monism, Pluralism, and Segmental Coordination: Toward an Alternative Thoery of Elite, Power and Social Stability," *Journal of The Chinese University of Hong Kong* 3(December 1975):187–206.

18. See Shao Ching-wen, *P'o-ch'u tsung-tsu kuan-nien* [Abolish Clan Concepts] (Kwangtung: People's Press, 1975), pp. 3–4.

19. Michael Banton, *Roles: An Introduction to the Study of Social Relations* (London: Tavistock Publications, 1965), pp. 28–29.

20. For a definition of the term "change agent," see Everett M. Rogers, "Change Agents, Clients, and Change," *Modernization among Peasants: The Impact of Communication* (New York: Holt, Rinehart and Winston, 1969), pp. 169–194.

21. See his "Group Communication and Development in Mainland China: The Functions of Social Pressure," in Wilbur Schramm and Daniel Lerner, ed., *Communication and Change: The Last Ten Years—and the Next* (Honolulu: The University Press of Hawaii, 1976), pp. 119–133. See also Godwin C. Chu, "Communication and Group Transformation in the People's Republic of China: The Mutual Aid Teams," in Godwin C. Chu et al., eds., *Communication for Group Transformation in Development* (Honolulu: East-West Center, East-West Communication Institute, 1976), pp. 151–174.

22. *Selected Readings on Agricultural Scientific Experimentation Activities*, p. 62.

23. Ibid., p. 33.

24. *The Fundamental Outlet for Agriculture Lies in Mechanization*, p. 39.

25. "Extensively Organize Scientific Research Activities, Render New Contributions to the Popularization of Tachai County," in *Chao-yang Agricultural School Marches Forward*, p. 83.

26. Party Committee of Hua-jung County, "With the Struggle between Lines as the Key Link, Consolidate and Develop the Four-Tiered Agricultural Research Network," in *Wu-ch'an ch'ieh-chi wen-hua ta ke-ming t'ui-tung wo-kuo k'o-hsueh chi-shu pen-po fa-chan* [The Proletarian Cultural Revolution Pushes Forward the Prosperous Development of Science in Our Country] (Peking: Scientific Press, 1976), p. 27.

27. According to a special report by the *Takung Pao* [Takung Report] of Hong Kong, in the Kwangtung Conference on Science and Educational Work held in Canton in October 1977, the Revolutionary Committee of Kwangtung Province expressed the urgent need to "re-organize and strengthen the four-tiered agricultural research network so as to promote agricultural development in the province. Inadequate equipment and funding on the part of the counties' agricultural science institutes had to be dealt with by the counties' revolutionary committees. Some of these institutes were deficient in their performance, and this situation had to be remedied" (*Takung Report*, October 13, 1977).

III
POLITICAL CULTURE

Communication in contemporary China has been an integral part of what Lucian W. Pye calls the "political culture" of the country. This refers to the values, beliefs, and social processes that are closely related to decision making on *societal means and goals.*

Pye, professor of political science at Massachusetts Institute of Technology, illustrates that the ways in which Chinese leaders utilize the media in their elite power relations reveal much about Chinese political culture. The press and radio in China are not just instruments for ruling; they are also institutions toward which the Chinese leaders have to react and which in turn reflect the processes of politics in the Party leadership. In spite of revolutionary rhetoric, Pye argues, the basic Chinese political culture, particularly the use of esoteric communication, maintains strong continuity with China's past.

As an example of esoteric communication, Merle Goldman analyzes two recent campaigns—concerning the dictatorship of the proletariat and the traditional novel *Water Margin,* respectively —to illustrate the role of mass media in political struggle, which in China is intimately related to cultural change. In the former, the radical group associated with Chiang Ch'ing initiated theoretical discussions in the mass media as a cover to attack the economic policies of Chou En-lai, thus seeking to reestablish the superiority of symbolic incentive over material incentive. In the latter, allegories from *Water Margin* were used by the radical faction to discredit Chou En-lai and Teng Hsiao-p'ing. The effectiveness of these campaigns, as well as their limitations, are noted in the light of subsequent developments. Professor Goldman is a member of the John Fairbank Center for East Asian Research at Harvard University.

The Cultural Revolution has been an episode of major importance in the People's Republic of China. Lowell Dittmer, associate professor of political science at the University of California, Berkeley, analyzes the Cultural Revolution as a series of communication events that were politically superimposed to accelerate cultural change. He discusses Mao's motives for launching the movement, and illustrates how Mao's ideas were communicated in the context of that tumultuous campaign. The impact of the Cultural Revolution on Chinese culture is examined in the perspective of its young participants, the Red Guards, as well as of those who were the targets of criticism. Professor Dittmer concludes his study by assessing the attempt of the Maoist group to continue the Cultural Revolution after 1969.

Political socialization of Chinese children apparently starts early. A major medium for conveying revolutionary ideology to Chinese children when they are still at an impressionable age is picture storybooks. Parris H. Chang, professor of political science at Pennsylvania State University, presents the results of an informal survey of 265 titles published during the period 1967–1977. He identifies eight major themes that are relevant to China's political culture and discusses the possible impact of the picture books on China's future generation.

7

Communication and Political Culture in China

Lucian W. Pye

From the establishment of the People's Republic until the Cultural Revolution, discussions of the relationship between the mass media and the Chinese Communists' political culture dwelt almost without exception on the ways in which the Party used communication systems to mobilize and control the population, raise the level of political consciousness, and generally speed the making of the Maoist Man and a more modern China. A somewhat lesser theme has been the ways in which the authorities have used and controlled writers at each turn in the Party's line.

Any study of the spirit and practice of governance in China today must still take into account the fundamental findings of such scholars as Alan P. L. Liu,[1] Frederick T. C. Yu,[2] and Franklin Houn[3] on how the Chinese use the radio and the press to disseminate their goals and change the attitudes of their people. And, of course, all students of Chinese politics will be permanently indebted to Merle Goldman for her blend of careful but exciting analyses of the political fates of Chinese writers.[4] Recent developments since the Cultural Revolution and through the "smashing" of the Gang of Four, however, call for some updating of these fundamental studies of the influence of the media on political culture and of political efforts to control culture. Visitors to China, limited as they are in what they are able to see, have generally been somewhat less impressed with the extent to which the media have been successful in changing the Chinese—a subject which in the past has commanded the bulk of scholars' attention—and more impressed with the suppression of intellectual creativity, a subject which has received less attention. In this chapter I shall not, however, seek to update these two subjects, important as they are.

Instead, I shall adopt quite a different focus and ask what can we learn about Chinese political culture from the ways in which

Chinese leaders utilize the media in their elite power relations. The press and the radio in China are not just instruments for ruling or the means whereby rulers influence the ruled; they are also institutions toward which leaders have to react and which in turn reflect, albeit vaguely, the processes of politics within the political leadership. From a review of the ways in which Chinese leaders use the media in their factional conflicts and in their policy "discussions," we can gain insight into some important dimensions of Chinese political culture.

Inside Out and Upside Down

The relationship between politics and communication media in China is distinctive, astoundingly paradoxical, and hard to explain. In one of the most secretive political processes in the world, the Chinese use their mass media at times to discuss bureaucratic policy matters which in other societies would be left to confidential channels of communication. In a peculiar reversal of practices, Chinese officials use public forums for what others would consider private political matters and, on the other hand (as far as we can determine), in their private communications with each other sound as though they were speaking in public. In the latter situation, they seem to want only to repeat to each other the established views of the moment.

For some time, Western analysts of Chinese politics have carefully perused the Chinese press and transcripts of Chinese radio broadcasts to spot policy issues and "debates" among advocates of different priorities. At times it has required an act of faith to believe that such subtle clues might be the hard stuff of real political jousting, but during the Cultural Revolution, and even more in the process of "crushing the Gang of Four," the Chinese have explicitly stated that newspaper articles and other mass media of communication truly revealed clashing intentions and differences of opinions. Moreover, the differences were not the general matters normally reported in the press and radio of other countries; they were more often the kinds of questions which governments throughout the world treat as highly confidential communications among decision makers that might only at times be "leaked" to the press.

As an adjunct to the mass media, we can include the Chinese use of wall posters *(tatzupao)*, which have the same startling characteristic mentioned previously: they frequently disseminate not only information of a confidential nature but different points of view as well. Matters that one might have thought could be handled with greater discretion through private channels suddenly surface in hand-scrawled wall posters—a method that would not seem to be consistent with the highly structured nature of Chinese society.

It is more difficult to make the case that Chinese officials in private comport themselves as though they were speaking in public; outsiders are rarely given a glimpse of how officials actually carry on "discussions" and "deliberations" about policies. Yet significantly, in all the revelations that have come with the denouncing of discredited leaders and their followers, remarkably few exposés of backroom deliberations have surfaced. Instead, from accounts of "struggle sessions" in offices and bureaus we get the picture of officials striving always to give voice to the current consensus and the proper line. Furthermore, those who have been privileged to talk with cadres and high Chinese officials uniformly report them to be more tightlipped, even in relaxed situations, than officials elsewhere. (This is true even in those cases where professional pride can cause a foreign listener to believe he has penetrated the Chinese wall of formalities and detected a revelation—such "revelations" are usually only confirmations of rumors or premature announcements of impending developments, and they rarely demonstrate that varieties of opinion are contending behind the scenes as policies are being worked out.)

We are clearly not suggesting that all of Chinese politics is revealed in the media. There is, of course, a vast world of secrecy, and we know that much goes on in officialdom which is never revealed in the media. When a senior official is purged, such as in the Lin Piao affair, cadres throughout the country are secretly instructed about what the crimes were; it may take one or even two years of such esoteric communication before the media are allowed to explain what the cadres already know. Presumably, such delays in public announcements are necessary to give the Doubting Thomases time to absorb the information that Lin Piao actually attempted to assassinate the sacred personage of the Chairman or that the Gang of Four were really "ultra-rightists" and not the "radicals" they were always thought to be.

Here again is another odd feature in the relationship of the media to politics in China: why such a long period of reliance upon secret, and often word-of-mouth, communications rather than the far more efficient mass media to disseminate information about a foregone development? In these situations, why don't the Chinese use the mass media to inform everyone about the authoritative position, thus greatly speeding up the process of eliminating the disgraced leader's followers? Instead, they initiate a prolonged process of local meetings throughout the country at which the new consensus is established and the supporters of the purged leader are in their turn purged. During this period the media, as we shall shortly note, are allowed to use only code names. One important reason this procedure is followed is that in Chinese politics personnel questions are always seen as far more important than policy issues. When a leading figure is purged, the first matter of importance is the elimination of all his sympathizers throughout the system. Only after this has been done is it possible to get around to the policy consequences. (Western analysts who tend to stress policy over personnel matters usually find themselves anticipating policy changes long before they take place. Foreign observers, for example, predicted immediately after the arrest of Chiang Ch'ing and her three associates that Chinese policies, especially in the cultural and educational fields, would change. Yet in the aftermath of the downfall of the Gang of Four, changes of substantive policies had yet to match the drama of the power and personnel reversals.) Since the mass media are less effective in dealing with personnel than with policy matters, they tend to lag behind events during a period of purging.

The communication system in China has three basic channels with somewhat paradoxical responsibilities. First, the public mass media, including wall posters, in addition to repeating the phrases of the day and the consensus views of the current policy line, will at times become the surprising forums for the advocacy of different policies and opinions. Second, the highly confidential, largely word-of-mouth, intraparty and intragovernmental system of informing cadres, which should encourage clashes of views according to the theory of the "mass line" and "democratic centralism," in practice is used largely to enforce consensus. Finally, some communication presumably exists among the actual decision makers, which may be characterized by the careful repetition of current "correct" views.

The explanations for these interesting peculiarities are complex.

Before moving on, let us note in passing two cultural features that probably contribute to this reversal of public and private modes of communication.

First, an important feature of the political culture in China is a deep suspicion that minority disagreement within the Party elite on any matter is a sign of potential intriguing. Clearly it is not easy for Chinese officials to disagree too sharply with each other; hence they are inclined to use indirect hints and avoid direct confrontations. Mao Tse-tung could call for more open clashes of views, but his threats to those who caused trouble seem to have carried far more weight in shaping cadre behavior. Mao's now frequently cited warning "Practice Marxism, and not revisionism; unite, and don't split; be open and aboveboard, and don't intrigue and conspire" has been read to mean that it would be foolish to go about mobilizing opinions contrary to the official consensus of the moment.

Second, modern Chinese culture still seems to reflect a Confucian tradition that requires courtesy in face-to-face relations but allows the abandonment of these strict controls when taking pen in hand to write for public print. Traditionally, people were more restrained in expressing disagreeable or aggressive views in face-to-face encounters, less restrained when speaking to an audience, and willing to be highly emotional in print—essentially the opposite of the norm in American culture.[5] This cultural pattern may therefore contribute to the current Chinese practice of being guarded in oral exchanges, somewhat more open in conferences and meetings, and willing to take the greatest risk in advancing contrary views when writing. Needless to say, these are finely shaded gradations, ranging from almost none to very modest contrary views; yet the steps in expressing aggression are the traditional ones—moving upward from oral to written. The difference is that the strongest expressions of aggression now take the form of fierce attacks in the mass media in support of the official consensus.

Aesopian Language

Given the surprising fact that the mass media is subtly used for factional advocacy purposes, it is not surprising that the Chinese are adept at using Aesopian language, historical allegory, and code words to make their points in public. In other cultures, such veiled messages are used to protect the author from reprisals by the powerful. In modern China, however, the use of allegory is not a monopoly of defenseless critics nor the tool of the impotent; it is used most often by the powerful and those who control the media. Thus, it is not always clear who is trying to speak past whom.

We need not dwell long on such classic examples of the use of critical allegory as Wu Han's play *Dismissal of Hai Jui,* which the still relatively obscure critic Yao Wen-yüan instantly recognized as being in fact an attack on Mao Tse-tung's dismissal of Peng Te-huai and not just the story of the removal from office of an official in the Soochow area in 1569–1570 because his heart was with the peasants. The incident, of course, was an opening shot in the Cultural Revolution and helped propel Yao Wen-yüan to the pinnacle of cultural power, from which he was only to fall with the ousting of the Gang of Four. Other well-documented examples of the use of allegory and allusion by critics of existing policies were the 1966 newspaper columns by Teng T'o entitled "Evening Talks at Yen-shan," and the "Three Family Village" essays by Teng T'o, Wu Han, and a third literary figure, Liao Mo-sha.

What is distinctive and indeed puzzling is the practice of the highest Chinese authorities of using allegory to make their points. Why is it that those whose words command attention and whose opinions prevail should have recourse to techniques that in other systems only the powerless fall back upon?

In some cases the reason is relatively simple: parables are a powerful method for reaching a mass audience, as any Christian can attest. When Mao Tse-tung put aside momentarily the role of helmsman for that of teacher, he frequently employed the Master's method. This was certainly the case when he spoke the parable of *The Foolish Old Man Who Moved the Mountain,* which also incidentally revealed the weakness of the technique—ambiguity and an uncertain moral—in that it referred to the powers of "God" and of "two angels." It must also have revived strange memories for some, since the story is almost word for word the same as the old folktale the ornithologist-missionary Dr. George Wilder of Pao-ting-fu used for his favorite Protestant-ethic sermon, which he enthusiastically delivered throughout North China in the nineteen twenties and thirties. In Dr. Wilder's version, the "two angels" were the Church and the School.

The fondness of Chinese leaders for using allegories and allusions goes far beyond the effectiveness of parables in reaching the uneducated. There are numerous examples in which Mao, in particular, used historical and other allegorical forms, not for clear and simple instruction of the masses but to make points that are at times highly obscure.

Consider as an example the way in which Mao Tse-tung jumped at the idea of suddenly requiring all 800 to 900 million Chinese to reflect on the "negative example" supposedly portrayed by the classic Chinese novel *Water Margin* (see chapter 8 in this volume for a more detailed examination of this campaign). Generations of Chinese had been brought up on the idea that *Water Margin* was an antiestablishment novel, with Sung Chiang as the Robin Hood–like leader of a band of rebels. Suddenly Mao announced that Sung Chiang had in fact been a revisionist, a leader who on the surface appeared to be revolutionary but whose ultimate actions supported bourgeois morality.

All Chinese by this time knew that revisionism was *bad,* and therefore if Sung Chiang was a revisionist he must be bad, but it was far from obvious who in the contemporary scene was being allegorically portrayed as a "Sung Chiang." For months throughout China millions of people taxed their brains trying to figure out "who Sung Chiang really was." Some saw him as the "Soviet Union," which had clearly gone the "revisionist" route; others thought that it might be Chou En-lai, who presumably wished for better relations with such "imperialists" as the United States; still others wondered whether it might not be Teng Hsiao-p'ing, soon to be the "capitalist roader who seeks to reverse correct verdicts."

Given the fact that the campaign could only have muddied the waters, how do we explain the enthusiasm of the leadership for this use of the allegory? Mao's own explanation was that everyone should read *Water Margin* because of the great advantage of "learning from negative examples."

A more fundamental explanation would refer to a basic feature of Chinese political culture: the Chinese are accustomed to being ruled by oracles, particularly ones that speak in riddles. For nearly two thousand years the Chinese have believed that they could realize a more perfect governance if they could only better understand all the meaning that might lie behind Confucius' cryptic remarks. Given this proclivity, it is appropriate that the oldest political artifacts of Chinese civilization should be oracle bones.

The Awesomeness of Code Names

Possibly nothing better illustrates the Chinese practice of associating the enigmatic with authority than their devotion to using code words and code names in their mass media. Even when everyone knows who is being referred to, an element of mystery is achieved by the use of cryptic and stylized phrases in place of proper names.

The tradition of the disgraced leader who becomes a "nonperson" goes back to Soviet practices. The Chinese, however, have added a category between that of the always-vilified name and the name that is removed from history never to appear again—the category of people vilified by a standardized expression, whose name is never mentioned.

In other cultures it is assumed that code names are used when it is desirable to keep some people from knowing the precise identity of the person referred to. But this seems not to be the case with the Chinese, who use in their mass media code names to which all have the key. Everyone in China must have known, for example, who "China's Krushchev" and "the Party person in authority taking the capitalist road" was, long before he was finally identified explicitly as the "renegade, hidden traitor, and scab Liu Shao-ch'i." Similarly, during the three years when the Chinese press reviled the "political swindler like Liu Shao-ch'i and his ilk," everyone knew that the man in question was Lin Piao. With the fall of the Gang of Four, the radio and the press in the provinces began to attack local leaders by code names: "That Rather Influential Person" in Kiangsi, "That Bad Man of Paoting Prefecture," "That Sworn Follower" and "His Sinister Henchman" in Liaoning, "That Confidant" in Honan, "A Major Leading Figure" and "Another Major Leading Figure" in Kwangtung, "The Tiger in Suchow," and "The Scoundrel, the Drummer and the Dog's Head Staff Officer" in Hunan, to mention just a few.

Why should those who are in control of China's mass media find it appropriate to disguise the names of the people they are vilifying? What does the Chinese public think when they are called to rallies of 500,000 people to denounce by code name individuals whose real names are well known? Who is trying to confuse whom? And for what purpose?

A generous but most un-Chinese legalistic interpretation would be that until a case has been "disposed" of, it is not appropriate to use actual names. In fact, code names were used for Liu Shao-ch'i and Lin Piao until the Central Committee finally verified their "crimes," but after it was official they were denounced by name. Also, the practice of avoiding naming names meant that the media never explicitly denounced Teng Hsiao-p'ing from the time of his fall after the death of Chou En-lai until his restoration over a year later—they only attacked "that capitalist roader who wanted to reverse correct verdicts." This Chinese convention has thus made it easier to reintegrate a rehabilitated purgee. For example, old associates who were spared the need to vilify Teng by name can now presumably brush off the fact that for nearly a year they had denounced "that capitalist roader who wanted to reverse correct verdicts," a label that is now a mere abstraction and a clear misnomer for the worthy Teng Hsiao-p'ing.

The Chinese practice of using code names for discredited leaders is, however, based upon more fundamental elements of Chinese culture than this. The practice of code names strikes very responsive chords in the Chinese public, stimulating a powerful combination of revulsion and activist participation, because of deep traditional Chinese attitudes.

The sense of revulsion comes from the Chinese belief that to be nameless is to be less than human. There is thus something ominous about someone the authorities declare a no-name. He is clearly a "dark spirit," capable of "devious scheming," and certainly a "monster and a freak" whose work must be "poisonous weeds." It is easy to imagine the worst of someone who is nameless. A named person, in contrast, is verifiable; people may instantly ask who originally vouched for him, who got him high office, and who formerly said good things about him.

The use of code names also has the peculiar effect of making the public a participating insider—the masses by word of mouth seem to know more than what the media reports, for, being knowledgeable about the actual name of the discredited figure, they possess confidential information which the media seems incapable of disseminating. The people are thus brought in on the side of those who are purging the public figure, and the feeling of knowing more than can be publicly stated in the mass media carries with it a sense of pseudo-responsibility: those who share secrets belong together.

This curious situation is another reminder that in China the relationship between the media and the political process is unique, defying not only the conventions of the "free" or professionalized press but the practices common to a submissive and totally "controlled" press. The adversary posture of the journalistic professional suggests that the media strive to provide a total picture of events, reporting all that is in the public domain and whatever can be pried out of the confidential realms of government; while, of course, the image of the controlled press is that of authorities manipulating attitudes and opinions, and limiting the spread of information. The Chinese, as has been extensively documented, use the media to shape opinions and values. Yet they also break with the tradition of government-controlled media by their strange practice of assuming that much of their audience knows more than the media are revealing.

The Destructive Power of Words

This Chinese way of positioning the media in relationship to both the authorities and the public might suggest a discounting of the potential powers of mass communication. Such an inference would be a gross misreading of Chinese attitudes. Few cultures elevate the power of the pen to a more exalted status. As we have already observed, Chinese generally express more aggression through the written word than they do orally. Moreover, they have always attached great meaning and significance to the printed word.

In Chinese political culture the power of words, with the noteworthy exception of those of Mao Tse-tung, is largely destructive, as might be expected given the propensity to express aggression in writing. Indeed, a major function of the media in the Chinese political process is to provide a vehicle for vilifying and hence "destroying" individuals. In pouring out venom against targets of abuse, Chinese writers are not just expressing the fury of their moral indignation; they also seem convinced that words of slander can truly demolish a person.

The basis of this view of the destructive powers of vilification seems clearly associated with the cardinal importance of the use of shaming in the Chinese socialization process.[6] Traditionally, parents freely practiced both teasing and shaming in disciplining children, and it seems that with communism there is even more use of "shaming" in schools and in criticism sessions. There is thus among Chinese a genuine appreciation of the horror of being singled out for public scorn. Indeed, the Chinese have, in a sense, revised the old Western adage to read, "Sticks and stones may break my bones, but words can utterly shatter me."

Over the years, with every campaign against discredited leaders, the media have been used not just to report on the crimes of the evil figures but actually to destroy them. And often the target of the vituperation is charged with having used words himself to harm others and to weaken the "people." For example, the Ministry of Culture Criticism Group in "Sometimes Shrilling, Sometimes Moaning—On Chu Lan's Big Poisonous Weed . . . " declared that "big careerist Chang Ch'un-ch'iao" had a "new plan to kill people with the pen," and Chu Lan's "hack writers group" had been "holding the pen and sharpening the sword to rabidly hack the Party and the people."[7]

The top leaders in the process of being removed by the Central Committee are not the only ones who are attacked in the media. On the contrary, lesser figures are usually those who are most seriously damaged by such public revilements. Such figures are often more vulnerable because they might escape political destruction if they were not singled out for public criticism. Yet such lesser figures are constantly caught up in media attacks because of the standard Chinese offensive strategy of "killing the horse to get the rider," that is, destroying followers to bring down the principal figure, and the defensive tactic of "expending horses and carts to protect the general."

Another form of the Chinese assumption of the automatic destructive power of words can be seen in their acceptance of the "dumbwaiter" principle: that is, if one rides to the top by one formulation of words, one will automatically crash to the bottom when that formulation is discredited. Merle Goldman has documented, for example, how Chou Yang rose to power in the context of implied attacks on Lu Hsun's literary tradition, and then, when the time came for the fall of Chou Yang, the stratagem used was to praise Lu Hsun.[8]

At the beginning of the Cultural Revolution there were numerous examples of the extraordinary vulnerability of Chinese leaders to any form of public criticism. Although in the end he was physically destroyed, Liu Shao-ch'i initially seemed to be numbed by the experience of being criticized in public by people he considered to be his inferiors.[9] Needless to say, the treatment Red Guards meted out to those they would destroy, even when limited to the verbal level, was hardly comparable to press criticism of public figures in other countries. Yet it is safe to say that current practices place China in that relatively small category of countries in which political figures can rise to the top and experience only praise and never the trauma of insult from a critical press. Whereas in most countries those who seek power must learn to live with varying degrees of public criticism, Chinese leaders do not have to pass through this particular form of hardening experience.

Words Can Unmask Demonic Powers

The Chinese feeling for the destructive power of words is fundamentally linked to a deep Chinese cultural sentiment which holds that what is hidden is usually bad, and that evil (as well as good) forces are constantly engaging in deceptions but can be utterly destroyed if unmasked. And, of course, the power of words and the media is the ability to unmask the hidden and hence devious motives of evil actors.

These basic sentiments were appropriately revealed in an editorial in the *People's Daily* of June 20, 1966, which praised the introduction of wall posters at the beginning of the Cultural Revolution:

> Chairman Mao Tse-tung says: "Posters written in big characters are an extremely useful new type of weapon."
> The revolutionary big-character posters are very good!
> They are a "monster detector" to unmask the monsters and demons of all kinds.[10]

The tradition of Chinese legends from *Monkey* to *The Woman Warrior* is filled with stories of ghosts and spirits who assume different guises, and it is the task of heroes to unmask them and hence destroy their potency. The psychological dynamics of this instinctive appreciation of the destructive potential of "unmasking" seems to be related to the same power of shaming in Chinese culture which we have already noted. To be unmasked is to be stripped of the protective shield that comes from conforming to one's expected role. That is to say, when one has experienced the humiliation of shame, one has also learned the destructive "consequences of being unmasked."

Similarly, in Chinese political culture motives are easily suspect. One must always be especially on guard against the tricks of the incorrigible, the "bourgeoisie," "former landlords," "feudal remnants," "rich peasants"—people who can be just about anyone born after Liberation. The Chinese political imagination permits the belief that individuals who have never owned land, had riches, or owned the material possessions associated in all other societies with a bourgeois lifestyle can somehow secretly, behind their masks of merely wishing "to serve the people," take on all the attributes of roles which were objectively destroyed a generation before in China.

Cultures that place great importance on shaming as a part of their socialization processes also tend in their legends to exploit the fantasy potentials of people becoming invisible or of changing their guises. In such cultures it is easy to appreciate the social advantages of being able to do this, but since the desire is beyond the reach of "good" people, it is usually "evil" ones who are most successful in becoming invisible or appearing to be different from what they really are.

The task of unmasking is never easy because of the trickery of the evil ones, who rarely reveal their true intentions. Indeed, manifest behavior is always suspect since it is well known that the foe practices "Waving the Red Flag to Oppose the Red Flag."

The act of unmasking consists essentially of, first, detecting devious motives and, second, applying a new label to the person. Just as the Chinese have turned traditional Marxism on its head by stressing human willpower over objective historical forces, so they have replaced objective class categories with subjectively defined class labels. The fact that China was devoid of a significant middle class has been ignored by the simple device of inventing implausible numbers of imaginary "bourgeoisie." If China in fact had had anywhere near the numbers of bourgeoisie, landlords, and rich peasants that the media have unmasked over the years, China would have been a remarkably rich country, regardless of income distribution.

In fact, however, the application of labels in the unmasking of opponents is a demonstration of the Chinese belief in the destructive power of words and not proof of objective sociological realities. Needless to say, the labels which the Chinese media employ have shattering powers.

The Limits of Constructive Power of Words

In contrast to the certainty which Chinese leaders seem to have about the destructive power of words, they seem to have doubts about whether the converse holds—that is, whether the media can be used constructively to build power. This is not to say that the Chinese have not tried to use the media to build up the image of

Hua Kuo-feng as the worthy successor to Mao Tse-tung, who, of course, was in his time ceaselessly extolled by all China's media. Yet the uninspired accounts in the Chinese press of Chairman Hua's visits to communes, factories, and conferences have more the quality of dutiful acts of ritualized homage than efforts to maximize political power. The unspoken assumption seems to be that if Hua is to consolidate his power, it will not be because of any magic in the media's use of words but rather through his actual political acts.

Although the media's attention to "model heroes" is related primarily to educating the masses and hence falls outside the purview of our study, the choice of which heroes to honor is at times a matter of interelite "struggles" and thus illustrates how the leaders use the media in their relations with each other, which is our subject here. Thus, the rise and fall of the popularity in the media of different "heroes" is a fairly good indicator of the fortunes of factions but not a very good clue to policy preferences. Recently, for example, in the military field we have seen, with the "crushing of the Gang of Four," a dramatic decline in attention to the once-popular "Good Eighth Company on Nanking Road" and a spectacular rise in coverage of the activities of the "Hard-Boned Sixth Company." The first outfit long received the accolades of the radicals, who never tired of telling of how the worthies of the "Good Eighth Company" were constantly devising new ways to help nearby peasants and workers. In contrast, the "Hard-Boned Sixth Company," the idol of the moderates, got its reputation from the ferocity of its fighting in Korea.[11] The change in blessing from one company to the other clearly reflected the political end of Chiang Ch'ing and the victory of the moderates, but the policy message was slightly more ambiguous. Whereas the "Good Eighth" was rarely noted for having martial skills, the "Hard-Boned Sixth" would accomplish three days of "hard military training" in two days and so have a free day to be helpful to peasants at their work.

All of this might have been a subtle way of announcing a change in military policy in favor of greater professionalism and a decline in revolutionary fervor, were it not for the fact that simultaneously the Chinese media stopped extolling the merits of the model warrior Chiang Tieh-sheng, whom the radicals described as a "bristly rebel," and again brought to prominence Lei Feng, a very unmartial soldier. Lei Feng compiled an awesome record of good deeds:

when travelling, he carried a broom so he could leap from the train at every stop and sweep the platform or, if time permitted, the entire station, before getting back aboard; pictures show him "selflessly" washing his comrades' underwear; and on innumerable occasions he helped old women with their baskets and young children with their reading, writing, and arithmetic.[12] Why have the victorious moderates, who certainly favor professionalism, decided that the Chinese press should revive memories of this unprofessional soldier? The answer lies not in speculations about the use of the media for policy advocacy but in the fact that Chou En-lai once had some kind words for the memory of Lei Feng. Presumably everyone is supposed to know this fact, and therefore can ignore the significance of the content of the model hero's behavior and concentrate on the issue of whose backing the model had once enjoyed.

Here again we return to our initial observation about how the Chinese media operate: on one hand, the audience is supposed to know more than what is told; yet, on the other hand, what is told seems designed to obscure what needs to be known. Everyone is supposed to know that the "radicals" once said that the "Hard-Boned Sixth Company" was "a sinister example of upholding a purely military viewpoint," and that Chou En-lai, the patron of the "moderates" once praised Lei Feng, but in the meantime the media are not permitted to give a straightforward statement about the currently correct military policy and what should now be the right mix of professionalism and revolutionary sentiments.

Exemptions from the Obligations of Reality

An important reason why the Chinese media do not feel compelled to give straightforward pronouncements on substantive policies and can indulge their tastes for Aesopian language is that Chinese political culture is not premised on the assumption that political leaders must ultimately submit to the disciplining effects of reality. It is, of course, true that politicians everywhere delight in occasions when unpleasant realities can be ignored and strive to insulate themselves from reality by pretending that the myth-world they have generated is a perfectly acceptable alternative to the world of hard facts.

In China, however, the ruling class operates as though it were completely exempt from the obligations of reality. There are several reasons why the Chinese leaders find themselves in such a situation. First, there are the peculiar Chinese alterations of Marxism-Leninism. The hallmark of traditional Marxists and particularly of the Bolsheviks was a deep respect for materialism which operationally was translated into a profound commitment to an objective analysis of the actual forces in any situation. Mao Tse-tung modified all of this by exalting willpower and giving supremacy to the human, and hence subjective, dimensions of history. In practice, Mao's worship of the human will meant that Chinese leaders were led to substitute desires and wishes for realities and accomplishments. To be correct in one's "Thoughts" and hence in one's sentiments became more important than substantive accomplishments.

Second, this turning of Marxism-Leninism on its head helped to preserve the traditional Chinese cultural propensity for attaching paramount importance to ideology and morality, thereby glorifying the value of subjective feelings and intentions at the expense of objective legal norms. The Chinese idealized rule by "good" men rather than the impersonal rule of law. Furthermore, Chinese officials traditionally preferred to have their actions judged by their skills at adhering to ritual and standards of etiquette rather than by the test of substantive performance or actual achievement.

Third, Chinese political culture is still strongly hierarchical, and the division between rulers and ruled lies precisely in the command of esoteric knowledge. Those who are ruled, when not passively accepting their stations and repeating the ritual words they have been given, are expected to inspire their superiors to be more dutiful in their search for moral perfection; they are never supposed to question whether the "emperor wears any clothes."

For these and other reasons, the Chinese media find it easy to cooperate with the political class in maintaining an elaborate world, filled with symbols, slogans, and code words and only weakly penetrated by reality. Thus, at a time when the policies and practices associated with Liu Shao-ch'i are being nearly universally adopted in China, it is possible to continue to pretend that everything Liu stood for was evil; and this is made possible by pretending that the consensus of the day is still "revolutionary" and "radical" because it has been decreed that, contrary to all evidence, the Gang of Four —the one-time "Maoist" radicals—were really "ultra-rightists."

The reason the Chinese are so indulgent about such gaps between public words and obvious realities is not an Anglo-Saxon appreciation of the social values of hypocrisy but rather a compelling Chinese cultural need to maintain at great cost the appearance of "consensus." The idea of challenging the collectivity seems unacceptable to Chinese for it suggests chaos, *luan,* and the possibility of being socially isolated. Everyone is expected to pay whatever may be the necessary price for preserving surface tranquility.

Consensus versus Interest

Even leaders who are about to lose power and position sometimes conspire to "play the game" of maintaining in public the impression of consensus even though behind the scenes they may be pouring forth their anxieties and bewailing their misfortunes.[13] Thus the media largely tap this surface layer of conformity and consensus and barely reflect any deeper tensions and conflicts. Yet in fact the Chinese political process is filled with conflicts that cannot be legitimately disclosed.

The problem is that Chinese political culture contains a fundamental tension between consensus and interests that reflect at the macrolevel a basic personality tension in individual Chinese between the imperative of conformity and the need for self-assertion.

Chinese children are taught *both* to conform and to achieve; they are supposed to be both selfless and capable of bringing honor to their lives. The values of conformity and selflessness are more openly acknowledged, but the expectation that one should try to excel over others is still there; hence a fundamental tension exists.

In Chinese political culture it is almost impossible to acknowledge the legitimacy of conflicts of interest. Although the rhetoric no longer speaks of the need for "harmony" as in the Confucian tradition, the concept of adherence to the revolutionary ideal of the "people" and the "state" has the same effect of upholding conformity and suppressing individual or limited interests.

The fact that the Chinese find it so difficult to legitimize the articulation of special interests is of fundamental importance in understanding their distinctive approach toward factional conflicts that might challenge the consensus of the day. Western analysts usually feel most comfortable in referring to policy issues when tracing possible factional alignments because they feel that such differences provide an entirely legitimate basis for factional groupings and tensions. It is important, however, to remind ourselves that it is a peculiarly parochial American view which holds that politics should revolve around policy choices, and we tend to be blind to other possibilities. There is indeed a tendency among American political scientists to employ a three-tiered scheme. At the highest and most legitimate level, there are basic "issues" over which "honorable men can disagree." At the next level, and slightly more shady, there are "interests" which may be either "legitimate" or "selfish," or both. Presumably, actors will more freely discuss "issues" than confess to having "interests." Finally, at the lowest, and almost unspeakable, level, there are "personality" preferences and clashes, a kind of "chemistry" in human relations that can be good or bad.

The Chinese tend to see politics in almost the reverse order. In their view it is self-evident, and hence legitimate, that the personal qualities of leaders are critical in attracting honorable followers or sinister "gangs." The very suggestion that people might have "interests" is taken to be a scandal; and, finally, most Chinese tend to suspect that discussions of issues are merely ways of throwing dust in the eyes of the naive.

A consequence of the Chinese hierarchy of legitimacy is that factional conflicts are treated primarily in the media as manifestations of the personal faults of the individuals involved. In the end, Liu Shao-ch'i, Lin Piao, and the Gang of Four will be remembered in the Chinese media for their personal sins and deficiencies, they will not be identified with any particular "interests," and their policy views will be treated cavalierly. They will all be seen as having opposed the "correct line" because of their distorted personalities. The general impression which the Chinese media strive to create is that everyone subscribes to the consensus; that is, orthodoxy can easily prevail, except for the deviant acts of a few corrupt personalities.

On the other hand, the realities of Chinese practice are that cadres are constantly seeking to get ahead, and therefore, in spite of the imperative of conformity, there is also the practical necessity of self-assertion. The media cannot deal explicitly with such forms of competition except after the fall of some leading figure, when of course the chorus in the media is one of denouncing the scoundrels and their "handful" of "sinister henchmen."

Elitist–Mass Politics

A principal reason the Chinese mass media have relatively little difficulty in maintaining the appearance of consensus in spite of cadre competition is that the Chinese political system, in spite of its revolutionary experience, remains a traditional elitist form of politics in which a sharply differentiated ruling class monopolizes the power in the society and manages, with whatever feedback it chooses to accept, the affairs of the masses. In such a system the rulers do feel a need to hang together and present to the masses the appearance of collective agreement, even as they compete for power among themselves.

Although it is in no way a deterministic "law" of history, the general pattern of political development in the building of the modern nation state has been one of moving from a stage in which personal ties are paramount in interelite relationships toward, first, a stage of institutionally based competition among those who do represent different governing or elite establishments, and then, finally, a stage where politics revolves around interests competing among themselves, with the "rulers" designing policies that are responsive to such conflicts.

China today still has a political system in which ruling power is responsive above all to the rulers' ideology and the network of career and personal relationships of officials. It has not yet openly entered the second stage, in which the clashes of the objective interests of the different agencies, ministries, and institutions are acknowledged as legitimate and the proper subjects of day-to-day political life. Although we know that such clashes must exist, the basic myth of the system, upon which its legitimacy ultimately rests, is that, through the powers of ideology, such interinstitutional conflicts can be trivialized, and that it should be possible to achieve the ideal of perfect harmony among all the governing institutions. Thus the conflicts which must arise in the planning process become "state secrets," and that strange amorphous institution, the "Center," resolves all problems so that the government and all the cadres can pretend that power struggles are unnecessary. Hence China still does not have a politics of open "policy issues." Only indirectly and in subtle ways can there be hints that clashes over policy are taking place.

Precisely because legitimacy would be threatened by any admission of difficulties over policy issues, such clashes among the leadership must be quickly transformed into issues about the personal morality of particular officials. Those who are defeated on policy matters have to be denounced for being inherently immoral and not merely for having poor judgment.

Needless to say, the Chinese political system is far from becoming one in which political life revolves around competing interests centered among the population at large. This is not a trite observation or merely another way of saying that the Chinese system is a variant of totalitarian politics. The intolerance of the Chinese political system for any concrete interests can be seen in the fact that even though region and locality can and do provide the bases for power groupings, there are no policy conflicts in China today which reflect regional differences beyond the traditional politics of each locality trying to get as much from the "Center" as possible and contributing the least possible. Moreover, distinctive economic and social interests arising out of geography simply do not surface in China. For example, those who used Shanghai as a power base advocated policies which could not by the widest stretch of the imagination be said to reflect the real interests of the citizens of Shanghai. The "Shanghai leaders" clearly felt no obligation to advance Shanghai's objective interests when they denounced the advantages of technology, called for autarchy and equal development in all provinces, and championed the sending of educated youth to the countryside, all policies which hurt the well-being of Shanghai.[14] Similarly, those who have had Kwangtung as their power base have not pressed for policies which would particularly benefit their area at the price of hurting other places.

Conflict and Legitimacy

With these observations about the nature of the Chinese political system in mind, we can now return to our earlier observation about their unique use of the media in intraelite politics. It now seems possible that the Chinese propensity to use the public media for semi-esoteric communications and to presume that the audience must know more than the media can tell is related to the basic tension in Chinese political culture which requires that the contradiction between conformity and self-assertion be contained on terms that preserve the appearance of consensus, which is the basis of legitimacy of the entire system.

Leaders and aspiring leaders feel a need to assert themselves but in ways that will not threaten the myth of consensus. This requires that assertion of interests and discussion of policy issues be muted as much as possible, or disguised in statements which appear to have more to do with morality, personal qualities, and aspects of ideology.

Since this situation is not strikingly different from what obtained under the traditional Chinese political system, it is not surprising that the leaders find it so easy to use allegories based on incidents in Chinese history and even forms of language very similar to traditional practices. Mao's style of using aphorisms and slogans as means for communicating policy directives conformed to the imperial tradition. Even the traditional Chinese tendency to exploit the mystique of numbers to accentuate and give greater potency to ideas has been used and enlarged upon. In the past the Chinese had their Five Sovereigns *(Wu Ti)* who matched their five elements, Three Model Emperors, Three Kingdoms, Five Dynasties, Three People's Principles; and now, of course, the use of slogans based on numbers seems to have no limits: "one guides two," "three comparisons," "three fixes and one substitution," "three reconciliations and one reduction," "the four togethers," "the three banners," "the three fames principle," "the four clean-ups," "the four modernizations," "five factors into one body," "the four olds," "the three manys and the one exception," "the ten shoulds and the ten should nots," and so on.

It was mainly Mao who invented such slogans for communicating priorities. But he was not alone. Indeed, the essence of the elite game under Mao, and even more so now, has been for senior leaders to float such slogans as ways of testing whom they might reach as potential allies. The question of who chooses to repeat whose slogan lies at the heart of the process in which power is accumulated in Communist China. The process has to involve a high degree of semiesoteric communications because, first, policy clashes cannot be openly admitted to and, second, the object is to mobilize potential supporters without creating explicit enemies.

In this manner, real problems are touched upon in the media through the use of cryptic forms, basic secrecy is preserved, and power alignments can be formed and reformed without any overt threats to the basic concept of legitimacy. Those who are most successful in this procedure can attract support and thus gain the power necessary for ruling, in a manner which does not create problems of legitimacy.

The public can follow the rise and fall of slogans and code words with a sense of confidence that, even though their rulers may be struggling among themselves, they need not fear that the system will be dramatically changed. Their only obligation is to understand that when victory comes to any particular element of the leadership they must instantly display two emotions, their pleasure for the victors and their hatred of the defeated. They have learned to be far more guarded in their expectations of the policy consequences of such victories and defeats. For even the least politically educated Chinese can appreciate that the defeat of Liu Shao-ch'i has not brought an end to Liuist policies, even though Liu was best known precisely for his policies; similarly, the fall of the Gang of Four will not bring an end to radical rhetoric, even though Chiang Ch'ing and her followers were best known for their dedication to rhetoric.

For both the leaders and the masses, there seems to be something comforting in having a political system in which there is a great gap between rhetoric and action, for this "gap" provides a zone of safety allowing one to get out of trouble by saying either "Heed my acts and not my words" or "Hear my words and overlook my acts," depending upon which is more convenient under the circumstances.

The Solution to the Chinese Puzzle

We can see that the "inside out, upside down" character of the relationship between the media and elite politics is not a manifestation of exotic cultural whimsy, but is functional for the stability of the system. The pieces of this Chinese puzzle fit together because of important structural and cultural features of Chinese politics.

The paramount rule of Chinese politics is the obligation of everyone to uphold consensus and practice conformity, under conditions in which the elite have a monopoly on initiatives and few can openly advocate any form of special interest.

The Chinese belief in the vital importance of consensus can be seen not only in their efforts, especially during campaigns, to ensure that everyone is thinking in the currently correct way, but more importantly in their practice of blowing up the downfall of every leader into a crisis of legitimacy for the entire system.

Since they are not inclined to acknowledge the legitimacy of intraelite conflict of interest, such clashes are managed at arm's length, that is, cryptically in the media. Unable to contend directly with each other as they seek different priorities, senior officials find it expedient to try to shade the interpretation of the media "consensus" in ways favorable to their interest.

It is of great significance that everyone seems to agree that the media's version of the consensus should be generally accepted as the correct one at any moment. The media thus have a major role in the maintenance of the legitimacy of the system. One consequence of this role is that they have inhibited the pace of change. Even during the era when Chairman Mao seemed to be the ultimate arbiter of Chinese politics, his mandates still had to be filtered through the communication process at the slow pace necessary for the maintenance of consensus and hence legitimacy. Similarly dramatic purges of personnel, such as the "smashing" of the Gang of Four, cannot bring instant changes of policies because rhetoric, policy choices, and new appointments have to be slowly blended to create consensus.

This process produced two important paradoxical consequences. First, there is the paradox that even though the media are vital for legitimacy, the very process that makes this true also operates to force the media to maintain a significant gap between its rhetoric and actual realities. The communication system, in the very process of upholding the fundamental realities of power and authority in China, has to create an imaginary world.

The second paradox is that even though the Chinese media present themselves on the surface as champions of revolutionary ambition, they are functionally a powerful conservative force, slowing the pace of change and striving always to uphold continuity. Because of its legitimizing function for the entire political system, the Chinese communication process must always strive to show that what is being proposed today is consistent with what was right yesterday. It is not just that everything which is to be done after the death of Mao Tse-tung must be made to seem consistent with Mao's wishes, but that all policies must be made to seem in line with the entire history of the Chinese Communist movement.

This basic obligation for maintenance of legitimacy explains in part the extraordinary attention devoted in the Chinese media to nostalgic accounts of earlier phases in the Party's history. The endless stories of past years are inspired not just by elderly leaders' love of reminiscence and their belief that youth should benefit from (admire?) their past accomplishments. They are necessary also because of the legitimacy function of the media.

Needless to say, this same vital political function which has forced the media to exaggerate the gap between rhetoric and reality in defining the present world also operates in such a way as to create a comparable gap between past realities and versions of history which must now be disseminated. The two paradoxes thus reinforce each other.

Pattern of Change

It is significant that in our analysis of the relationship of the media to Chinese political culture it has been repeatedly necessary to refer back to traditional Chinese cultural patterns in order to explain contemporary practices. In spite of revolutionary rhetoric, basic Chinese political culture in the critical area of attitudes towards authority and concepts about the workings of power maintains strong continuity with China's past. Twenty odd years of essential isolation from the rest of the world and prolonged periods of intense inward focus of policy has meant that Chinese political culture, in spite of adopting a new ideology, has changed less than the political cultures of most of the new states that emerged after World War II.

Godwin Chu in his introduction to this volume has identified the important fact that Chinese culture accentuated ''affect oriented'' relationships and the value of hierarchy and compliance. Chinese political culture of today remains one in which supreme importance is attached to the affective dimensions of relationships—the state of cadres' ''thought'' and ''revolutionary fervor'' are more critical than their technical skills or objective accomplishments. And as we have seen, hierarchy and compliance continue to be of supreme importance as everyone strives to uphold the appearances of consensus, even as they try to climb the ladder of the hierarchy.

Presumably with the downfall of the Gang of Four, a new era of Chinese politics is possible, but it is still far too early to judge what degree of change is most likely. What is clear, however, is that nearly two years' time following the defeat of the ''radicals'' has not been enough to change in any significant degree the relationship between the media and China's political culture. At present the Chinese political system seems to be wavering between the one possibility of becoming more disciplined and technocratically ruled (possibly reminiscent of the 1950s) or the other possibility of a more relaxed and tolerant one-party system (possibly like some of the Eastern European Communist states). Movement in either direction probably would not alter our basic analysis of the media and elite politics.

NOTES

1. Alan P. L. Liu, *Communications and National Integration in Communist China* (Berkeley: University of California Press, 1971).
2. Frederick T. C. Yu, *Mass Persuasion in Communist China* (New York: Praeger, 1964).
3. Franklin Houn, *To Change a Nation* (New York: The Free Press, 1961).
4. Merle Goldman, *Literary Dissent in Communist China* (Cambridge, Mass.: Harvard University Press, 1967).
5. This is an important point for Westerners to understand. Americans and Japanese, for example, seem to have quite different instincts: Americans generally feel that they can be more intemperate in their language and more revealing of their thoughts and feelings when speaking in private and "off the record," and that they should be far more guarded, circumspect, and above all more precise and less extreme in their use of language when in a public forum or when writing for the record. In contrast, Japanese, both politicians and intellectuals, can be extremely sensitive to the views of those with whom they are conversing in private, intensely anxious to be agreeable, but in public print the same individuals, on the same subject, can give uninhibited vent to immoderate views. This difference between the American sense of verbal openness in speech and the need for precision and qualification in print and the reverse Japanese practice has caused considerable misunderstanding between the intellectuals of the two countries. In the 1950s and 1960s, when Japanese intellectuals were often critical of aspects of United States policy, American scholars were often dumbfounded because they thought they had achieved a meeting of minds in private conversations and then the Japanese would publish a statement of the same unqualified views. No doubt the Japanese intellectuals at times must have felt that they had been misled when Americans used more cautious and guarded language in print than they had used in private conversations.
6. For discussion of "shame" in Chinese culture, see Francis L. K. Hsu, *Under the Ancestor's Shadow* (New York: Columbia University Press, 1948); and Lucian W. Pye, *The Spirit of Chinese Politics* (Cambridge, Mass.: M.I.T. Press, 1968).
7. Peking Radio, July 1, 1977, in *Foreign Broadcast Information Service,* July 6, 1977, p. E14.
8. Merle Goldman, "The Fall of Chou Yang," *China Quarterly* 27 (July–September, 1966): 132–48.
9. For Liu Shao-ch'i's first attempts at refuting Red Guard criticisms, see Lowell Dittmer, *Liu Shao-ch'i and the Chinese Cultural Revolution* (Berkeley: University of California Press, 1974).
10. Quoted in "Quarterly Chronicle and Documents," *China Quarterly* 27 (July–September, 1966): 211.
11. For a typical example of how the moderates raised the "Hard-Boned Sixth Company" to be a model in the military field comparable to Tachai in agriculture and Tach'ing in industry, see Chairman Hua Kuo-feng's speeches during a tour of the Northeast, *Foreign Broadcast Information Service,* May 6, 1977, p. E4.
On the first anniversary of Mao's death, the Hard-Boned Sixth Company explicitly recognized that it had been the object of criticism by the Gang of Four, who had "stirred up an evil wind" and, "braying that consolidation meant restoration,"

claimed that, by "constantly paying attention to military training," the Hard-Boned Sixth "was restoring the bourgeois military line." In its own defense, the Company claimed it was second to none in "forging close ties with the masses" and helping to "build the economy." In short, the Hard-Boned Sixth has been as anxious as any unit to appear to be "revolutionary" and to show that it had seen through the "ultra-rightist" character of its "radical" critics who followed the Gang of Four.

12. As an aside, we should take note of the fact that most Chinese model heroes had short lives. A living "model hero" might unforeseeably become an embarrassment in the future, given man's unpredictability, but a deceased "hero" is easier to manage and, furthermore, the sentiments evoked by his death can touch responsive chords in the public mind, given mankind's anxieties about death and immortality.

13. We cannot here go into the contradictory features of the Chinese socialization process, which on one hand stresses the imperative of repressing personal feelings and striving for the good of the collectivity (whether it be the family, clan, or the commune and the "people"), and on the other hand teaches the importance of reducing internal tensions by giving voice to grievances (when one "eats bitterness" and wants others to know about it, because of the hope that authorities, like one's parents, can be moved by sympathy). The important point is that the process of learning to control one's emotions to defer to the collectivity is consistent with developing a style of seeking sympathy from authority figures.

14. The relationship of Shanghai to national policies is of great interest for understanding both the realities and the myths of China's political economy. Historically, Chinese nationalism and, more particularly, the Chinese Communists, depicted Shanghai as a place where foreign interests were "bleeding away" China's strength and thus the very essence of foreign "exploitation" of China. After 1949, the Chinese authorities were clearly in a quandary: should they not take advantage of the impressive "capital plant" Shanghai represented with all of its human talents, from management to a skilled labor force, to speed China's national growth? Or, should they reverse matters and start to "exploit" Shanghai by draining it of its "advantages" and scattering them about the rest of the country? Either choice was difficult since it would make a mockery of the pre-Liberation viewpoint. Hence the peculiar ambivalence of the Peking authorities toward Shanghai. The answers to these questions will hopefully emerge from a book which Christopher Howe is now editing.

8

The Media Campaign as a Weapon in Political Struggle: The Dictatorship of the Proletariat and *Water Margin* Campaigns

Merle Goldman

The People's Republic of China has repeatedly mobilized the energies and resentments of the population in a series of campaigns on political, economic, and social issues. These campaigns have directed both the elites and the masses in surges of activity for a number of different purposes: to introduce new policies, transform values and attitudes, correct deviations from established norms, rectify leadership practices, and purge intellectual and political opposition. At different times, they have included one or all of these tasks. Whether localized or nationwide, such campaigns were the major channel through which the population learned of new initiatives, priorities, and "enemies" of the regime. They functioned as the most intensive, directed form of political communication.

A generally accepted axiom is that these campaigns espoused the Party's official policy. Supposedly, China's population was exposed solely to the prevailing line at the time with no room for differing or divergent views. Such an axiom may have been appropriate before the Great Leap Forward, but even then, as in the Hundred Flowers movement, it was not altogether accurate. After the Great Leap Forward and until the purge of the Shanghai group in 1976, the Chinese population was exposed in the process of a campaign to a number of views that at times differed from the official line and even from Mao.

Because of the factionalization of the leadership in the era after the Great Leap Forward, the various factions were able, most of the time, to present divergent views within the context of a campaign. In the second Hundred Flowers movement of the early 1960s, the Party apparatus dominated the media. Intellectuals associated with it subtly criticized the Maoist methods of mass mobilization and ideological struggle used in the Great Leap Forward. At the same time, a group of radical ideologues linked to Mao and his wife, which was to become the core of the Cultural Revolution group, defended Great Leap Forward practices and articulated many of the arguments that were to be used against the Party apparatus in the Cultural Revolution. Even in the early stages of the Cultural Revolution, these contrasting views were still expressed.

Similarly, in the post–Cultural Revolution period, though the Shanghai faction dominated the media, the bureaucratic faction under Chou En-lai and Teng Hsiao-p'ing also injected their views in the course of a campaign. The two sides presented opposing views of the Cultural Revolution: the Shanghai group sought to continue its programs and values; the bureaucratic group sought to do away with them. Moreover, neither faction necessarily conveyed Mao's views in the post–Cultural Revolution period. In addition, some even expressed views that diverged from the major factions as well as from Mao. In the aftermath of the Cultural Revolution, China's population was, in fact, exposed to divergent approaches on a number of issues.

With the exception of *Hsüeh-hsi yü P'i-p'an (Study and Criticism),* no one journal or newspaper represented a specific viewpoint in contention with another, as had happened at the beginning of the Cultural Revolution. The major newspapers and journals reflected the views of both factions. This seemingly controlled arrangement, however, did not reflect a compromise. Rather, it demonstrated that, although the Shanghai faction had the predominant voice in the media and cultural organs, the bureaucratic faction which controlled the political-economic-military apparatus had the power to insert its ideas into a campaign even though it did not control the media.

The Shanghai group headed by Mao's wife, Chiang Ch'ing, initiated a series of campaigns in the aftermath of the Cultural Revolution in order to regain the initiative lost to the bureaucratic faction in the early 1970s. But in each campaign—the Anti-Confucian/Anti-Lin Piao, Dictatorship of the Proletariat, and *Water Margin*—the bureaucratic leadership, using similar methods, deflected the attack and reinterpreted the slogans of the campaign to communicate a contrary political message.

The Dictatorship of the Proletariat

The Shanghai group launched the campaign "Study the theory of the dictatorship of the proletariat" in early 1975, shortly after the fourth National People's Congress. Though the campaign was a continuation of the Shanghai group's offensive against Chou En-lai and the rehabilitated Party leaders, begun in the Anti-Confucian/Anti-Lin Piao campaign, it was also sparked by the happenings at the fourth National People's Congress. The Congress confirmed Chou En-lai's efforts since the conclusion of the Cultural Revolution to restore stability and emphasize economic modernization.

Along with the issuance of a relatively pragmatic program, the fourth National People's Congress gave a number of the major positions in the reconstituted government to Party officials purged in the Cultural Revolution. Many of the rehabilitées were returned to the economic ministries. Teng Hsiao-p'ing became the first vice premier and chief of staff of the army. Even the minister of education, the supposed domain of the Shanghai group, was filled by Chou Jung-hsin, a close associate of Chou En-lai's and former vice minister of higher education before the Cultural Revolution. The Shanghai group fared poorly in the distribution of governmental posts. The Peking opera star Yu Hui-yung, an associate of Chiang Ch'ing's, became the minister of culture, but the only member of the Shanghai group to be given real power was Chang Ch'un-ch'iao, who became vice premier and head of the General Political Department of the People's Liberation Army.

Though Mao may have approved of attention to economic matters, the rehabilitation of specialists, managers, and administrators may have rekindled a persistent fear that had obsessed him throughout his career: the reestablishment of an elite bureaucratic class that would suppress the revolution. This fear was expressed in a number of new Maoist quotations that the Shanghai group cited to demonstrate Mao's blessing to its campaigns. These quotations supposedly were expounded in late December but first appeared in a *People's Daily* editorial on February 9, 1975, shortly after the close of the National People's Congress. Like all Mao's recent instructions they were ambiguously worded, but taken together they expressed concern with economic inequalities:

> Why did Lenin speak of exercising the dictatorship over the bourgeoisie? This question must be thoroughly understood. Lack of clarity on the question will lead to revisionism. This should be made known to the whole nation.
> China is a socialist country. Before liberation she was much the

same as capitalism. Even now she practices an eight-grade wage system, distribution to each according to his work and exchange by means of money, which are scarcely different from those in the old society. What is different is that the system of ownership has changed.

Chairman Mao also pointed out: so far as the bourgeois rights are concerned, "These can only be restricted under the dictatorship of the proletariat."

Taking off from these quotations, followers of the Shanghai group warned that emphasis on economic modernization would ensure the continued existence of, and even an increase in, bourgeois rights, defined as an unequal wage system, higher wages for skilled workers, and small private enterprise. These practices, they said, would produce a new class of skilled workers, cadres, intellectuals and well-to-do peasants who will hinder China's transition to an egalitarian communist system.

Liang Hsiao, the writing group of Peking University and Tsinghua that was under the control of the Shanghai group, asserted that to reach communism, "the proletariat must carry out the most radical rupture with traditional property relations."[1] In this article of early February, however, Liang Hsiao took an unhurried view of the time required to make that radical rupture in economic relations. "We cannot all at once get rid of the traditions and the birthmarks of capitalism."[2] In the interim, the rupture must be made ideologically rather than economically. Liang Hsiao and others called for repeated struggle against the bourgeoisie in the ideological realm because that is where the bourgeoisie exerts the most influence.

Equally important as ideological struggle was the use of ideology to stimulate production. Instead of material incentives, a Shanghai group writer, Chou Ssu, recommended symbolic incentives and volunteer labor in order to inspire the workers with such idealism that collective interest would override all thought of individual gain. He quoted Lenin: "Communist things only began to come into being when Saturday volunteer labor emerges. . . . This is not the neighborly help often seen in the rural areas, but large scale and organized labor to meet the needs of the whole country without remuneration."[3] Volunteer labor, also a feature of the Great Leap Forward, was this time not to be an uncontrolled mass movement from below, but organized labor under firm leadership from above. However, Chou Ssu stopped short of calling for its full adoption right away. He explained that it was the "first step" toward communism, but "today it is still necessary to apply the principle to each according to his work."⁴

Indirectly acknowledging that their proposals might be unpopular, several writers vowed that deemphasis on material incentives did not mean lack of concern with the material well-being of the working people. On the contrary, material well-being was to be raised by increasing production, but again they stressed that this would be accomplished by means of ideological rather than material incentives. As one article explained, "Our party has never used [material incentives] as a means to stimulate production, but has given priority to carrying out education on socialism and communism for the masses and the people."⁵

At the end of February, Yao Wen-yüan, a prominent figure in the Shanghai group, published his first signed article since the height of the Cultural Revolution seven years earlier. The article, entitled "On the Social Base of the Lin Piao Anti-Party Clique," was greeted with great fanfare in the media. Until the Dictatorship of the Proletariat campaign, members of the Shanghai group spoke through writing groups such as Liang Hsiao and Lo Ssu-ting rather than in their own names. Yao more vividly than the writing groups spelled out the social costs of the bureaucracy's approach to development. He predicted that if the new elite were not suppressed, they would usurp power as the "new bourgeoisie" had done in the Soviet Union.⁶

Though the "new bourgeoisie" was in the forefront, Yao declared that it was really the "old bourgeoisie," a euphemism for the pre–Cultural Revolution Party leadership returning to power, who were directing their activities. "Inexperienced newly engendered elements openly break the law, while cunning bourgeois elements of long-standing direct them from behind the scenes—this is the common occurrence of class struggle in our society today."⁷ With a premonition of what might happen to his associates and himself if the "old bourgeoisie" gained full power, Yao warned that they "will carry out a bloody suppression."⁸

To counter these forces, Yao called for the whittling away of bourgeois rights by means of struggle. But Yao's concept of struggle, unlike the earlier pronouncements of his followers, went beyond struggle against the bourgeoisie in the ideological sphere to include the bourgeoisie in the political sphere. "We must carry out such class struggle and two-line struggle and continually defeat the bourgeoisie and its agents working for revisionism, for a split, and for intrigues and conspiracy."[9]

Yao also leveled a new charge against the bourgeoisie, that of empiricism. He pointed out that Mao, in opposing the Peng Te-huai anti-Party group in 1959, had declared that "at present, the main danger is empiricism."[10] By asserting that Mao had warned of this danger many times after that, Yao implied that Mao was alarmed by the danger of empiricism in the present. Yao did not define empiricism, but he claimed that Mao sought to overcome empiricism by having the Central Committee and senior and intermediate Party cadres read Marxist-Leninist works. By implication, therefore, empiricism was defined as disregard for ideology and those who disregarded ideology were the top Party administrators.

Following Yao's signal, a number of articles subsequently appeared attacking empiricism. Those guilty of empiricism were accused of despising theory, that is, ideology, and regarding it as "outdated." The short commentary in *Red Flag* of April 1975 accused "empiricists" of rejecting the view that "the correctness or incorrectness of the ideological and political line decides everything."[11] They "belittle the guiding role of revolutionary theory in revolutionary practice."[12] Moreover, these "empiricists" were indirectly accused of opposing Cultural Revolution policies. They were depicted as resistant to new things. They could not discern the development of revolution and the changes in objective conditions, but used "old rules to handle new problems."[13]

Some articles attacking empiricism and urging struggle against the bourgeoisie repeated Yao's arguments, but a number of others called for even more radical action than Yao had proposed. Whereas Yao demanded struggle under Party direction, several articles called for struggle arising from the masses in the manner of the Cultural Revolution. One of these pointed out that Mao "inspired the vast numbers of the masses to expose our dark side in the open, all-around way and from the lower level upwards."[14] Whereas Yao had cautioned that the suppression of bourgeois rights should be done gradually, "step by step," and primarily in the ideological-political realm, a new Liang Hsiao article, in the same March 1975 *Red Flag* as Yao's, called for a struggle in the economic sphere against bourgeois rights with little mention of the gradual approach espoused in its February article.[15] A number of articles used quotations that recalled the uncontrolled revolutionary fervor of the Cultural Revolution. The phrase "no construction without destruction" was repeatedly cited, as well as the quotation from Mao that "before a brand new social system can be built on the site of the old, the site must be swept clean."[16]

There was also a demand to return China to the revolutionary spirit of the guerrilla days that was reminiscent of similar calls in the Great Leap Forward and the Cultural Revolution. Much attention was given to Mao's report at the Second Plenum of the Seventh Central Committee of March 5, 1949, in which he expressed the fear that once the Party was in power, the feelings of arrogance, inertia, love of pleasure, and distaste for hard work would prevail. Mao was quoted: "We must maintain the same vigor, the same revolutionary zeal and the same death-defying spirit as displayed in the past revolutionary war and carry our revolutionary work through to the end."[17]

In contrast to the guerrilla days, however, one article observed, "People do not compare their work, zeal and contributions to the revolution with those of others; they only compare with others for wages, treatment and material comfort, chasing after and extending bourgeois rights in every way."[18] At this time some comrades preferred to make revolution peacefully; if this practice continued, the article concluded, it would mean the end of the revolution. The demands for mass movements, guerrilla spirit, and radical change in economic relationships, however, were minor counterpoints to the dominant tone of controlled ideological and political struggle.

Another minor counterpoint at this time, from the other direction, subtly expressed the views of the fourth National People's Congress. The difference between these articles and those that sounded the dominant line was one of emphasis. With some exceptions, most articles approved of the gradual process of the whittling away of bourgeois rights. But a number of them, instead of emphasizing the inevitable overthrow of the bourgeoisie and the establishment of an egalitarian society, stressed the inevitability of inequality in the present early phase of socialism. As pointed out in a *Kwangming Daily* article, "These shortcomings are unavoidable in the first stage of Communism—the socialism that is born out of capitalist society. . . . The principle of each according to his work in the historical period of socialism still has its historical assumptions that must be implemented."[19] Furthermore, as opposed to the articles by the writers for the Shanghai group, this one emphasized the use of material incentives rather than ideology as the stimulus to productivity. "We must also make use of commodity, value, money price and other economic categories to develop a socialist economy in town and country and make use of the form of money as the means for the distribution of consumer goods to the individual."[20]

A *People's Daily* editorial of February 22, 1975, was more specific. It explained that in the near future the small commodity producers "cannot be driven out or crushed; we must live in harmony with them." They can be changed "only by very long, prolonged, slow, cautious and organized work."[21] The concept of "the middleman," a view of the Liu-ist early 1960s in which some writers described the Chinese masses as caught between the old and new society, was expressed in this editorial. Though the ordinary worker wanted revolution, he was not ready to carry it out in deed. Therefore, revolutionary action was not appropriate at present. "The worker is building the new society, but he has not yet become a new person who wipes out the mire of the old society. He is still standing in the mire of the old world. He can only dream of making a clean sweep of this mire. If we think that this can be done immediately, it is nothing more than a stupid pipe-dream which is in practice a pipe-dream of moving the socialist world into mid-air."[22]

As if in response to these two opposing counterpoints, Chang Ch'un-ch'iao, another leader of the Shanghai group, appeared in the April *Red Flag* with his first signed article since the Cultural Revolution. "Overall Dictatorship over the Bourgeois Class," like Yao's article, was given widespread and repeated coverage in the press and radio. It was presented as the authoritative interpretation of Mao's views on bourgeois rights. Although it appeared as an effort to direct the campaign along the "correct" path, the article was somewhat defensive; it rejected the call which some articles had issued in March of that year for a radical rupture in property relations.

Perhaps Chang was reflecting Mao's own reservations about moving too fast. Apparently Chang was also responding to expressed fears of another Great Leap Forward that were aroused by the campaign. He accused others of sabotaging the movement by spreading rumors of "communization," a reference to some of the radical practices introduced during the Commune movement of 1958, such as abolishing private plots. As if to dispel these fears and rein in more radical cadres, Chang vowed that the "wind 'of communization' . . . shall never be allowed to blow again."[23] He promised that even when the commune should finally be made the basic accounting unit (instead of the production team), it would remain under collective leadership, thus continuing "commodity production, exchange through money and distribution according to work."[24]

He rejected the Great Leap Forward volunteerist approach of achieving communism economically in a short period of time. There will be no quick transition, he stated, to common ownership and the abolition of private property; thus, in the short term, no basic change would occur. Instead, he presented a more traditional Marxist approach, affirming that communism will come only when an abundance of goods exists. Change will be slow because "our country does not yet have a great abundance"[25] of commodities. Thus, in the pursuit of communism's economic goals, Chang was more cautious than some of his associates. In this article, he was willing to tolerate the "harmful" effect of bourgeois rights in the economic sphere in order to develop the economic potential necessary to ensure the transition to communism. Still, he warned, there can be no backsliding nor widening of the gap in the distribution system.

While he cautioned against radical action in the economic field, Chang was not so cautious about action in the political and social arenas. Though he assured that one need not worry about the "wind of communization," he warned that "the bourgeois wind blowing among the Communists, particularly leading cadres, does the greatest harm. . . . "[26] His main concern was not so much with economic class enemies as with political enemies among the leading cadres. Chang granted that historically the slaveowners, landlord class, and old bourgeois class of the early days "did some good for humanity," but the new bourgeois class elements were instigators of evil.[27] "Poisoned by this evil wind, some people have got their heads full of bourgeois ideas . . . looking at everything as a commodity, themselves included."[28] They joined the Party just to move up the political ladder and benefit themselves and are "Communists in name, but new bourgeois elements in reality."[29]

Returning to the guerrilla-base paradigm, Chang compared the need to attack present-day bourgeoisie with the attack on the counterrevolutionaries in the guerrilla bases in the 1930s. He recounted an incident Mao cited in his speech "The Situation and Our Policy after the Victory of the War of Resistance against Japan." Mao described a fortified village held by a handful of counterrevolutionaries close to the Party headquarters at Pao-an that refused to surrender until the Red Army finally stormed it in 1936 and destroyed it. Chang compared this incident to the present situation, but whereas Mao had mentioned a handful of enemies, Chang speaks of many within numerous "fortified villages." The struggle against these enemies, he implied, would be protracted and violent. "Today, there are still many 'fortified villages,' held by the bourgeoisie; when one is destroyed, another will spring up and even if all have been destroyed except one, it will not vanish itself if the iron broom of the dictatorship of the proletariat does not reach it."[30]

Chang's milder attack on bourgeois rights in the economic sphere coupled with his intensified attack on the "bourgeoisie" in the political sphere were subsequently echoed by others in the press. The mass criticism group at Peking University and Tsinghua University explained that "the new bourgeois elements have an exceedingly greedy appetite and are not merely after economic interests. There is no doubt that they will try to take over political power."[31] These elements were accused of using the tactics of the Monkey King, who wormed into the belly of his adversary and took over the leadership—a charge Mao had leveled against Liu Shao-ch'i and his associates in the Cultural Revolution.

The Shanghai group's purpose was to create a hostile public opinion against the old and new elite. This was succinctly spelled out in the *Red Flag's* April 1975 commentary: "We simply want to create a strong public opinion among the masses to intimidate the class enemies and all social forces and social groups that oppose social revolution, and hate and sabotage socialist construction. We want to create such an opinion so that we can keep the capitalist forces from surfacing and make them give up."[32]

At the same time that they were building up public opinion against the bureaucratic leadership and the National People's Congress' stress on economic development, the Shanghai group reinterpreted the new Maoist quotations for their own purposes. Whereas Mao was primarily concerned with bourgeois rights in the economic sphere, Chang Ch'un-ch'iao and his followers were primarily concerned with expelling the bourgeoisie from the political sphere. The bureaucratic leadership and even Mao in the aftermath of the Cultural Revolution stressed the more traditional Marxist approach of change in the economic base in order to change the superstructure; the Shanghai group continued to stress the volunteerist approach of the Cultural Revolution of changing the superstructure in order to change the substructure.

Moreover, the Shanghai group attributed views to Mao that he had not expressed and, in fact, opposed. In the purge of the Shanghai group, it was revealed that at the end of March, Yao had revised a New China News Agency report to include a denunciation of empiricism and sent it to Mao for approval as an official document. Allegedly, Mao on April 23, 1975, responded by commenting that revisionism was not just empiricism but also includes dogmatism. Mao is quoted as having said, "It seems that the formulation should be: Oppose revisionism which includes empiricism and dogmatism. Both revise Marxism-Leninism. Don't mention just one while omitting the other." "Not many people in our Party really know Marxism-Leninism. Some who think they know it in fact do not know very much. They consider themselves always in the right and are ready at all times to lecture others. This in itself is a manifestation of a lack of knowledge of Marxism-Leninism."[33]

These statements of Mao were interpreted in 1977 as an attack on the Shanghai group, and Yao and Wang Hung-wen were charged with blocking their dissemination at the time. Whether these charges are accurate or not, Mao's statements in this campaign did not criticize empiricism nor advocate struggle against the bourgeoisie in the political sphere. The Shanghai group apparently took advantage of Mao's blessings on their drive against material incentives to influence public opinion in ways Mao had not intended.

Though Mao's comments on empiricism were not relayed to the public at that time, criticism of empiricism gradually petered out by the late spring of 1975. There was even direct criticism of those who acted radically or arbitrarily in the economic sphere. Whereas Chang Ch'un-ch'iao had inferred that some overzealous cadres had exceeded the prescribed measured effort to curb bourgeois rights, Chi Yen in the same April *Red Flag* directly called these cadres "leftists." He charged that those who advocated outright abolition of material incentives, rural private plots, sideline production, and free markets committed "leftist" mistakes.

Chi Yen acknowledged that material incentives caused inequality and a gap between mental and manual labor, but he rejected the Cultural Revolution approach of an all-out effort to close these differences. Instead, he proposed a more traditional Marxist approach to restrict bourgeois rights by producing favorable economic as well as ideological conditions. "By restriction, here, we mean gradually reducing the scope and role of bourgeois rights and actively creating ideological and material conditions for their eventual abrogation in the future. But they are unlikely to be abolished for a considerably long time to come."[34] The present effort was meant not to encourage but to resist the pressures to change the existing economic relationships. "Attention must be paid to guard against such sentiments which are divorced from reality."[35] Bourgeois rights were to be not only recognized but protected for a protracted period.

By June 1975, the Shanghai group's attack on bourgeois rights became muffled by this intensifying counterattack that stressed stability, unity, and economic development. A June *Red Flag* article criticized those who emphasized ideology in opposition to unity: "The idea and practice which set deepening the study of theory against the promotion of stability and unity are wrong."[36] People were advised to analyze in their areas and units the impact of the campaign's negative factors that "adversely affect stability and unity."[37] In contrast to its role in the initial stage of the campaign, the theory of the dictatorship of the proletariat was now used to promote, not undermine, stability and unity. Once again, Chou En-lai's economic program enunciated at the fourth National People's Congress came prominently to the fore. Several articles in the June *Red Flag* paraphrased Chou's National People's Congress speech. They underlined the need for "strengthening the material basis of the dictatorship of the proletariat, specifically modernizing our agriculture, industry, national defense, science and technology before the end of the century."[38]

The exact causes of the labor unrest that erupted in localized areas in the late spring and summer of 1975 are unclear. But it can be presumed that the contradictory arguments presented by the opposing factions in the campaign aggravated an already factionalized conflict in some industries between managers and workers who identified with the bureaucratic leaders on one hand and cadres and workers who identified with the Shanghai group on the other. As the unrest grew in the late summer and troops were dispatched to squash labor disputes, the campaign virtually died out.

From the very beginning, the campaign organizers, if not all of their followers, had accepted certain inherent limitations. Most of the articles, including those of Yao and Chang, did not have the messianic quality of the Cultural Revolution or the bitterness of the later campaigns against Teng Hsiao-p'ing. With some noted exceptions, most of the articles of the Shanghai group advocated a "step-by-step" narrowing of economic and social inequality. The complete elimination of money, wages, and all forms of private property was a long-range goal that was not to be implemented overnight. Both Yao and Chang had not yet incited through their writing groups mass movements against the bourgeoisie. Both talked more of study than of action in the implementation of their ideas. Hence, when the campaign appeared to provoke more disruptive acts in the economic realm than Mao and perhaps even its organizers originally intended, it was terminated.

Water Margin

In August 1975, the Shanghai group turned away from the broad economic and social issues of the Dictatorship of the Proletariat campaign to more narrowly focused factional issues when it launched its subsequent campaign against the popular novel *Water Margin*. It used discussion of this epic indirectly to attack specific individuals such as Chou En-lai, Teng Hsiao-p'ing, and the rehabilitées of the Cultural Revolution.

Deep as the ideological disputes were—as revealed in the campaign on the dictatorship of the proletariat—the personal cleavages in the top leadership were even more severe, as reflected in the campaign against *Water Margin*.

Rehabilitation of officials purged in the Cultural Revolution accelerated in the summer of 1975. Teng Hsiao-p'ing had restored a sizable number of his old associates to key governmental and Party positions, among them five provincial first Party secretaries. Several members of Peng Chen's former Peking Party Committee and the former chief of the General Staff of the army, Lo Jui-ch'ing, were seen around Peking. Some of these rehabilitées had personally been treated harshly by the Shanghai group during the Cultural Revolution. The group had every reason to believe that the rehabilitées might retaliate against them.

Like the Anti-Confucian/Anti-Lin Piao and Dictatorship of the Proletariat campaigns, the *Water Margin* campaign was couched in ideological phrases. But this drive was more directly concerned with personal animosities between the Shanghai group and Chou En-lai followers than were the other two movements. There was also less leeway for subtle rejoinder. The bureaucratic leaders were able to dull the attack, but they were less able than in the previous campaigns to use it to convey their own views. Even the editorials were less independent of the line taken in the *Water Margin* articles. What produced the Shanghai group's virtual monopoly of the media on ideological issues by the fall of 1975 is unclear. It could be that Teng Hsiao-p'ing's increasing power and proposals for a return to more conventional educational and scientific practices and increased material incentives may have pushed Mao to turn against him and throw his complete support to the Shanghai group's attack on Teng in the *Water Margin* campaign.

Like the tale of Robin Hood in the West, *Water Margin* had fired the imaginations of generations of Chinese. For centuries its heroes had been sung about in opera and its tale retold by storytellers in villages and marketplaces. Based on a series of popular tales and legends gradually compiled during the Yüan dynasty, the story concerns a peasant uprising in the Northern Sung dynasty in the early twelfth century, led by a group called the Hundred and Eight Heroes and made up of peasants and ex–government officials who were persecuted by corrupt officials. Originally their leader was Chao Kai, who had built up a base in the area of a water margin *(liang-shan).* He died of his wounds and was succeeded by Sung Chiang. Under Sung Chiang, the water margin rebels defeated a group of corrupt officials led by Kao Ch'iu. Following their victory, Sung Chiang accepted amnesty from the Emperor and then helped the regime quell other rebellions such as that of Fang La. So went the original version. At the end of the Ming dynasty, however, the scholar Chin Sheng-t'an condensed the novel from one hundred to seventy chapters and deleted the section where Sung Chiang accepted amnesty from the emperor and suppressed other rebellions. Chin's was the version used in the People's Republic of China until the Cultural Revolution.

Though they had rejected much of China's past, the Chinese Communists and Mao himself until 1975 extolled *Water Margin* as a progressive novel. Unlike their treatment of *Dream of the Red Chamber,* there had been no long exegesis or campaign to reinterpret *Water Margin* in Marxist-Leninist terms. It was accepted simply for what it was, a romantic account of heroic peasant rebels who waged battles against corrupt officials. Mao spoke of *Water Margin* as one of his favorite stories and it was one of the few books he carried along with him on the Long March. During the Cultural Revolution, however, as part of the renewed effort to reject China's "feudal" past, *Water Margin* was subjected to mild criticism. Sung Chiang was portrayed as a dual personality who was both revolutionary and compromising. Nonetheless, in 1972 *Water Margin* was recirculated as a good example of peasant rebellion against corrupt bureaucrats. Though Sung Chiang was criticized in some respects, *Water Margin* continued to be treated as a progressive book.

Suddenly, in the late summer of 1975, *Water Margin* was used to instill in the population hostility to the current bureaucratic leaders and their politics. *Dream of the Red Chamber* had been similarly used in the early 1950s to indoctrinate the population in Marxist values of class struggle. These classics were convenient media for changing attitudes because they were known by all, literate and illiterate; in the campaigns, however, the sense and characters of the stories were distorted in order to communicate a particular message.

Thus, on August 25, 1975, in a new bimonthly "Literature" column in the *Kwangming Daily,* Sung Chiang became a traitor and *Water Margin* abruptly became a reactionary novel. Sung Chiang was no longer portrayed as a hero or even a dual personality, but as one who betrayed the revolution because he capitulated to the Emperor and suppressed peasant rebellions. His battles against corruption in government were no longer praised because he only eliminated corrupt officials but did not change the political system and its values. This "Literature" column was prefaced by an editor's note which explained that the story of *Water Margin* demonstrated how a revolution ends in failure because it "opposed only corrupt officials and not the emperor." Unless the top leadership is overthrown, the revolution is bound to fail. The study of *Water Margin,* therefore, "will enable people . . . to draw a clear line between revolution and capitulation."[39]

"Capitulation" was further defined in the "Literature" column that appeared next in the *Kwangming Daily* on August 30, a week ahead of schedule, written by Liang Hsiao. It defined "capitulation" not only as surrender to the emperor but as a downplaying of struggle and conflict, an implicit criticism of Chou En-lai's approach since the conclusion of the Cultural Revolution. Liang Hsiao attacked the view "that as long as we pledge allegiance to the Emperor, oppose corrupt ministers and rely on several 'good officials,' all contradictions will be wiped out and all problems will be resolved." Liang Hsiao also criticized the top leadership for tolerating corrupt officials. Kao Ch'iu, an apparent analogue to Liu Shao-ch'i, committed his crime "under the indulgence and connivance" of the emperor. Yet the "Emperor was invariably embellished as the wisest and most august ruler."[40] Because the emperor was not removed and corrupt officials continued to govern, the revolution failed.

The day following the Liang Hsiao article, August 31, 1975, the *People's Daily* appeared with its first article on *Water Margin,* "Commenting on *Water Margin*" by Chu Fang-ming. It presented a vivid description of the power struggle at the water margin that could be interpreted as a description of the current power struggle. After Sung Chiang, an obvious analogue to Chou En-lai and/or Teng Hsiao-p'ing, was given amnesty by the emperor, "he used persuasion and force to reject and suppress the revolutionaries." At the same time "he recruited deserters, renegades, hereditary aristocrats, generals of the royal court, and landlords and assigned them to important positions."[41] Chu warned that capitulationists like Sung Chiang who look like revolutionaries but were actually counterrevolutionaries had appeared in revolutionary ranks throughout history and in the present.

The reader would have no trouble, as he might in the more complex Anti-Confucian/Anti–Lin Piao campaign, in connecting these *Water Margin* "counterrevolutionaries" to present "counterrevolutionaries." Had not Chou En-lai and Teng Hsiao-p'ing suppressed the radicals and brought back purged officials, as was so evident at the fourth National People's Congress? Moreover, it was well known in official circles that when Teng was secretary of the Southwest Region in the period after the communist takeover, he had conferred names of the heroes of *Water Margin* on his associates and conferred on himself the title Sung Chiang. The description of Sung Chiang and his associates was more obviously analogous to Chou En-lai, Teng Hsiao-p'ing, and their associates than were the more erudite allusions used in the two previous campaigns.

Then, in a September 4, 1975, editorial in the *People's Daily,* new Maoist quotations on *Water Margin* suddenly appeared.

Mao's first statement merely summarized what had already been said in the August articles. "The merit of the book *Water Margin* lies precisely in the portrayal of capitulation. It serves as teaching material by negative example to help all people recognize capitulationists." But his next statement made certain that Mao would be identified not with the emperor but with Chao Kai, the original founder of the peasant movement before it was taken over by renegades such as Sung Chiang. "*Water Margin* is against corrupt officials, but not against the emperor. It excludes Chao Kao from the [Hundred and Eight Heroes]."

Mao then expressed the negative view of Sung Chiang that had been presented in August. "Sung Chiang pushes capitulationism, practices revisionism, changes Chao Kao's Chü-i [Justice] Hall to Chung-i [Loyalty] Hall and accepts the offer of amnesty and enlistment. Sung Chiang's struggle against Kao Ch'iu is a struggle waged by one faction against another within the landlord class. As soon as he surrenders, Sung Chiang goes to fight Fang La." Mao's view, which charged that Chao Kai's principles had been changed by his successor Sung Chiang, appears to accept the Shanghai group's argument that like Chao Kai's successors, Mao's successors perverted his revolutionary principles.

Though these statements were later dated to August 14, 1975, there is no explanation of why they had not been cited at the start of the campaign in August rather than almost two weeks later. In the purge of the Shanghai group, it was charged that Yao Wen-yüan had delayed the publication of Mao's quotations in order to orient the campaign to serve the interests of the Shanghai group. Still, the quotations were presented in an editorial that was more moderate in tone than were the August articles. Moreover, it expressed a desire to limit the campaign and keep it strictly under the control of the Party, an approach that more likely reflected Mao's wishes than that of the Shanghai group. It warned against turning the campaign into another Cultural Revolution with another Maoist quotation which in the campaign against the Gang of Four was cited as an example of Mao's efforts to rein in the radicals: "Practice Marxism and not revisionism; unite and don't split; be open and aboveboard; don't intrigue and conspire."[42]

Nevertheless, this campaign that dominated China's major journals and newspapers from September through November was more in tune with the articles of August than with those of the more moderate editorial of September 4. It, like the Dictatorship of the

Proletariat campaign, went beyond the limits that Mao had set in his statements. Here again, the sense of Mao's instructions as presented in quotations was distorted by the Shanghai group. There is evidence that Mao was once more becoming disenchanted with Teng Hsiao-p'ing, but there is no evidence that he sought to attack Chou En-lai. As the campaign progressed, however, there was little doubt that it was directed against Chou as well as Teng.

Also, though Mao did not mention the character Lu Chün-i in his statements, much attention was given to him in the campaign. Repeatedly and increasingly, it was stressed that Sung Chiang had put Lu Chün-i, labeled "an out-and-out reactionary," into the number two position in the political hierarchy to "consolidate the rule of the capitulationist line at the water margin."[43] Sung Chiang invited Lu to the water margin "not for the sake of transforming him into a leader of the revolutionary peasant army, but for the sake of making use of his reactionary character and using him as a chief accomplice to push his capitulationist line."[44] Originally, Sung Chiang had wanted to put Lu in the number one position, but the firm opposition of Chao Kao and especially of his followers compelled Sung Chiang to put him in the second position.

Allegorically, this interpretation of *Water Margin* charges that Chou brought in Teng to help him retreat from Cultural Revolution policies and had even wanted to put Teng in charge, but was stopped by Mao and the Shanghai group. Without the insertion of Lu Chün-i into the discussion, the reader would have identified Teng with Sung Chiang, but with so much attention given to Sung Chiang's having made Lu Chün-i the number two official under him, the identification of Sung Chiang with Chou was made explicit. The *Water Margin* campaign was used to project an image of the Shanghai group as being in alliance with Mao as fighters against reaction.

In the context of the campaign, Chou and Teng were treated as traitors. Most articles stressed that the enemy within the revolutionary ranks was much more dangerous than the enemy without. Officials such as Kao Ch'iu need not be feared because their corruption and brutality were obvious, but leaders such as Sung Chiang subtly subverted the revolution before others became aware of it.

Lu Hsün was repeatedly quoted on this subject: "In most cases the revolution is ended with the infiltration of opportunists. This also means that its insides have been eaten through by worms."[45]

Liang Hsiao directly related these opportunists to capitulationists in the present. Though Lu Hsün made his critique in 1929, it "was a militant manifesto and criticism of the capitulationist faction of the time and we still feel it is correct when read today."[46] The lesson to be drawn from *Water Margin* was that a fortress was most vulnerable when attacked from within—as was happening within the current regime.

While Chao Kai, who was presented as the embodiment of revolutionary spirit, was alive, Sung Chiang did not act openly. He played a dual game. He openly showed respect to Chao, but secretly infiltrated his associates and covertly sabotaged the movement. In reality, he made Chao Kai "a commander without an army."[47] Disregarding Chao Kai's preeminent position, Sung Chiang "went ahead to give assignments and make decisions arbitrarily by himself. . . . He purposely left out Chao Kai, cultivated his own prestige and paved the way for the usurpation of leadership."[48] In time, Chao Kai was reduced to a figurehead while Sung Chiang wielded the real power. He then filled the administration with his own men and made the policy decisions. This theme, with its obvious allusion to a weakening Mao and an increasingly powerful Teng Hsiao-p'ing leadership, was given more and more attention as the campaign evolved.

The campaign was also used to denounce Chou's and Teng's efforts to curtail the political power of the Shanghai group. It criticized Sung Chiang's acts of vengeance against Chao Kai's closest supporters such as Wu Yung, Li K'uei, and the Yüan brothers. Though some of these characters in the actual *Water Margin* story were ambivalent and even friends of Sung Chiang, in the campaign they are depicted as representing the interests of the masses and as being suppressed by Sung Chiang. At the beginning of the revolution, the Yüan brothers were seated among the first ten officials at meetings of the water margin rebels. But in a short time the "deserters and renegades" whom Sung Chiang brought into the movement were placed ahead of the Yüan brothers in the hierarchy. Sung Chiang kept Chao Kai uninformed about this reassignment of positions. This scenario resembles the experience of the Shanghai group at the fourth National People's Congress, where, with the exception of Chang Ch'un-ch'iao, its members received few important positions while rehabilitated Party members gained prominence in the reconstituted state government.

Anticipating what might happen to them when Mao died, the Shanghai group, through the *Water Margin* campaign, warned of their impending demise unless action was taken against the current leadership. When Chao Kai died, "revolutionary generals, like the Yüan brothers, who adhered to Chao Kai's revolutionary line were oppressed and their military powers curbed in every possible way."[49] Though Chao Kai in his directives had expressed his opposition to Sung Chiang as his heir, his directives were ignored. Consequently, as soon as Chao Kai died, Sung Chiang made him into an idol in order to fool the population while he enthroned himself and his "reactionary" associates. He and his associates then demoted and executed those who had upheld Chao Kai's line. Even though action was subsequently taken against Teng Hsiao-p'ing, this prophecy of its own demise by the Shanghai group proved accurate.

Sung Chiang and his associates were charged with obstructing the revolutionary movement not only because of their thirst for vengeance and power, but because of their antirevolutionary stance. Their water margin uprising did not succeed because although it eliminated corrupt officials, it "did not touch the economic base and superstructure."[50]

In this context, the phrase "capitulation to the emperor" could be interpreted as the unwillingness to change the prevailing economic and political system. While Sung Chiang agreed with Chao Kai and his associates on the need to throw out corrupt officials, he did not agree that the main focus of the water margin struggle should be on the question "Whither the revolution?"[51] Like Chou En-lai in the Cultural Revolution, he was willing to go along with the purge of a group of "corrupt" officials, but was unwilling to carry the revolution through to the end and abandoned it halfway. It was charged that Sung Chiang regarded all revolutionary activity as being "totally devoid of respect of law and order and simply unthinkable."[52] He refused to violate the laws and institutions of the state and devised all ways and means to uphold them and use them to suppress the insurgents, a description of first Chou's activities and then Teng's in the aftermath of the Cultural Revolution.

By contrast, Chao Kai's associates, the analogues to the Shanghai group, were described as not only more revolutionary than Sung Chiang, that is, Chou and Teng, but even more revolutionary than their leader, Chao Kai, that is, Mao himself. In the campaign, little attention was given to Chao Kai's revolutionary feats, but much attention was given to those of his followers. They not only opposed existing laws and institutions in their ideology, but "were not afraid to manifest the heroic spirit of insurgent peasants by destroying them in action."[53]

The example was given of Li K'uei, who is not merely against corrupt officials but "holds sovereign power in contempt and looks on state laws as dung and dirt."[54] Since Chao Kai's associates believed that corruption was produced by the existing political and economic system, the only way to rid government of corrupt officials was to overthrow the system that produced them. Corruption, bureaucratism, and elitism were not aberrations or the doing of certain "reactionary individuals," but were inherent in the prevailing system. To purge corrupt officials only helped to stabilize the existing system because the elimination of corrupt officials lessened the resistance of the peasants and, therefore, weakened their revolutionary will.

Such action was described as comparable to that of the Ming official Hai Jui, the historic villain of the Cultural Revolution, who ousted corrupt officials and placated the masses, but continued the exploitation of the peasants by the bureaucracy. As a December *Kwangming Daily* article pointed out, "the logic of the peasant revolution is that those who oppose corrupt officials also oppose the emperor . . . but opposing corrupt officials and serving the emperor loyally are basically antagonistic."[55]

This campaign, therefore, advocated more radical action than either the previous campaign on the Dictatorship of the Proletariat or Mao had advocated. Where that campaign had recommended the gradual change of the economic system along with ideological struggle against the leadership, this one advocated complete overthrow of the existing political and economic system. It was the Cultural Revolution approach of changing the personnel in order to change the prevailing political and economic arrangements because "without the seizure of power, it is not possible to touch fundamentally the economic base and superstructure."[56] It legitimized once again the Cultural Revolution's slogan "rebellion is justified." Revolution cannot rely on the evolution of economic forces; therefore, the leadership must be purged in order to change the system. Here again, Mao may have wanted to dispense with some of the "capitalist roaders in the Party" but not with the bureaucratic leadership itself. His statements in this period preached unity and denounced factionalism.

Unlike the Anti-Confucian/Anti-Lin Piao and Dictatorship of the Proletariat campaigns, there was only slight representation of the moderate position within the confines of the *Water Margin* campaign itself. Some articles were very academic, as if they were purposely contrived to divert the discussion toward historical rather than current questions. For example, along with descriptions of *Water Margin* as an aborted peasant rebellion, there were erudite discussions on whether peasant rebellions should or should not be considered part of the class struggle and, therefore, a motive force of history. As Peng Chen had been charged with diverting the attack on Hai Jui into an academic discussion in the Cultural Revolution, so Teng Hsiao-p'ing was charged in the *Water Margin* campaign with using the same device.

While these methods were subtle and, to the uninitiated, perhaps hard to perceive, the bureaucratic leaders used more direct methods of resistance outside the *Water Margin* campaign. The campaign developed in the cultural and educational realms where these leaders had less control, but it did not spill over into the economic and political sphere where they had more control. Some factories and communes in Shanghai and in a few other areas discussed *Water Margin*, but this campaign generally did not have the widespread mass participation of the Anti-Confucian and Dictatorship of the Proletariat campaigns. Thus, while the bureaucratic leaders had less leverage in the media at this time, they had more in the economic realm and even in the media discussion of nonideological issues.

The success of the bureaucratic leadership in limiting the campaign to the cultural realm was reflected in the November issue of *Red Flag*. Alongside the articles on *Water Margin* were several on the need for agricultural mechanization, stability, and unity. While the *Water Margin* articles stressed that criticism of *Water Margin* and study of the dictatorship of the proletariat would help the economy, these articles made little mention of *Water Margin*. Instead of ideology, these articles emphasized that "mechanization not only provides the only way to develop large-scale socialist agriculture, but is the important link in . . . achieving modernization of agriculture, industry, national science and technology."[57] Also, production would increase not because of the overthrow of capitulationists as learned through the study of *Water Margin,* but because "if we foster the idea of agriculture as the foundation, organizing initiative of industry to support agriculture, [and] have old factories lead new ones . . . it is possible to form a stronger production capacity.''[58] The articles on production and mechanization reflected Chou En-lai's view of development, not that of the Shanghai group.

Moreover, these articles criticized the Shanghai group, though not with the same passion the Shanghai group itself used in the *Water Margin* campaign against the bureaucratic leaders. They pointed out that economic development is dependent on unity and stability, but a small handful "try to create confusion, sow seeds of discord and spread rumors in order to fish in troubled waters.''[59] Despite the disturbance of this small handful, however, the approach toward them, unlike the crusading zeal advocated toward the "capitulationists" in the *Water Margin* campaign, was to be the mild treatment of "cure the sickness to save the patient.''[60] Farm mechanization and increased output needed stability, unity, and discipline. The crusading zeal espoused by the *Water Margin* campaign could only undermine the current efforts to impose discipline and oppose factionalism.

In addition to the press attention given to agricultural mechanization and economic development, coverage was also given to the fortieth anniversary of the Long March, in which the joint editorials in the army and party newspapers paid respect to the martyrs of the Long March and by extension to the veterans still alive, among them Teng Hsiao-p'ing and the rehabilitées. This drive, along with the wide coverage given to the agricultural mechanization movement, was launched about the same time as the *Water Margin* campaign and appeared to be a concerted effort to relegate the *Water Margin* campaign to minor status. But by December 1975, the *Water Margin* campaign became absorbed into a more direct movement against Teng Hsiao-p'ing's educational policies and, after Chou's death, against Teng Hsiao-p'ing himself. Then coverage of the agricultural development drive and the Long March virtually disappeared.

After the death of Chou En-lai and the purge of Teng Hsiao-p'ing, the *Water Margin* discussion was revived in the summer of 1976. Now, it no longer appeared to be directed against Chou and Teng so much as against Hua Kuo-feng. The same incident was recounted of Sung Chiang handing over his position to Lu Chün-i. This incident could still be applied to the Chou-Teng relationship, but in the context of the summer of 1976, with conflict building between the Shanghai group and the bureaucratic leaders now led ostensibly by Hua Kuo-feng, it was more likely directed against him.

Moreover, the 1976 scenario appeared more applicable to the Teng-Hua relationship than to the Chou-Teng relationship. Sung Chiang wanted to hand over his post to Lu Chün-i because "although he already occupied the number one position, his position . . . is insecure."[61] But this transfer of power was termed a trick to keep power away from the revolutionaries. As before, *Water Margin* was called a good negative teaching example, but this time it was not so much because it taught one how to discern capitulation. Rather, it taught that "conceding one's post" to someone else was done to maintain the status quo. The lesson to be drawn was that there was collusion between Hua Kuo-feng and Teng Hsiao-p'ing's followers against the Shanghai group. This resurrection of the *Water Margin* campaign, however, was cut short by Mao's death and the subsequent purge of the Gang of Four.

The Effectiveness of Media Campaigns in Political Struggle

The Dictatorship of the Proletariat and *Water Margin* campaigns raise the question of how much a media onslaught of articles and editorials, accompanied by forums and discussions in universities, factories, and communes, can be transformed into actual power. Can a campaign create public opinion for or against a certain policy, or certain individuals, to the point where that public opinion will influence policy makers?

It is true that one objective of these campaigns—denial of the premiership to Teng Hsiao-p'ing—was achieved, but that denial had more to do with Mao's opposition than with the campaigns themselves. The other objectives of these campaigns—rejection of pragmatic methods and of the bureaucratic leadership—were not achieved. It is true that the pragmatic approach became unrepresented in the media with the direct attack on Teng in 1976, but that did not mean this approach was disregarded in important economic and political decisions. The minister of education, Chou Jung-hsin, was purged at the time that Teng was attacked, but the bureaucratic leadership continued in office virtually unscathed. No matter how zealous and persistent their efforts, the Shanghai group's domination of the media could not be translated into political power because they did not have the full support of their leader Mao and were opposed by the political-economic-military apparatus.

Still, their domination of the media was sufficient to set the general ideological tone and prevent the opposing faction from publicly defending its views in a sustained and extensive way. Their impact, therefore, was negative. They could create the impression of great popular indignation against certain policies and certain people, but could not create popular support for their policies or people. Thus, they created the impression of popular indignation against the dismantling of Cultural Revolution programs that may have slowed the dismantling of such programs in the short run but did not stop their dismantling. At the same time, they could not build up public support for continuation of Cultural Revolution policies and for their own leadership.

That the Shanghai group was purged without much public resistance and, in fact, with ostensible public delight indicates not only the unpopularity of their programs and rejection of their leadership, but also their ineffectuality in influencing public opinion. They failed in part because the bureaucratic faction's ability to insert its views into the media made it impossible for them to build up a unified public opinion in support of their cause.

It appears that public opinion was confused rather than congealed by the messages conveyed by the media. In the Dictatorship of the Proletariat campaign, as in the prior Anti-Confucian campaign, the public was assaulted by a bifurcated ideological offensive. Each faction used the discussions of Confucianism-Legalism and then of Marxist ideology to communicate its views and struggle against each other.

In the *Water Margin* campaign, the public received a message on ideological issues that conflicted with the one it received on economic issues. Confronted with an onslaught of contradictory, erudite, ideological exegeses, there is evidence that the public turned off both of them or made their own interpretations. Criticisms were made in the *Water Margin* campaign of individuals and groups who refused to comment on the *Water Margin* with the excuse that their work gave them no time or that the discussion had nothing to do with them.[62] We may speculate that the nonparticipation and diverse interpretations of events caused in part by the contradictory media campaigns of the post–Cultural Revolution may prove more destructive to the reimposition of the Party's overall ideological control than will any other legacy of the era of the Shanghai group.

NOTES

1. Liang Hsiao, "It Is Necessary To Enforce the Dictatorship of the Proletariat over the Bourgeoisie," *People's Daily*, February 10, 1975, p. 1. *Foreign Broadcast Information Service*, February 11, 1975, p. E3.

2. Ibid.

3. Chou Ssu, "This Historical Mission of the Dictatorship of the Proletariat: Study of 'A Great Unprecedented Action,' " *Hung-Ch'i* [Red Flag] February 1975, p. E7.

4. Ibid., p. E5.

5. Ching Hua, "Restrict the Bourgeois Rights and Consolidate the Dictatorship of the Proletariat," *People's Daily*, February 28, 1975; *Survey of People's Republic of China Press*, no. 5810, p. 138.

6. Yao Wen-yüan, "On the Social Base of the Lin Piao Anti-Party Clique," *Peking Review*, no. 10, March 7, 1975, p. 6.

7. Ibid., p. 7.

8. Ibid., p. 6.

9. Ibid., p. 8.

10. Ibid., p. 9.

11. A short commentary in *Red Flag*, reprinted in *People's Daily*, April 3, 1975, p. 1: *Foreign Broadcast Information Service*, April 3, 1975, p. E3.

12. Ibid.

13. Ling Yüeh, "To Continue the Revolution, It Is Necessary to Overcome Empiricism," *People's Daily*, April 12, 1975; *Survey of People's Republic of China Press*, no. 5843, p. 150.

14. Nan Yü, "The Masses of People Must Be Relied upon to Consolidate the Proletarian Dictatorship," *People's Daily*, March 16, 1975, p. 2.

15. Liang Hsiao, "Criticize Following the Beaten Path and Sticking to the Old, Persevere in Continued Revolution," *Red Flag*, March 1975; *Selections from People's Republic of China Magazines*, no. 814–815, pp. 44–45.

16. Mao Tse-tung, "Introductory Note to a Serious Lesson," quoted in Chou Ssu, *Foreign Broadcast Information Service*, February 10, 1975, p. E6.

17. Yen Ch'ün, "Forever Preserve the Proletarian Revolutionary Spirit," *Red Flag*, March 1975; *Selections from People's Republic of China Magazines*, no. 814–815, p. 54.

18. Ibid., p. 55.

19. Ch'i Hsien, "The Dictatorship of the Proletariat Must Restrict Bourgeois Rights," *Kuangming Jihpao* [Kwangming Daily], February 18, 1975, *Survey of People's Republic of China Press*, no. 5819, p. 119.

20. Ibid.

21. "Marx, Engels and Lenin on the Dictatorship of the Proletariat," *Survey of People's Republic of China Press*, no. 5803, p. 40.

22. Ibid.

23. Chang Ch'un-ch'iao, "On Exercising All-Round Dictatorship over the Bourgeois Class," *Red Flag,* April 1975; Foreign Languages Press, 1975, p. 21.

24. Ibid., p. 22.

25. Ibid., p. 21.

26. Ibid., p. 23.

27. Ibid., p. 23.

28. Ibid., p. 23.

29. Ibid., p. 23.

30. Ibid., pp. 14–15.

31. "The Dictatorship of the Proletariat and the Renegade Lin Piao," *Red Flag,* May 1975; *Selections from People's Republic of China Magazines,* no. 823–824, p. 26.

32. "Study Well and Have a Good Grasp of Integrating Theory with Practice," *Red Flag,* April 1975; *People's Daily,* April 3, 1975, p. 1; *Foreign Broadcast Information Service,* April 3, 1975, p. E4.

33. "The Whole Story about the Farce of Opposing Empiricism Staged by the Gang of Four," New China News Agency, March 2, 1977; *Foreign Broadcast Information Service,* March 7, 1977, p. E19.

34. Chi Yen, "The Weapon for Restricting Bourgeois Rights," *Red Flag,* April 1975; *Foreign Broadcast Information Service,* April 9, 1975, p. E3.

35. Ibid., p. E6.

36. Yüeh Hai, "Deepen the Study of Theory, Promote Stability and Unity," *Red Flag,* June 1975; *Selections from People's Republic of China Magazines,* n. 827–828, p. 3.

37. Ibid., p. 2.

38. Ibid., p. 5.

39. Liu Chen-hsiang and Nien Ching-hua, People's Liberation Army members, "*Water Margin* Is Teaching Material Using a Negative Example to Advertise Capitulationism," *Kwangming Daily,* August 23, 1975, p. 2.

40. Liang Hsiao, "Lu Hsun Has Effectively Criticized *Water Margin*—'A Study of the Evolution of Rascals,' " *Kwangming Daily,* August 30, 1975, p. 2.

41. Chu Fang-ming, "Commenting on *Water Margin,*" *People's Daily,* August 31, 1975, p. 2.

42. *People's Daily* editorial, "Promote Comments on *Water Margin,*" September 4, 1975; *Foreign Broadcast Information Service,* September 4, 1975, p. E13.

43. Po Ching, "Commenting on the Capitulationist Sung Chiang," *People's Daily,* September 17, 1975; *Survey of People's Republic of China Press,* no. 5943, p. 139.

44. Ku Feng, "*Water Margin* Is a Black Specimen Publicizing the Extolling Combine Two Into One," *Kwangming Daily,* December 9, 1975; *Survey of People's Republic of China Press,* no. 6022, p. 10.

45. Cheng Chi-shen, "About the Offer of a Plan by Hou Meng," *Kwangming Daily,* November 28, 1975; *Survey of People's Republic of China Press,* no. 2999, p. 16.

46. Liang Hsiao, "Lu Hsun Has Effectively Criticized *Water Margin,*" p. 2.

47. An Chan, "Comment on Sung Chiang, the Capitulationist," *Red Flag,* October 1, 1975; *Selections from People's Republic of China Magazines,* no. 844–845, p. 50.

48. Preface to the reprint of *Water Margin* (People's Literature Publishing

House, September 1975); *Foreign Broadcast Information Service,* November 4, 1975, p. E4.

49. Chen Ta-kang, "On the Yüan Brothers," *Study and Criticism,* no. 9, September 9, 1975; *Selections from People's Republic of China Magazines,* no. 842, October 14, 1975, p. 8.

50. Mass criticism groups of Peking University and Tsinghua University, "A Textbook by Negative Example Advertising Capitulation—A Critique of *Water Margin,*" *Red Flag,* no. 9, 1975; *Foreign Broadcast Information Service,* September 9, 1975, p. E4.

51. Wu Chien-fan, "Secrets of the 'Stone Tablets with Heaven's Command,' " *People's Daily,* September 24, 1975; *Survey of People's Republic of China Press,* no. 5953, p. 114.

52. Mass criticism groups of Peking University and Tsinghua University, *Foreign Broadcast Information Service,* September 9, 1975, p. E1.

53. Yüan Liang, "Sung Chiang and 'Law and Institutions,' " *Kwangming Daily,* November 9, 1975; *Survey of People's Republic of China Press,* no. 5982, p. 40.

54. Mass criticism groups of Peking University and Tsinghua University, "A Song Singing the Praise of the Capitulationist Line," *People's Daily,* September 5, 1975; *Survey of People's Republic of China Press,* no. 2938, p. 165.

55. Ku Feng, "*Water Margin* Is a Black Specimen," p. 8.

56. Che Pien, "Historical Materialism Brooks No Distinction," *Kwangming Daily,* September 25, 1975; *Survey of People's Republic of China Press,* no. 5955, p. 83.

57. Tan Fang, "Quicken the Pact of Farm Mechanization," *Red Flag,* November 1, 1975, *Selections from People's Republic of China Magazines,* no. 848–849, p. 25.

58. Ibid., p. 29.

59. Pa Shan, "Develop the Excellent Situation of Stability and Unity," *Red Flag,* November 1975; *Selections from People's Republic of China Magazines,* no. 844–845, p. 82.

60. Ibid., p. 83.

61. Jen Hsiu-ling and Chao Shen-t'ien, "What Is Sung Chiang's Abdication For?" *People's Daily,* July 20, 1976; *Survey of People's Republic of China Press,* no. 6148, p. 1.

62. Party branch of Palimiao Brigade, Kansu, "Set the Masses in Motion in Commenting on *Water Margin,*" *Red Flag,* no. 12, 1975; *Selections from People's Republic of China Magazines,* no. 852–853, p. 25.

9

Cultural Revolution and Cultural Change

Lowell Dittmer

You can't just force people to believe in these things, right? You can't force people to believe in anything; I spoke about this the day before yesterday. In matters of the mind, you can't force a person to believe; nor can you force a person not to believe.[1]

—MAO TSE-TUNG

The purpose of this chapter is to analyze the Cultural Revolution as a series of communication events that were politically superimposed in order to accelerate cultural change.

We begin our inquiry with an examination of Mao's motives for launching the movement, attempting to reconstruct the theory and method of psychocultural change implicit in his relevant statements. We next look at how his ideas were communicated in the context of the mass movement and at the impact they had on its participants. Finally we shall review and assess the attempt by the Maoist group to continue the Cultural Revolution from 1969 to 1976 in order to preserve the revolutionary gains for the successor generation. The study is based on a combination of documentary and media sources and on interviews conducted in 1977 with recent Chinese refugees in Hong Kong.

The Maoist Theory of Cultural Change

In the decade between Krushchev's secret denunciation of Stalin and the launching of the Great Proletarian Cultural Revolution, the gravest threat to the continuation of the Chinese revolution was, in Mao's view, "revisionism." As Mao and his colleagues elaborated this term in their polemics with the Communist Party of the Soviet Union, it came to refer not merely to the alteration of Marxist doctrine but to a congeries of social trends and policy tendencies that seemed to conspire to turn the clock back on the revolution and effect a gradual, nonviolent counterrevolution back to capitalism.

In his contributions to the Sino-Soviet polemic, Mao tended to attribute this complex of trends to the leadership. He was to continue to do so when he brought the antirevisionist polemic home to China in the form of the Cultural Revolution's mass criticism of elites. Nonetheless, implicit in Mao's various statements is a set of assumptions which point to a coherent argument about the psychological origins of revisionism among both elites and masses.

Mao's resort to an implicit psychology betrayed his growing inability to make sense of such tendencies within the theoretical vocabulary of classical Marxism. Persisting capitalist tendencies could no longer be based on capitalist ownership of the means of production, for private property had been essentially expropriated by the end of the Party's first decade in power.

Djilas offered an alternative materialist explanation. He defined ownership as tantamount to "the right of profit and control," which implied that the Party apparatus had become the functional equivalent of the bourgeoisie by dint of its "monopolistic administration and control of national income and national goods."[2] Although he occasionally flirted with this notion (as when he referred to bureaucrats as a "class"),[3] Mao was unwilling to accept its ultimately anarchist implications, but felt impelled to grasp for more subjective, attitudinal criteria.

The key attitude to which Mao turned as a substitute for ownership as a defining criterion of revisionism was *selfishness*.[4] An attack upon selfishness was entirely consistent with Chinese philosophical and cultural traditions and could therefore be relied upon to provide an overwhelming natural constituency. Many other revisionist deviations could be seen to derive from selfishness: Inequality was of course considered a direct consequence of selfishness by a few, but bureaucratism was also implicated because it tended to isolate the self from the masses, as did nearly all intellectual pursuits. Rational calculation of costs and benefits was inherently self-interested. Even the desire to "extinguish" various forms of struggle in favor of compromise betrayed an obsession with self-control, with not letting the self go in conflictual situations, all of which arose from a selfish desire for personal survival and well-being. The negative disposition of "revisionist" elites toward mass criticism and cultural revolution betokened their selfish desire to preserve their own power and suppress all dissent.

At the roots of selfishness, according to Mao, was the emotion of fear. One refused to share, to open oneself to the masses, because of one's fear of losing something. Mao referred to such emotions in explicitly therapeutic terms as "encumbrances," mental "baggage":

> "To get rid of the baggage" means to free our minds of many encumbrances. Many things may become baggage, may become encumbrances, if we cling to them blindly and uncritically. . . . Thus, a prerequisite for maintaining close links with the masses and making fewer mistakes is to examine one's baggage, to get rid of it and so to emancipate the mind.[5]

Mao's works are filled with embittered testimonials to the crippling effects of fear upon the Chinese masses. "What should we not fear? We should not fear heaven. We should not fear ghosts. We should not fear the dead. We should not fear the bureaucrats. We should not fear the militarists. We should not fear the capitalists."[6]

In 1955, he chided colleagues who had approved the dissolution of 200,000 agricultural production cooperatives for their excessive caution: "Too much carping, unwarranted complaints, boundless anxiety and countless taboos—all this they take as the right policy in the rural areas."[7] His works contain numerous tributes to the glory of fearlessness, which Mao equates with potency. "He who is not afraid of death by a thousand cuts dares to unhorse the emperor," he quotes.[8] And in his poetry Mao makes similar references. In "Changsha," for instance, he alludes to the likely reason for his infatuation with youth:

> We are young,
> sharp as a flower wind, ripe,
> candid with a scholar's bright blade
> and unafraid.[9]

And in "The Long March," Mao praises the fearlessness of the Red Army:

> The Red Army is not afraid of hardship on the long march,
> Ten thousand waters and a thousand mountains are nothing.
> . . . .
> The far snows of Minshan only make us happy
> and when the army pushes through, we all laugh.[10]

How can people be brought to "get rid of the baggage" and "emancipate the mind" from fear and thus attain this potency?

Within the Chinese Communist Party canon, there are two theories. The first and most common is that "curing" people requires long and patient ministration. This is an allopathic form of therapy in which the patient's anxiety is counteracted by reassurances and support. Among Chinese it often is referred to as "cultivation," after the original title of Liu Shao-ch'i's seminal work on this subject, "On the Cultivation of Communist Party Cadres" (usually translated as "How to Be a Good Communist").[11] Three years after the appearance of Liu's essay, Mao endorsed this approach: "So long as a person who has made mistakes does not hide his sickness for fear of treatment or persist in his mistakes until he is beyond cure, so long as he honestly and sincerely wishes to be cured and to mend his ways, we should welcome and cure his sickness so that he can mend his ways and become a good comrade."[12] Again, in a speech given immediately prior to the launching of the Hundred Flowers campaign, Mao said:

> We must oppose the method of "finishing people off with a single blow." This remolding of the intellectuals, especially the changing of their world outlook, is a process that requires a long period of time. Our comrades must understand that ideological remolding involves a long-term, patient and painstaking work, and they must not attempt to change people's ideology, which has been shaped over decades of life, by giving a few lectures or by holding a few meetings. Persuasion, not compulsion, is the only way to convince them.[13]

Even on those occasions better remembered for his more militant statements, Mao has reaffirmed his commitment to cultivation therapy—witness this passage from his "class struggle" speech to the Tenth Plenum in 1962:

> As to how the Party should deal with the problem of revisionism and the problem of a bourgeoisie within itself, I think we should adhere to our traditional policy. No matter what errors a comrade may commit . . . if he should change himself earnestly, we should welcome him and rally with him. . . . We permit the commission of errors. Since you have erred, we also allow you to rectify them.[14]

As the most widely endorsed form of political therapy, cultivation has become institutionalized in the Chinese Communist organization system in the form of "criticism and self-criticism" and "study" *(hsueh-hsi)* meetings, which are held routinely among members of work units, Party committees, and other small groups.

The intensity of such sessions varies according to the magnitude of the error and the stage of the mass movement in progress at the time. At its most intense, members of the group are completely isolated from their environment, families, and friends for a matter of months and segregated into study groups dedicated exclusively to thought reform. These more intransigent cases might be ostracized and obliged to write self-examinations for some time before acceptance.[15] In its more everyday form, members of the group also interact on an occupational or residential basis and are allowed to maintain contact with a normal outside circle of friends and relatives. How study groups operate is discussed in Martin Whyte's chapter in this volume.[16]

Although it is true that Mao endorsed cultivation therapy, he is perhaps better known for his espousal of a second therapeutic technique, one that is not "long-term, patient and painstaking" but short and abrupt: not gentle but "rough." A classic exposition may be found in his "Oppose Stereotyped Party Writing" (February 8, 1942): "The first thing to do in the reasoning process is to give the patient a good shake-up by shouting at him, "You are ill!" so as to administer a shock and make him break out in a sweat, and then to give him sincere advice on getting treatment."[17] This is a homeopathic form of therapy, which consists of an induced exacerbation of the symptoms of the illness in order to build up the patient's resistance. Mao makes this clear in his frequent comparisons with "immunization."[18] Using a different metaphor to make the same point, Mao speaks of "tempering": "Tempering means forging and refining. Forging is shaping by hammering and refining is smelting iron in a blast furnace or making steel in an open-hearth furnace. After steel is made, it needs forging, which nowadays is done with a pneumatic hammer. That hammering is terrific! We human beings need tempering too."[19] To this form of "shock" therapy Mao attributed both subjective and objective value. The subject, finding himself suddenly confronted with the object of his fear, should discover that the feared thing is not as terrible as he had imagined it to be, and his ability to cope with his fear will be correspondingly enhanced. His cure will permit him to realize untapped potential, as Mao put it.[20]

The experience was gratifying not only because of the power it unleashed, but because the source of this power was also an emotional wellspring of certain deeper truths. In a passage from his speech at the Yenan Forum on Art and Literature in 1942, Mao claimed that by boldly confronting his own fear of filth and defilement, he was able to undergo a conversion, to transfer his most basic loyalties from one class to another.

> I came to feel that compared with the workers and peasants, the unremolded intellectuals were not clean and that, even though their hands were soiled and their feet smeared with cow-dung, they were really cleaner than the bourgeois and petty-bourgeois intellectuals. This is what is meant by a change in feelings, a change from one class to another.[21]

The "change from one class to another" that Mao discusses here had nothing to do with the relations of production. It involved rather a "change in feelings," from the fear of "dirt" (which Mao —apparently in common with most members of his audience— tended to associate with the workers and peasants) to admiration and respect, through direct contact with the object of fear.

Mao was convinced that confrontation with the feared object could not only transform subjective emotions but actually undermine the power of the object as well. The object, having previously relied upon fear to exercise dominion over a cowed subject, will be so taken by surprise upon being so boldly confronted that he will reassess the power balance and probably retreat.

The original experience from which Mao drew this conclusion may well have been his confrontation with his father, which he described to Edgar Snow. From this he learned that if an authority is "dared" he will usually back off, whereas "when I remained meek and submissive, he only cursed and beat me the more."[22] Thus did Mao conceive the "paper tiger" nature of oppressive authorities.[23]

Sensing that their power is based upon fear rather than shared values, the oppressors are apt to panic and to resort to extreme measures at the first sign of fearlessness on the part of the oppressed. It is good tactics for the oppressed to reinforce this panic and to throw their oppressors into utter rout, thereby permanently reversing the relationship between the feared and the fearful:

> People swarm into the houses of local tyrants and evil gentry who are against the peasant association, slaughter their pigs and consume their grain. . . . Doing whatever they like and turning everything upside down, they have created a kind of terror in the countryside. This

is what some people call "going too far," or "going beyond the limits in righting a wrong," or "really too much." Such talk may seem plausible, but in fact it is wrong. . . . To put it bluntly, it is necessary to create terror for awhile in every rural area, or otherwise it would be impossible to suppress the activities of the counterrevolutionaries in the countryside or overthrow the authority of the gentry. Proper limits must be exceeded in order to right a wrong, or else the wrong cannot be righted.[24]

"Shock" therapy has not been institutionalized into the Chinese organization of thought reform, but it has been employed on a number of occasions in the form of "mass criticism" *(p'i-p'an* in Chinese, as distinguished from the normal type of criticism, *p'i-p'ing)* or "struggle" meetings. Struggle and mass criticism differ from criticism and self-criticism not only in the intensity of the sanctions imposed on the target, but in the nature of the audience. That of the former tends to be a large and relatively inclusive "rally" of anonymous individuals, a "mass" rather than a hierarchically organized face-to-face group that interacts routinely. Students of mass behavior have suggested that this type of gathering tends to reduce the inhibitions of group members against intense emotional expression and radical political action.[25] Mass criticism or struggle has arisen in many of the more intense Chinese mobilization campaigns, usually to eliminate enemies of the campaign in question (e.g., landlords in the land reform campaign). To my knowledge, however, it has been used as a conscious instrument of thought reform for the targets of criticism only twice.

The first such occasion, the Hundred Flowers movement, was notoriously brief and abortive. There had been violent popular uprisings in Poland and Hungary, and Mao expressed keen interest in them. He remarked with some bravado in November 1956: "Since there is fire in Poland and Hungary, it will blaze up sooner or later. Which is better, to let the fire blaze, or not to let it? Fire cannot be wrapped up in paper. Now that fires have blazed up, that's just fine."[26] But in 1957 he began to express concern that the Chinese leadership might be similarly assailed. He claimed that "certain people" even hoped this would happen, that "thousands of people would demonstrate in the streets against the people's government."[27]

Though the frequency with which he returned to the subject betrayed his real concern, he ridiculed any such possibility: "If a handful of school kids can topple our Party, government and army by a show of force, we must all be fatheads. Therefore, don't be afraid of great democracy. If there is a disturbance, it will help get the festering sore cured, and that's a good thing."[28] Thus Mao issued his famous invitation to critics to do their worst:

> In my opinion, whoever wants to make trouble may do so for as long as he pleases, and if one month is not enough, he may go on for two, in short, the matter should not be wound up until he feels he has had enough. . . . Don't always try to keep a lid on everything. Whenever people utter queer remarks, go on strike or present a petition, you try to beat them back with one blow, always thinking that these things ought not to occur. Why is it then that these things that ought not to occur still do?[29]

When rightists among the students, bourgeois democratic parties, and middle-class intellectuals seized the initiative during the campaign to deliver some telling criticisms of the Party and of Mao himself, Mao expressed anger.[30] The Hundred Flowers movement had to be terminated short of its therapeutic objectives.

During the Cultural Revolution, Mao again faced intra-Party opposition to his rectification plans, but this time he defied his opposition and allowed the campaign to develop in a much more spontaneous fashion. His experiment with encouraging people to emancipate themselves from fear seemed again to coincide with his own fear that if the regime did not open itself to criticism it might become a target for a second revolution. This fear was ambivalently combined with nostalgia for his old rebel role and a desire that this second revolution should somehow be allowed to succeed.

In sum, Mao's theory of psychocultural dynamics is one that presumes attachment to the status quo—not so much to a given arrangement of relations of production as to emotional inhibitions against loss. His method of psychocultural change pays lip service to institutionalized processes of "cultivation," but relies for more fundamental change on a form of "shock" therapy that challenges the individual to confront and overcome the object of his fears boldly and directly.

This technique is not altogether exogenous to the cumulative body of social scientific research findings. Social anthropologists are familiar with the sort of forcible violation of taboos that Mao recommends to detach emotional commitments to the status quo;

they consider this a characteristic ingredient of "revitalization" or "millenarian" movements. Such movements typically succeed in unleashing "extra untapped sources of energy and resolution" and in binding their participants together "in mutual guilt and mutual support in opposition to all those who still accept the old beliefs." To this extent, they coincide with Mao's expectations for the Cultural Revolution.[31]

About this aspect of the experience the psychoanalysts have a contribution to make: they would find Mao's head-on approach to thought reform quite similar to what is known clinically as the "counterphobic defense" against latent anxiety. This consists of a deliberate attempt to precipitate the event most dreaded in order to obtain a "flight to reality" from the torments of one's imagination. The counterphobic defense, like taboo violations in the revitalization movement, is successful in dissipating immediate anxieties and in bolstering self-confidence; but because it fails to comprehend or resolve the underlying source of anxiety, new anxiety tends to accumulate and to require repeated discharges.[32]

In view of the different research conditions in which these findings were obtained, it would not be justified to extrapolate more than a few tentative hypotheses. I propose two for discussion in this chapter: (1) The Cultural Revolution will succeed not only in provoking dramatic short-term changes in the action patterns of its participants but in effecting a significant long-term attitudinal transformation. (2) The inherent limitations of the counterphobic approach will leave the problem open-ended and necessitate either a repetition of this approach or a search for new solutions.

The Dynamics of the Cultural Revolution

As Mao once aptly put it, "There are two aspects to socialist transformation. One is the transformation of institutions, and the other is the transformation of people."[33] We shall accordingly turn to the impact of the Cultural Revolution first on the Chinese institutional framework and then on the attitudes of the movement's participants.

Mao's focus during the Cultural Revolution was on the "transformation of people"; institutions were simply grist for his mill. That they should be heavily damaged in the course of his construction of a new socialist man indicates his impatience with their bureaucratic inertia. Based on the principle of "destruction before construction," the institutions and the officials who staffed them quickly emerged as the principal targets of the mass movement.

Two communication strategies were used. "Cultivation" therapy generally took place within the existing institutional framework and concentrated its sanctions against individual deviants from institutional norms. As a counterphobic approach, however, "mass criticism" involved free recruitment of members into informal groups which were often based on former institutional associations but were nonetheless outside, and often opposed to, existing institutions. Moreover, while normal criticism and self-criticism tried to rectify the individual target, in mass criticism the target was not seriously expected to rectify his or her errors. Rather, the magnitude of errors seemed to be increased as new targets or new problems were brought up for additional criticism.

Thus, in mass criticism as a communication strategy, there was a splitting of the roles of target and audience: the target was no longer a significant participant in the communication process, but rather a pedagogic device for polemical speeches made by critics to inflame a mass audience. Indeed, if the target should succeed in rectifying his errors, he would tend to inhibit further escalation of the movement, and this was therefore opposed by those leaders who had a stake in its continued expansion.

Although Mao attributed one of his reasons for launching the Cultural Revolution to the allegation that none of his colleagues paid attention to him any more, the fact that he was able to create an artifically coercion-free public realm conducive to such a movement is evidence of his still unrivalled power and prestige. He achieved this by cementing his hold over the People's Liberation Army through his alliance with Lin Piao, and by prohibiting members of the Party apparatus from interfering in the free mobilization of the masses.

To the young rebels Mao gave the "four freedoms," and many other freedoms besides. They were at liberty to organize, travel through the country free of charge (for a brief period), recruit new members, publish handbills and tabloid newspapers, and choose their own targets. The mass communication network was devoted exclusively to criticism of the bureaucratic establishment, and intrabureaucratic communication became so thoroughly penetrated by "leaks" that it began to lose its autonomy. The mass communication network consisted not only of the official press, now under control of the Central Cultural Revolution Group, but of a congeries of decentralized informal communication media: big character posters, Red Guard tabloids, handbills, and traveling rally speakers such as Chiang Ch'ing, Ch'en Po-ta, and Chou En-lai.[34]

Within this loosely structured social context the revolutionary masses were encouraged to rise and liberate themselves. They did so by demonstrating, criticizing and/or "struggling" against the authorities whom they had most feared and resented, and by engaging in other behavior (chiefly conflictual) previously forbidden to them. To engage in such behavior, the young rebels had to overcome their inhibitions. These inhibitions were represented in their polemic rhetoric by an imagery of "shackles," "frames," a "fortress," and so on.

This metaphorical "line of demarcation" divided their world into two antagonistic sectors: on one side was light (symbolized by the sun, fire, and so on), publicity, purity, and heroic activity; on the other was darkness, concealment, filth, and dependent passivity. The young rebels considered it scandalous to ignore this line of demarcation, or to pass freely between these two sectors. Yet the barrier dividing the two worlds should be "smashed," "bombarded," "crushed," or otherwise vigorously penetrated: "With the tremendous and impetuous force of a raging storm [the rebels] have smashed the shackles imposed on their minds by the exploiting classes for so long."[35] The rebels were (with some justification) indebted to Mao's Thought as the "telescope and microscope" *(wang-yüan ching ho hsien-wei ching)* that helped them to perceive this segmentation.[36]

In several remarkable *obiter dicta,* Mao encouraged such revolutionary breakthroughs despite the chaos they unleashed: "Do not be afraid to make trouble. The more trouble you make and the longer you make it the better. Confusion and trouble are always noteworthy. It can clear things up."[37] The rebels responded with enthusiasm: "We want to wield the massive cudgel, express our spirit, invoke our magic influence and turn the old world upsidedown, smash things into chaos, into smithereens, the more chaos the better!"[38]

The young rebels experienced a sense of euphoria and omnipotence that led them to discount their previous fears and adopt a more optimistic assessment of the mass revolutionary potential. This was expressed in the imagery of catastrophe: "with the fury of a hurricane," "with the force to topple mountains and upturn seas," "with the power of thunder and lightning from the heavens, this [Cultural Revolution] has enveloped all China and shaken the world."[39]

The consequences of the Cultural Revolution may be assessed in terms of its impact on the institutional structure and on the attitudes of individual participants. We shall discuss both briefly:

1. The purge of an overwhelming majority of career officials from the Party and government bureaucracies resulted in a dispersion of power from the Center to the local levels. The subsequent purge of Lin Piao and his followers seems to have contributed to the same trend in the People's Liberation Army. This was consistent with the ideological objective of "self-reliance," but seems also to have attenuated the regime's hold on the countryside.

2. The distinction between internal bureaucratic and public communication channels was abridged by the widespread tendency to "leak" information to extrabureaucratic constituencies, who would often circulate it publicly. This information was not the usual promotional material designed to provide mass reinforcement to the leadership, but rather highly damaging revelations of arrogance, corruption, and hypocrisy among leading officials. The relatively free circulation of such information seemed to aggravate cleavages among elites and masses and to render cooperation more tenuous.

3. There was a significant influx of junior officials (who had joined the rebel ranks during the movement to oust their superiors) and young rebel celebrities into the ranks of the Revolutionary Committees and later into the reconstructed Party apparatus. Despite repeated injunctions from the Center to welcome them, these new cadres never managed to ingratiate themselves among their senior colleagues. They tended to form separate factional groupings with distinctive interests.

4. There was a significant reduction in the number and the degree of stratification of material incentives; most bonuses and piece rates were eliminated from the industrial sector, there was unsystematic reduction of the incomes of the higher-paid strata, and there were experiments in agriculture with more egalitarian work point allocation systems.

The impact on attitudes was significant, but more difficult to measure. So far as the targets of mass criticism or struggle are concerned, the impact was deep and unforgettable, according to the reports I have been able to gather through refugee interviews, but not usually conducive to a genuine transformation to the proletarian standpoint. The criticism targets were held to account for many things that had been beyond their control. The only politically appropriate response, it sometimes seemed, was simply to confess to all crimes of which they were accused. The lesson the target drew from the experience was often a political rather than a moral one: it was necessary to bend with the stronger wind, be more discreet and equivocal in revealing one's ideological preferences, and anticipate changes in line with a preemptive self-criticism. A former Central cadre told me:

> Struggle didn't change my thoughts, it caused me to resist. If they're wrong, they can't change my thoughts. If they're right, they don't need to [use] struggle. . . . The more you are struggled, the more you resist. You superficially relent, but in your heart, you hate it. . . . If you utterly deny any trace of correctness in a person; he can't accept it.

The attitudes of the targets of criticism were for the most part not transformed but underwent what was called an "inner migration" among anti-Nazi Germans, while their overt behavior became detached from their attitudes—on lease, as it were, to the political exigencies of the day.

For those who participated in mass criticism, the impact of the movement on their attitudes was equally profound and usually somewhat more consistent with Maoist objectives. "During the mass criticism I changed my thoughts because I thought: 'Oh, what that person did was wrong,' " recalled one former participant. By symbolically transforming their own inhibitions into various external "barriers" and then using verbal aggression to penetrate these barriers, many were able to achieve a catharsis, realize untapped skills of leadership or symbol manipulation, and undertake many audacious (and normally impermissible) exploits. The "barriers" of social distance that had divided elites and masses seem to have been permanently attenuated by this assault. My informants indicate that local leaders, for instance, became much more assiduous about consultation with their colleagues and fraternization with their constituents.

> Before the Cultural Revolution I didn't even know who was the unit secretary. The [cadres] didn't talk to us, didn't know our names, lived in separate cadre residence halls [kao kan lou]. . . . After the

Cultural Revolution, they moved in and lived in the same apartment building with us. They were closer to the masses: their children played with ours, they walked around in the yard, talked with us, and if we had something [to discuss] we could talk with them. They didn't necessarily solve your problems, but you could go talk with them.

The masses for their part became much bolder in voicing demands or grievances, sometimes resorting to big character posters or letters to superior officials (many wrote to Chou En-lai, for example, some to Mao himself) if they failed to obtain redress within their units. " 'The movement' made people smarter, more capable of doing things for themselves, always willing to ask 'why?'—it became more difficult to mislead [yü-nung] people. For example, the Tienanmen incident [in April 1976] could never have occurred earlier." In short, the Cultural Revolution seems to have succeeded in reducing arrogance among elites and subverting the "docile tool" mentality among the masses at least marginally, generating a somewhat more democratic attitude toward authority.

That this more irreverent attitude was no unalloyed blessing soon became apparent. Many Red Guards and revolutionary rebels found their counterphobic emancipation so intrinsically rewarding that they continued to indulge in such behavior even after it was no longer considered heroic or socially useful. There was no place in Mao's thought for such a contingency; he seems to have regarded the political system as a sort of pressure cooker—once the lid was taken off, people would give vent to their grievances, and then everyone would feel much better. Or, as he put it more prosaically in a post mortem justification of the Cultural Revolution:

One big-character poster, one Red Guard, and the whole country is in an uproar. The order that had been established over more than a decade was disrupted, and at the Center and in the localities, cadres who were dissatisfied [sic] with the status quo panicked. Most of them had good intentions—they were afraid that it would throw us into chaos. Actually, it only disrupted the enemy and tempered the good people. . . . [With the appearance of] a Liu Shao-ch'i, a Lin Piao, a Great Cultural Revolution, and a Campaign to Criticize Lin Piao and Confucius, people said that the Party was suffering from internal disorder. We wanted it to be disordered so that we could cure it. Without the disorder, how would it be possible for us to discriminate between the good and the bad people; how could we have forced Lin Piao to jump out? . . . We allowed disorder so that we could catch those hands that were muddying the water. Then *the water would clear up of its own accord.*[40] [Emphasis added]

To sum up the impact of the Cultural Revolution on Chinese political culture at the end of the spontaneous mobilization phase in 1968, the "transformation of institutions" seems to have drastically impaired the functioning of normal administrative processes without yet introducing altogether satisfactory organizational alternatives. The "transformation of people" was on the whole consistent with Maoist objectives and quite impressive, so far as the "people" (as opposed to the targeted "enemies") were concerned. However, it became evident that the transformation of people in the context of institutional disintegration led to economic and other costs on the system that could in the long run prove intolerable. If the Cultural Revolution were to continue, some way had to be found to lock it in an institutional "cage" without causing it to die in captivity. Much of the next decade was to be dedicated to this elusive objective.

A Revolution Continued?

In this section I assess the more lasting consequences of the Cultural Revolution, beginning with the attempt to institutionalize the Cultural Revolution in the 1968–1976 period and its results.

Transformation of Institutions

The radical attempt to institutionalize the Cultural Revolution consisted of a war on three fronts, waged more or less concurrently.

The attempt to infuse existing institutional structures with a more revolutionary spirit was made through the introduction of many new ideas designed to enhance mass participation, such as the "open-door rectification" of the Party (which involved the non-Party masses in the purge and reconstruction of the Party), the regular rotation of leaders between on-line labor and desk jobs, replacement of the "branch" principle with the "committee" principle in regional and local Party committees (which implied more influence by militant amateurs and less by functional specialists), a general simplification and decentralization of the bureaucracy (to facilitate community control), and so forth.[41] In fact, however, most of these innovations proved ephemeral: the military leaders and veteran cadres who in turn seized control of the old institutional structure lost little time in demonstrating their ability to ignore or interpret self-servingly these directives, and the radical Center, severely weakened by the purge of its control organs, found that with the demobilization of the masses its exhortations often availed little. Thus the attempt to infuse a more revolutionary spirit into the bureaucracy quickly developed into a competition for appointments to key decision-making offices.

The radicals were at a disadvantage in this competition because it was generally acknowledged, as early as the introduction of the Revolutionary Committees to replace the Paris Commune concept in February 1967, that their lack of bureaucratic experience disqualified them for top leadership positions; the most they could hope for thereafter was a quasi-apprenticeship under the "three-in-one union" formula, which tacitly allotted them one third of all representative positions. And the radicals did, indeed, achieve visible gains under this arrangement. The percentage of mass representatives (most of whom were Cultural Revolution radicals) on the Central Committee increased from 26 percent at the ninth Central Committee to 34 percent at the tenth, for example, and Wang Hung-wen became first vice chairman of the Party.

Yet these gains were more apparent than real. With the reconstruction of the Party at the provincial and local levels, the radical position there diminished even as it improved at the Center: none of the mass representatives at the tenth Congress were first or second Party secretaries of their provincial Party committees, and twenty-eight of the forty-eight did not even have positions on the standing committees of their provincial Party committees.

In general, the appointment strategy tended to succeed only in those areas still under Mao's immediate jurisdiction (particularly the Politburo) and only as long as he was still alive, leaving the radicals in the position of a head without arms or legs.

In their attempt to foster the creation of new and more revolutionary organizations, the radicals were prolific indeed. Beginning with their rise to influence in 1973, they introduced a bewildering series of models in rapid succession: there was the Fang Hua Lien model army unit in Chekiang, the Hsiao Chin Chuang Brigade's political night school, the Ch'ao-yang model agricultural college, the July 21 Worker Colleges and May 7 Peasant Colleges, the armed workers' militia, and so on. The radicals' modus operandi was to notice a mass initiative that seemed worthy of emulation and, with little or no further spot testing, proceed to give it great fanfare in the media, encouraging other units to adopt the model. Most of these model organizations did not prove viable, however. They usually contained few intrinsic rewards—they did not improve productive efficiency or increase unit income, and in fact usually imposed added sacrifices on their participants. On the other hand, if the organization did meet the needs of a mass constituency and promised to thrive, the Party could either coopt it or otherwise frustrate radical attempts to use it as a base. This was the fate of the poor and lower-middle peasant associations that sprang up in the years following the Cultural Revolution, and of the reorganized mass organizations that strongly supported the 1973 call to "go against the current."

The radicals' dominant influence over the media dates from the first stage of the Cultural Revolution, when the propaganda department of the Central Committee was disbanded and the Central Cultural Revolution Group took over all propaganda channels. Yao Wen-yüan represented the Politburo in receiving broadcasting and press delegations from abroad, and was considered to be in day-to-day control of propaganda output. All the major organs, including the *People's Daily, Kwangming Daily, Red Flag,* the Central Broadcasting Administration Bureau, New China News Agency, and Peking Television, were influenced by the radicals, who also controlled the publication of literary artistic magazines, university journals, and books and pamphlets published in Peking and Shanghai.

Even so, radical control of the culture and propaganda "system" was never complete. During Lin Piao's ascendancy, his imprint on this sphere was unmistakable. The purge of the Lin Piao clique left Chou En-lai in ascendancy as the only active member remaining in the Politburo Standing Committee besides Mao. The moderates also gained some editorial influence over the *People's Daily* and *Red Flag,* and consolidated their control of the provincial media.[42] Given their organizational weakness and the persisting moderate challenge to them even in the propaganda sector, the radicals had to contend with the likelihood that any new initiative that threatened bureaucratic interests might be blunted, ignored, or reconstrued.

For as long as Chou En-lai was alive, this form of resistance was extremely subtle and effective. One technique consisted of immedi-

ate and apparently forthright compliance with the radical demand
—this tended to disarm those radicals who were genuinely concerned with the issue in question, while frustrating those who
hoped to use that issue as a lever to target other members of the
leadership.[43]

A similar tactic was to join in the assault upon the ostensible
target of criticism as if that target had no ulterior referent among
the leadership, and in fact to convey the impression that the leadership was solidly united—thus when Chiang Ch'ing began to make
more frequent public appearances in the spring of 1974 to promote
the burgeoning Anti-Confucius/Anti-Lin Piao campaign, Chou
took pains to appear with her as frequently as possible in order to
dispel any impression of a rift between them.[44] When the ulterior
referent of the criticism was fairly obvious and quite sensitive, the
objective simply had to be reinterpreted. Perhaps the best example
of this is the *Red Flag* verdict that the campaign to go "against the
tide," apparently initiated by Mao himself,[45] was entirely compatible with Party discipline:

> Going against the tide is completely consistent with observing Party
> discipline. . . . In the course of the struggle between the two lines
> within the Party, our great leader Chairman Mao always unwaver-
> ingly abides by Marxist-Leninist principles and dares to go against
> the tide; he also firmly safeguards the Party's organizational princi-
> ples and observes the Party's discipline. Chieftains of the opportunist
> lines within the Party, because they want to push the revisionist line,
> always sabotage the Party's organizational principles and oppose the
> Party's discipline.[46]

The first drawback, then, to the radical attempt to revolutionize
culture from the "towering heights" of the Central propaganda department was that their organizational control remained incom-
plete and their propaganda initiatives were hence sometimes reinterpreted in the light of various vested interests in the process of
their dissemination.

The second problem was more intractable, because it was intrinsic to the content of the revolutionary culture that was being pur-
veyed. Chiang Ch'ing supervised the production of eight revolutionary operas *(yang pan hsi)* during this period and proscribed the
performance of nearly everything else. Although the eight productions were initially well received, they began to pall and finally grew

so obviously tiresome that Teng Hsiao-p'ing could jeer about the difficulty in selling tickets.[47]

Similarly, although the radicals produced the study materials for the various study meetings that were held throughout the country, and although these meetings were held much more frequently after the Cultural Revolution than before, the participants became bored with the proceedings as they were meeting from two to five times a week (and during campaigns often meeting before work in the morning and again after work at night). The same study materials would be used repeatedly, and the discussions remained at the level of simple sloganeering. According to my informants, people did not even bother to conceal their apathy: "During the meeting, people would do other things—write letters, knit, chat—sometimes the chatting was louder than the person making the report, and the leader would have to ask people, 'Don't talk so loud.' People would go to sleep. Some people didn't even bother to attend."

What emerges from this brief survey of the post–Cultural Revolution institutional structure is a picture of pervasive internal cleavage. In the Party committees, the radicals were confined to the plena and rarely received other responsible elite positions. At the Center, they also made visible gains in the plena of the Central organs, but their most substantial gains were in grasping significant executive power and in exerting dominant sway over the culture and propaganda sector. They had no influence over economic or financial matters. Thus the cleavage became one between those having control of the material base and those having control of the cultural superstructure, between the powerful but silent and the weak but shrill.

Transformation of People

My impression is that the radicals tended generally to adhere (willy-nilly, perhaps) to "cultivation" therapy during this period. Although they took temporary recourse to the older pattern of free mobilization, public posting of big character posters, and so on, these liberties were rescinded as soon as economic disruptions ensued. The counterphobic approach lost some of its political effectiveness because bureaucratic elites under Chou En-lai avoided drawing a rigid "line of demarcation" that would justify rebels in mobilizing for dramatic breakthroughs and pursued a more pliant, yielding strategy. As a form of therapy, the counterphobic shock had succeeded in detaching commitments to the status quo but managed to implant no new set of positive values. It contributed to selflessness in the sense of fostering the courage to defy conventions regardless of personal cost, but failed to demonstrate how altruism, as a revolutionary value, could lead to harmonious and fruitful cooperation.

Psychologists have determined that one of the preconditions for the exercise of social altruism is the absence of risk and the presence of stability and certainty of conditions.[48] The pattern of institutional cleavage and instability during this period entailed that this precondition could not be met. The delicate balance of power among elites induced the radicals to use all sorts of arcane circumlocutions. They were deterred from making the contemporary relevance of their criticism themes explicit by the power of the interests they sought to attack. And if they did become more explicit, those interests would intercede to reconstrue the criticism, with much the same effect on the public. The criticism themes in the various campaigns during this period tended to be academic and irrelevant to the concerns of working people, most of whom had never read Confucius and could not understand the importance of differing periodizations of Chinese history or the relative merits of legalism versus feudalism.

One campaign followed another, usually inconclusively. For example, the criticisms of *Water Margin* in the summer of 1975 focused on the tendency toward "capitulationism," but what specifically was involved? It did not become clear that Teng Hsiao-p'ing was the ulterior target of these attacks until Teng became politically vulnerable in February 1976. And this was unusual; most of the campaigns conducted from 1972–1976 remained at an abstract level and never descended to specific targets. The general atmosphere conveyed was one of obscure menace, tending to discourage the masses from becoming involved.

For the leaders, the nature of the uncertainty was less obscure but no less hazardous. By interpreting shifts of nuance in the press they were able to follow the subtle and constantly seesawing line struggle among elites, but the fact that the struggle remained inconclusive tended to discourage unreserved commitment. There were at least two fairly rational strategies of adaptation: one was to bank all on one line during its high tide in an effort to achieve power or celebrity in the short term,[49] and the other was to try to avoid becoming dangerously overcommitted to either line while opportunistically utilizing both. Neither strategy accorded with bureaucratic rules of step-by-step promotion, and both undermined discipline by appealing to forces outside the organization. A general atmosphere of insecurity was engendered that was conducive not to resolving policy decisions and serving the people but rather to prudent self-protection.

This persisting institutional cleavage tended also to vitiate the effectiveness of the communication campaign as a method of generating mass enthusiasm and willingness to sacrifice for the public interest. Given that control of the Party apparatus and propaganda machine fell into the hands of elite factions who were opposed to each other, the *apparatchiki* below saw little reason to cooperate in leading campaigns that might redound to their own criticism. The People's Liberation Army withdrew its propaganda teams sometime after Lin Piao's purge, and according to my informants the Party no longer dispatched propaganda teams after the Anti-Confucius/Anti-Lin Piao campaign wound down in 1974. Attempts to mobilize the masses tended to become self-defeating in the absence of any institutional support, for mobilization then passed into the hands of informal groups, who tended to clash vigorously with the authorities and with one another. Thus when the mass movement reached a certain threshold, it tended persistently to degenerate into factional strife, strikes, and other forms of civil disorder.

Preliminary Post Mortem

To what may we attribute this failure to institutionalize the gains of the Cultural Revolution, so fateful in its consequences? This in part may be attributed to some rather obvious political factors, chief among them the rapid and massive rehabilitation of veteran cadres beginning in 1972, which established a strong political base for opposition to the revival or continuation of Cultural Revolution policies.[50] Although caught off guard in 1966, this contingent of veteran and rehabilitated cadres had won experience in polemical in-fighting and was now prepared to render determined and skilled resistance to the revival of policies inimical to their interests and convictions. As Chiang Ch'ing observed, "More than 75 percent of the old cadres inevitably turn from members of the democratic faction into members of the capitalist-roaders' faction."[51]

Yet even more important than bureaucratic opposition in defeating the institutionalization of the Cultural Revolution were certain unresolved internal contradictions within the radical program. First among these was the ambivalence toward institutionalization itself. To Mao and the radicals, institutionalization entailed the diversion of energies from ultimate objectives to the side payments necessary for maintenance and enhancement of the organization itself. But in the absence of a stable organizational structure and a set of rules to ensure the consistent allocation of sanctions and incentives, the Maoist coalition was ceaselessly wracked by disputes over allocative priorities. If the goals of the revolution were to be achieved, these disputes had to be permanently settled so that people could get back to work—that is, some degree of institutionalization seemed necessary. Still the radicals remained ambivalent: they became a force that was in but not of the organization, dependent on it for achievement of many of their objectives but performing no clearly useful organizational role and assuming no responsibility for organizational maintenance, but rather maintaining a hypercritical stance toward organizational shortcomings.

The second internal contradiction involved the need to reinforce altruism. To offer rewards for being altruistic would be self-negating, and yet without some inducement to do so, why should people serve the people rather than themselves? Individuals of exceptional dedication (Joan of Arc, St. Francis of Assisi) have occasionally attained a relatively pure form of altruism, but it has always been difficult for large groups to do so, particularly when they are involuntary. The way in which churches and other philanthropically motivated associations typically solve this dilemma is to offer nonmaterial compensations, such as honor or rectitude, for material sacrifices.[52] But the radical definition of altruism was even more uncompromisingly self-denying than that used by most churches. For example, during the Anti-Confucius/Anti-Lin Piao campaign they warned cadres against performing services to the people for the wrong reasons (i.e., in hopes of accruing political debts among one's constituents).

> We will run counter to Chairman Mao's teaching on serving the people "wholeheartedly" and lack the thoroughgoing revolutionary spirit of the proletariat if we want to gain some personal benefits while doing things for the people, if we think that because we have performed meritorious service for the people we are entitled to see personal "rights" and privileges in certain matters, and if we, after doing something good for the people, relax the strict demands on ourselves and begin to plan for our personal future. . . . [53]

In their important articles on "bourgeois right" published in the spring of 1975, Yao Wen-yüan and Chang Ch'un-ch'iao criticized Lin Piao for offering political favors to his constituents, for "handing out official posts and making some promises, inviting guests and giving them presents, wining and dining, and trafficking in flattery and favors. . . . When his sworn followers are exposed by the masses, he used his position and power to . . . protect them and help them slip away." All of this transforms the relations among people into "relations of buying and selling of commodities," according to Yao.[54] In sum, the radical definition of true service to the people precluded the acceptance of compensatory values of any kind for one's sacrifice, even such nonmaterial values as gratitude or feelings of indebtedness.

Insofar as the radicals sought to enforce the rigorous self-denial implied by their definition of altruism, they were prevented from using positive reinforcement to promote their programs and were almost bound to encounter difficulties. As a former Peking middle-school student put it in trying to explain the unpopularity of the *hsia-hsiang* (sent down to village) program, "Because life is tough [in the countryside], people hate it, and this makes it difficult to change their thoughts. Mao seems to think participation in labor will make people very happy and be a transforming experience, but when they find that it's tough *[k'u]*, they complain." The radicals seemed at times to be equally oblivious to the need to make positive appeals to a mass constituency. During the movement to study proletarian dictatorship, for example, Mao made a statement attacking "small production" *(hsiao sheng-ch'an)*. Yao Wen-yüan wrote an article echoing this attack, as did Chang Ch'un-ch'iao in his article of April 1, which identified the peasantry as "small producers" and asserted that small production engenders capitalism continuously. Although China's peasantry has always been (with the army) Mao's basic constituency, Chang also made invidious comparisons between agriculture and industry, contending that while the more advanced "ownership by the whole people" predominated in industry and commerce, [local] collective ownership still held sway in agriculture.[55] In pursuing such arguments the radicals were theoretically consistent but politically insensitive.

Much more prominently featured in the radical arsenal of sanctions was the negative reinforcement of criticism: in the decade following the Cultural Revolution, mass criticism as a communication device was used with great frequency against a wide array of targets, from Lin Piao to Jonathan Livingston Seagull. Western psychologists generally consider negative reinforcement to be inferior to positive reinforcement because of its imprecision, and because of its negative side effects (e.g., resentment).[56] Imprecision is deliberately employed in Chinese mass criticism to induce everyone guilty of the error in question to take warning from the criticism and rectify the error before criticism becomes more severe and specific. The problem with this type of stimulus generalization is that the negative side effects tend to become general as well. As China's most vociferous public scolds, the radicals reaped a whirlwind of resentment: there was apparently great delight in the subsequent *tu quoque* discovery that they had been guilty of many of the same crimes for which they had criticized nearly everyone else.

The third contradiction in the radical program was not a logical one, but it was nonetheless very serious. This was the contradiction between the repeated calls for greater equality and for reduction of special privileges for the few, and the also frequent criticisms of various aspects of economic production, which conveyed the impression that the radicals were in favor of redistribution but opposed to production. This would be an untenable position, of course, because shortfalls in production tend to foreclose redistributive programs and place economics in command. The radicals were nevertheless quite critical of attempts to reimpose industrial discipline (as Teng had apparently proposed in one version of his "Twenty Articles on Accelerating Economic Development"), viewing these as a pretext to purge all radicals from the industrial sector.[57] As the debate intensified, there was an increasing polarization between the culture/propaganda and the financial/economic systems, creating a gap between ideological ends and economic means that was difficult to reconcile without another major upheaval. But the delicate balance of power among elites allowed this gap to exist unreconciled for some time, causing considerable bewilderment among the masses. A peasant posed the following excellent question: "Since distribution according to work is about the same as in the old society, why is it sill in existence now? And since it is allowed to exist, why is it necessary to restrict it under the dictatorship of the proletariat?"[58] The editor's reply explained that although "to each according to his work" did embody "bourgeois right," at the same time "We must not say, 'Long live distribution according to work.' The fact that we recognize it and allow it to exist at the present stage does not mean that we should extend or develop it.'' To what ends was revolutionary thought reform to be directed under such equivocal circumstances? The task of the radicals was no longer dramatically and drastically to transform, but to restrict what seems to have been tacitly accepted as a necessary evil.

Conclusion

Our purpose was to explore the impact of the Cultural Revolution on cultural change in contemporary China. I would conclude that the impact has been more significant than anything at least since the great campaigns of the 1950s. The impact on people was one of shock, as it was intended to be, but this shock did not always detach their commitments to the status quo but tended to have a polarizing effect, depending on whether one was a victim, critic, or spectator and on such factors as age, class background, and ego strength. For most participants, the impact seems to have been liberating, to have generated leadership skills and high expectations of politics. Authority relationships seem to have become more informal and democratic, engendering problems of discipline not usually associated with authoritarian systems.

For targets of criticism, however, the impact seems to have been counterproductive. Although with more or less enthusiasm most went along with the movement to participate with the masses and in manual labor, they seem to have developed an abhorrence for the chaos of the Cultural Revolution itself that inclined them to be increasingly negatively inclined toward the ''newborn things.''

The impact on institutions was to purge them and open them to public scrutiny, allowing the masses to participate in their reorganization along more revolutionary lines. This resulted in at least a temporary reduction in the size and complexity of the bureaucracy and certainly shook things up, but its general effect was highly disruptive. The breakdown in the institutional structure also exacerbated the problems associated with the transformation of people, permitting mass mobilization to fall into the hands of informal groups who tended to come into conflict with one another.

The events of the ensuing decade have tended to transform and sometimes obscure the effect the original experience had on its participants. The massive rustication program seems to have been almost as much a shock to the millions of former rebels as their sudden emancipation, for they had been led to believe that their status and power would be enhanced by the Cultural Revolution.

The focus shifted from the transformation of people to the transformation of institutions, but the demobilization of the masses seemed to attenuate the force behind the radical cause while the rehabilitation of cadres strengthened bureaucratic resistance to it. The radicals were also beset by several internal contradictions in their own program, which gravely impaired their political efficacy.

Thus, during a decade of ceaseless organizational experimentation, the only change that endured was the introduction of the radicals to the bureaucracy as a team of in-house critics. They failed to ingratiate themselves with their colleagues and in fact the relationship between radicals and bureaucrats tended to polarize, creating a vertical cleavage that ran all the way down to the local levels. Under these circumstances the attempt to continue the transformation of people became inextricably involved with the power struggle among elites, and the didactic value of the criticism themes was obscured by the need to attack powerful bureaucratic elites without specifying them. The polarization between one faction in control of propaganda and the other in control of the economy led to a deep chasm between "is" and "ought" that was at least bewildering and at most led to a sense of cynicism or moral outrage. The pervasive institutional instability detracted from the attempt to make men altruistic and led to the rise of careerists with more rhetorical flair.

The rise of Hua Kuo-feng provides an opportunity for the Chinese to restore a unity of views to their system that is more consistent with its structure, to enforce an order and predictability that is more compatible with social altruism, and to realign norm and reality so that they are far enough apart to inspire, without being so far apart as to incite irrational and desperate action. The problem will be in the structure: can it be arranged to restore order and discipline while still accomodating the more democratic attitude toward authority that was introduced during the Cultural Revolution? If not, the same stresses that precipitated the first Cultural Revolution could lead to a troubled future.

NOTES

1. "Concluding Remarks at the Supreme State Conference" (March 1, 1957), in *Mao Tse-tung ssu-hsiang wan-sui* [Long Live the Thought of Mao Tse-tung] (Hong Kong: n.p., 1969), pp. 90–100. (Hereafter *Wan-sui*.)

2. Milovan Djilas, *The New Class: An Analysis of the Communist System* (New York: Praeger, 1962), p. 35 et passim.

3. "The class of bureaucratic officials on the one hand and the working class together with the poor and lower-middle peasants on the other are two classes sharply opposed to each other." Mao's original statement was made in 1964 but not publicly quoted until 1976, in a joint editorial. Cf. *Red Flag,* no. 7 (July 1, 1976), p. 6.

4. Cf. Mao's essays, "In Memory of Norman Bethune" (December 21, 1939), in *Selected Works,* vol. 2 (Peking: Foreign Languages Press, 1965), pp. 337–338; "Serve the People" (September 8, 1944), in ibid., vol. 3, pp. 227–229. (Hereafter *Selected Works.*)

5. "Get Rid of the Baggage and Start the Machinery" (April 12, 1944), in *Selected Readings from the Works of Mao Tse-tung* (Peking: Foreign Languages Press, 1971), p. 306. (Hereafter *Selected Readings.*)

6. "Toward a New Golden Age" (July 1919), in Stuart Schram, *The Political Thought of Mao Tse-tung* (New York: Praeger, 1963), pp. 105–106.

7. "On the Cooperative Transformation of Agriculture" (July 31, 1955), in *Selected Works,* vol. 5 (1977), p. 184.

8. "Speech at the 2nd Plenary Session of the Communist Party of China" (November 15, 1956), ibid., p. 344.

9. "Changsha," in *The Poems of Mao Tse-tung,* trans. Willis Barnstone (New York: Harper & Row, 1972), p. 33.

10. "The Long March" (October 1935), ibid., p. 65.

11. *"Lun kung-ch'an-tang yüan ti hsiu-yang"* (July 8, 1939), in *Liu Shao-ch'i wen-t'i tzu-liao chuan-chi* [A Special Collection of Materials on Liu Shao-ch'i] (Taipei: Chung-kung wen-t'i yen-chiu so, 1970), pp. 25–69.

12. *Selected Works,* vol. 3, p. 50.

13. "Speech at the Chinese Communist Party's National Conference on Propaganda Work" (March 19, 1957), in *Selected Readings,* pp. 493–494.

14. "Speech at the 10th Plenary Session of the 8th Central Committee," in *Chinese Law and Government* 1, no. 4 (Winter 1968–1969):91.

15. Cf. Robert Jay Lifton, *Thought Reform and the Psychology of Totalism: A Study of "Brainwashing" in China* (New York: Norton, 1963); also Philipp Lersch, *Zur Psychologie der Indoktrination,* bk. 3 (Munich; Beck, 1969).

16. See also Martin King Whyte, *Small Groups and Political Rituals in China* (Berkeley: University of California Press, 1974).

17. *Selected Works,* vol. 3, p. 56.

18. "Talks at a Conference of Secretaries of Provincial, Municipal and Autonomous Region Party Committees" (January 1957), *Selected Works,* vol. 5, pp. 369–370.

19. "Beat Back the Attacks of the Bourgeois Rightists," (July 9, 1957), ibid., p. 459.

20. "A Study of Physical Education" (April 1917), in Schram, *Political Thought,* pp. 94–102.

21. *Selected Works,* vol. 3, p. 73.

22. Edgar Snow, *Red Star over China,* rev. and enl. ed. (New York: Grove Press, 1968), p. 168. An account of a similar experience in the development of a revolutionary outlook is found in *The Autobiography of Malcolm X* (New York: Grove Press, 1966), p. 8.

23. "U.S. Imperialism Is a Paper Tiger" (July 14, 1956), and "All Reactionaries Are Paper Tigers" (November 18, 1957), in *Selected Works,* vol. 5, pp. 308–312 and 517–518, respectively.

24. The translation is from "Report on an Investigation of the Peasant Movement in Hunan" in *Selected Works,* vol. 1, p. 28.

25. Cf. Sigmund Freud, *Group Psychology and the Analysis of the Ego,* trans. James Strachey (New York: Liveright, 1949); and Elias Canetti, *Crowds and Power,* trans. Carol Stewart (New York: Viking Press, 1962).

26. "Speech at the 2nd Session of the 8th Central Committee," *Selected Works,* vol. 5, p. 337.

27. Sidney Gruson's unexpurgated edition of the speech "On the Resolution of Contradictions among the People" (via Warsaw), in *New York Times,* June 13, 1957, pp. 1, 8.

28. "Talks at a Conference of Party Committee Secretaries," *Selected Works,* vol. 5, p. 358.

29. Ibid., p. 374.

30. "Concluding Remarks at the Supreme State Conference" (March 1, 1957), in *Wan-sui* (1969), pp. 90–100.

31. Peter Worsley, *The Trumpet Shall Sound: A Study of "Cargo" Cults in Melanesia* (London: MacGibbon & Kee, 1957), pp. 250–251; see also Anthony Wallace, *Culture and Personality,* 2d ed. (New York: Random House, 1971), chapter 4.

32. Otto Fenichel, "The Counterphobic Attitude," *Collected Papers* (London: Routledge and Kegan Paul, 1955), pp. 163–174.

33. *Wan-sui,* pp. 90–100.

34. Three Red Guard tabloids—*Hsin Pei-ta* (Peking University), *Red Flag* (Peking Aeronautical Institute), and *East is Red* (Peking Geological Institute)—had national circulations, while a fourth, Tsinghua University's *Ching-kang-shan,* for a while in 1967 had a national circulation second only to that of the *People's Daily.* Red Guard liaison stations and tabloids sometimes communicated information across the country more quickly and efficiently than did the official press.

35. "Sweep Away All Freaks and Monsters," *People's Daily* editorial, June 1, 1966, in *Survey of China Mainland Press,* no. 3712 (June 6, 1966), p. 2; see also H. C. Chuang, *The Great Proletarian Cultural Revolution: A Terminological Study* (Berkeley: Institute for International Studies, University of California, August 1967), passim.

36. *Ching-kang-shan* editorial, no. 5 (December 26, 1966), p. 3.

37. "Chairman Mao's Important Instructions," in *Joint Publications Research Service,* no. 49826 (February 12, 1970), p. 23.

38. "Long Live the Revolutionary Rebel Spirit of the Proletariat," *Red Flag,* no. 11 (August 21, 1966), p. 27.

39. "A Proposal by 57 Revolutionary Organizations,"*Hsin-hua* (Peking), January 29, 1967, in *Joint Publications Research Service,* no. 41202 (May 29, 1967), pp. 23–27; "Behind-the-Scenes Story of the Yielding of Power in the Seven Ministries of Machine Building," *Fei Ming Ti* [Flying Whistling Arrowhead], February 17, 1967, in *Joint Publications Research Service,* no. 41779 (July 11, 1967), pp. 101–105; *People's Daily* editorial, June 8, 1966, in *Current Background,* no. 392 (October 21, 1969).

40. "Mao's Talks to Liberated Cadres and Cadres from Wuhan" (Autumn 1974), *Fei-ch'ing yüeh-pao* [Studies in Communism] 17, no. 12 (February 1975):78–79.

41. For a more detailed accounting, see my "Revolution and Reconstruction in Contemporary Chinese Bureaucracy,"*Journal of Comparative Administration* (February 1974):443–87.

42. At Chou En-lai's banquet soiree preceding National Day in 1975, there were some indications that he was preparing to mount an even stronger challenge to the radicals: twenty percent of the forty-nine pre-Cultural Revolution officials whom he allowed to reappear at that time were active in the culture and propaganda sector before the Cultural Revolution. These included four former vice ministers of culture (meaning the entire membership of the vice ministers of culture from the 1965 period had been rehabilitated!), two vice directors of the Central Committee propaganda department, two assistant editors of *Red Flag,* and others.

43. For example, the moderates reacted quickly to the "against the current" campaign that was initiated at the tenth congress. They immediately abolished the cultural test at the entrance to colleges and readmitted those candidates who had been rejected after having failed to pass the test. In the factories where rebellious workers had attacked "regulations and systems," study classes were held to listen to their complaints, and education on discipline was applied to them. When Huang Shuai's letter criticizing her teacher was published in the *People's Daily* on December 12, 1973, the authorities also responded quickly. On December 28, the *People's Daily* published a report side by side with the reprint of Huang's letter, stating that everything had been rectified at Huang's school and that teachers, students, and parents were closely united and helping one another. "Going against the current does not mean that the students should oppose the teachers. Together they should open fire on ɪevisionism" (Peking Radio, February 13, 1974).

44. On the five occasions when Chiang Ch'ing appeared publicly from December 1973 to March 1974, Chou was also present. Each occasion was marked by a close-up photograph of the two together with foreign guests. Teng Hsiao-p'ing also attempted to ignore the ulterior implications of the campaign to criticize *Water Margin* in the summer and fall of 1975, but without going to the trouble of demonstrating public amity with the radicals.

45. According to Ming Ming in *Tung-hsi Feng,* the article "The Spirit of Going Against the Tide," which appeared in the *People's Daily* on August 16, 1973, was written by Mao himself. Cf. Yen Ching-wen, "Power Struggle in Peking Moves to a New Climax," *Chan-wang* [Prospect], no. 283 (November 16, 1973), pp. 6–9.

46. Fang Yen-liang, "Going Against the Tide Is a Marxist-Leninist Principle," *Red Flag,* no. 1 (December 1, 1973), pp. 23–27.

47. To fill the aesthetic gap, "black dramatic troupes," "underground clubs," "underground concerts," and "underground story-telling gatherings" made their appearance, organized by "loafing actors" to give performances by "loitering all over the country."

48. Cf. Gerald Marwell and David R. Schmitt, *Cooperation: An Experimental Analysis* (New York: Academic Press, 1975); also Leonard Berkowitz, "The Self, Selfishness and Altruism," in J. Macaulay and L. Berkowitz, eds., *Altruism and Helping Behavior: Social Psychological Studies of Some Antecedents and Consequences* (New York: Academic Press, 1970), pp. 143–151; and Roland N. McKean, "Economics of Trust, Altruism and Corporate Responsibility," in Edmund S. Phelps, ed., *Altruism, Morality, and Economic Theory* (New York: Russell Sage Foundation, 1975), pp. 29–44.

49. This strategy could yield spectacular dividends for young radicals. Chu Ke-chia graduated from a Shanghai high school at eighteen in 1969 and volunteered to go down to the countryside in Yunnan, where he founded a school in an isolated mountain village and undertook to begin a factory. In 1973, at the age of twenty-

two, he was made a candidate member of the Central Committee, and two years later he became a member of the Standing Committee of the fourth National People's Congress. Chang Li-kuo, a former Red Guard, became vice chairman of the Hupei Revolutionary Committee in 1968, and in 1973 became secretary of the Communist Youth League in the same province.

50. Cf. Hong Yung Lee, "The Politics of Cadre Rehabilitation since the Cultural Revolution," (unpublished manuscript, 1977).

51. *Kwangming Daily,* December 14, 1976; January 22, 1977; as cited in Lee, ibid., p. 41.

52. Bruce Bolnick, "Toward a Behavioral Theory of Philanthropic Activity," in Phelps, *Altruism, Morality, and Economic Theory,* pp. 29–44; see also Nicholas Rescher, *Unselfishness: The Role of the Vicarious Affects in Moral Philosophy and Social Theory* (Pittsburgh, Pa.: University of Pittsburgh Press, 1975), p. 23 et passim.

53. Kan Ko, Chuang Ning, "Persist in the Method of Seeking Truth from Facts," *Red Flag,* no. 1 (January 1, 1973), pp. 9–15.

54. Yao Wen-yüan, "Dictatorship of the Proletariat and the Renegade Lin Piao," *Peking Review,* June 27, 1975, p. 8; as quoted in Tang Tsou, "Mao Tse-tung's Thought, the Last Struggle for Succession, and the Post-Mao Era," *China Quarterly,* forthcoming.

55. Chang Ch'un-ch'iao, "On Exercising All-Round Dictatorship over the Bourgeoisie," *Red Flag,* no. 4 (April 1, 1975), pp. 3–13.

56. Cf. B. F. Skinner, *Beyond Freedom and Dignity* (New York: Knopf, 1972), pp. 56–78.

57. *Survey of the People's Republic of China Magazines,* no. 926 (May 23, 1977), pp. 8–30.

58. "Correspondence on Bourgeois Right," *Study and Criticism,* no. 3 (March 16, 1975).

10

Children's Literature and Political Socialization

Parris H. Chang

> In order to guarantee that our party and country do not change their color, we not only must have a correct line and correct policies, but must train and bring up millions of successors who will carry on the cause of proletarian revolution.
>
> —MAO TSE-TUNG, 1964

Since 1949 China has been a land of revolution. Substantial changes have occurred not only in political spheres and systems of economic ownership and production, but also in social institutions, values, and attitudes, even though many of these changes have fallen short of the proclaimed goals of the government. Communication has been instrumental in the revolutionary transformation of China.[1] This chapter examines one communication medium—children's literature or, more specifically, children's picture storybooks.

Since coming to power in 1949, the leadership of the Chinese Communist Party has maintained control over the agents and processes of political socialization and communication. To create a new socialist society and a new political culture, the Chinese Communist leaders realize that they must eradicate many existing attitudes and orientations and instill new values in the Chinese people. Toward this end, they have sought to change the process of socialization as well as to establish new patterns in structure and content of communication.[2]

At what age should political socialization begin? Is it possible to shape a child's political orientation even in preschool years? Will early impressions have significant impact on political behavior in later years? These and other questions concerning primary political socialization have been discussed for centuries. Many Western writers, notably Plato and Rousseau, have argued for an early start in political education.[3] They assume that what is learned during the first few years of life is less easily dislodged later.

Persuasive as it may be, this view is by no means accepted by all social scientists. Such alternative theories as Lucian Pye's personality theory, for example, have been advanced.[4] What concerns us here, however, is not the theoretical controversy but policies the Chinese government applies to children's early political socialization. There is no question that the Chinese leaders believe in early political socialization, and this belief is clearly reflected in children's literature as well as in other media of communication.

Chinese Picture Storybooks

Picture storybooks are among the most popular types of reading in China today. These are small paperback books (mostly 5 by 7 inches) with large attractive pictures and a brief caption (or text) on each page. Written in simple language, they are intended for children (preschool and school age) but also attract adults; thus they help bridge the illiteracy barrier and are "favorites with children and adults who can only read a little."[5] By 1956, more than 100 million copies of picture books had been printed.[6] In the past two decades, the number must have increased many times, although precise information is not available.

This form of literature had existed in China long before 1949. Illustrations on the pages of the stories of the Sung and Yüan dynasties and character portraits and pictures in many popular romances and novels of the Ming and Ch'ing dynasties are said to be the forerunners of picture storybooks.[7] According to the French sinologist Jean Chesneax, "something like the modern comics were used as early as the fourteenth century to propagate the teachings of Confucius."[8] Only after the May Fourth movement of 1919, however, did modern picture storybooks begin to appear and become widespread as a popular form of literature.

Before 1949, this medium of communication rarely carried clearcut political messages, as it was intended primarily for entertainment, diversion, and escape. Most books were based on Chinese classics such as *Romance of the Three Kingdoms, Monkey,* and *Water Margin,* and on other popular novels such as *White Snake, Cases of Shih Kung* and *Living Buddha Chi Kung.* A large number of picture books also were adapted from Western thrillers (e.g., *The Three Musketeers, The Count of Monte Cristo*), Hollywood movies (e.g., Tarzan, Charlie Chan), science fiction, and Chinese translations of American comics. They are still very popular reading among children in Taiwan and Hong Kong today. In the opinion of one Chinese Communist writer, such books poison the people's minds and constitute a particularly pernicious influence on children.[9]

In China today, picture storybooks are an important medium of communication and serve as an instrument to transmit officially sanctioned messages to readers. A large proportion of the picture storybooks published in the 1950s, for example, were on revolutionary struggle and socialist construction—stories about the anti-Japanese war, the Communist-Nationalist civil war, and the Korean War, and propaganda on agricultural collectives, communes, and the Great Leap Forward. Some of these publications featured heroic men and women who were worthy models for younger generations. Another large percentage of the books carried stories of historical figures, revolutionary struggles, patriots of the past, and pioneers in the search for freedom and truth (Figure 10–1). At that time, many picture storybooks based on traditional novels (such as *Monkey* (Figure 10–2) and *Romance of the Three Kingdoms,* and old legends, fables, dramas, or folktales, also were still published because they were extremely popular among readers in the 1950s (as they were before 1949), according to the Chinese writers previously quoted.

By the mid-1960s, however, books portraying "emperors, generals, prime ministers, scholars, beauties" had come under severe criticism.[10] This was a time when Chiang Ch'ing and other radical elements in the Party were attacking the influence of the past and bourgeois ideas in Chinese society in order to rectify China's cultural and ideological spheres.[11] Reflecting this political trend, books portraying traditional stories ceased to be published.

Meanwhile, a major shift in emphasis was taking place and a greater degree of politicization can be discerned in the children's literature from the mid-1960s on. If "science" and "conscience," according to Jean-Pierre Dieny, were two main themes of picture storybooks before the Cultural Revolution of 1966,[12] the former received less and less emphasis with each passing year. And in fact, greater attention was paid to education in class struggle, revolutionary traditions, and proletarian internationalism.

A large number of stories during this period praised soldiers'

Figure 10-1. Li Shih-chen, a well-known medical doctor and pharmacologist of the Ming Dynasty.

love and helpfulness toward the people, devotion to the Party, and similar virtues. They featured such People's Liberation Army models as Lei Feng, Wang Chieh, and Ouyang Hai, who were objects of nationwide emulation campaigns in 1964–1966. Stories about the conflict in Indochina also gradually increased as the Vietnam war escalated; anti-American themes appeared in many of these books. Other titles reflected the Chinese leadership's stress on solidarity with the revolutionary peoples of the world by portraying international friendship and the revolutionary struggle of Asians, Africans, and Latin Americans.

The storybooks of the 1970s have mirrored the political and policy changes that came as a result of the Cultural Revolution. They condemned the evil life and influence of Confucius during the campaign to criticize Lin Piao and Confucius. They also publicized such "newborn things" of the Cultural Revolution as the barefoot doctor (Figure 10-3), the sent-down youth, and the spirit of "going against the tide." Since the fall of 1975, a spate of storybooks has

FIGURE 10-2. From *Monkey Subdues the White-Bone Demon.*

appeared to criticize the classic *Water Margin* (Figure 10-4) and to depict Sung Chiang (the main character in it) as a "capitulationist," (see Merle Goldman's chapter in this volume). Now that the Gang of Four has been purged, one can expect new storybooks that will reflect the ideological values and policies favored by the post-Mao leadership.

FIGURE 10–3. A young barefoot doctor in action with acupuncture; from *The Small Barefoot Doctor.*

FIGURE 10–4. From *Exposing the Capitulationist Sung Chiang.*

Major Themes

This section describes a set of values and orientations abstracted from a random survey of 175 picture storybooks. Nine tenths of them (251 titles) were published after 1971, while 25 titles were published before the Cultural Revolution of 1966 (during 1967–1970, publication of storybooks appears to have stopped as a result of the political turmoil). Out of the 251 titles published since 1971, 39 are 1977 editions. Close to half (127) of these books were published by the Shanghai People's Publishing House: the rest were published by Peking's People's Art Publishing House and fifteen provincial (municipal) People's Publishing Houses including those of Kwangtung, Hopei, Kiangsu, Tientsin, Kansu, Inner Mongolia, and Liaoning.

With a few exceptions, the pictures in these books are drawn with a professionalism on a par with that of the best comic strip artists in the United States. Action is conveyed with forcefulness and economy of line. Facial expressions are rendered with crisp and careful strokes. Unlike American comics, however, there is nothing pornographic about Chinese picture storybooks. American comics have no dearth of sex; women are busty love objects and even heroines are leggy and use sex as a weapon. Chinese picture books, by contrast, do not show women as sexy; a woman's strength is usually her correct ideological belief.

Another interesting contrast is the absence of political and social humor in Chinese picture books. Many American comic strips poke fun at American life and society and satirize public policies as well as the nation's leaders. Chinese picture books are too serious to permit satirical social criticism. Moreover, whereas Batman, Superman, and Mandrake are heroes to many Americans because of their superhuman power, and other antiheroes such as Dagwood and Charlie Brown are loved for their buffoonery and ineptness, we find neither clowns nor supernatural heroes in the Chinese repertoire.

Undoubtedly, a basic difference underlies Chinese and American comics. American comics are intended for amusement and diversion; Chinese comics, for education and indoctrination. Tracing this a step further, one can say that American comics reflect and comment on what American artists see in their society and culture, whereas Chinese comics are an instrument of the authorities to create and develop the society and political culture they desire.

Indeed, intense political socialization is the outstanding characteristic of China's picture storybooks. The Party not only controls the publication of the picture books but approves in advance themes and values going into them. The writer-artists work for the Party and state—their mission is to transmit the Party's ideology and policy, to instill correct political attitudes and orientations in their readers.

What are the values and attitudes which the Party leadership seeks to inculcate? How are they different from the traditional ethos? The following eight themes emerge from my readings of the sample picture books. As no quantitative analysis was attempted, these themes are proposed on a tentative and impressionistic basis as core values of China's political culture.

Support for the New System

Running through a large number of stories is the theme of allegiance to the Chinese Communist system.[13] The objects of devotion range from institutions (e.g., the Party, the People's Liberation Army, the commune, and so on) to policies (e.g., collectivization, communization, rustication of youth) to worthy individuals. Among those praised in the stories are Chairman Mao and Marshal Chu Teh[14]; (Figure 10-5); martyrs who fought against the Japanese, the Kuomintang, and the Americans in Korea; model workers like "Iron Man" Wang Chin-hsi of the Tach'ing Oilfield and model peasants who excel in the task of socialist construction; and a host of model functionaries and People's Liberation Army heroes (e.g., Lei Feng, Wang Chieh, and Ouyang Hai)—all of whom died in the line of duty while building the new society (Figures 10-6 and 10-7).

It should be pointed out that every political system, East or West, has utilized a multitude of devices, including early socialization of those new to the system, to marshal support for it. During the Ch'ing dynasty in China, for example, the authorities used schools, lectures, and ceremonies to extol filial piety, respect for elders and superiors, peaceful and industrious conduct, observance of the law, and other tenets of Confucianism—all as a basis for instilling positive loyalty and compliance to imperial rule.[15]

What distinguishes current Chinese efforts at early political socialization is perhaps their highly centralized approach to propagating the new social and political ethic. Furthermore, the wide-

FIGURE 10-5. From *Stories of Commander Chu Teh.*

FIGURE 10-6. Lei Feng denouncing a landlord; from *The Boyhood of Lei Feng.*

FIGURE 10-7. Wang Chieh jumped over a mine, sacrificing his own life to save his comrades; from *The Story of Wang Chieh*.

spread and highly conscientious use of models as a tool of political socialization is an ingenious Communist innovation. It is true that Confucius long ago taught that "teaching by example is superior to teaching by words," and that the use of models in moral education had a long tradition.[16] It is the Chinese Communists, however, who have developed an impressive array of skills and systematically employed both positive and negative models to instill new behavior and change the old. The selection of many ordinary men and women and even children, rather than national leaders, as models for emulation seems to make good sense in terms of observational learning theory,[17] for it is easier for people to emulate the common people than it is to identify with the elites.

Collectivism

Another major theme that frequently appears in the stories can be characterized as collectivism. Instead of stressing obligations to the family and kinship groups, as in traditional China, children are now taught to focus their loyalty on the collective and the nation state. Group interests must always be put ahead of individual interests. The story of Li Shuang-shuang embodies this orientation. As a good commune member, she worked hard, cared for the collective interest and public property, and dared to "struggle" against wrongdoings of neighbors, relatives, and even her own husband; she once actually put up a big character poster to expose her husband and other commune members for stealing workpoints.

To put the interests of the local collective ahead of individual interests, however, is not enough. In traditional China, too, the individual was taught to subordinate his interests to those of a group, although this group usually meant a kinship unit, native village, or locality and did not extend beyond those who shared these memberships or relationships. The current emphasis calls for subordinating the interests of a small exclusive collective to those of a larger and more inclusive one. Thus, in *Song of Dragon River (Lung Chiang Sung)*, we see a female Party branch secretary, Chiang Shui-ying, help the leader and other members of the Lung Chiang Brigade overcome their tendencies to be concerned with their own group interests and salvage the crops in 90,000 *mou* of the country, even though this means destroying 300 *mou* of crops that belong to the brigade (Figure 10–8).

Included also in the broad theme of collectivism are stories that display the attitude/behavior of being helpful to other people, emphasizing group action and cooperation in a common effort, and decrying the tendency toward individual concern. The attitudes expressed in such slogans as "serve the people" and "fight self" are highlighted in many stories portraying dedication to the public cause, conscious suppression of private interests, and heroic self-sacrifice, including loss of life, to serve the revolution.

Struggle

Many stories published since the 1960s have portrayed post-1949 China as rife with class struggle and internal enemies of the revolution. The aim is perhaps to sensitize readers to be on the lookout for class enemies in their own environment (e.g., villages, schools, neighborhoods) and to struggle against them. The struggle is to be conducted not only against class enemies; it is also against those who belong to the ranks of the "people" but whose actions harm the cause of revolution.

Contrary to the traditional orientation, which emphasized the maintenance of harmonious social relations and avoidance of con-

FIGURE 10-8. Chiang Shui-ying convinces other villagers to forego the interests of a small collective in favor of those of a larger one; from *Song of Dragon River.*

flict or disorderly action, children are now being taught to dare to struggle against neighbors, friends, relatives, and superiors.[18] Indeed to "go against the tide" and to criticize one's parents, teachers, and particularly higher authorities are actions prominently featured in some of the post–Cultural Revolution picture books.

Activism

Closely related to the theme of struggle is the principle of political activism. This requires the Chinese to overcome old inclinations toward passivity and dependency and to assert themselves in striving for desired goals.

In addition to taking an active role politically, Chinese children are also taught to employ their own initiative and capacities to overcome obstacles in life. Rather than being resigned to one's fate or to a seemingly insurmountable difficulty, as a new socialist man or woman one must learn the moral of *The Foolish Old Man Who Moved the Mountain* and exert oneself to accomplish the tasks that lie ahead. In so doing, one must overcome superstition and a "fatalist" orientation in society.

Self-Reliance

Intimately connected with the teachings of struggle and activism is an emphasis on self-reliance. Many stories stress the power of the human will that persistently "dares to think and act" to overcome obstacles; they discourage dependence on material resources or recourse to higher authorities or foreigners.

Fiery Years, for instance, is a book that embodies the spirit of self-reliance. It depicts a group of Shanghai steel workers who, in the face of an economic blockade instituted against China by an unnamed socialist country, set their minds to make, from domestic material, a special alloy steel needed for building China's warships. They work day and night at their experiments, struggling against the thinking of some officials who have blind faith in experts and rely on importing the needed steel.

Violence and Pro-social Aggression

Readers of China's picture books can hardly fail to notice the quantity of graphic pictorial representation of violence. In story after story we see violent behavior—in battles against the British, the Japanese, and the Americans, and in the struggle against invaders from Taiwan. For example, in a story about the atrocities of the British during the Opium War, *San-yuan-li,* one hapless English soldier is shown having his skull split open by a Chinese peasant attacking him from behind with a long-handled hoe. In *The Little Coast Guards,* Little Hung (a girl in her early teens) is shown shoving a bulky enemy spy down a steep cliff after a bullet has hit the man's wrist and caused him to drop his dagger (Figure 10-9).

Many stories that feature models for national emulation also vividly portray their heroic deaths. Aggression against "bad people," in action or attitude, is approved and rewarded.

Women's Liberation

The Chinese Communist leadership has sought to elevate the status of women. The picture storybooks reflect this new orientation. Indeed, girls and women not only appear on the brightly colored covers of many picture books but also are the main characters of the stories.[19] Women have been given prominence especially in

FIGURE 10-9. Pro-social aggression; from *The Little Coast Guards.*

books published in the post–Cultural Revolution era; in *Song of Dragon River (Lung Chiang Sung), On the Docks (Hai Kang),* and several others based on Chiang Ch'ing's revolutionary operas, the principal model character is invariably a heroine. The message in these stories is significant: whatever a man does, a woman also can do, and do better (Figure 10-10). These heroines are not sex objects, as in American comic books; their strength lies in their proletarian outlook and devotion to the revolution.

As one analyst has pointed out, older women are portrayed as peasants and wives, while girls and young women are shown as teachers, medical workers, educated youth, and so on—models capable of taking on approved roles or responsibilities.[20] This may indicate actual social change as well as the official policy of achieving equality of sexes.

In line with the theme of women's liberation, one story portrays the unselfish female commune member mentioned earlier, Li Shuang-shuang, who defies male authority and struggles against her lazy and selfish husband. Similarly, *Female Street Cleaners* tells the story of an educated youth who fights the old orientation of subordination to paternal authority.

Figure 10-10. A woman liberated from household chores to work in the factory; from *The Female Steelworker.*

Beware of Enemies

Mao's teaching "never forget the class struggle" constitutes a main theme in many stories. Children are encouraged to be vigilant against class enemies, especially those who live in their own environment (Figure 10-11). Through the sharp dichotomy between positive and negative characters portrayed in the books, children are taught to be sensitive to the distinction between friends and enemies and to develop a keen class consciousness.

The Impact of the Picture Books—Some Hypotheses

We shall now consider the possible implications of early political socialization. But a few caveats must first be made.

Although this study assumes that early socialization does make an impact, there is no direct evidence of the validity of the assumption. The possibility that what is learned in the early years of life is more influential than what is learned later, remains only a plausible working hypothesis. Thus the following sketch of the systemic impact of political socialization via picture storybooks is based largely on impressionistic, circumstantial evidence.

FIGURE 10–11. Little Hung, a third grader, catches a Soviet spy (who happens to be her grandfather); from *Duel by Wit*.

What social and cultural consequences may be expected from the proliferation of revolutionary picture storybooks? We offer a set of tentative observations as hypotheses for further study. Though largely consistent with some of the existing literature, these observations are certainly debatable and require verification by more concrete evidence.

1. While acceptance of the substance of the new Chinese political culture seems uneven, its continued propagation through indoctrination could heighten a consciousness in the Chinese people of their identification with the national community leading to a substantial degree of national integration.[21]

2. Exposure to the major themes in revolutionary picture storybooks could lessen superstitious and fatalistic tendencies among the Chinese, and inspire more confidence in their own ability to subdue nature and overcome obstacles through collective human endeavor. Such modernizing attitudes are indispensable for a country seeking political and economic development.

3. As a result of vigorous propagation of early political indoctrination, the Chinese may develop a high degree of political awareness. Most people in China seem to realize that politics is an important part of their lives and that to be indifferent toward politics will

FIGURE 10-12. "Severely Criticizing Lin Piao and Confucius" by Tsui Hung-ling, age 10; from *Pictures by Chinese Children.*

have adverse consequences. As attested by the example of the Red Guards during the Cultural Revolution, the primary emphasis on politics in the thinking and lives of Chinese people may have created in Chinese adolescents an impatient, precocious desire to participate in adult activities (Figure 10-12).[22] The realism of Chinese storybooks—namely, the depiction of a real world that does not encourage children to pursue inner dreams and fantasies or to engage in make-believe—could reinforce the trend toward precocity.

4. Heightened political sensitivity and precocity, if prolonged, could in turn be conducive to widespread political participation. Although the involvement of enormous numbers of Chinese people in the political process is not "political participation" as the term is generally understood in the West,[23] there is no question that China's political culture is no longer a traditional one (in which individuals display little or no awareness of the national political system).[24] Whether or not China will fully develop a participant political culture, it seems apparent that during the Cultural Revolution, at least, individuals and groups engaged in the articulation of demands and came close to the making of decisions, leaving a

political/ideological legacy that encourages mass political participation. In some respects, however, such a legacy can be debilitating to the system. As Samuel Huntington has pointed out, a rapid increase in popular mobilization and participation without the development of effective political institutions to channel such participation produces not political development, but "political decay."[25]

5. As outside visitors and refugees from China have often reported, the Chinese now possess a heightened class consciousness. They know that to have a correct class background is a matter of importance that could affect one's career and welfare. They tend to be suspicious of outsiders and are apt to look closely at the people they encounter to see who are friends and who are enemies. (The sharpening of class consciousness begins early in life, as is seen in the revolutionary picture storybooks.) This tendency, coupled with what Alan Liu calls a "dual standard of political civility" (aggression against the "enemy" and comradeship with the "people"), could have wide ranging implications. The systemic indoctrination of a dual standard of political civility, in Liu's view, accounts for the factionalism and group violence characteristic of the Cultural Revolution.[26]

6. Because Chinese children have been taught two sets of behavioral standards, pro-social aggression or violence against negative elements may be considered legitimate. While no political system completely outlaws violence against enemies of the system, China would seem to be unique in accentuating pro-social aggression in its political socialization process and in the extent to which it changes the definition of enemies according to the prevailing political climate. This type of socialization appears to have contributed to violent group conflicts in China both during and after the Cultural Revolution. Heightened political sensitivity and the teaching of dual standards of political civility which sanctify pro-social aggression constitute what Alan Liu calls the "subjective precipitating factor" in the mass conflict of the Cultural Revolution.[27]

NOTES

1. See, for example, Godwin C. Chu, *Radical Change through Communication in Mao's China* (Honolulu: The University Press of Hawaii, 1977).

2. Ibid.; also, Alan P. L. Liu, *Communications and National Integration in Communist China,* new enl. ed. (Berkeley: University of California Press, 1975).

3. David Easton and Jack Dennis, *Children in the Political System* (New York: McGraw-Hill, 1969), pp. 75–77.

4. Ibid., pp. 77–81; also, Lucian W. Pye, *Politics, Personality and Nation Building* (New Haven, Conn.: Yale University Press, 1962), pp. 45–46.

5. Chiang Wei-pu, "Chinese Picture Story Books," *Chinese Literature,* no. 3 (March 1959), as translated in Ralph C. Croizier, ed., *China's Cultural Legacy and Communism* (New York: Praeger, 1970), p. 164.

6. Ibid., p. 165.

7. Ibid., p. 164.

8. Quoted by Gino Nebiolo in *The People's Comic Book* (Garden City, N.Y.: Doubleday, 1973), p. xii.

9. Chiang Wei-pu, "Chinese Picture Story Books," p. 165.

10. "Do Not Let Serial Pictures Poison the Minds of Children," *Worker's Daily* (Peking), May 18, 1965, as translated in Croizier, *China's Cultural Legacy,* pp. 166–167.

11. See Merle Goldman, *Literary Dissent in Communist China* (Cambridge, Mass.: Harvard University Press, 1967).

12. Jean-Pierre Dieny, *Le Monde est à vous: La Chine et les livres pour enfants* (Paris: Gallimard, 1971), ch. 1.

13. This general theme is highly similar to an analysis of stories in elementary readers published in 1963 and 1964 by Charles P. Ridley, Paul H. B. Godwin, and Dennis J. Doolin; see *The Making of a Model Citizen in Communist China* (Stanford, Ca.: Hoover Institution, 1971).

14. A picture biography of Chu Teh, *The Story of Commander Chu,* was published in June 1977, almost one year after his death. No other living top Party officials, except Mao, have ever been featured in the books.

15. Kung-Chuan Hsiao, *Rural China: Imperial Control in the Nineteenth Century* (Seattle: University of Washington Press, 1960), ch. 6.

16. The functions of models are analyzed in Donald J. Munro, *The Concept of Man in Contemporary China* (Ann Arbor: University of Michigan Press, 1977).

17. See, for example, A. Bandura, *Psychological Modeling* (Chicago: Aldine-Atherton, 1971), and I. S. Rohter, "A Social Learning Approach to Political Socialization," in D. C. Schwartz and S. K. Schwartz, eds., *New Directions in Political Socialization* (New York: The Free Press, 1975).

18. The commitment to political activism and struggle has been a serious problem in Chinese political culture. See Richard H. Solomon, *Mao's Revolution and the Chinese Political Culture* (Berkeley: University of California Press, 1971).

19. According to Blumenthal, who conducted a detailed study of the picture books, women have not achieved equality (equal prominence) in these stories; males are much more prominent in cover illustrations, as main characters, and as officials and models, while women still play a very minor role. See Eileen Polley Blumenthal, "Models in Chinese Moral Education: Perspectives from Children's Books" (Ph.D. diss., University of Michigan, 1976), pp. 114–115.

20. Ibid., p. 115.

21. Cf. Chu, *Radical Change,* ch. 8.

22. Alan P. L. Liu, *Political Culture and Group Conflict in Communist China* (Santa Barbara: Clio Books, 1976), pp. 19–20.

23. See James Townsend, *Political Participation in Communist China,* new ed. (Berkeley: University of California Press, 1969).

24. The definition is taken from Gabriel Almond and G. Bingham Powell, Jr., *Comparative Politics* (Boston: Little, Brown, 1966).

25. Samuel Huntington, *Political Order in Changing Societies* (New Haven, Conn.: Yale University Press, 1968), ch. 1.

26. Liu, *Political Culture and Group Conflict in Communist China,* pp. 24–35. A different conclusion about the consequences of teaching pro-social aggression has been suggested by Ridley, et al., *Making of a Model Citizen,* pp. 144–145, 198–199, and Blumenthal, "Models in Chinese Moral Education," p. 195. The experience in China, particularly during the Cultural Revolution, would tend to confirm Liu's observation.

27. Liu, *Political Culture and Group Conflict,* p. 35.

IV

VALUE CHANGE

An important component of culture consists of the values, beliefs, and social processes that are essential to the *maintenance of primary relations.* Marriage norms and kinship relations are part of that component. Over the past three decades in China, the Party has promulgated a new marriage law and made various attempts to establish a proletarian basis of social relations in place of the traditional kinship ties. However, what Francis L. K. Hsu, formerly professor of anthropology at Northwestern University and presently director of the Center for Cultural Studies in Education, University of San Francisco, found from his personal observations indicates considerable continuity with the past and relatively little change in these important areas of Chinese culture. What some Western visitors mistook for changes, Hsu argues, could be attributed to the fact that their information prior to 1949 came from individuals who were close to Westerners and who were not representative of the Chinese people as a whole.

What are some of the new values and beliefs being communicated to the people of China? Ai-li Chin, assistant professor of sociology at the University of Massachusetts, seeks an answer by analyzing the content of popular short stories published in China since the 1950s. Although the main body of her data comes from stories published in 1976–1977, she is able to present a picture that includes the 1960s and the 1950s. As one might expect, she found that the content of the short stories was very much affected by the prevailing ideological interpretation at the time. Nevertheless, on the whole certain recurring values stand out clearly from the short stories throughout the last three decades.

Vivienne Shue, assistant professor of political science at Yale University, presents a case study of the effect of communication campaigns in the 1950s in changing some of the traditional values of the Chinese peasants. She shows how the Party skillfully began by appealing to old values and then altered the messages to carry new values; the peasants' behavior could then be explained on the basis of both the old and the new. In her opinion, however, the final stage, that of new values fully supplanting old ones, was in no case achieved.

Hsia-hsiang, or rustication, is a mass movement intended to bring up a new generation of Chinese by exposing them to the peasant culture while in their teens. Thomas P. Bernstein, associate professor of political science at Columbia University, traces the development of the movement, which espouses the ideal of selfless service. The whole movement, however, seems to involve a dual communication pattern. On one hand, revolutionary values are being officially communicated to the young people, to encourage them to go and stay in the villages. On the other hand, other more subtle messages from the government tell the students in effect that it may not be necessary to subscribe to the new value system. The incongruence of the messages, Bernstein suggests, tends to reduce the effectiveness of the official communication.

William L. Parish, associate professor of sociology at the University of Chicago, presents findings based on quantitative measures and statistical analysis that illustrate the impact of communication on changing rural life in Kwangtung. Indices of newspaper reading and political study were found to be moderately related to measures of collective altruism. In other realms of village life, similarly modest correlations were found. Other indices of communication—for example, movie teams, wired broadcasting, and private radios—showed no consistent correlations with collective life in the villages. It seems that most peasants know fairly well what the new ideals are but in everyday action they respond largely to the constraints and incentives of their immediate local situation and to the mixed collective structures created by the Party in the 1950s.

11

Traditional Culture
in Contemporary China:
Continuity and Change in Values

Francis L. K. Hsu

Nobody can deny that China after 1949 has changed. The world's oldest surviving civilization has undergone a drastic change. For China, some of these spectacular changes are unprecedented. Yet they are still very Chinese.

The principal force for these changes has been communism, an exogenous ideology and practice (as were also Christianity and democracy). Compared with societies such as those of Western Europe, China historically exhibited no great internal impetus toward change, and politically she had revolts but no revolution until the coming of the West in force.[1] But the psychocultural soil in which the new exogenous seeds were sown is Chinese.

In the following study, I shall analyze certain characteristic Chinese values rooted in their kinship system, show how these values are manifested in some aspects of Chinese behavior, and indicate how they have fared under communism, with its new system and means of communication.

Human beings in all societies relate to one another and to ideologies and spiritual matters, as well as to material things, by way of role or affect. *Role* is usefulness. In this approach, the objects to which one relates are tools for rewards or satisfactions beyond them. In human relations, it means what I can do for you in return for what you can do for me. The utmost in role is what money can buy; it involves, at any rate, a high degree of calculation. Every social organization defines role in terms of its two components: the position of the individual in it and the duties, obligations, and privileges specific to the individual's role.

Affect has to do with how the individual feels about the objects to which he relates, about his role and the duties, obligations, and privileges associated with his role. Affect can be described chiefly in such terms as devotion, worship, love, hate, friendship and comradeship, sympathy, and sacrifice. True affect is totally incommensurate with money or calculation. The utmost of affect may involve giving up one's life or worldly riches for the sake of one's good name, kinsmen, lovers, leaders, or causes, not because they are profitable but because one is deeply committed to them.

Affect is at the foundation of the values of all societies. The values of a society will persist if a majority of its members is affectively committed to them. Conversely, the values will fail to last when a majority is not so committed to them.

Role patterns are learned in families, in schools or workshops, by way of reading and studying, and in contacts throughout life. New jobs or new skills can be mastered even at age fifty or sixty. But affective patterns are inculcated primarily and principally in the kinship arena of parents and children. Growth and later developments are mostly expansions or permutations of those which the individual acquired in the early years of life. In this way kinship exerts its influence in human behavior not only where a specific kinship link can be traced but also where such obvious links are absent.

The Characteristic Patterns of Affect
in Chinese Kinship

In every social organization, the individual's role rests on a variety of bases—kinship, contract, hierarchy, ideology, sex, and so on. But the kinship basis comes first everywhere. In the course of growing up, the individual may discard the kinship base for others, but a Chinese is less likely to do so than Westerners because one of the attributes of his kinship system is *continuity*. That is, once a relationship is established, the Chinese individual tends to maintain it for a long time, often indefinitely.

Consequently, a Chinese tends not only to be reluctant to leave his or her first role position—regardless of age—he or she is also reluctant to replace it or sever connection with it even when he or she assumes other role relationships with other individuals. Thus, when a man becomes a husband, he keeps his close ties with his parents; his husbandly role is simply added to his role as son; and when he has to make career decisions, his elders' wishes are likely to figure largely in them.

Continuity of the first role (e.g., as sons) leads to the second characteristic of Chinese kinship: *inclusiveness*. The longer the first role lasts (is continuous), the more numerous will be other roles added to it.

If parents and unmarried children alone have to maintain their ties, a nuclear family will be the result. But if parents and their married sons and the sons' children have to maintain close ties, the situation naturally becomes commensurate with a joint family. By extension, if there are close ties among lineal ancestors of many generations past and yet to come, then the number of collateral relatives involved will be large and some kind of clan or other form of kinship-related larger grouping must necessarily come into play. In other words, inclusiveness is a function of continuity and is a kind of continuity itself.

The attributes of continuity and inclusiveness lead Chinese kinship roles to perpetuate themselves but also to expand their influences outside the kinship arena even when no kinship ties can be traced. For example, good friends become sworn brothers and they often take each other's children as dry sons or daughters.

The attribute of *authority* in the Chinese kinship system makes it relatively easy for the father and mother to exercise their authority. In fact, the authority of any superior relative tends, by extension due to inclusiveness, to be as readily exerted as that of the father.

Some sociologists have tried to differentiate authority and power. In my opinion, power is only one of three bases of authority. First, authority may be enforced by brute power of the physical or economic kind. But this is the least reliable base, for the authority will immediately become untenable if, for any reason, the force is withdrawn or weakened. Second, authority may result from charisma. The usual sense in which the term "charisma" is used is confined to the political, following Max Weber. To me, charisma simply means a kind of attraction to a multitude of people for any reason whatever—technical, sexual, oratorical, and so on. In this sense Marilyn Monroe and Babe Ruth had charisma, as did Franklin D. Roosevelt and Abraham Lincoln. A person enjoying charisma has influence and can command the voluntary following of a very large number of people. Such authority is easier to maintain than that of brute force, but it is also subject to change because charisma fluctuates and does not last forever.

The third basis of authority is tradition. Here the most important consideration is whether one should obey another person's commands for no other reason than it is one's view of life to do so. Thus, where a system of slavery prevails, the master does not have to explain to the slave why he must obey. The fact that the master holds the position of master and the slave holds that of slave is enough reason for the slave to obey the master's commands. Similarly, in a caste society the duties, obligations, and privileges of members of the higher and lower castes also do not have to be explained on any rational basis.[2]

The chief basis of the Chinese father's authority was tradition. The Chinese son had to obey his father by virtue of the roles occupied by the father and the son, respectively. Hence the dictum: "No parents are wrong [vis-à-vis their children]" *(t'ien hsia wu pu shih tzu fu mu)*.

Of course, force and charisma were not entirely absent in the Chinese paternal authority system. For example, fathers could report disobedient sons to the authorities and secure immediate arrest and punishment. Also, fathers who had great fame and were very learned probably had their authority affirmed and reinforced in many instances.

Tradition as the basis of authority is less likely to be challengeable, discontinuous, or temporary than is charisma or brute force. Hence, the attributes of continuity and authority are commensurate with each other.

The attribute of *asexuality* in the Chinese kinship system finds expression in the custom of confining sex to strictly defined areas but not extending it to others. The Chinese have never considered sex, as such, bad. It is only bad if it occurs with the wrong person (such as someone else's wife), in the wrong place (for example, in a public park), at the wrong time (such as during broad daylight) or indulged in excessively (as illustrated by the fictional character Hsi Men Ching in the well-known novel *Chin P'ing Mei [Golden Lotus]*.[3] They view sex as one of the necessities of life, like food. In short, the Chinese never had the notion of sexual repression in their traditional culture and they have not developed it under the new regime.

Courtship in China Today

With this background of characteristic patterns of affect in Chinese kinship, let us analyze two areas of life, courtship and marriage, to see whether and how far traditional values have changed in China today. We shall deal with courtship first.

Anyone who had a little experience in China before World War II and who visits her today may come away with the impression that mores between the sexes have changed a great deal. Traditionally, women were spoken of as being either the "good family" *(liang-chia fu-nu)* variety or the "wind and dust" *(feng-ch'en)* kind. The former consisted of "virtuous wives and kind mothers" *(hsien ch'i liang mu)* whose business was the home and children. The latter consisted of females of easy virtue, including actresses, singers, and streetwalkers.

It was the second kind of Chinese women who used to appear frequently in public, decked in their colorful best, with fancy coiffures and scented cosmetics. They also did not hide some public display of their practiced charm toward men. Before 1911, the "good family" women showed themselves in public only on the occasion of festivals and other special events, such as funerals and weddings. Women of well-to-do families commonly rode in carts or sedan chairs when they went anywhere, properly chaperoned. "Exposing one's head and face" *(p'ao-t'ou lu-mien)* was a colloquial Chinese expression depicting the involuntary condition of a woman being forced by circumstances, usually poverty, to be seen frequently in public. It was an expression often heard in Chinese operas and songs lamenting the misery of an unfortunate female.

"Good family" women from less favored circumstances did indeed appear in public in south and southwest China more than in north China. In the north, women went to the fields to bring the midday meal to their fathers, husbands, and brothers, but they did not as a rule work in the fields. They might occasionally go to markets for some purchases. In the south, farmers' wives and daughters worked side by side with men. A common sight was waterwheels being moved by the feet of men, women, and children. In such areas of southwest China as Yünnan Province, women not only regularly worked on farms but were equal traders in markets with men. They often carried merchandise on their backs or at the two ends of a pole and walked long distances, up to ten or fifteen miles.

But in public these working women dressed in blue or in other subdued colors, many in trousers. Nor did they wear fancy hairdos. As a rule, they conducted themselves demurely, attracting as little male attention as possible. They did all this, it should be noted, without the benefit of communism.

Since the early twentieth century and after the advent of modern schools and colleges of Western origin or inspiration, it was not uncommon to see "good family" girls and women in public with "war paint." Dating of a sort existed on college campuses and elsewhere. But these activities were restricted to a fraction of the population and to the treaty ports and metropolitan centers such as Tientsin, Shanghai, Peking, and Canton. Even in these places, the conduct of Chinese youngsters could not compare in daringness with what went on in America at comparable times and places. In the 1930s, the deans of missionary women's high schools (often European or American ladies) as a matter of regulation used to censor all incoming mail. A girl student found guilty of corresponding with a male would be reprimanded or threatened with expulsion. In some schools a girl had to show parental permission in writing to correspond with a boy to whom she was betrothed.

After 1949, the new government institutionalized, without much fanfare, equality between the sexes in work and play. The changes are not yet evident at the highest levels of leadership. For example, there are still no female commanders of the People's Liberation Army. But one result of the change is evident in schools, factories, banks, shops, the professions, and many offices of government, where women are ubiquitous. More Chinese women than ever before are seen in public. But the Chinese females, although they dress more colorfully in the summer than in winter and with greater variety in 1972 than in 1952, as a whole tend still to be more somber in appearance than they were when Westerners last saw or read about them before the Communist Revolution.

As for relations between the sexes, a case did come to my notice recently in which the female took the initiative with unusual enthusiasm. Our informants in Hong Kong were a noted musician and his wife who left China after the Cultural Revolution. While performing in Shanghai he was the object of much female admiration. One young lady wrote to him many times and kept pestering him on the phone. When he finally told her that he was not interested in her because he was married, she demanded "to be shown his wife before she would believe it." He did, and the young lady, crestfallen, left him alone.

Those who did not know about Shanghai before the Revolution might conclude that such female aggressiveness came with the Revolution. But in 1936 one of my former middle school mates had some unusual experiences. He was a member of what was then China's number one basketball team, nationally known as "The Five Tigers of Nankai" (Nankai Middle School of Tientsin). When the Tigers hit Shanghai on exhibition matches, this very handsome young man was showered with fan mail and romantic proposals from numerous young ladies.

As for relations between the sexes, a majority of Chinese women, even those in schools and colleges, do not appear to have taken on an aggressive role. The pattern of public interaction between young Chinese males and females, moreover, simply does not measure up to Western romantic standards. It often involves encouragement by relatives, friends, or co-workers, and it will be seen by most Americans today as painfully slow moving. Chinese men and women did date before 1949, as they do today. On one July 1972 evening (about 9:00 p.m.) I counted some 175 couples, mostly in their twenties or thirties, within a two-block area on the river side of the Shanghai Bund.[4] However, even though the street lights were darkened by the thick foliage of trees and some lovers held hands or had arms around each other's waists, none showed any more external signs of passion than that. Reflecting on my student days in that same city in the thirties, I judge that these young couples today were doing as much (or as little) in the art of romance as those of us attending the then missionary-run University of Shanghai did in comparable circumstances.

In broad daylight, the Chinese are of course even more subdued by American standards. My family and I saw hundreds of couples in the Temple of Heaven and the Summer Palace of Peking, the East Lake of Wuhan, and the Botanical Garden of Shenyang. We even saw one couple perched inside a large lookout hole on the side of the Great Wall facing Mongolia. But none of them even held hands, which might have been the cause of some Western visitors' misperception. Most fail to realize that the quantity and quality of romantic expressions are subject to cultural conditioning. It can safely be said that a Chinese girl would still not allow herself to be photographed with a boy unless she has already decided to marry him. Another common practice of so many Chinese young males and females is to go out in groups, which do not preclude mild romancing.

The case of Comrade Tung of Shenyang will fill in some details of the present Chinese manner of courtship leading to marriage. Comrade Tung and his wife first met in 1949 when both were members of the same factory. Then Tung was assigned to work in the party-sponsored labor union elsewhere in the same city. They did not begin what Comrade Tung described as a "special relationship" until 1955. Here is how Comrade Tung related to me the sequence of events that followed:

> While working in the labor union, I went back from time to time to visit my old friends in my old factory. Please understand, *I did not go to visit her at first* [emphasis his], I must reiterate. But by 1955 she became older. I went one Sunday to see her. Then the next Sunday she came to my dormitory to see me. It was then that I became a member of the Party. She did the same about the same time. In 1956 I was assigned away to serve as Secretary of Youth Corps of a factory in Peking. I was elected by my co-workers to that post. We corresponded. We saw each other during summer and winter vacations. Always I came back to Shenyang to see her except once when she went to Peking to see me. Through all that correspondence and visits we never promised marriage to each other, but "our hearts knew the score" *[hsin li ming pai]*. The subject of our letters and conversations? They were about our work, study sessions, the good and worthy things we separately saw, and so forth. Even then we two only "understood each other in our hearts but never announced in our words" *[hsin chao pu hsüan]*. We never said "I love you" or "Will you marry me?"
>
> But when she came to see me in Peking in the winter of 1956, we toured the sights and took a picture together. That was serious, you know. We never said so, but it was clear. Three or four months before that, I told my parents. My wife's parents died early; she was brought up by her older sister in Dairen [south Manchuria]. So she told her.[5]

Comrade Tung and his wife were married in Shenyang in the fall of 1957. He traveled from Peking to Shenyang for this. His former colleagues and her friends and co-workers, about forty-five in all, assembled in the conference room of her factory, in the early evening. According to Comrade Tung, the ceremony was as follows. They ate candy and drank tea. The younger members of the assembly sang revolutionary songs. The chief administrators of her factory each gave a short speech—encouraging the new couple to learn, to strive ever more for the country, to live harmoniously, and to raise the next generation. Comrade Tung remembers that watermelons were also served. After that, the newlyweds went to their new quarters provided by her factory: one bedroom and kitchen for their honeymoon. After twenty days Comrade Tung went back to his work unit in Peking while his wife remained in Shenyang. They lived separately for over two years before Tung was reassigned to his present position in Shenyang and reunited with his wife in one household. In 1972 they had two sons, aged fourteen and nine.

The "Puritan Ethic" Nonsense

Recent observers have gathered a variety of impressions about China. One of the earliest and still most persistent is the notion that the Chinese under communism have developed a sort of Puritan ethic. For example, the Chinese government extols the importance of work and the people show zeal for it; idleness is a rarity. Perhaps because of this apparent zeal for work and partly because of the predominance of blue-colored formless clothes worn by Chinese men and women on the streets, in factories, and in the fields, some Western observers have even applied the term "blue ants" to the Chinese.

Some observers add more embellishments to the same theme. An Austrian newspaperman is struck by the fact that both men and women wear trousers, not well cut—"more noticeably on the women, they seemed to have been made from a single ill-fitting pattern"[6]—that the Chinese women exhibit little variety in the way their hair is worn, and that they seem to use little or no cosmetics. Above all, the same reporter says, Chinese men and women do not appear to exhibit a fervor for romance. And he quoted the principal of a Peking high school: "Our young people grow up in the spirit of the Revolution and social progress, and they have no time for love or the problems of sex."

Although this school principal was merely taking a categorical, zealous, and official line that is untrue to reality, as most Chinese know, Barbara Tuchman, visiting China in 1972, parroted the same thing. "I can say that any overt interest in sex was simply nonexistent." "When the subject came up in conversation with one female interpreter, it produced a grimace of disgust as if we had mentioned a cockroach, and the same expression contorted the face of a doctor of mental health when he was asked about perversions and homosexuality."[7]

Are these then not all significant elements of the Puritan ethic? The Puritans exalted work. The Puritan women with their clumsy clothes in black and white certainly did not care to exhibit sartorial or bodily charms. The Puritans made it elaborately clear that sex was only an instrument for procreation to be resorted to sparingly

and without enjoyment.[8] In fact, doesn't the Chinese zeal in march-
ing into uninhabited frontiers and making sand traps bloom remind
some Americans of the famous "Mr. Hooker's Company," when
the Reverend Thomas Hooker led his church congregation along
the Connecticut River valley, traveling overland and driving their
livestock along the narrow trails? Is there not an atmosphere of
conformity in China? There is, after all, no night life in China today as old China hands once knew it and as Americans understand
it. The new government had stamped out prostitution and also
raised the status of actresses and singers to professional ranks. The
Chinese go to bed early and get up early; by five o'clock in the
morning many men and women, old and young, are already out on
public squares, parks, and river banks, doing their calisthenics.
Isn't such austerity and the emphasis on hard work and frugality
easily translatable in Western minds into the general joylessness
well known among the early Puritans?

Appearances are, however, deceiving. The Chinese have not developed a Puritan ethic, and much of the error on the part of Western observers comes from their lack of understanding of Chinese
cultural ways before the Revolution. They simply have projected
their own Western psychological background onto the current
Chinese scene.

The Chinese have always placed high value on personal industriousness. The traditional couplets in red or gold that adorned the
lintels of Chinese homes during the New Year celebrations were full
of praise for the glorious results of hard work and scholarship.
Chinese biographies and autobiographies usually spoke of these
qualities as indicating the high merit of their subjects.

But the difference between the Chinese value of industriousness
and that of the Puritan is deep-seated. Whereas the Puritans
worked for God, the individual Chinese traditionally worked for
his parents and for the rest of his family so that his ancestral line
would continue and prosper. Although insisting on direct communication with God, the Puritan could not see Him; consequently,
working for God turned out to be working for the sake of work.
The Chinese had no comparable aspirations. His parents were
manifest links with his ancestors. Working for the prosperity and
continuation of the family line thus involved a high degree of selflessness under external sources of authority that is different from
what the Puritan would and could embrace. Puritan selflessness

was based on individualism. When the chips were down, it was individual conscience which guided them, not any external authority. The Chinese never had individualism in their past, and the Communists have certainly not created it. The Communist leaders have simply tried to mobilize and transfer that same selflessness from kinship authority to political authority. In fact, the following ubiquitous exhortation attributed to Mao today is actually traditional to China and is certainly not Puritan:

> Hard work first,
> Enjoyment later.[9]

The "later" refers to the future of the individual and his fellow men as well as to generations yet to come. The Chinese emphasis has always been on this world, not on some unknown paradise in heaven as the Puritans would have it. Their religious hell, moreover, was not like the Protestant model, from which there is no return, but somewhat akin to the Catholic purgatory. The soul would go through various tortures as punishment for wrongdoing before death, but the final punishment and reward usually involved reincarnation: low birth (including birth as an animal) and a life of misery would be the lot of the wrongdoers, while high birth and a life of ease, wealth, longevity, and social esteem awaited the meritorious. Confucian classics and popular collections of stories such as *Liao Tsai*[10] bear unmistakable witness to this.

Nor can the Puritan ethic be attributed to the Chinese today on the ground of new sex mores. For example, had Mrs. Tuchman been in a position to raise the question of sex with any of the college girls before 1949, she would not have received a more welcome response than the one she received from the female interpreter in 1972. For the average unmarried "good family" Chinese, Communist or otherwise, simply regards her question as being out of order unless it is in the proper context, such as in a hygiene class.

Another source of Western confusion is the peculiar relationships between Westerners and Chinese in China. Since only a fraction of Westerners in China could speak Chinese even for purposes of daily conversation, their contacts with Chinese were always limited and superficial, as they still are today when Westerners meet non-Western peoples in many parts of the world. Before 1949 they used to command their Chinese servants and subordinates in pidgin English. The manner in which the officers and men in the

U.S. gunship *San Pablo* interacted with their Chinese servants in 1926, portrayed in the novel *The Sand Pebbles,* is a typical example.[11] Some Westerners were friends with a few of their Chinese equals and their families; these Chinese could speak excellent English (or some other Western language) because they usually received some of their education in the West. Others patronized Chinese women of easy virtue with whom they needed little verbal communication. Outside of these contacts, they had few opportunities to know Chinese life in any but the most superficial way. They toured the Chinese streets and saw the sights very much in the way Americans still tour Chinatowns.

Now, since most Western visitors today still roam or are driven through the streets of Peking, Shanghai, and Canton with no better language skills than before, they miss the colorfulness of the gaily decorated ladies of easy virtue. There also is no longer the tiny but visible minority of school-and college-educated ladies who in the 1930s used to sport fancy hairdos, colorful attire, and high heels. The new emphasis is on reducing the distances that separate the more affluent from the less affluent so that social prestige accrues to the simply clad rather than to the expensively dressed. The common and unavoidable sight everywhere (streets, offices, factories, fields, schools) is of the conservatively clad "good family" types. Add to this the new sex equality, which tends to minimize sartorial differentiation between men and women everywhere, and the new emphasis on devotion to the revolution, in which Party zeal and nation-building efforts take precedence over personal needs and desires, and we have a picture that easily confuses observers steeped in Puritanism but only superficially acquainted with Chinese life before or after 1949.

Marital Life in China Today

One feature of Chinese marital life today which has attracted much attention in the Western press is that some Chinese spouses live apart from each other for most of the year because of their separate work locations.

In the early days after Liberation, when the communes were being developed, quite a few Western reporters wrote that not only were children taken from parents but also spouses were permanently separated from each other. There were titillating reports in American communication media of husbands and wives contriving to meet in privacy for two hours on Saturday night. Sympathy was showered on the "poor Chinese" deprived of a normal sex life by the harsh dictates of an "inhuman" government. That was, of course, pure nonsense. Conjugal life is remarkably unaffected by communization in rural areas. The couples we speak of later who are physically separated by work dwell principally in cities today.

Before the Revolution, the cities would be crowded with the highly educated such as doctors, lawyers, teachers, officials, and engineers, while the villages had no professionals of any kind. Many of these city dwellers would be seen accompanied by their wives and children and parents. But many others were refugees from the grinding poverty and squalor of the villages who could do no better than move into the equally grinding poverty and squalor of the cities. Many of these, too, often had with them their wives and children.

Between the affluent and the slum dwellers, however, were village lads who found places in city stores or workshops as apprentices or journeymen, or in rich peoples' homes as servants and retainers. Most of these had parents in the villages. If they were married, their wives and children would remain with their parents in the villages. Once in three years, they would go home to spend three months with their families; such was the custom. That was what hired hands in my parents' home in Manchuria did, as did most of the shop assistants in Peking, Tientsin, Taiyuan, and other cities who had families in villages or in smaller towns. For as long as possible, traditionally, Chinese kinsmen tried to live together, if not under the same roof, then in the same neighborhood or same village. It was not practical to take all their kin with them to their places of work even if they could manage it financially.

This picture has changed since 1949. The villagers no longer have to (nor are they allowed to) roam the cities for work; they are more than fully occupied in their communes. Nowadays, city-dwelling families of professionals or white-collar workers are the ones more frequently separated by assignment to *hsia fang* (sending educated youth or older persons down to rural areas for learning, discussed by Bernstein elsewhere in this volume), or by work. Some spouses who work regularly in separate locations get together for one month a year at government expense.

Several factors in the new society have increased the likelihood of the latter arrangement. First, all work assignments are made under central planning according to overall national needs. This means that situations will arise when the talents of one spouse are needed in one location while those of the other are needed elsewhere.

Second, educational opportunities today are nearly equal between the sexes. Among over 90 percent of the people we met in the summer of 1972 between the ages of twenty-five and fifty from Canton to Shenyang (old Mukden), both spouses worked. The Chinese term for this today is *shuang chih kung* or "double work force." If the wife possessed no special skills, she could easily find work where her husband is employed. We have seen small factories under the direction of Street Revolutionary Committees where three or four women make glass flowers or do tailoring around two or three sewing machines. In one such factory in Shanghai, one woman worked as a barber who cuts boys' hair at five cents each. The higher the female's qualifications, however, the greater the chance she may be needed in areas other than where her husband is employed.

Finally, even without central direction, the possibility exists that employment opportunities and suitable talents do not occur at the same time in the same location. We know quite a few junior high graduates who, tired of waiting for assignment to a more desirable and therefore less available locality, volunteered for a less desirable and therefore more available locality. Even today, most Chinese who are used to cities prefer cities to villages. And of all cities, Peking and Shanghai are the most desirable; consequently it is very difficult to get an assignment there. In some families the wife worked in Peking and maintained her residence there, while the husband was assigned to a location some distance away but went home once a month. In some of these instances, the work of the wives was less specialized than that of their husbands, and they certainly did not all live separately because of overall occupational needs.

We might well ask the question: Do all Chinese spouses living separately from each other hate the arrangement? The Western temptation is to give an unconditional answer, yes. I have even heard a visiting Hindu professor of law in the United States vehemently expostulate: "Who wouldn't like to be with his wife? That is simply human nature!" There was no room for discussion. That kind of statement reminds me of protestations by the happily married to whom being single is unimaginable and by the confirmed bachelor who would not be caught dead in wedlock.

It may come as a surprise to many Americans, but Chinese reactions to this separate-but-equal arrangement are not at all uniform. For example, there is Miss H., a guide working for the China Travel Service International Division in Shenyang, Manchuria. Three years ago and through relatives, she was introduced to a young man who worked in Yung Chia, Szechuan, some 2500 miles away, when he came to Shenyang to spend a month with his parents. (Unmarried men and women can have a month's leave and travel at government expense to be with their parents.) Miss H. and the young man were soon married. He left for Yung Chia when his leave was up. Two months a year, one for Miss H.'s leave and one for her husband's, have been the time Miss H. and her spouse have spent together in their married life so far.

I asked her whether she would not like to be with her husband all year round. The following dialogue ensued between us:

"I don't want to go to Yung Chia, that's why."

"Why not?" I persisted.

"That's such a far-away place. I don't know anyone there and I can't leave my mother here."

"Don't you have some brothers and sisters to take care of your mother here?"

"Yes, but . . . this way I am free to work and play . . . I don't have to live with a mother-in-law . . . "

This was the only occasion in the nine weeks of our China trip that I heard the word "free" used to express an individual wish. But the gist of her response was not hard to understand. In the mother-in-law problem she hit upon a traditional note that we both understood instantly, even though she was over thirty years my junior. Apparently, the traditional authority of the mother-in-law is still a force to be reckoned with in modern China.

Obviously, not all married ones who are separated most of the year like it. I know some couples who did not appreciate it at all: for example, a north China couple who both graduated from college and were high school teachers at the time I met them. The husband was in one town and lived with his mother and his two young sons in a house he and his wife owned, while his wife was in a town some hundred miles away. The wife came home to be with her family not only for the one month a year to which she was entitled but also during any other and shorter intervals that she could manage. So, when the husband heard that his school needed an additional math teacher with a university degree, coinciding with his wife's qualifications, he at once submitted an application on her behalf for transfer. His first application was rejected, but she has since been reassigned after a lapse of several years.

Of course, we cannot draw authoritative conclusions from a few cases such as these, but we can make some inferences of a more general nature. To begin with, those today most likely to be dissatisfied with separation during most of the year are the former intelligentsia or the once affluent, who usually had their families with them where they were employed. People who are used to one set of conditions of life cannot help but find it hard to switch to another.

Then inferentially, the sons and daughters of the former intelligentsia or the once affluent who grew up before the Revolution or who were born shortly after it are next in line for possible dissatisfaction. After all, they were raised by parents with pre-Liberation approaches to life. Of course, many young people of such backgrounds have made special efforts to dissociate themselves from the disability of their social origin, but that is, of course, not a condition anyone can achieve in a very clearcut manner except in an external sense.

To a vast majority of Chinese whose pre-Liberation lifestyle was far humbler, however, the separate-but-equal marital arrangement is not something repugnant, as it would be to most Americans. As we have seen, to them such an arrangement is, by tradition, not unnatural.

Role Versus Affect

To what extent, then, have these new developments seriously changed Chinese courtship and marital behavior? From what little we know, we can safely say that the society has changed greatly in terms of role, but the interaction between the sexes has not departed much from the age-old affective pattern characterized by what I described as asexuality. For Chinese girls to appear at work or in the streets wearing formless blue and seemingly unmindful of matters of sex appeal, or for Chinese couples to converse unromantically about locomotives and commune production—these are perfectly in keeping with Chinese feeling on how men and women should conduct themselves where they can be observed.

Since the young are more involved in government-sponsored activities than before, they are bound to be less subject to parental influence than before. Mate selection is no longer a parental prerogative; married sons and daughters tend to live under different roofs and locations from their parents; betrothal, wedding, and funeral ceremonies are reduced to the bare minimum; "five-generations-under-the-same-roof" households, rare even in traditional times, no longer exist as objects of public admiration (although three-generations-under-the-same-roof households are still common); late marriage is widely practiced; most wives do gainful work outside the home; the new retirement system in employment means that many children do not need to support their aged parents. These are some new structural arrangements in which the individual finds himself or herself in new roles.[12] Other developments along the same line are the elimination of clan temples and annual clan worship services, the necessity of burial in public cemeteries, and the diversion of attention from genealogical studies to greatly expanded efforts at village, commune, manufacturing, and mining histories.

Nor have the Peking leaders been slow in cultivating new patterns of affect. For example, honors are accorded communal production heroes while filial piety as a virtue has disappeared from public view; new art, literature, drama, and music eulogize devotion to the Party and national causes; birth control, which goes contrary to the traditional desire for sons, and cremation, which is a far cry from the traditional concern for the body, are being widely promoted—to name a few of the most obvious.

Since the revolutionary goals aim at greater identification with communal and national well-being, the Communist government, through new art, literature, and other public media, tries to lower romantic or sentimental fervor in the interest of such goals. This in essence is not unlike the situation during early Christendom when the early Fathers also tried to divert sexual energy to the work of God; it was why St. Paul thought celibacy to be much better than the marital state. The difference is that the Chinese under Communism do not have to expend so much effort "repressing" their sexuality in the Western sense. The attribute of asexuality means that sex was not so pervasive in their scheme of things as it was in the pre-Christian West.

The attributes of continuity and authority are contradictory to the Communist call for a break with the past. The operation of these two attributes made true revolution in Chinese history impossible before the coming of the West. That was why the new Chinese leadership had to stage not only public confessions of past errors, work-study programs, and extensive rectification campaigns but also Anti-Confucius and Anti–Sung Chiang (hero of the popular novel *Water Margin*) movements.

While attempting to reduce the undesired aspects of these attributes, however, the Chinese have not left them behind. For example, although the imported new ideology is indeed established by breaking with the past, its realization is carried out under the influence of the characteristic Chinese attribute of authority. Power struggle and elimination of rivals notwithstanding (these were not rare in Chinese history), the elderly Mao continued in supreme command till his death. There is evidence that Chiang Ch'ing, leader of the fallen Gang of Four, made ample use of her husband's authority to vent her own hatred against the social inequities of the past or even to further her own aggrandizement.[13] In this situation the personal feelings and the actions they inspire in some individuals cannot possibly coincide with the public good in all cases. The task of achieving a break with past authority in ideology, but making use of the authority of the seniormost person in the promotion, maintenance, and development of the new ideology, is full of perils. Probably that is why, in recent years, political changes have been manifested in sudden twists and turns. The contention between those who insist on "redness" first and those who prefer "expertise"—that is, ideology or pragmatism—is as yet unsettled.

The new patterns of affect have by no means replaced the old in the romantic and marital spheres. Young people today can select their mates as they please, but matches are still made by older relatives; those who have married through some such arrangement still speak of it with pride. Consent of parents is still sought by couples who have met on their own. Moreover, the nuclear family of parents and children has not been broken up by the Revolution. As a whole, the feelings between parents and children seem to be just as strong as they were before. There is also no present indication that aged parents who have some grown children will ever live alone. Also, workers are given paid periods off each year to *sheng ch'in,* the traditional term for visiting parents. Finally, the Chinese New Year, which has always been a time of family reunion, remains the most important festival in China. Of the eight public holidays a year, it alone is a three-day affair. In the early fifties, during some of the public criticism and self-confession movements, instances of children turning in their parents were not unknown. A famous case was the daughter of President Lu Chih-wei of the then Yenching University, who publicly denounced her father. Later, the daughter of Lin Piao also informed on her father. But this pattern did not proliferate.

The Communist leadership's call for *lao chung ch'ing san chieh ho* ("solidarity of the old, the middle-aged, and the young") and Mao's dictum *yang wei chung yung, ku wei chin yung* ("use foreign elements for Chinese goals, use old elements for new purposes") can only be interpreted as attempts to reconcile the traditional attributes of continuity and authority, which are still important in Chinese patterns of affect, with new requirements born of new revolutionary goals.

The attribute of inclusiveness is still evident in Chinese ways of courtship and marital life today, as we have seen. But the nature of Chinese marital life bears clearest witness to this. Whenever possible (that is, if not assigned to work in other localities), married sons and daughters live with parents, not only in rural communes, which we visited near Peking, Shanghai, Wuhan, Tientsin, and Shenyang, but also in cities. Public child care centers are flourishing, but grandparents are still preferred to mind preschool-age youngsters.

Shorn of their customary power to tyrannize daughters-in-law, older women today seem to be unusually helpful toward their sons' mates and their little ones. This helpfulness on the part of the old seems to be reciprocated by the young. Chinese couples tend to share the affections of their children with their own parents or parents-in-law to such an extent that it must astonish most Americans.

I shall use my own observation to illustrate. My seventy-nine-year-old mother-in-law, who lives in Wuhan with her son and his wife, has always been surrounded by some of her grandchildren, who enjoy her as much as she does them. But now the grandchildren are no longer children and most of them are assigned to work posts away from home. When we visited my mother-in-law in Wuhan, she was saying how nice it would be if she could have her great-granddaughter with her for a spell—to love and share her bed as some of her grandchildren used to do when they were younger. That wish did not, however, look realistic to me at the time.

Later we traveled to Shenyang, 1300 miles away, and spent a few days with our young nephew, his wife, and their four-year-old daughter. There were plans for his mother to come to Shenyang to bring the little girl to Wuhan to stay with her great-grandma. But each time we brought up the idea to the little girl, she would retort that she was not going to go. Quite firmly so, in fact. We left China in August. In November my brother-in-law wrote that he had a new granddaughter and his wife had returned to Wuhan from Shenyang with their four-year-old granddaughter. He quoted the little girl proudly announcing to visitors: "My mother loves me a lot. But my great-grandma cannot live without me. So I came to keep great-grandma company."

The patterns of household composition, suitable matches, and duties and obligations are matters of roles and their performance. But the patterns of how the young should relate to the old and how spouses and lovers should behave toward each other in public are matters of affect which govern how the individual feels about his or her roles and their performance. Matters of role can be learned and unlearned from childhood throughout adulthood so that new ones may be easily substituted for old ones. This applies not only to skills and the use of tools but also to occupation and location and condition of work. Matters of affect are not easily modified or replaced. Extreme changes in the affective patterns of a society of several hundred millions, even under a regime which aims at its total redirection, must therefore depend upon accumulated changes through many generations.

Perhaps this is why Chairman Mao spoke of continuous revolution. But even Mao could not refrain from using the old Chinese story of *The Foolish Old Man Who Moved the Mountain* (part of the *Little Red Book*) to convey to his followers the way of continuous revolution. Noting that the two problems confronting China are feudalism within and imperialism without, he compared these with the twin peaks of the old man's mountain. The old man was ridiculed when he began the task of moving the mountain. But he replied, "I may not be able to get rid of it in my lifetime, but my sons and my sons' sons will continue the effort after I die. The mountain will not grow but my descendants will." Thus are revolution and the traditional duties of kinship inextricably joined.

NOTES

1. Francis L. K. Hsu, *Psychological Anthropology* (Cambridge, Mass.: Schenkman, 1972), pp. 509–567.

2. Although some mythological episode may be used by the people practicing slavery or caste to "explain" it as a whole or in part.

3. One complete English translation of this book is entitled *Golden Lotus,* by Clement Egerton. London, 1939, in four volumes.

4. See Eileen Hsu-Balzer, Richard Balzer, and Francis L. K. Hsu, *China Day by Day* (New Haven, Conn.: Yale University Press, 1974).

5. Private communication.

6. Hugo Portisch, *Red China Today* (Chicago: Quadrangle Books, 1966), p. 36.

7. Barbara Tuchman, *Notes from China* (New York: Collier Books, 1972), p. 11.

8. As Edmund S. Morgan's researches reveal, this was not the view of the original Puritans; see his *Puritan Family: Religion and Domestic Relations in Seventeenth Century New England* (Boston: Trustees of the Public Library, 1944; new rev. ed., New York: Harper & Row, 1966). Instead, this view of sex was the product of the later Victorian era in the United States.

9. Two traditional sayings are *hsien ku hou t'ien* ("bitterness before sweetness") and *ch'ih te k'u chung k'u, fang wei jen shang jen* ("superiority among men is achieved by enduring the bitterest of the bitter").

10. Pu Sung-ling, *Liao Tsai.* Translated into English by Herbert Giles as *Strange Stories from a Chinese Studio* (Cambridge: Cambridge University Press, 1908).

11. See Richard McKenna, *The Sand Pebbles* (New York: Harper & Row, 1962). A more recent example is a book entitled *A Life Time with the Chinese,* by Wilfred V. Pennell (Hong Kong: *South China Morning Post,* 1974). Mr. Pennell's life with the Chinese as a newsman with various English publications turns out to be a life with Westerners in China. He met a few Chinese warlords, Nationalist leaders, and politicians, but he lived and mostly socialized with his fellow "old China hands." In the end he "feared that the coming [communist] revolution would . . . become the most far-reaching" in China's history. "This was obviously far more important," he lamented, "than the disappearance of the Concessions and the special privileges. It could mean no privileges at all . . . " (p. 279).

12. These new structural arrangements generally apply more to urban areas than to rural villages.

13. Judging from her biography, *Comrade Chiang Ch'ing,* by Roxane Witke (Boston, Mass.: Little, Brown, 1977), there is little doubt about the depth of her feeling in this regard. Such seething emotions are bound to lead their possessors to extremes.

12

Value Themes in
Short Stories, 1976-1977

Ai-li Chin

Fiction, especially short stories, has been a deliberately structured, consciously directed way of channeling popular communication for cultural change in the People's Republic of China. Chinese political leadership, from Mao through various levels of bureaucrats and cadres in charge of cultural affairs, has exerted strategic influence on the creation and dissemination of short stories to further the cause of the revolution. The main instruments have been the Marxist-Leninist epistemology and theory of literature as they have evolved and been transformed in the Chinese context.[1]

These theories and concepts have shaped not only the themes and characterization but at times the form and language of stories for nearly three decades. Yet the correspondence between political ideology, literary doctrine, and story content, though close, is not always perfect; the relationship is by no means deterministic. Careful examination of story content during different periods has revealed not only expression of the dominant ideology but also indications of value conflict, as well as some interpersonal and group relationships, which may be unexpected consequences of political policy.

In this chapter, we take a close look at short stories from a relatively brief period characterized by intense factional struggle at the top: January 1976 through June 1977. During this eighteen-month period, there was first a rapid rise of radicalization in politics and in the popular media, and then, following the death of Chou En-lai and Mao Tse-tung, the consolidation of power by moderates in the party and government bureaucracy. Not unexpectedly, short stories produced in this period include some of the most political, as well as the most diverse, ever written in the People's Republic. Although we will discuss the content of these stories primarily in relation to shifting political and ideological emphases, we will also examine their meaning in the evolving Chinese society and their implications for some of the recurrent or enduring cultural values.

In focusing the analysis on the relationship between political change and story content, I do not mean to imply that the sole function of short stories in China is to serve as a political instrument. Short stories are read for entertainment, for improving one's knowledge of the language, and for cultural identification. While we know virtually nothing so far about the actual readers and their response to the stories, it would be a mistake to assume that the stories have no appeal because of their political purpose. For many of the stories do include homegrown humor, lively dialogue, and local color.

The primary source for this study is the *Jenmin Wen-hsueh* (People's Literature) monthly, January 1976 through June 1977. *People's Literature* is the official production created in 1949 under the All-China Federation of Literary and Art Circles, an organ of the All-China People's Political Consultative Conference. The magazine publishes short stories, criticism, and essays related to the theory and practice of fiction. Poetry is also included, although there is a separate magazine of comparable status, *Shih K'an* (Poetry). Nationwide in circulation, *People's Literature* was in continuous publication from the beginning of the People's Republic until the early stage of the Cultural Revolution; after closing down for ten years, it resumed publication in January 1976. It is a monthly except for the first half of 1976, when it was a bimonthly. With the fourth issue of that year, and some change of policy, the magazine reverted to monthly publication.

People's Literature exercises its leadership in the domain of short story writing, if not over fiction in general, in the following manner: (1) The first issue appeared almost immediately after the birth of the People's Republic on October 25, 1949, signifying the important role it was to play as a medium for communicating the values and ideology of the new state. (2) The first issue opened with a statement of the magazine's mission by Mao Tun, a leading literary figure from the May Fourth movement who had joined the revolution. He also delivered an official report on the new literature in Liberated Areas to the first All-China Conference of Literary and Artistic Workers, a report which was summarized in *People's Literature.* (3) In December 1964, the editors of the magazine issued solicitation for "New Hero Stories," responding to the policy of moral education for the "new socialist man." A year later, a collection of more than 1600 such stories was reported. The announcement was repeated in each issue until just before the magazine abruptly ceased publication in 1966. (4) When the magazine reappeared in January 1976, it began with a full-page calligraphy of its title by Chairman Mao, and the reproduction of two of his poems. The *Ching-kan-shan* poem, on scaling the heights of the Ching-kan mountain where Mao began his career as a revolutionary, perhaps suggested the motto of the magazine at that time. (5) Since the beginning of 1976, there has been a special section of stories reprinted from provincial publications, thus serving to establish national standards or reinforce major policy directions regarding short story writing.

Before undertaking the main task of relating political change to literary ideology and story content for 1976–1977, we shall briefly outline major themes in earlier stories in the People's Republic.

The Short Story until 1975

In the first few years of the People's Republic, the revolutionary short story celebrated the military valor of members of the Liberation Army and their spirit of dedication and self-sacrifice. Among civilians, the value of cooperation among the poor and the oppressed was stressed, as well as the necessity of mutual dependence between the Liberation Army and the peasants. Members of the family, often the elders, who held onto traditional beliefs or who did not work for the common good, would be persuaded to adopt views more in keeping with the new society. Feelings of hatred and indignation against class enemies were given legitimacy, and the right to revenge for past oppressions was elevated to a creed. In fact, a certain degree of revolutionary stature accrued to those who had suffered oppression, although to be ideologically correct and progressive in political thinking was of supreme importance. A spirit of activism prevailed.

During the period of brief relaxation immediately preceding the Hundred Flowers movement, greater diversity appeared in story themes and values. There was a noticeable increase in humanistic values and a decrease in ideology. During the latter part of 1956, romantic themes occupied a significant proportion of the story line, with ideological matters often taking a secondary place. Slightly greater latitude was also given to material values, such as the occasional portrayal of a positive character who displayed a hint of a new middle-class lifestyle.

At the height of the Great Leap and Commune movements, stories not unexpectedly glorified collectivity at the expense of home and family. During these years stories emphasizing the nearly limitless physical energy of individuals emerged. This value undoubtedly had its origin in the close interdependence of precarious lives in the pre–1949 liberated areas, but as a focus of short stories, it came into its own in the portrait of the selfless local party secretary at the end of the 1950s and beginning of the 1960s.[2] It was also in these latter stories that one of the main humanistic values, that of concern for the well-being of others and service to the ordinary, humble *lao-pai-hsing* (common people) was most clearly celebrated.

Stories of the early to mid-1960s took a decidedly different turn.[3] Family values clearly emerged to an unprecedented height, occupying center stage in characterization, plot development, and artistic attention, with rather casual references to ideological correctness. Of course, basic values of socialistic society were not neglected, but they were more assumed than vigorously fought for in these stories, while family, or even wider kinship relations, and the process of mate selection were the kind of subject matter lovingly developed. Interpersonal relationships, such as the close collaboration between the generations, between husband and wife, and between a young man or woman and "the chosen one" seemed to preoccupy story writers. Humanistic values were not so much paramount as pervasive. Much artistic attention was lavished on casual, though personally meaningful, everyday encounters, with the liberal use of light humor in characterization and dialogue to enliven the atmosphere.

Two surprising themes turned up in these stories. One was the reappearance, in a limited and qualified way of course, of the traditional *yen* father, signaling a partial revival of the personal qualities of sternness and distance, and the value of unquestioned authority. The other complementary theme, though not uncontested in some stories, was the sometimes demure, though basically capable and socially competent, *ta-fang* female, willing to sumbit partially to the wishes of her meddling parents or demanding mother-in-law. In short, submissiveness in favor of family unity emerged as a positive value in these stories.

Conflict and competition had their place in these story themes, but they arose from a mixture of personal clashes and differences in ideology. Circumstances around which conflict and competition developed illustrate some value dilemmas expressed in these stories: whether to build up intergenerational dependence or autonomy and assertiveness of individuals; whether to stress equality between the sexes or the subordination of women to family roles.

The Cultural Revolution brought an interruption in the movement to popularize the writing and dissemination of short stories. In the political realm, the Cultural Revolution came to represent the turbulent assertion of the value of youth, their right to rebel and to question tradition and authority.[4] It meant the downplaying of familial and other stable ties.

Due to the unsettled state of affairs and the cessation of literary journals and other regular channels of publication, short stories intended for the general reader in China were scarce. A search through Red Guard newspapers yielded a few extremely sketchy, rudimentary "stories." An early anthology after publications resumed is a volume called *Wo-men shih Mao Chu-hsi ti Hung-wei-ping* (We Are Chairman Mao's Red Guards).[5] The stories are all about Red Guards and may have been written or collected especially for youth of the Red Guard generation. Yet the fact that the anthology was published in 1971 means that these stories represent not so much the revolutionary message at the height of the Red Guard movement but rather the reintegration of revolutionary youth in its aftermath.

These post–Cultural Revolution Red Guard stories depict the struggles and accomplishments of demobilized youth in the countryside or in factories. Some distinguishing features are: (1) prominent references to Chairman Mao as the source of personal strength, wisdom, and inspiration; (2) the frequency of maxims denoting willingness to undergo hardship and personal sacrifice in serving the masses; and (3) the prevalence of natural instead of human obstacles, such as illness, injury, wind, rain, or flood. The message is clear: these ex–Red Guards are not out remaking society but helping to build it, with the accent on sacrifice and dedication.

As the dust settled on the Cultural Revolution, the short story in the early to mid-1970s resumed its place as one of the major means of communicating new values and norms and reintegrating revolutionary youth into society.[6] A systematic campaign was initiated to recruit potential writers from among the workers, peasants, and soldiers—that is, the spare-time writers—and to organize writers' workshops. There was an upsurge in the publication of collected volumes of short stories from all over China.[7]

In these stories published between 1971 and 1975, the focus of interest was divided between the new political and work roles of youth and the wisdom and experience of age. Parental authority was now more likely to be open to questioning by sons and daughters, with the young generation just as likely to emerge more competent, or more correct, than their elders. Respect was no longer something which came with age and family status, but rather something to be earned through either past revolutionary experience or present position of responsibility and spirit of dedication. Equality between the sexes again became important, as did the sheer fact of being young. Indeed, a favorite character at this time was the young heroine barely turned twenty. She was competent and self-assured, straight-speaking and fearless, at times even brash. An aggressive quality in both heroes and heroines, especially in youthful ones, prevailed in these stories.

Humanistic values, however, were not lacking. These were found in an elder with a revolutionary lesson to teach the young, or a master worker who lovingly cultivated the revolutionary spirit in an apprentice. A strong affective dimension emerged in these roles, giving emotions a heightened role in nonfamilial or romantic relationships.

Ideological Controversy and the Short Story, 1976–1977

The middle 1970s witnessed the beginning of an intense struggle for domination between the radical faction identified with Chiang Ch'ing and the moderates associated with Chou En-lai and Teng Hsiao-p'ing.[8] This coincided with the renewed publication of *People's Literature* after a ten-year interval.

As 1975 drew to a close, the moderate Teng Hsiao-p'ing as senior vice premier spoke on behalf of ailing premier Chou En-lai and his policy of unity, stabilization, and increased production through modernization. Chou's policy had won the endorsement of the National People's Congress earlier that year. While the radical faction did not do so well in capturing top cabinet positions, Chang Ch'un-ch'iao did become vice premier and Yu Hui-yung, a supporter of Chiang Ch'ing, became minister of culture. A controversy between the moderates and radicals was surfacing on educational policy, especially over the quality of education and increasing attention to science and technology at the university level, and the achievements of the Cultural Revolution were still being debated.

Perhaps because of their precarious power position, the radical faction, with Mao's apparent consent, waged a battle against Chou and the party bureaucracy during 1975 through two campaigns: to "study the theory of the dictatorship of the proletariat," and to criticize the novel *Water Margin* as a veiled attack against Chou and Teng.[9] By the end of the year, control over the media was concentrated in the hands of the radical faction. In all the debates, criticism from the left was justified on grounds of class struggle and efforts to combat and prevent revisionism.

The revival of *People's Literature* in January 1976 was obviously part of a coordinated program to revitalize the cultural front and to provide regular channels for publishing creative works. *Poetry*, or *Shih K'an*, also reappeared after a lapse of ten years, and in March the publication of several new national magazines was announced: *People's Drama, People's Music, People's Dance*, and *People's Fine Arts*.

A Liberal Start

The new issue of *People's Literature* clearly attempted to establish continuity with the original publication and inherit its mantle as the official organ of the literary sphere. Yet the magazine appeared eager to shape a new identity for itself. The cover had a new design, with its title in calligraphy by Mao and a felicitous message on the promotion of even better creative writing. The contents opened with the reprint of Mao's two 1965 poems which had just appeared in the *People's Daily, Red Flag*, and *Liberation Army Daily*, and had been much editorialized about in the media. The message in one of the poems was: Nothing is impossible if you dare to scale the heights of Ching-kan mountain.

The first issue in 1976 also had a special end-piece entitled "To the Reader," an editorial statement well worth examining as an indication of the ambiguous political stance of the magazine at the beginning of the year. The article called attention to Mao's calligraphy written especially for the magazine as indicating his great concern with proletarian revolutionary literature. It proclaimed itself to be vigilant against revisionism as the socialist fatherland entered the new post–Cultural Revolution era and undertook the movement to criticize Lin Piao and Confucius. Aside from paying lip service to the goal to "combat and prevent revisionism," nothing was said about "capitalist roaders," or the "new bourgeoisie." And, on the literary front, the magazine wished to celebrate the appearance of many new writers from among the workers, peasants, and soldiers, and many publicatons from various provinces, cities, and autonomous regions. Because these developments in short story writing had already taken place during the early 1970s, this part of the statement signaled no departure in policy.

Then came a pronouncement on literary policy that was remarkable for its liberal position, foreshadowing developments a year later. The article pledged itself to "let a hundred flowers bloom and a hundred schools contend," to "adopt the old to serve the new," and to "borrow the foreign for Chinese use." The article ended by declaring that the magazine would allow "the free development of different artistic forms and styles," "critically inherit national artistic forms," and "promote free discussion, and broaden criticism and rebuttal." It urged writers inside and outside the party to unite, and "old, middle-aged, and young ones to work together." A surprising document for early 1976, in light of the factional struggle then in progress.

Let us now examine some of the stories in this issue. "One Day in the Life of the Chief of the Machinery and Electricity Bureau" seems to fulfill the promised new directions, or at least to mark a departure from previous stories. This story is prophetic for several reasons: (1) It portrays complex motivations of local party secretaries and government officials as well as conflicts among them, (2) it depicts "middle characters," and (3) it leaves room for a bit of psychological character study. In the past (at least in stories in anthologies and in *People's Literature*), local party secretaries and administrative personnel had usually been lone figures of authority, impeccable in motivation and behavior; the emphasis was on the positive, unitary nature of political authority. During the Cultural Revolution, revered public figures and the party hierarchy itself came under merciless attack, and the image of the exemplary public functionary was tarnished. There was, however, a delay of several years before the failings of public figures appeared in short stories. With the first issue of *People's Literature,* the way was apparently open to descriptions of human weaknesses and political conflict in the public arena.

"One Day in the Life" concerns a hero, Huo, whose socialist character seems beyond reproach: He is quick and decisive, willing to assume responsibility, and eager for workers to bring up contradictions about production. He also neglects his own health in the pursuit of duty. As chief of a machinery and electricity bureau, he has various responsibilities, including that of overseeing the production record of a mining equipment factory. Not quite measuring up to standard are two others with official responsibility: his deputy chief, Hsu, an old cadre, and the party's deputy branch secretary, Yu. Thus, Huo's refusal to go to the hospital for his high blood pressure contrasts with Hsu's hypochondriacal complaints and his eagerness to occupy a hospital bed. Huo's willingness to assume responsibility shows up Hsu's philosophy that it is better to avoid action than to make a mistake. Hsu's motto is "everything in moderation." But even though Hsu gets in the way of effective action, he is a sad rather than a "black" character, almost comical with his hundreds of pills, his rotund figure, and a "good-natured, Buddha-like face." He is, furthermore, slow to anger and fond of joking with subordinates.

Yu, the deputy party secretary at the bureau, provides a different sort of contrast to Huo. Yu is a complainer. He feels that Huo blames him for "pursuing fame and fortune" and letting production drop, and he objects to the difficult rush assignment imposed on the factory. Yet Yu is not without redeeming virtues. He takes well to criticism and suggestions at meetings, and is the first to pick up the collapsed Huo and carry him to the hospital, blaming himself in the meantime for not being reprimanded enough by the Party. Yu is more weak than "bad."

As we shall see, this new practice of depicting weaknesses in party secretaries and bureaucrats is also found in stories published while the radical faction controlled *People's Literature,* but Hsu and Yu receive a kinder treatment in this story than do their counterparts in the later, more politicized "radical" stories.

"One Day in the Life" shows considerable restraint in political slogans and didactic passages. The few that are present are uttered by the hero Huo: "Heightened production is necessary to strengthen socialism," "With two imperialist powers competing like demons, world war is inevitable," and "Production without sound management leads to ruination." These statements clearly reflect the moderate policies of the Teng Hsiao-p'ing–Chou En-lai group.

The other two stories in the first issue of *People's Literature* will be briefly noted to provide added contrast to the stories of the next few issues, in which political struggle becomes more intense and characters more polarized. The heroine of "Story of a *Lao-shih* [solid] Person" is a middle school student named Lo who, despite her academic excellence, chooses to go down to the countryside and become a peasant. Her added virtue is to convert a lazy, spoilt, and comfort-loving classmate to do the same, and to encourage her to use her scientific talents for the agricultural experimentation station. The second girl thus begins as a weak character but turns into another model youth. A third character is the head counselor of the school, who "incorrectly" believes that the brightest student should be cultivated as the *chien-tzu* or "outstanding element" and should take the college entrance examination. The counselor also takes undue pride in his middle school being *chung-tien chung-hsüeh,* one of the select schools.

This story is something of an anomaly. The fact that it is reprinted from an earlier provincial magazine may partly account for this circumstance. The coeducational philosophy criticized was in fact already being modified, although stylistically the story is in keeping with the literary doctrine of this issue of *People's Literature.*

The third story portrays another "middle character," the company commander of the agricultural station of a military unit. He is smugly pleased with the production prize received by the unit, but the heroine, a *hsia-hsiang* girl sent down to the village to be a swinekeeper, points out that the sacrifice is too great: pigs have to be sold to buy fertilizer for the increased yield. Her bluntness and courage in speaking out eventually win over the commander.

Radicalization

This policy of liberalization, however, had no chance to prove itself, for in the next few months the political winds changed. With the new year came the death of Chou En-lai. On February 7, Hua Kuo-feng became acting premier, bypassing Teng. By April, Hua was elevated to premier and first vice chairman of the Party, and Teng was dismissed from all posts in and out of the Party. Teng was increasingly attacked as an "unrepentant capitalist roader" for his policy of giving priority to unity, stability, and economic development, thus putting production on a par with class struggle. He was also accused of underrating the accomplishments of the Cultural Revolution and opposing the "three-in-one" principle of leadership attributed to Mao and appropriated by the radical faction—namely, participation of elder, middle-aged, and young cadres at all levels and in all settings. In the meantime, the educational controversy was also being cast as a struggle between two lines and two classes. In industry, the left was advocating putting all management of productive enterprises and supervision of cadres in the hands of workers' control teams, known as "mass democratic management." The struggle against revisionism now included the "restriction of rights against the bourgeoisie" within the socialist society.

On the cultural front, several new developments reflected the stamp of Chiang Ch'ing and the ascendance of the radical faction. In January, the National Dance Festival was held, and in March, the National Acrobatic Festival. A theatrical festival was also announced. The media lost no time in making use of various anniversaries—May 4, May 7, and May 16—to send forth ideological messages. Then, on May 23, the thirty-fourth anniversary of the Yenan Forum, the keynote of media messages was to deepen criticism of Teng and to persevere in revolution in literature and art.

Beginning with the second issue, March-April, *People's Literature* applied increasingly stringent political standards to short stories. A piece called "A Brief Report from the Literary and Artistic Circles" praised the *san-chieh-ho* or "three-in-one union" method of literary production[10] as a "newborn thing" of the Cultural Revolution, and attributed forty-six volumes of fiction, poetry, and reportorial writing to this format. Between 1972 and 1976, the "three-in-one union" method was also credited with the nurturing of over four hundred creative writers under the wing of the Editorial Office of the Shanghai Publishing House. Some of the new writers who began writing short stories under this plan were said to have matured into novelists. In terms of literary doctrine, the report proclaimed that the "three-in-one union" format by bringing peasants, workers, and cadres into the creative process "limited the bourgeois rights of the literary and artistic workers," a goal not included in the pre-1975 statements of writers' workshops.

By July, *People's Literature* reverted from a bimonthly to a monthly and intensified its campaign to politicize the short story. The heading "Essays" *(Lun-wen)* in the magazine was changed to

"Criticism" *(P'ing-lun)* at this time. An editorial statement described the first half year of the renewed magazine as "a time of criticism against Teng Hsiao-p'ing under Chairman Mao's initiative and leadership," and "the great victory in the struggle against rightist restorationism." Several stories were cited as exemplifying the struggle of the revolutionary masses against the rightist Teng Hsiao-p'ing, with all the ideological phrases associated with his position.

Beginning with the second issue of *People's Literature,* characters became polarized and political slogans and didactic passages intruded more heavily into the stories. In "A Stiff Examination" (1976, no. 2), the hero is Party Secretary Chang of the bureau in charge of a brick factory. When he was a boy of fifteen, he ran away to join the Red Army after his father was executed by a landlord. Now, as bureau chief, he respects workers' opinions and follows their advice in solving problems with machines. He tears off the bureau's own poster to leave room for the workers' wall posters. All this he does in the name of combatting "Liu-Lin revisionism" and "capitalist agents within the Communist Party." By contrast, Deputy Party Secretary Li is fat and flabby, lounges in a sofa, and rides the elevator; he ignores the masses and understands only power. He is the "capitalist agent." The other negative character is Tung, a team leader of the technical improvement group at the factory. He sports a white Dacron shirt and relies on foreign books on technology. It is he who covers the workers' wall posters with a bureau poster to curry favor with his superiors. He is obviously a "capitalist sympathizer."

In "Conquest of the Iron Army" (1976, no. 2), Party Secretary Kao, who is concurrently political committee chairman of a petroleum drilling station, believes in self-reliance and has faith in the masses. His opposite number is Technical Director Li, who ridicules a former girl worker who had been sent to college by the masses but listens only to an engineer recalled from the May 7th school. Again, the plot in the story is summed up by its author as class struggle.

A brother-sister pair in "Hai Lan" (1976, no. 2), the story of a fishing enterprise, is likewise put on opposite sides of the ideological divide. The brother, the team leader, wants to hire someone to build the last boat of the fleet. The sister, despite everyone's skepticism, volunteers a group of girls to build it. In this story, the mother's doubts about the daughter's ability are called "thoughts of Confucius and Lao-tze," and the brother's proposal to employ paid help is labeled "a crooked way," a "capitalist solution."

Although this story contains some banter which lightens the atmosphere, the term *ya-t'ou,* used affectionately for girls in stories of the early seventies, now has a negative connotation of "gossipy females" *(tsui-k'uai-ti ya-t'ou).*

Articles of literary criticism, more accurately political commentary, also became highly ideological. Critics assessed characters as "full of hatred of capitalism," "shielded by capitalist roaders," or "determined to wrestle power from them." Young factory workers as heroes are described in these articles as "daring to go against the tide" when they accuse the deputy party secretary and factory director of "using material incentives to lead the workers down the capitalist road" and "cheat the masses by deflecting the direction of class struggle." The ideological campaign in *People's Literature* was comprehensive and intense.

That such a campaign was being waged is best illustrated by a critical article in the July issue about the story discussed earlier, "One Day in the Life of the Chief of the Machinery and Electricity Bureau" (1976, no. 1). The author of the story, Chiang Tse-lung, was charged with depicting the hero as "following Teng Hsiao-p'ing's capitalist road," "pushing production and management at the expense of class struggle and the struggle between two roads." The fictitious bureau chief Chiang created, in the words of the critic, "is not a hero," but "at the most a technician," "someone without political thought, blind to the laws and characteristics of class struggle in the history of socialism." In a later issue that year, the editors admitted to their own error in publishing the story, attributing their poor judgment to the same influence: Teng's revisionism and his three-point program.

Chiang's self-criticism included all the negative slogans and policies attributed to the "evil" Teng faction, using the same phrases as his accusers and adding some more. The rest of his piece, however, gives the impression of a man subtly defending himself. "I thought I was building up a hero in an old cadre who is in firm support of the continuous revolution," he said, and went on to itemize all the admirable attitudes and activities of his hero in the past. However, he concluded, since this character was "politically blind," "no other qualities could redeem him"; thus, "the more he works hard, the greater harm he renders to socialism." About his own efforts, Chiang said, "Subjectively I thought I was using my writing to help the masses in their political struggle; objectively I ended up doing more harm than good."

Chiang then went on to describe his own class origin as a worker and how he came to write in response to Chairman Mao's call for the masses to engage in creative writing. His first story was based on his own political struggle as a steel worker—again, an apparently admirable record. We may speculate that perhaps Chiang was made an object lesson in this ideological warfare because he was one of the more successful writers, with at least five more published stories to his name.

A story in the issue just before the criticism/self-criticism issue, *Wu-wei* or "Fearless," deserves brief notice. County Committee Secretary Liu is a veteran of the Yenan Revolutionary Army, was criticized during the Cultural Revolution for taking the capitalist road, and after reform became county chief before assuming the present post. Usually lacking in initiative, he is contemptuous of cultural programs and is now pushing a wage policy stressing work points and material incentive. He also schemes with a higher official to transfer young Party Secretary Tu who is critical of him. In short, here in one person are concentrated many political issues the radicals stood against. In fact, the dialogue in this story is full of political discourse or ideological arguments by this and other characters.

An incidental point of interest in this story is a reputed romance between the hero, Party Secretary Tu, and Deputy *Hsien* Secretary Cheng. The young pair were rebels together during the Cultural Revolution and have now become leaders of the revolutionary group in the *hsien* in opposition to Liu. Both are against the work point policy, and together they help various party branches to carry out criticism meetings. From the radical point of view, they appear to be model young people.

What is unusual is to find a minor love theme in an extremely politicized story, especially when romantic interest is seldom found in post–Cultural Revolution stories. The hearty enjoyment of food is also not associated with the hero figure. Our hero, however, indulges in both. I have no explanation for the appearance of these two features except a negative one: Whatever has been out of fashion in the literature produced by one faction may be reason enough for their opponents to include it in their own.[11]

Moderation

The death of Mao on September 9 was swiftly followed by the arrest in October of the four leaders of the radical faction. And although the campaign to criticize Teng deepened into October, by the end of the month the tables were turned and an all-out campaign to criticize the Gang of Four was launched. Hua Kuo-feng, elevated to the chairmanship of the Central Committee of the Chinese Community Party and successor to Mao, made his first major policy statement in December and outlined his program for 1977. He reaffirmed Chou and Teng's policy to push economic growth while pledging to carry on the mass study of the Communist doctrine. Also on the agenda was rectification of purged members of the Party.

People's Literature devoted the entire October issue to the death of Mao, and by November the magazine changed tunes completely, following the lead of the *People's Daily, Red Flag,* and *Liberation Army Daily.* Editorials and articles attacking the Gang of Four from these publications were reprinted in *People's Literature.* Several short stories condemned by the radical faction were now reappraised, including "Song of the Gardener" which had been criticized for "advocating the primacy of culture" *(wen-hua chih-shang).*

A new signature, "An Editorial Committee," appeared under an important article specifying the harmful influences of the Gang of Four on literature and art. The article complained that under the Gang of Four, every piece of creative work had to include a capitalist roader, and all works that failed to meet this specification were suppressed. Furthermore, the article charged, the Gang of Four equated a democratic roader with a capitalist roader, or dubbed "a capitalist roader with the cloak of an old revolutionary." The Gang of Four was further accused of turning many pieces of work dealing with internal contradictions among the people into contradictions between the enemy and the people, "forcing any character with problems in thinking to commit antirevolutionary activities." The Gang also maintained, the charges continued, that not many capitalist roaders were reformed, or that reform was not "real" or "permanent," and that they were "dishonest, stubborn, and vindictive," "worse than landlords or Japanese aggressors."

In terms of literary or artistic concepts, the article attacked the practice under the Gang of Four of turning all characters in fiction into "fixed models" *(tien-hsing-hua)*—"all out of the same mold" and "in their own image." Heroes, they said, seemed to be born with correct knowledge and proper class consciousness, did not need to go through any process of improvement, and had to attain the upper hand in every situation. These approaches to characterization were denounced "formalism" *(hsing-erh wei-shang)*. The article concluded by quoting Mao on the necessity in literary and artistic work of "including weaknesses in work and outlook" instead of committing the error of "pitting one half against the other half."

In the same issue of *People's Literature* appeared a remarkably outspoken piece called "My Overall Reaction Is: Liberation!" by Wang Yüan-liu, who identified himself as a "writer from the broad masses." While his specific complaint against the Gang of Four was the banning of a film, he went on to generalize: "In recent years, those of us who try to write according to Chairman Mao's thought on literature and art, and produce works for the use of workers, peasants, and soldiers have been experiencing great difficulties. Chairman Mao's thoughts and policies on literature and art were wantonly distorted. The masses in creative work suffered suppression and control from so-called 'principles' and 'direction from above,' resulting in the 'swinging of clubs and the flying of hats.' We were full of anxiety, not knowing when something we wrote might offend them, thus being consigned to oblivion, never to have a chance for a comeback." He then called the type of control he had experienced as "fascistic dictatorship" and characterized the oppression as "white terror."

The change in *People's Literature* was quick, thorough, and decisive. The first half of 1977 witnessed a consolidation of power by the moderates under Hua and the reinstatement of Teng by mid-spring. Criticism against the crimes of the Gang of Four proliferated in the media while a "completely new situation of political liveliness and economic prosperity" was forecast in the New Year's Day joint editorials in the *People's Daily, Red Flag,* and *Liberation Army Daily.* Science and technology with the goal of modernization were reemphasized, and an improvement in the people's livelihood was promised. One of the Party's main tasks was to strengthen its internal structure to prepare for the new tasks ahead. Moreover, the campaigns to learn from Tachai in agriculture and from Taching in industry were to be continued.

In 1977 ideological criticism of stories in *People's Literature* virtually disappeared. Instead, articles continued to attack literary policies and practices under the Gang of Four and to give fresh interpretations of the Party's position on literature and art.

Criticism of the discredited literary doctrines now centered on the "three breakthroughs" *(san-tu-ch'u)*. This principle, developed in the early 1970s, has to do with the "gradual emergence of the hero model out of the story material depicting the life of the masses." The first breakthrough is to describe positive characters and have them stand out from the rest, the second is to distinguish heroic figures out of the positive ones, and the third is to select and construct the true hero model, the *ying-hsiung tien-hsing,* to exemplify the essence of the revolutionary spirit of the masses.

The critics in 1977 had much to say about this principle. The most pragmatic complaint was that the heroes created under this approach were so perfect that they became impossible to emulate. "The ordinary worker has no place in this kind of literature and art." The critics compared the doctrine to the "eight-legged essay," condemned it for stifling creativity, for negating the Hundred Flowers spirit, and for being the instrument to separate the "fragrant flowers" from the "poisonous weeds." Advocates of the *san-tu-ch'u* were also accused of "violating the literary creed of uniting socialist realism with revolutionary romanticism" and of elevating *san-tu-ch'u* to a "supreme creative principle for the concrete realization of Chairman Mao's literary and artistic line," placing it at times above the word of Mao. Finally, the critics charged that by labeling the seventeen years of revolutionary literature and art a "black line under revisionism," the Gang of Four "wanted to destroy everything."

What, then, did the moderates propose as the new approach to creative work? They began by referring back to the basic Marxist statement that the creative arts were a "reflection of reality," and by quoting Lenin as saying that "it is absolutely necessary to preserve individual creativity, and the limitless world of thought and imagination, form and content." The proletarian struggle, proponents of the new approach pointed out, was now manifested in "rich, complex phenomena"; therefore writers should be allowed to use different methods of expression, different forms and styles. Writers should be free to reflect either class struggle or scientific experimentation, to portray either struggle against a class enemy or internal contradictions among the people, and to describe either the politically mature hero or heroes in the making. Stories could also include one or two negative characters. And, to add to the legitimacy of the new doctrine, a quotation was found from the newly published fifth volume of Mao's *Selected Works* on the promotion of "all kinds of forms and styles" in literature and art as well as in science, letting those who specialize in these fields judge the issues: "Questions which arise from literature, art and science should be discussed by people in the literature, art, and science circles, go through literary, artistic, and scientific practice, and should not be settled in any simplistic fashion."[12]

For four months, beginning in October 1976 through January of the next year, there were virtually no short stories in *People's Literature*. When they reappeared in the February issue, the stories bore little resemblance to those published during the months when the radical faction had control over the media, and reverted to earlier types that had prevailed between the Great Leap and the Cultural Revolution. The focus was again on "contradictions among the people" and the story atmosphere was much less political and the pace more leisurely, although there was a sprinkling of stock ideological phrases, such as the "destructive efforts of the Gang of Four." Compared with the 1976 stories, there was again space devoted to storytelling for its own sake or for the development of a plot, and fewer passages of concentrated ideology. Dialogue could again be included to contribute to character or to lend a touch of humor or local color. Interpersonal relations now were explored, not for ideological differences alone, but for revealing a shared past, or for giving meaning to a chance encounter. Heroes, heroines, and supporting characters did not have to be all good or all bad, but appeared as socialist citizens with human weaknesses and failings in the past.

Let us now examine some of the "new" themes and "new" types of heroes and heroines presented in these stories. They were new in representing another turn in ideological emphasis, yet mostly old in recalling similar characteristics found in stories of the early 1960s and again in the 1970s.

The first prominent theme is the need of young workers and cadres for training and guidance by experienced elders. This motif occurs in a number of stories, but only three will be cited here to illustrate varying emphases within this broad theme.

In a simple story called "Flying Alone" (1977, no. 5), a young helicopter pilot is envious of the more glamorous fighting pilots on training maneuvers in the sky. One day he goes up with his commanding officer, who had done heroic work during the T'angshan earthquake. The older pilot had rescued a *hui-hsiang* ("sent down to the villages") girl, who had returned to the village after education, and a petroleum technician, and had himself been injured. Now recovered, he and the young pilot visit the village. The girl takes them to see an old woman to whom the officer had airlifted food after the earthquake. From this visit, the young pilot learns the lesson that all assignments are important, and that he must find a purpose in his chosen career of serving the people. The focus of this story is not class struggle between hero and villain, but rather the struggle to overcome human weakness by an ordinary young man with whom the reader can, presumably, identify. The young trainee learns from the guidance and example of the older pilot, who expresses affection for him—a theme first found in stories of the early 1970s.

This story still contains some ideological slogans, though less so than do the more political stories. Some sample phrases: "recouping losses in training brought about by the Gang of Four" or "the importance of following regulations in training." Even the old woman, when asked how she is, replies, "Good, good. Ever since that 'destructive gang' was seized, I have not had a single worry on my mind!" Present also is the usual expression of gratitude to Chairman Mao and the Party—by the girl for being rescued and brought back to health, and by the old woman for being given food for her New Year celebration.

The story "Awaken" (1977, no. 5) contains a variation on the theme of the young worker learning from the older. The image of the *yen* elder had gained prominence in stories of the early sixties, when family relationships were stressed over political themes. In the early seventies, this stern master worker or older peasant was again a prominent character, this time in the context of encounters between the experience of age and the revolutionary zeal of youth. And now, in the post–Gang of Four period, when production, knowledge, and competence are considered important, the *yen* authority figure has reappeared.

The elder figure in "Awaken," the commander of a fishing fleet, teaches a young captain who is somewhat cocky and lacking in self-discipline. The commander fails the young man in a test and takes him out to learn from experience, to make him realize the importance of navigational rules. The young man's boat loses its anchor and is saved by a spare anchor tossed from the commander's boat nearby. The older man takes the opportunity to send over a message and a political lesson: this place was precisely where the youth's father had drowned under the oppressive fishing conditions before liberation.

The *yen* elder appears also in "Startled" (1977, no. 5), a story about a young student driver looking for a master: "I am not afraid of strictness, because a *yen* master produces skillful apprentices." The young man, however, has a "childlike," "mischievous and fun-loving spirit." While on assignments, he would stop for a meal or a nap. Although he is reprimanded by the transport team captain, it is the master driver to whom he is apprenticed who teaches the young man, with patience and affectionate concern, the value of time.

A second theme is dedication to work, including overcoming physical limitations. In a story called "On a Windblown Snowy Road" (1977, no. 4), an elderly man in charge of supplies and services carries a load of firewood on a snow-covered mountain road. This is the seventh day of his border patrol duty. Despite a painful leg injury sustained on duty three years before, he insists on catching up with his unit because he detests physical limitations, and is concerned for his hungry comrades in need of firewood. He loses his way, and after gathering scrap branches for a fire signal, he is reunited with his unit.

In this simple tale of endurance and dedication, a political note is almost mechanically tacked onto the story by having the wife insert a pair of slogans in his shoes: "Fight revisionism" and "Continue the revolution." His forthcoming transfer to work in his village is somehow put in terms of "limiting the rights of the capitalist class" and "narrowing the three big differences."

The theme of inexhaustible energy was prominent in stories of the Great Leap period, when natural obstacles were conquered by determination. In the next story, "Adventure on the Water Lily

River'' (1977, no. 3), however, the idea of overcoming physical limitations is an incidental part of a more complex plot. The young director of a water control project works days without sleep to cope with a drought. The river transport team that benefits from his efforts happens to be headed by his grandfather, who had brought him up when he was an orphan but whom he has not seen in years. The main drama of this story thus comes not from political struggle or even the struggle against obstacles, but from the chance circumstances that result in the young man's helping his grandfather.

A third theme is political conflict or intrigue at the local level, a theme infrequent in pre–Cultural Revolution stories but found in stories of either the radical or the moderate persuasion. In the short story called ''Preface'' (1977, no. 4), no fewer than eight characters are crowded into seventeen pages. The deputy head of a production team, Chen, described as an old intellectual fond of carrying a gold cigarette case, covets the post of deputy chairman of the revolutionary committee at a factory making industrial pipes. In his scheming for the position, he has as his accomplice the responsible person of the city's revolutionary committee and the technical director of the production team, who echoes Chen's words in return for a promotion. Chen tries to make use of a worker, a crabby old cadre nicknamed ''Old Man Stone,'' who turns out to be incorruptible. The old worker succeeds in stopping the conspirators from starting a controversial project.

Political authority, which in pre–Cultural Revolution stories was usually presented as unified and unshakable, is in this story subject to factions and realignments. The political ideology that demarcates the two sides is *ching-yen chu-i* or ''empiricism,'' in this context signifying ''reliance on experience.'' Thus Chen's faction tries to get rid of Old Man Stone because he stands for experience instead of revolutionary fervor, while the old cadre proudly stands on the record of his work.

Another story on the theme of factional conflict is called ''Snowy New Year's Eve'' (1977, no. 5). A rebel clique dubbed ''the clique that reaches for the sky'' tries to obstruct the production of fertilizer in the name of promoting ''revolution above production'' and ''taking orders from the Center.'' Opposed to this clique are an old cadre, an experienced master worker, and young workers of the fertilizer factory, all of whom believe in taking initiative on the local level, giving priority to needs of the commune, and not being intimidated by orders from higher authority. This group faces a difficult technical problem by working all night and overcoming natural obstacles.

Change and Variations in Story Values—A Summary

We have examined changes in short stories between January 1976 and June 1977, and demonstrated some of the ways in which stories respond to political and ideological change. The correspondence between ideology and story values, however, is not always close or simple. The human situation, as depicted in even the simplest of short stories, is more complex than the bare idea embodied in a political slogan or ideological declaration.

Characters in stories take on flesh and blood, and the beliefs they hold or actions they undertake arise out of motivations and antecedents and have consequences for other people. If material for stories bears any resemblance to the social nexus in which people live and work, stories are found to contain some basic and enduring values which modify the more immediate, transient values that rise and fall with the political fortunes of the dominant group in the real world. Furthermore, incompatibility between values makes resolution or compromise necessary, and such solutions give us insight into either prescribed patterns or unanticipated consequences in behavior and relationships.

We shall therefore summarize the findings in terms of core values and some of their variants, as well as transient values.

Ideological correctness is the primary core value in stories of all periods since 1949, but the particular form it takes depends on the dominant ideology at the time. In 1976 this value rose to a position of prominence, and the form it took included attacks on class enemies from within the socialist society and challenges directed against those in positions of authority. In 1977 it became a matter of bending all efforts toward production and learning rules and regulations of the work to be done.

Willingness to work hard, to engage in physical labor, and not to shirk public responsibility collectively forms the next core value. This value is fundamental and pervasive: negative characters are often shown to be lazy, fat, or comfort-loving. Variants, however, do come and go, such as stretching one's physical capacity to the limit, working deep into the night, and disregarding signs of fatigue or illness. This syndrome appeared repeatedly and in explicit terms during and immediately after the Great Leap and makes its reappearance in the 1977 stories, at a time when production has again become important, at least as important as class struggle and ideological correctness. There is no obvious or intrinsic reason why such an extreme variant should not be associated with more radical politics as well, but in fact it is not found in the more politicized 1976 stories. One critic, writing from the radical standpoint, even poked fun at stories of the other camp whose heroes would "give up eating, sleeping, or family affairs as soon as they meet with some difficulty."

Activism is another recurrent value, often expressing itself in quick thinking and decisive action, goal-oriented behavior and forward motion. It means taking fate into one's own hands. This value is in clear contrast to the traditional tendency to wait and see, toward caution and contemplation. During the height of radical politics, action meant not weighing the consequences, not caring whose toes were stepped on. The phrase "daring to go against the tide" was often used to describe the hero or heroine in early 1976 stories.

Honesty, trustworthiness, and sincerity comprise a value relating to personal characteristics. The old Chinese term *lao-shih,* with roots deep in Chinese culture, reappears in the 1976–1977 stories. *Lao-shih* means dependable, straight-talking, not devious, deceptive, or scheming. Yet one can also be too *lao-shih,* thus becoming easy prey for others to take advantage of.

Speaking out is a seemingly simple virtue, but the Chinese *lao-pai-hsing,* ("plain folks"), accustomed to the hierarchical society of prerevolutionary days, would consider their private opinion of no consequence to strangers or superiors. In the new society, the worth of each person is assured. Several stories concern old women who never before spoke out and, having learned to do so, have become responsible persons whose words are reckoned with in the village. But speaking *out* shades into speaking *against,* and thus, as the quality highly valued in young rebels during the Cultural Revolution, it appears frequently in the 1976 stories.

Affection and caring for others, a characteristic prominent in the post–Great Leap stories about local party secretaries, makes a comeback in the stories of 1977. This value is now associated with the current father figure, again described as *yen,* stern and distant, as was the father in stories of the early to mid-1960s. In the 1977 stories, care and concern compensate for the sternness of the master worker in relation to the young apprentice.

Implicit values: there are two unresolved value dilemmas implicit in revolutionary stories since 1949. One concerns family unity versus equality between the sexes, and the other concerns youth versus age, wisdom, and experience. Generally speaking, stories have sought to preserve basic familial values while advocating the independence of women and equality between the sexes. But there have been times, such as during the height of the Great Leap and Cultural Revolution movements, when serious inroads have been made on family values. As stories of the early and mid-1960s reveal, there are limits to the compatibility of these values when translated into behavior. Variations of the value dilemma between youth and age have also been found in stories of the past two or three decades: youth exemplifying activism and the spirit of rebellion, and age representing experience, wisdom, and continuity.

In addition, a significant change has taken place in the portrayal of political authority. It has often been said that Maoist political philosophy is based on the assumption that human nature is malleable and that, when shown the way, people will correct their mistaken attitudes and behavior and remake themselves into useful citizens of the socialist society. We have seen that this assumption has generally been depicted in short stories through the lives of ordinary people, as distinct from class enemies who are often abstract, minor characters whose past history may be revealed but whose *possibilities* for reform are not explicitly explored. In recent stories, the depiction of the vulnerability and changeability of human nature has been extended to include those in positions of responsibility and authority: it has become permissible to portray human weakness in authority figures as well.

The other extreme of this value dimension—the relative unchangeability of human nature—was stretched to the limit when radicals were in control of the media. Revolutionary heroes and heroines then embodied the spirit of socialism without allowance for weaknesses or improvements, and, conversely, negative characters possessed traits that were persistent and deep-seated despite apparent changes or professed self-reform. Perhaps this fundamental rigidity in value assumptions about human nature contributed to the unpopularity of the radical position.

With the return to a less stringent view of human nature, that mirror of perfection showing the image of the local political authority now has cracks in it. A degree of realism has been introduced into short story writing which will be difficult to reverse.

NOTES

1. Ai-li S. Chin and Nien-ling Liu, "Short Stories in China: Theory and Practice, 1973-1975," in *Popular Media in China: Shaping New Cultural Patterns,* ed. Godwin C. Chu (Honolulu: The University Press of Hawaii, 1978), pp. 124-183.

2. A. S. Chen [Ai-li S. Chin], "The Ideal Local Party Secretary and the Model Man," *China Quarterly* (January-March, 1964): 220-240.

3. Ai-li S. Chin, "Family Relations in Modern Chinese Fiction," in *Family and Kinship in Chinese Society,* ed. Maurice Freedman (Stanford, Ca.: Stanford University Press, 1970), pp. 87-120.

4. See David Raddock, *Political Behavior of Adolescents in China* (Tucson: University of Arizona Press, 1977).

5. Shanghai jenmin ch'u-pan she [People's Press of Shanghai], 1971.

6. Chin and Liu, "Short Stories in China."

7. Ibid., pp. 19-23. See also Hsu Kai-yu, *The Chinese Literary Scene: A Writer's Visit to the People's Republic* (New York: Vintage, 1975).

8. For the chronology of political events in this section, I relied mostly on the "Quarterly Chronicle" of the *China Quarterly.*

9. See Merle Goldman's chapter in this volume.

10. The term refers to three kinds of people assigned to help the writers: party representatives, editors from newspapers and publishing houses, and experienced writers. See discussion in Chin and Liu, "Short Stories in China."

11. *Shanghai tuan-p'ien hsiao-shuo hsüan* [Selected Short Stories from Shanghai] (Shanghai: Shanghai pao-k'an ho wen-i ch'u-pan she [Journalistic and Literary Press of Shanghai], 1974).

12. Referred to in *People's Literature,* 1977, no. 5, p. 4.

13

Peasant Culture and Socialist Culture in China: On the Dynamics of Structure, Behavior, and Value Change in Socialist Systems

Vivienne Shue

All Marxist governments have among their declared goals the promotion of continuous cultural reforms leading eventually to a total cultural transformation of their societies. China of course has been no exception in this, and in fact, students of comparative communism have tended rather regularly to come to the conclusion that the Chinese leadership may well have made the most determined and creditable attempt of all the present-day Marxist governments actually to nurture and promote the widespread cultural change of which they speak.[1] But despite our customarily granting to the Chinese an "A" for effort in this sphere, Western observers still have not been able to acquire a very adequate understanding of how the Chinese themselves have conceived of the process of cultural change in which they are engaged, or of how they have thought they might best promote and consolidate the transformations they desire.

There has been a tendency to suppose that what the Chinese mean by cultural change really can be summed up as the alteration of people's attitudes, beliefs, and values through a program of constant propaganda/education, criticism/self-criticism, personal cultivation, and model emulation. On this view, the Chinese program of cultural change takes effect essentially at the level of individual psychology. It consists, only to a limited degree, of rational argumentation; it is made up primarily of ideological and emotional or psychological appeals to people to give up their selfish, bourgeois values and lifestyles and to dedicate themselves to self-sacrifice for the collective good.

There is of course some justification for taking this view of Chinese efforts at cultural change, since the Chinese Communist Party has always appeared to put much store in the positive value of propaganda/education and re-education. But since, in the West, it has mainly been political scientists who have written about Chinese propaganda/education programs and other attempts to create the new socialist citizen, there may be a different kind of reason for this concentration on the personal subjective or psychological aspect of cultural change in China. For as Tucker has shown, when the concept of 'culture' made the transition from the anthropologists' vocabulary to the political scientists', it lost some of its content—it underwent what Clifford Geertz has called a "radical subjectification."[2] When the early workers in the field, such as Almond, Verba, and Pye, began defining the scope of 'political culture', they talked mostly in terms of symbols, values, and beliefs, and were ambivalent about how to relate these to the objective political behavior of a people. They referred to a society's political culture as its "subjective orientation to politics."[3] In so doing, as Tucker says, "political scientists have parted company with the great majority of anthropologists. Viewing culture as the socially learned and transmitted way of life of a society, the anthropologists have treated it as a behavioral *as well as* a psychological concept."[4]

One consequence of the political scientists' narrower focus on subjective, psychological aspects of culture, as Pateman has pointed out, has been to give greater weight to problems of early childhood socialization when looking for the essential elements of political cultures,[5] because it is believed that in childhood basic psychological patterns are formed. In the field of Chinese studies, this approach has been reflected in a number of efforts to analyze the implications for politics of what might be peculiarly Chinese modes of child-rearing, most notably, perhaps, in Richard Solomon's monumental work on Chinese ambivalence toward authority and preference for avoiding conflict.[6] Writers like Solomon have been interpreted, fairly or unfairly, as implying that the political culture of China is so deeply imbedded in the secret, unconscious desires, needs, and predilections of her people that to set about changing it as radically and as openly as Mao Tse-tung and the Party have tried to do is a basically naive but still agonizing folly, doomed to failure. Although this approach does not explicitly deny that cultural change is possible, it seems to put the wellsprings of political culture so deeply into the private spheres of life that it must necessarily remain well out of reach of ordinary government- or Party-organized reform efforts. These writings have thus been seen as implying that the political culture of the Chinese people must be taken to be more or less given.[7] This has been partly the fault of the writers, for failing to give sufficient emphasis to other structural or environmental determinants of individual personalities, attitudes, and beliefs that contribute to the formation of political cultures. And it is partly the fault of their readers, who, children of their own cultures, tend to accept as an article of faith that predispositions acquired in the crib are most painfully, if ever, overruled by adult experience.

Partly in reaction to the apparent over-determinism of the political culturists' conception, then, some scholars in the field, especially sociologists and political sociologists, have recently been offering more structural analyses of the origins of Chinese attitudes, beliefs, and political (and nonpolitical) behavior. Focusing on the existence of political and social subsystems and organizations in the Chinese environment to which Chinese adults must learn to adapt in making their way through life, these analysts have attempted to show that "there are good, rational reasons," not only subconscious, psychological motivations, for the attitudes and values the Chinese adhere to and for the behavioral choices they make.[8] This type of analysis has progressed to the point where it has even been possible to distinguish between those organizational subsystems operative within Chinese society that are more conducive and contributory to genuine attitudinal and behavioral modifications, and those that are less so.[9]

In line with similar findings by students of other communist systems,[10] these studies have been very concerned to demonstrate the ways in which the Chinese Communists have themselves created political and social subsystems that serve to reinforce traditional cultural orientations among the people, rather than to facilitate the desired change to new ones. It is assumed that the Party's creation of such seemingly self-defeating structures in the environment has been either unwitting or unavoidable (or both). Yet it is maintained that the real functioning of these political and social subsystems, by their very nonconformity with the regime's propagandized cultural goals, has taught important lessons to individual Chinese trying to adapt to the total system. And the Chinese people's learning of these lessons from experience, more than any nonrational or psychological motivations on their part, provides a most powerful explanation for what lately has been judged to have been uneven and sluggish progress toward the Party's goals of popular cultural transformation.

This type of analysis, which regards invented or inherited political and social structures essentially as potential (and probable) limits on the extent of possible cultural transformation, has constituted a positive step forward in our understanding of the issues. It has served somewhat to demystify the concept of Chinese political culture, while at the same time reconfirming the complexity of the matter. It has not, however, taken us very far in the effort to develop a truly dynamic conception of the relationship between culture and structure in socialist society. And it has not helped us to understand very much at all about the very process of cultural change—if and when it is possible, and how it happens at all.

In treating culture and structure as essentially parallel systems imposing limits on each other, the analysis has not squarely addressed the question of whether and how these systems might interact in ways that promote change rather than block it. Even Whyte, who has gone the farthest in examining the differential effects of a variety of organizational settings in producing what he refers to as a "strict political atmosphere," does not offer a hypothesis about when or whether the maintenance of a strict political atmosphere graduates to an instance of cultural change, or how this happens, or how we can tell if it does. We have yet to outline a model of the relationship between structure and culture when cultural change *is* being successfully brought about. This chapter is intended as a step in that direction.

The method here is to focus on problems in effecting changes in Chinese peasant culture during the early years of land reform and socialist transformation. From the Party's perspective, peasant culture was clearly the dominant culture of China, and insofar as it was incompatible with modern socialist precepts, it required efforts at transformation. Those early years produced a rich written record of the Party's hopes and frustrations in confronting peasant culture. So, in the first section below, we begin by selecting and sketching three important areas where peasant values were grasped by the Party and were understood to be at odds with preferred socialist values.[11] The next section draws further on the written sources in an attempt to extract from them the Party's own conception of the value change process, which, it is argued, is implicit there.

The outline formula for value change thus reconstructed is admittedly still rudimentary and unadorned. But it has the advantage of setting behavioral change into a more dynamic relationship with value change. And it provides the framework for more sophisticated constructions of possible relationships between institutional or structural change and changes in values and culture.[12] This formula also illustrates and explains the Party's explicit conviction that it could best create a new socialist culture by building on appropriate elements already present in traditional peasant culture. In view of what has been said above about the initial, more superficial Western assumption that the Chinese depended almost entirely on propaganda/education and psychological pressure to achieve a degree of cultural change, this last point is perhaps the most significant one.

From the reconstruction of the Chinese value change formula given here, it is clear that the process was expected to occur over very long periods of time, and the final outcome was therefore expected to remain uncertain for years, perhaps for generations. Nevertheless, in the third section of this chapter, we offer a preliminary assessment of the progress made in effecting change in each of the three areas of peasant culture explored. In each case the evidence suggests that progress during the first few years of socialist transformation was only partial. In some cases peasant value change was less well consolidated than in others, and some of the reasons for this are discussed. In the concluding section we return to the issues of culture, structure, and change raised here, and relate them to some common misapprehensions about the Chinese "new socialist citizen."

Peasant Culture and Socialist Culture: Three Areas for Change

We begin by outlining three traditional value orientations of Chinese peasants that were regarded by the revolutionary government as needing change. The efforts to bring about the desired changes followed a similar pattern, but the outcomes of the three cases were not alike.

Farm Family Autonomy or Collectivism. Chinese peasants were traditionally organized for production by individual households, consisting usually of a single extended family. These farming families made most of their long-term and short-term plans on the principle of strengthening the economic independence of the unit. They preferred to own all the land they farmed and to avoid tenancy or sharecropping. They strove to purchase most of the other basic means of production as well, so as not to have to share, borrow, or rent from others. They hoped to build up their personal savings to a level where, for most small emergencies at least, they would not need to depend on extensions of credit from others. They wanted if possible to have their own carts and oxen to take their produce to market, and to avoid dealings with middlemen and jobbers. They prayed for sons who might grow up and work for the family, thus, among other benefits, reducing the need for hired labor. With only a few unavoidable concessions to commerce and cooperation, the goal of the poor peasant family was generally to come as near as possible to self-sufficiency in production and marketing.

There were sound reasons for this in the prevailing village economy. Interest rates on loans, even when they could be gotten from friends or kin, were generally high and not infrequently ruinous. Landlords did not by any means always reduce the crop share they took in bad harvest years and were often known to increase it, leaving tenants hungry. At the rates poor independent farmers could afford to pay their hired laborers, they knew they could only expect laziness, shoddy work, and probably pilfering. To have to rely on someone outside the household for a vital function or production input was regarded as most likely to bring trouble and expense. Even in the better times, when market prices were up, interest rates down, and landlords could afford a show of generosity, most of China's peasants appear to have remained determined to try to keep their liabilities within the household, and to acquire ownership or control for the family of all the things it would need to sustain itself.

In fact, of course, this guiding principle of family self-sufficiency was usually not entirely practicable and therefore often compromised.[13] Poor peasant families routinely worked out a variety of mutual aid and cooperative activities with one another, to stretch scarce resources and make the most efficient use of what was available.[14] Trading manpower for ox-power, setting up rotating credit

unions, arranging for joint labor on embankments and waterworks
—these are just some of the more common cooperative undertakings resorted to by poor and not-so-poor peasants to help make
ends meet.

Even so, most traditional peasant mutual aid schemes tended to
be short-term or purely temporary.[15] Many were in fact used only
in times of emergency, to combat floods or locusts or bandits.
Others, although they might involve the same partners many times
in succession, were still only seasonal arrangements, and were subject to rupture or renegotiation each time. This was so because the
needs and attributes initially bringing cooperating families together
might easily change: an ox might die, a well go dry, a son be con-
scripted. What had been a mutually beneficial agreement could
quickly become a disadvantage. Peasants preferred to keep their
choice of partners flexible, with the terms of partnership fixed on
an ad hoc basis. They shied away from long-term commitments,
because even families that seemed solidly established could at any
time suffer a calamity preventing them from keeping their part of
the bargain.

Occasional cooperation was, for most, both necessary and valuable. Yet while strict autonomy may have been impossible, independence was still highly valued by peasant households and basic
self-sufficiency remained their goal. Even when times were relatively good, the Chinese countryside was a place where most families
were living close to the subsistence margin and where neither custom nor the degree of social cohesion gave them much hope for
charity or for official assistance should they falter. In their own
agreements and dealings, therefore, they took care not to have to
pay for the mistakes or the misfortunes of others.

When the Chinese Communist Party came to power, this preference for independent family production and reluctance to join in
long-term cooperation were clearly among the characteristic peasant values regarded as most urgently in need of change.[16] During
the agrarian reform movement itself, the preoccupations of the
small-holder were actually useful in giving impetus to village revolution, and therefore official promotion of cooperation in production was notably absent.[17] But as soon as the redistribution of land
and livestock and tools was complete, central policymakers began
pressing for more long-term cooperative ventures among farmers,
for two basic reasons.

First, independent family farming patterns were regarded as inefficient in their use of resources and far from maximizing total agricultural output.[18] The cropping decisions, water use, and labor allocation demands dictated by a small-peasant subsistence system were judged to be irrational, wasteful, and unlikely to permit rapid technological improvement because of the extremely low levels of capital accumulation attainable in individual farming households. In short, peasants were to be urged to make mutual aid and cooperative arrangements because this would raise their productivity and their income.[19]

Second, the central leadership regarded mutual aid and cooperative arrangements as important methods of making up for remaining inequities in the distribution of land and other means of production across households. Less well-off mutual aid team and co-op members would, by these arrangements, gain access to needed labor power or tools essential to keeping up their production and keeping them out of debt.[20] Not only would this be beneficial for the production of an overall agricultural surplus, it would also help prevent the reemergence of markedly richer and poorer, exploiting and exploited, strata in the villages after the homogenizing creation of an enormous middle-peasant class, which was the result of the land reform.[21] Cooperative work arrangements among peasant families were to be valued, therefore, not only for their productive effects, but also on grounds of equity—what they would do to preserve and enhance a more equitable distribution of village wealth.

Like other socialists, Chinese Communists did not adhere to the goal of collectivism merely for its own sake, but rather because of their attachment to the underlying principles of equality and economic growth which were believed to depend for their sure development on a greater degree of cooperation and collectivism in work. It was for these reasons, then, that the Party regarded the peasant tendency to shun entangling alliances and promote family autonomy as a counterrevolutionary cultural inhibition in need of change.

"Risk Aversion" or the Ethic of "Progress." Like peasants in other societies living near or at the subsistence margin, poor Chinese peasants traditionally followed the "safety first" principle in making their own production and marketing decisions. Crop selection, seed selection, and field selection, soil preparation, fertilizer use, and irrigation practices were all affected by the peasants' need to insure—what was by no means certain—that they obtain

from their labors at least "enough" to sustain their families until the next harvest. Insofar as the logic of the "safety first" principle counseled against the adoption of new tools or technique, experimentation, specialization, or capital investment, these poor peasants were aptly regarded as "risk averse." This, when associated with the demonstrable technological primitiveness and stagnation of Chinese agriculture in the early part of the century, helped earn Chinese peasants the reputation for stubborn backwardness, conservatism, and opposition to progress that peasants in most other societies have sooner or later also come to enjoy.

Like other revolutionary and modernizing political elites, the Party has at times tended to regard the "risk averse," "conservative thinking" Chinese peasant as an obstacle to progress and economic development. Of course, with their long experience of rural revolution, Party cadres did not make the mistake of treating the peasantry as an undifferentiated mass, politically backward and "endlessly dark." They classified the village population into more and less progressive segments, very well aware that the success of their own movement was largely due to the real revolutionary potential to be found among the peasantry. Nevertheless, around the time of national liberation, the communist literature contained many references, in rather pitying tones, to the backward and benighted state of the peasant, held captive and dragged down for so long by feudal economic and social relations, superstition, and isolation from modern science and technology.[22] Party cadres obviously considered it part of their job to try to wipe away all backward tendencies, outdated values, and conservative ideas left over from the "old society" that might prevent peasants from responding well to the government's intended programs for agricultural modernization and development. It should be noted, however, that their goal was not only to lead peasants to accept centrally initiated rapid change and progress, but also to develop the capacity of peasants to innovate, evolve new technique, and plan for progress in their own communities. They hoped to give peasants some insight into how their own work in the village fit into the national economic program, and on this basis to bring peasants to the point where they would value progress in the community for its own sake, and for its contribution to the development of a more prosperous and powerful Chinese nation.

Other revolutionary and modernizing elites have at times hamhandedly tried to wrench their peasant populations into economic and technological modernity. In China, party cadres were also guilty at times of superciliously and ill-advisedly enforcing change and "progress" in production and marketing on skeptical villagers. Yet in China the Party did at least seem to recognize early that the problem with peasants was not mere stupidity and stubbornness. It was, rather, the product of generations of risk-taking and dying and learning about disaster. Thus the Party acknowledged that, where risk and investment and scientific farming were concerned, the changes it meant to bring about in the countryside would have to be as much cultural as economic and technological.

Harmony and Withdrawal or Conflict and Political Participation. The final example is actually the clearest case of a desired change in the rural political culture. It involves some of the fundamental assumptions of Chinese peasants about the proper conduct of village political affairs, their own roles in the local political process, and the nature of relations between leaders and led.

From the beginning it was constantly reiterated by the Party that village revolution and socialist transformation could not be genuinely accomplished without the full, unrestrained, and continual participation of the mass of peasants in all the important decisions affecting them and the village. The object of the revolution, it was stressed, was not merely to crush the old ruling class and redistribute the spoils, but also to put the reins of power firmly and permanently in the hands of those who had formerly been part of the oppressed classes. These beneficiaries of the revolution were to inherit not only new rights, but a few heavy responsibilities: the responsibility of exercising principled dictatorship over the reactionary classes and that of conducting village affairs justly and in a progressive manner. Entailed in this, on the Party's analysis, were one unassailable general prescription and two necessary corollaries.

The general prescription was that the broad mass of peasants must be brought *willingly* to participate actively and decisively in village affairs. It was endlessly proclaimed that without the conscious and deliberate participation of the masses in decision making and in policy implementation, even "good" decisions and policies could not be well executed. This principle was fundamental.

Following this, it was held that in their seizure of local control and conduct of village affairs the broad masses must inevitably encounter sharp struggle, especially class struggle, and they must be prepared to wage the struggle resolutely. Conflict was unavoidable. The revolution and the subsequent development of socialism would not go unopposed. The majority of peasants would have to come to understand this and be willing to join the fray—to do principled, class-conscious battle with enemies of the revolution.[23]

In particular, it was held, the mass of peasants would necessarily have to be willing to challenge all people in positions of authority in the village—old village elites at the time of power seizure, and new village elites during the subsequent extended transition period. Determination to eliminate the privileges and powers of old elite members and aggressively to supervise new elite members (i.e., village cadres) was considered essential to prevent counterrevolutionary backsliding and betrayal of basic revolutionary ideals.

All of this was clear enough. It was in Mao's writings, and it was repeatedly explained and emphasized in the training of cadres with responsiblity for village work. The problem, however, was that the Party perceived the "revolutionary masses" often to be falling far short of the necessary levels of revolutionary enthusiasm for political participation, and of the required determination to provoke and face up to village conflicts, especially conflicts with village power-holders, whether old or new. They noted a disappointing political apathy among peasants; a fear of precipitating overt conflict, a desire to find peaceful solutions to problems, and a marked reluctance to face down village leaders even on issues involving fundamental questions of justice and propriety.[24]

The Party had no difficulty in explaining why peasants, even poor and middle peasants, evinced a preference for conflict avoidance and were pessimistic in general about the value of political action. In the "old society" the rural balance of power had been so weighted against poor peasants that attempts at popular political action were most often doomed to failure, and in conflicts with local powerholders ordinary villagers generally stood to lose. They now could not help but view the Party's call to action with healthy skepticism; nor could they be blamed if they hesitated to cross swords with the "local bullies" (or later, with the "commandist" cadres).

Before Liberation, local powerholders were not only frequently in a position to do great harm to troublesome poor peasants, but virtually the only ones in a position to do them much good in a crisis. They were the ones who could negotiate with the authorities for a village tax reduction in bad harvest years; they had the connections outside the village to locate part-time labor opportunities; they were the ones best able to extend a small loan in an emergency. Cultivating good, stress-free relations with these people often provided poor peasants the only access they were likely ever to have to special protection or privilege.[25]

Yet, in the revolutionary era, a rural political culture marked by patterns of deference and *noblesse oblige,* by conflict avoidance, compromise, and widespread nonparticipation in village affairs, could no longer be regarded as acceptable, no matter how functional it may once have been for poor peasants living an otherwise politically voiceless and economically precarious existence in tightly knit and small communities heavily influenced by tradition and the demands of lineage loyalty. Thus, there were some real political attitudes or preferences which were characteristic of the supposedly most revolutionary poor and middle peasants and which, according to the Party, would unavoidably work to impede the development of social revolution and the maintenance of a militant political atmosphere in the villages. Because these attitudes could be serious obstacles to the proper development of a revolutionary socialist political system, they were subjected to strong pressure immediately upon Liberation and targeted for protracted challenge all through the transition period.

The Party's Outline Formula and Initial Strategies of Cultural Change

Accepting for the moment, then, that the Party was at least to some degree conscious of its need to alter certain cultural patterns associated with peasant life as a complement to its intended political, economic, and technological changes in the countryside, we may now turn to the question of how the Party imagined and proposed that it might actually go about inducing and promoting the kind of cultural change that it was after. Since it was a Marxist party, it generally did not address independently the problems of culture and cultural change in its publications and analyses, but dwelt instead on questions of class structure, relationship to the means of production, and changes in the economic base. For this reason, there is to my knowledge no major theoretical work of the period that contains an authoritative presentation of Party conceptions of the origin and process of cultural change. Still, the voluminous official and semiofficial literature on rural problems of the period often did deal with matters of peasant attitude change, value change, behavior change, and the relationships among these. And implicit in the many published parables and analyses of the time can be found a rough model of the process of revolutionary cultural change as the Party conceived of it. It may be summarized in an outline formula, as follows.[26]

Outline Formula. An appeal is made to a group of people to change their behavior, to act in some way differently from before. This appeal is made, in whole or in part, on the basis of one or more traditionally accepted values. That is, the revolutionary leadership calls upon the people to act in new ways for the attainment (or restoration) of already popularly valued ends. But the leadership has *in addition* other (new?)[27] values in mind, values also consistent with the requested behavior, which it hopes to promote in the course of events.

If the appeal takes hold and people do begin to behave as they are led to behave, an ambiguous situation has been created with regard to the informing values. It becomes possible to interpret and justify the new behavior first in terms of the old values, second in terms of the new values promoted by the leaders, or third (in what will probably be a majority of cases, since the two sets of values are unlikely to be mutually exclusive) in terms of both new and old values. At this point people are acting in response to Party demands, frankly initially motivated by traditional values, but they may possibly be coming to find it convenient and meaningful to explain their own actions to themselves and to others at least partly in terms of more recently articulated values. If true value change is to occur, then this undoubtedly is the critical moment.

The Party will, at this stage, actively seek to promote the new values over the old, through propaganda/education and persuasion. It will use all the peaceful resources at its command to lead people to find these new dimensions of worth and meaning in their own activity. Yet Party leaders have been aware that they may fail in this attempt. There is always the possiblity that new valued ends will be rejected, especially if the older valued ends are not readily achieved by the Party's recommended means. But if, as a minimum, the initially desired goals *are* basically attained, then it is expected that participants will be open to accepting the other values ascribed by the Party to their acts. At this stage their old values may be thought of as coexisting with the new ones. And if, to push it a step further, the initially desired goals become rather routinely attainable by the adopted means, if indeed those goals come to seem practically guaranteed, then it is hoped that they may also come to seem the less critical or salient of the values actively pursued. In these conditions, the newer values promoted by the Party may emerge from mere coexistence with the old to a position of primacy in the minds of the people. At this point in the ideal formula for value change, it might be said that both the people and Party leaders were taking the same old values for granted and were together most actively pursuing other, newer values—values consistent with their changed behavior but not initially motivating it.

Old values may, through careful direction, give rise to new forms of behavior that, in altered environmental conditions, may in turn give rise to new values.[28] It is a deceptively simple conception of the origin and process of value change among the masses, somewhat more sophisticated in fact than it may at first appear.

First, it assumes what we in the West have learned from modern anthropology, that culture is not innate but learned, and it presumes what we in the West have learned from modern psychology, that human learning can be facilitated by reinforcement of desired responses in an at least partly controlled environment. Thus it treats the problem of cultural change primarily as a problem of teaching and learning, and it addresses both the rational thought component of learning and the environmental reinforcement component.

Second, this formula takes a firm stand on the relationship of behavior to culture. It treats human behavior as both a product of culture and a source of cultural change. Whereas in Western political science we have tended to look to behavior as one possible indicator of degree of value change where value change is being promoted, in this Chinese conception altered behavior is only the first step in the change process; it coexists with both old and new values and can be explained in terms of each, and therefore it alone is an unreliable indicator of how much cultural distance has been traversed.

Third, this formula clearly accepts that the process of cultural change is a protracted one.[29] It depends on constant environmental reinforcement as well as prolonged rational persuasion; interruption of either would be likely to set back the process. This in turn would indicate that the Party harbored few illusions about the speed with which Chinese peasant culture might be thoroughly transformed. It suggests instead a high degree of tolerance for only partially remolded value responses and for inconsistencies in peasant attitudes and behavior. Cultural change, the creation of the new socialist man and woman, is on this outline formula to be a very gradual development, and one that may well proceed unevenly. With this in mind we can now turn to a brief examination of the strategies of value change actually followed by the Party after 1949 where the three problematical peasant value orientations discussed above were concerned.

Initial Strategies. First, how did the Party try to influence peasants to drop their original preference for independent family farming and to convince them to join in mutual aid teams and cooperatives? It was noted above that the Party had two sets of motives for promoting cooperation: increased efficiency and productivity, on the one hand, and enhanced equity or social justice, on the other. It is interesting therefore that in its appeals to peasants in favor of cooperation, the Party almost always argued in terms of the first set of values, and almost never in terms of the second. This second advantage of cooperation was something which peasants were obviously expected to value explicitly only after the more immediate goal of improved productivity had been attained in practice.

The revolutionary leadership clearly judged that, contrary perhaps to appearances, peasants did not value family economic independence so much for itself as for what, on the basis of their experience, they thought it would bring them—short-term minimization of risk and long-term maximization of family income. They therefore made their appeals for peasant cooperation almost exclusively on the basis of these two more fundamental values, and set about reordering the rural economic environment to make mutual aid and cooperation arrangements more consistent with what they perceived to be the peasants' most important valued ends—greater security and a better harvest for the family.

Examples of the ways in which the revolutionary government linked promises of improvements in individual family security and livelihood with participation in mutual aid and cooperation are legion. They have been detailed elsewhere,[30] and will therefore be only very briefly summarized here. The chief method employed was to make it clear that preferential treatment would be given to mutual aid team members or co-op members in the granting of low-interest loans, or the sale of limited quantities of superior seed grain, or the signing of advance deposit marketing contracts, or the deployment of scarce technical advisory personnel to help with double cropping, and so on.[31]

The use of such material incentives to individual households to join up was quite overt. This was a time when private sources of credit were drying up,[32] when thanks to state trading companies and supply and marketing co-ops good private marketing deals were getting more difficult to find,[33] and when price stabilization and tax regulations[34] were making it more imperative than ever to increase output so as to increase income. Peasants clearly found these promises of special access to needed inputs and reliable marketing outlets to be quite attractive.

Furthermore, the risks associated with cooperation must have appeared to peasants to be diminishing. If they ran into serious troubles, mutual aid teams and co-ops were frequently allowed to renegotiate or even default on public loans without penalty.[35] Local cadres were instructed to work for the adoption of dependable workpoint and accounting systems within teams and co-ops, systems which, while they were undoubtedly often cumbersome and annoying, also were intended over time to help insure that exchange relationships and the assignment of work within production groups were more rational and less onerous than they might otherwise have been.[36] Of course, if the situation were yet to become intolerable in a production grouping and a family came to regret its decision to join, it was always promised the option of withdrawal.[37]

All alterations in the economic environment considered, then, and especially in view of the seemingly ever-shrinking opportunities for independent private entrepreneurship outside the teams and co-ops, most peasants were rapidly being brought to the conclusion that joining in production cooperation with other families might now be in the best interest of their own families' security and livelihood. It was never any secret that the new authorities were attracting peasants into co-ops with out-and-out promises of advancing the well-being of their own households. Perhaps the classic example came during the "high tide" of 1955–1956, when it was declared a matter of policy that upon joining a co-op (or upon making the transition from elementary to advanced cooperative organization) no less than 90 to 95 percent of participating households should experience an immediate rise in income.[38] And there is evidence, in those years, of a considerable spurt of state investment in the agricultural sector, used in part to make good on this declaration.[39]

On the problem of the "conservative" or the "progress" orientation, as noted above, the revolutionary leadership approached peasant risk aversion with the knowledge that in a precarious subsistence economy, risk-averse behavior where cropping patterns, irrigation technique, or investment choices are concerned is not only usually not irrational, but often in fact the most rational strategy for the peasant to adopt. A risk-averse strategy will not maximize income, but it should minimize loss and therefore provide the greatest security that actual income will at least be "enough." Thus the new government began its program of peasant attitude change not by asking them to take, for the sake of progress or development or modernism, what they must inevitably have regarded as irrational risks, but by deliberately moving instead to restructure some key aspects of the peasants' economic environment that were dictating conservatism. They appealed to farmers on their old "safety first" principle, and by including a greater measure of security or a larger margin for error in the deals they offered peasants during the early years, they were able to induce peasants into some startling changeovers.

The government offered tax breaks, for example, to peasants who would open virgin land,[40] preferential prices to peasants who would cultivate cotton and other cash crops where production had been depressed by the war,[41] comprehensive guaranteed purchase and supply contracts to peasants who would agree to produce needed handicraft or other sideline goods,[42] modest amounts in low-interest loans to peasants who would dig wells or undertake other irrigation projects,[43] and limited assistance with seed and equipment for peasants willing to try double cropping or other new techniques.[44]

Almost all such overtures were met with rapid and enthusiastic peasant response—sometimes too rapid and enthusiastic: more wells were dug than were needed, for example, and within a few years peasants were producing more cotton than the planners had bargained for.[45] As soon as minimum guarantees were made available, some security in case of disaster, China's peasants were clearly prepared to adopt new cultivation patterns and techniques and to make investments they judged might pay off in better harvests or more income. Many more such security incentives were offered to good effect throughout the transition period. While the new revolutionary government was not yet, nor would it soon be, in a position to remove all the serious risks from farmers' calculations, it was able to recast the odds sufficiently so that, in the years immediately following 1949, many peasants were drawn into production-expanding, commodity-diversifying, and growth-promoting investments and ventures they would before have judged too dangerous.

In promoting higher levels of overt conflict and political participation in villages, the Party also achieved some striking successes early on. The Party's various techniques for mobilizing peasants into aggressive political action have been discussed many times and do not need to be rehearsed in detail here. Especially during land reform, the creation of peasant associations and even of poor peasant associations, the rent reduction small group and mass meetings, the antidespot and antitraitor mass meetings, the "speak bitterness" sessions and the process of "settling accounts," along with the actual seizure and redistribution of land and other property, brought the mass of village dwellers into an openly conflictual and politically highly charged relationship with the small group of landlords, other elite members, and "local bullies" who were separated out as the enemy. If at first Party cadres were unable to stir the peasants of an area from their accustomed fear and apathy to join in the struggle, then workteams of cadres and activists were repeatedly sent in to press and organize the movement until most people were drawn into participation and every family was classified among the friends or among the enemies of the revolutionary masses. While the level of actual physical violence was probably a good deal lower than had been the case in some earlier periods of the revolutionary movement, there can be little doubt that the way the Party carried out its land reform after 1949 still brought the great majority of peasants deliberately into new political roles and decisively disrupted, if it did not absolutely eliminate, the old tendency to preserve outwardly harmonious patterns of authority and deference in village affairs.

After the land reform movement subsided, sustaining high levels of peasant political participation and sustaining attitudes of struggle among the rural masses became somewhat more problematical. The Korean War was probably of fortuitous assistance in organizing an extra degree of patriotic mobilization in rural areas. All ordinary peasants were also made responsible for keeping a watchful eye on the activities of landlords, "bad elements," and other class enemies who remained "under surveillance" after land reform. Elections were held in most areas for new village governing councils. And there were, in addition, several centrally-orchestrated mass political campaigns, like the Three-Anti Five-Anti campaign, which filtered down to some villages and involved peasants there in another round of criticism and struggle.

But probably the major political responsibility that remained on the shoulders of ordinary peasants in the years after agrarian reform was participation in the small group and mass meetings for the rectification of errors and workstyle of local cadres. In these years, rectification was still "open door," that is, not yet confined to Party members, and ordinary peasants were enjoined to speak out in a spirit of direct, constructive criticism—or if the situation warranted, of hostile, angry criticism—of their new village leaders. If the discussions were frank and the presentations of grievances were principled, then it was thought that these meetings in the rectification process would do much to maintain the spirit of anti-elitist struggle and mass participation that had been at the core of the land reform effort. As explained in the next section, however, these conditions of progressive rural political participation often proved difficult to preserve.

More on Strategies and Some Evidence on Outcomes

Although in several important respects the outcomes in each of the three cases were to be dissimilar, it seems pretty clear that, in all three, the revolutionary government was rapidly successful in achieving the first step—the stage of motivating new behavior by appeals to old values—in the ideal formula for value change sketched above.

On Collectivism. Where the values of family autonomy and collectivism were concerned, peasants clearly were not expected at the beginning to love or value the collective for its own sake, or for what it did for others. Their attachment to it was admitted to be entirely conditional on its delivery of personal and family benefits otherwise not attainable. The many available reports of internal bickering, individual family withdrawals, and team and co-op collapses confirm this general picture.[46]

Once peasants had been drawn into teams and co-ops, however, the Party did move on to the second stage, deliberately attempting to foster attitude change. It began issuing considerable propaganda/education material urging peasants who had manifestly joined for personal advantage to stop thinking entirely in those terms once inside. They were, for example, admonished not to do slipshod work for the group, not to concern themselves only with how many workpoints they personally were awarded, and not to volunteer only for easy jobs, leaving the disagreeable tasks to others.

There was abundant evidence, of course, that these were precisely the kinds of self-interested behavior that peasants continued to exhibit after teams and co-ops were formed.[47] But now the leadership urged them to think (sometimes, at least) about working for the good of the group as a whole, so as to raise its overall production and income. It was pointed out again and again that a general rise in productivity would be managed to the benefit of each and every individual member in the long run. In other words, there was a deliberate attempt to convince peasants that their own self-interest and the interest of the collective could and did overlap, that working for oneself and working for the collective could be one and the same thing.[48] It was an attempt to create that ambiguous situation, described in the ideal formula outlined above, wherein individuals might find it meaningful to justify and describe their new behavior both in terms of new values and in terms of older ones. And in teams and co-ops that were successfully run over a period of a few years, it is very probably the case that peasant members did begin to see their old and new values coincide in some ways in work for the collective.[49]

The final step in the formula, as it has been outlined here, would have been for peasants to come to value the collective welfare not just when it reinforced their own, but even in preference to their own welfare. With this degree of value change, they would have been prepared willingly to make sizeable personal sacrifices for the sake of the group. But a careful reading of the literature of the period reveals quite plainly that, with very few exceptions, the Party never even tried to propagandize this degree of value change among peasants. Farmers were never asked during the transition period cheerfully to sustain a loss only for the co-op's sake. What was emphasized was that if it *seemed* they had to take a small loss temporarily, in the long run they would still make a bigger personal gain since their transitional sacrifice would serve to strengthen the co-op organization and make it more profitable for all members.

Even at the high tide of transition from elementary to advanced co-ops, when a certain percentage of co-op members stood to lose a part of their personal income to the group, it was rarely suggested that they should like it. As a rule, these transitions were presented as the result of the demands of poor and lower-middle peasants who had waged a class struggle against exploiting elements in the group, and had won the struggle.[50] By that time it was clear that with the advance of the semisocialist cooperative economy, those under pressure could not have expected anymore to make a go of it outside the group if they tried to withdraw. They had little choice but to acquiesce. Few of them pretended to any sentiment that they ought to put the collective interest before their own. Those who did were probably not believed.

The problem of self-interest versus collective interest is central to the cultural transformation of any socialist society, and I have included consideration of it here in order to emphasize the very modest degree of value change among peasants that was attempted and expected by the Chinese leadership during these years. The ideal formula for value change outlined above was probably being consciously followed over these years, but there is little evidence that the leadership ever tried seriously, or were able in many cases, to proceed beyond the stage of creating an ambiguous situation for peasants with regard to their value orientation. In any case, the elapsed time before the onset of the disruptions of the Great Leap Forward was insufficient for a very full change of values to have come about. If there were illusions on the part of some leaders about the readiness of peasants to put the interest of the collective ahead of that of their own families, those illusions were very shortly to evaporate. As Mao said at the Chengchow Conference "Before last autumn it seemed as if the peasants were running ahead of the workers, but after autumn they were immediately concealing output and dividing it privately among themselves. These then are the two sides of the peasantry: peasants are still peasants."[51]

On Conservatism. Where risk aversion and peasant conservatism were concerned, again there is little doubt that the leadership was able to induce peasants to adopt new behavior by altering somewhat their economic environment and then appealing for change on the basis of old valued ends such as enhanced security and a better harvest. But in contrast with the first example, here it is unclear that the attempt at value change actually moved very much beyond this first step.

Quite a bit of propaganda/education material was issued, it is true, urging its readers to adopt a modern, progressive, scientific, nonsuperstitious approach to daily problems. But it seems doubtful whether most of this ever penetrated to the villages and the peasantry. Much of it appeared in journals and articles intended for Party workers, students, and youth, who were felt perhaps to be most amenable to such ideas. Even if these people were influenced and did pass on to others what they read, however, they were often not the ones whose opinions were taken most seriously by peasants when making difficult production decisions.

Numerous model experiences of innovations leading to higher crop yields were, of course, widely publicized and probably relayed through cadres and activists to large numbers of peasants. They tended to be quite specific about technique and results, however. It is questionable whether they did (or were even meant to) convey a general value preference for progressive behavior and adoption of new methods, or if, instead, they merely made peasants more aware of certain promising options potentially available to them.

Very early on, then, it became obvious that peasants all across the country would react rationally and rapidly to government programs for agricultural modernization, economic diversification and development, and also that peasants could and would improvise their own improvements if the environment could be made reasonably favorable. The main problem for the authorities then became, first, the extension of their control over the rural economy to make it in fact more favorable to local entrepreneurship, and second, the development of usable improved agricultural techniques for systematic extension. Although the intention to banish residual superstitious, nonscientific, conservative peasant attitudes and values was never abandoned, a change in attitudes was, it seems, quickly realized not to be the top-priority need of the transition period.

On Conflict. Finally, the evidence on value change among peasants where conflict and political participation are concerned is also mixed. During the earliest stages of village revolution, and especially during the land reform movement, there would seem to be plenty of evidence that peasants were indeed, for the sake of old valued ends, brought to participate actively and to set aside their doubts about the need for struggle. The Party's appeals to peasants to take bold action were largely articulated, in those days, in terms of old values, or at least old notions about justice, fairness, and the basic minimum dimensions of socially observed human rights. "Speak bitterness" meetings, after all, were precisely forums in which old norms of decent, moral behavior were implicitly used as the standard against which to measure the behavior of those on trial. The ritual (and actual) "settling of accounts" with landlords during the movement were clear examples of leadership appeals to old rural attitudes and values designed to provoke, and to strengthen peasant determination for, new revolutionary action. These themes, plus the obvious appeal by the Party to the traditional desire of peasants to own more land, make the fit with stage one of the formula for value change quite perfect. Peasants acted in revolutionary new ways within their villages in hope of restoring old norms of village justice and in hope of gaining more land for their families.

During the excitement of land reform, the stakes were very high and most peasants undoubtedly were at least moved far enough from their customary apparent political apathy to attend the struggle meetings and to participate in overt conflict with other, more powerful villagers. There is much evidence, however, that this participatory behavior was still not easily won.

Peasants hung back and were fearful of committing themselves.[52] They, and even the locally recruited cadres and activists, frequently expressed a preference for avoiding public struggle and strife, and for carrying out the land reform as peacefully as possible.[53] And even when they were brought to carry on real struggle, the Party leadership complained that the struggle was not guided by principles of class conflict. Peasants were influenced by kinship ties to refrain from targeting certain individuals for struggle; or they mercilessly attacked some villagers who happened to be personally despised, regardless of their class status.[54]

In sum, while it is true that the Party generally succeeded in eliciting a high degree of peasant participation in land reform struggle, it is also true that the reform process had to be repeated more than once (and often several times) before the leadership was satisfied that this participation was genuine enough, universal enough, and principled enough to establish a solid foundation on which to build a new village political order. [55]

After the completion of land reform, the problems of peasant political participation and continuation of the class struggle became only more acute. It was widely conceded that peasants and activists alike staged a large-scale retreat from politics and the cares of public affairs once the land was redistributed and the government's general injunction to farmers became "settle down and get rich."[56] Most peasants obviously preferred to leave the conduct of village political campaigns to the remaining active cadres, concentrating themselves on their own problems of production. Local cadres, for their part, were continually reminded by the Party that they should be seeking ever wider and more active mass participation in all aspects of policy implementation. The problems involved here for village cadres, in getting assigned tasks done and in getting the mass of peasants to participate, without resorting to elitist or "commandist" tactics, were to characterize the entire transition period.

The truth was that cadres were often more than happy to leave out the mass of poor peasants when it came to certain programs to be administered in the villages. There are numerous accounts of cadres showing favoritism to people classified as middle and even rich peasants in the distribution of state loans at low interest, or in the signing of commodity purchase contracts. This they did because better-off peasants had more collateral and made better risks for venture capital—and these were important considerations for cadres expected to administer such programs efficiently and profitably.

Village cadres also were often not sorry to see peasants reassume their original preference for deferential, non-stressful relations with members of the village elite. This made the prospect of Party-ordered criticism/self-criticism sessions and cadre rectification campaigns quite a bit less terrifying for them.

As the revolutionary government got more and more into the business of supplying special investment and other inputs on a preferential basis, the government's local cadres likewise predictably came to be seen by villagers as their best and only links to outside assistance. In this respect cadres were regarded as performing a patronage function very similar to that associated with the more benevolent roles of traditional village elites. While peasants were being urged to challenge, criticize, and in a principled fashion call to account those local cadres who had been leaders in earlier struggles but who had lately been guilty of mistakes in class policy or transgressions in political style, they were also painfully aware of the potential costs to the village and to themselves of going so far as to demoralize or humiliate their cadres. Above all they would not have wanted to make their own local cadres look so bad in the eyes of their superiors as to reduce their credibility or their leverage in negotiations affecting village welfare.

The emerging danger of the routinization of elite-mass struggle, of only pro forma, ritualized performance of criticism sessions, was constantly deplored by the Party leadership during the transition period. If cadres and villagers went through the motions of bringing conflicts frankly to the surface, but did so only within mutually understood limits, so that the conflicts were controllable and ultimately relatively unthreatening to any individual, then the Party's desire to impress on peasants the lasting value of political participation informed by conscious class struggle could never be realized. The fact that this possibility was so much the subject of worried warning during these years is the best indication we have of the power of various forces in the villages threatening to reduce the salience of peasant political participation.

But even if potential cadre-mass conflicts remained less well explored than the leadership ideally would have wished during these years, it is still quite clear that in most villages the poor peasant masses retained the power to act decisively, from time to time, in determining the course of village affairs, by uniting to press the issue of class struggle. The best example of this power came with the "high tide" of 1955–1956, especially with the extraordinary speed of conversions from elementary to advanced production co-ops. There is no denying that the Party, and the Chairman in particular, were the instigators of the "high tide" of collectivization in the countryside. But the movement could not have been brought off with such speed and thoroughness without the willingness on the part of poor peasants in the villages to face up to the confrontation with better-off villagers over the issues of rent payments and private ownership within co-ops.[57] This was a stage in the development of village class struggle when poor peasant militant participation was essential and where, to all appearances, it was widely attainable. It is true that, by that time, the inroads already made by elements of the cooperative economy had considerably altered the balance of power in the villages. Better-off co-op members had few realistic options remaining by 1955–1956 but to give in to poor members' demands. This surely was sensed by the "broad masses," and their willingness to precipitate the conflicts entailed in the conversion from co-op to collective probably reflects their confidence that the outcome would be positive. The risks of participation, if not the unpleasantness of it, were in this sense, anyway, somewhat reduced for poorer peasants.

What all of this suggests is that the Party was able at times to appeal to some old values, override others temporarily, and bring peasants into active political conflict and struggle for specific ends. It suggests further, however, that peasant tolerance and taste for political engagement and community upheaval remained limited. The Party was apparently most successful at motivating peasants to join in short-term, specific, class-based village conflicts where those who entered the fray stood to gain land or other property as well as a measure of vengeance and a sense of vindication. It was less successful at motivating them to enter into long-term, generalized cadre-mass conflicts where the purpose was to preserve a democratic, class-conscious style in the running of village affairs.

Where the patterns of conflict and political participation were concerned, the traditional valued ends of the poor peasants—restoring old norms of justice and obtaining more land—were accomplished exceedingly quickly through the deliberate heightening of village conflict. These ends were accomplished in dramatic, once-for-all efforts that patently consumed much emotion but little time. As for the new valued ends associated with the conflictual mode in village affairs—continuation of principled class struggle, anti-elitism, antibureaucratism, and a mass-participatory style of village politics—these were not afforded the time they needed to take hold. The very shortness of the village upheaval probably prevented the crystallization of the ambiguous situation regarding values that is called for in the ideal formula. Abruptly, and with fear in their hearts, poor peasants achieved their most cherished ends through land reform and collectivization, and then, often it seems with a shudder, they released their grip on the means. While the Party stridently pressed on with propaganda about the importance of continuing village struggle and mass participation, it is evident that it often faced a peasantry (and also a cadre force) no longer objectively motivated to persevere. In this respect at least, the Party's own rapid success at delivering to peasants their basic demands may have deprived it of the period of ambiguity it needed to further the transformation of their values.

Comparisons. The three case studies explored here illustrate outcomes that are clearly somewhat different. In the first case, involving the values of collectivism, the Party was best able to adhere in practice to the ideal formula. The period discussed here was short and the reactions of peasants were by no means conclusive, but both the structural alterations and the propaganda efforts were sustained, so that the Party did appear at times actually to harness old habits and beliefs for the creation of new ones.

The second case, involving peasant conservatism, was more of an abortive effort. The restructuring of the economic environment to encourage peasant entrepreneurship was a complex process demanding continuous assessment and readjustments by the leadership. But when it *was* able to restructure the environment, the Party appears to have found peasants very receptive to new, more modern, and technologically advanced economic undertakings. Peasants generally did not seem to need tutoring in the virtues of upgrading quality, capital accumulation, infrastructural investment, and commodity diversification. Although they were still far from being fully citizens of the twentieth century, the gap between the attitudes of ordinary peasants and those of the new socialist farmers the Party hoped to nurture proved not to be so formidable. The new government in fact had its hands full trying to plan ways to meet the existing capital and technical needs of farmers; and so, as the leadership exerted itself to cope with the more pressing problems of shortages and difficulties in setting an effective extension service in place, the originally perceived urgent need to modernize peasant thinking dulled somewhat by comparison.

In the third case, involving the values of struggle and participation, the Party's own early victories had the effect of undermining its linkage of old attitudes and new ones. The ideal progression of the formula for value change was interrupted and the new socialist, democratic, antibureaucratic values were not fully reinforced. Through vigorous political campaigns and rectification movements it continued over the years to attempt to reestablish the linkage, but with the countervailing tendencies present in village cadres' roles and identities, the project was often frustrated.

The formula for value change the Party tried to employ depends for its success on a delicate balance among attitudes, behavior, and environmental factors. Sequence and duration of stages are also important. As the second case illustrates, early gains may exceed the Party's expectations and capacities, and the need to press for further value change may then appear to evaporate. But as the third case suggests, an opportunity missed, on this formula, may not readily be regained. And as all three cases together demonstrate, the formula might show some success in one area but also allow for slippage in others.

Conclusions

During the early transition to socialism, the Party pursued a wide-ranging program for the transformation of traditional peasant culture. In this pursuit, it did not rely solely or even primarily on the tools of persuasion, exhortation, and psychological pressure. On the contrary, the Party conceived the process of directed cultural change to involve the balancing, sequencing, and reinforcing of complementary changes in three areas of human experience: environmental systems, behavioral patterns, and articulated values. Changes in all three areas were seen as necessary conditions of genuine cultural transformation; and the changes in each sphere were regarded as intimately interrelated—mutually dependent and possibly mutually reinforcing. Changes in environmental systems, it was hoped, would produce changes in behavior patterns, which might, as they became elaborated, reinforce and even further the initial environmental modifications to which they were the response. Meanwhile, directed change in the third area of articulated values could help to consolidate and make sense of developments in the other two.

This was the basic insight. Faltering or stagnation in any one sphere might work to undermine the process; and attention to only one or two areas, not all three, could not be expected to produce genuine cultural transformations. The responsibility of the Party to establish and maintain reinforcing conditions in all three spheres at once, then, was a heavy one. Since, in their view, the relationships among the levels of human experience were not inevitable, but uncertain and dynamic, there was ample room, if the reinforcements were imperfect, for backward movement as well.

If we as observers are concerned to evaluate the degree of real value change attained at a given point in such a system, then the core, problematical Party conception is that of the value ambiguity of human behavior and the simultaneous value-creating and confirming potentialities of behavioral change. Since to alter peasant behavior is not to guarantee value modifications but merely to establish the possibility of reinforcement of new socialist values, the process requires an indeterminate period marked by modified peasant behavior and the confusing coexistence of both old and new underlying values. On this conception of the change process, it would be insufficient to look only at the structural determinants of peasant behavior, or to look only at peasant behavior itself if what we wish to know about is the extent of value change. For within identical structural patterns and identical behavioral patterns there may be different value orientations slowly taking shape.

If this is not a terribly satisfying formulation for social scientists looking for answers about the political cultures of socialist systems, it does at least clarify one misapprehension about the Chinese Communist Party and the new socialist citizen. Armed with this kind of understanding of the process of cultural transformation in which they were engaged, Party leaders would be able to show great tolerance for the persistence of old cultural orientations and for the only partial acceptance of new ones, well into the socialist era. If there have been times in more recent Chinese history when the leadership has been intolerant of lingering traditional value orientations and has tried to force the pace of cultural transformation, these have been times of departure from the basic conception described in this chapter.

The formula outlined here is one on which new socialist men and women do not spring into the world as entirely fresh and modern creations. They are, rather, the products of an evolutionary process that begins from and continues to incorporate, as it modifies, many ancient and venerable themes and values in Chinese culture. What is called for is not the total rejection of past culture, but the sifting, modernizing, and recasting of its elements for new purposes.

It is one of the ironies of China's twentieth-century development that her leading political reformist intellectuals so often gave the impression of being repelled by their own traditional culture as they called for a thorough reorientation of the Chinese spirit, while her practicing revolutionaries, who might have been expected to dream dreams of total destruction, applied themselves instead to finding ways of using popular old cultural orientations for new revolutionary purposes. Thus Hu Shih and Liang Ch'i-ch'ao (at least in his early years) discerned in China's cultural history a reprehensible femininity, an embarrassing weakness yielding perpetual reaction, and a simultaneously self-deluding and self-congratulatory inability to cope with the genuine and abiding dilemmas of individual, society, and nation. But by contrast, as Friedman has shown for Sun Yat-sen and the Chinese Revolutionary Party, and as Selden has shown for Mao Tse-tung and the Chinese Communist Party, successful revolutionary work in the early twentieth-century Chinese environment consciously depended on its resonance with tradition, on its use of familiar cultural themes and expressions, and on its acceptance of only half-modern elements into the ranks of those who would create a new society and a new future for the people.[58] They perceived that traditional culture held not only the weaknesses to be overcome and the fetters to be broken, but also the precedents for heroism and defiance, for determined bitter sacrifice, for guile and treachery, ambition and imagination that must all be recalled and invoked to bring individuals and masses into the movement, at once legitimating it in past terms and giving it license to change the face of China. This vision of the relationship of Chinese tradition to revolutionary transformation persisted beyond Liberation and into the period of building socialism and of nurturing the new socialist citizen.

NOTES

The author is grateful to Richard Baum for helpful comments on an earlier draft, and to Victor Falkenheim for insights and information leading to the capture of a better focus for this chapter.

1. For just one of the more recent judgments of this kind, see Archie Brown and Jack Gray, eds., *Political Culture and Political Change in Communist States* (New York: Holmes and Meier, 1977), pp. 263–264. In the conclusion to this comparative volume with essays on Yugoslavia, Hungary, Poland, Czechoslovakia, the USSR, and Cuba, Jack Gray writes: "The attempt to create a new socialist man, the end product of the official political culture, has been on the whole a depressing failure. . . . Almost everywhere apathy, privatism and 'economism' are prevalent and tolerated and sometimes even encouraged. Only China and perhaps Cuba (although bureaucratism is growing apace there too) still pay more than lip service to the idea; and only in China has there been a consistent and vigorous attempt to create a new kind of social and political organization which will (it is hoped) provide a milieu in which the new man can grow" (pp. 270–271).

2. See Robert C. Tucker, "Culture, Political Culture, and Communist Society," *Political Science Quarterly* 88, no. 2 (June 1973): 176–177.

3. From one of the classical definitions, in *Political Culture and Political Development,* ed. Lucian Pye and Sidney Verba (Princeton:Princeton University Press, 1965), p. 513.

4. Tucker, p. 176 (emphasis added).

5. Carole Pateman, "Political Culture, Political Structure, and Political Change," *British Journal of Political Science* 1, pt. 3 (July 1971): 292 and passim.

6. Richard Solomon, *Mao's Revolution and the Chinese Political Culture* (Berkeley: University of California Press, 1971).

7. Pateman makes the same charge against Almond and Verba and other writers on Western political cultures who have likewise focused too heavily on the psychological elements of personality formation.

8. For one excellent example of this kind of argument, see William J. Parish, Jr., "Socialism and the Chinese Peasant Family," *Journal of Asian Studies* 34, no. 3 (May 1975). The phrase "good, rational reasons" is his, p. 616; and a more explicit reference to the structural orientation of Parish's analysis can be found on p. 615.

9. This is the contribution of Whyte's very valuable work. See Martin King Whyte, *Small Groups and Political Rituals in China* (Berkeley: University of California Press, 1974), esp. chap. 10.

10. Among the most intelligent and rigorous of these has been the work of Kenneth Jowitt on Rumania. In an extremely rich early article describing his own approach, Jowitt wrote: "Political culture will be studied in conjunction with political structure; structure and culture will be viewed as establishing mutual, though not necessarily equal, limits for one another." See Kenneth Jowitt, "An Organizational Approach to the Study of Political Culture in Marxist-Leninist Systems," *American Political Science Review* 68, no. 3 (September 1974): 1172.

11. Note that most of the discussion to follow is cast in terms of peasant 'values', although at times there are also references to peasant 'beliefs' and to peasant 'attitudes'. While there may be analytic distinctions to be made here, such as those proposed by Rokeach and others, they are deliberately passed over in this chapter. 'Values', 'attitudes', and 'beliefs' are all generally treated here as learned orientations among the more subjective elements of culture. Instead of seeking to clarify possible distinctions among them, an effort is made to explore the possible relationships between these subjective elements of culture, on the one hand, and the more objective, behavioral elements of culture, on the other. In particular, the effort is to explore this changing relationship during the very process of cultural change.

12. In these two ways, the effort here is similar to that of Richard Fagen in his landmark study of institutional innovation, popular participation, and directed cultural change in Cuba; see Richard R. Fagen, *The Transformation of Political Culture in Cuba* (Stanford: Stanford University Press, 1969), esp. chap. 1. The Chinese formula for value change sketched below should be compared with Fagen's central observation that " . . . in revolutionary institutions where participation in a wide range of activities is encouraged, behavior is frequently modified even when there is no initial change in attitude. Such behavioral changes may lead in turn to new ways of perceiving and evaluating the world, and thus a permanent nexus for relating the two types of change is established. In short, participatory activity—not in itself dependent on the internalization of new norms—may eventually lead to very basic changes in the value and belief systems of those who are swept into participation" (p. 10).

13. Good accounts of traditional mutual aid practices can be found in "Investigation of the Situation Regarding Temporary Mutual Aid Teams in Ch'ing-liang Village, Ch'ang-sha County [Hunan] . . . ," *Hsin Hunan Pao*, 14 April 1954; and in the report of the Office of the Huang-kang [Hupeh] CCP Land Committee, "Preliminary Research into Problems of Temporary Mutual Aid Teams," *Jen Min Jih Pao*, 11 February 1954.

14. On the advantages to peasants of various forms of mutual aid, see *Mutual Aid and Cooperation in Agricultural Production [Nung-yeh sheng-ch'an hu-chu ho-tso]*

(Peking: Hua-pei jen-min ch'u-pan-she, 1952); and "In Various Places in the Central South Peasants . . . Organize Mutual Aid in Labor and Develop Production," *Ch'ang-chiang Jih Pao,* 8 April 1952.

15. See "Investigation of the Situation . . . "

16. See Teng Tzu-hui, "Basic Tasks and Policies in Rural Areas," in *Mutual Aid and Cooperation in China's Agricultural Production,* (Peking: Foreign Languages Press, 1953), esp. p. 27 ff.

17. See *Study Questions and Answers on Land Reform [T'u-ti kai-ko hsueh-hsi wen-ta]* (Shanghai: Wen-kung, 1951), esp. p. 12.

18. For this type of argument, see Hsueh Mu-ch'iao et al., *The Socialist Transformation of the National Economy in China* (Peking: Foreign Languages Press, 1960); and Huang Nan-sen and Wang Ch'ing-shu, *On the Objective Foundation of the Cooperativization High Tide in China [Lun wo-kuo nung-yeh ho-tso-hua kao-chi ti k'o-kuan ken-yuan]* (Shanghai: Shang-hai jen-min ch'u-pan-she, 1956). Also, *Basic Information about Cooperative Economy [Ho-tso-she ching-chi chi-pen chih-shih]* (Canton: Hua-nan jen-min ch'u-pan-she, 1954).

19. It would incidentally also serve to make agriculture more amenable to central planning and therefore better serve national industrialization. See Fang Ch'ang, *The Relationship between Developing Agricultural Production and Developing Industrial Production [Fa-chan nung-yeh sheng-ch'an ho fa-chan kung-yeh sheng-ch'an ti kuan-hsi]* (Peking: Jen-min ch'u-pan-she, 1956).

20. On the class policy for mutual aid teams and co-ops, and the explicit intention that they serve the interests of the poor, see, for example, "Questions and Answers about Several Labor Mutual Aid Policy Problems" *["Tui lao-tung hu-chu jo-kan cheng-ts'e wen-t'i ti chieh-ta"],* in *Reference Material on Agricultural Production Mutual Aid Teams [Nung-yeh sheng-ch'an hu-chu-tsu ts'an-k'ao tzu-liao]* (Peking: Chung-yang jen-min cheng-fu nung-yeh-pu, 1952), pp. 15–20; and *Model Regulations for an Agricultural Producers' Cooperative* (Peking: Foreign Languages Press, 1956), esp. article XI; see also *Talking about Some Problems in the Class Policy for Agricultural Cooperativization [T'an-t'an nung-yeh ho-tso-hua chieh-chi cheng-ts'e ti chi-ko wen-t'i]* (Peking: Chung-kuo ch'ing-nien ch'u-pan-she, 1956), esp. pp. 16–19.

21. The perceived possibility of such a class repolarization is explicitly discussed in both Su Hsing, *The Socialist Road of China's Agriculture [Wo-kuo nung-yeh ti she-hui-chu-i tao-lu]* (Peking: Jen-min ch'u-pan-she, 1976); and T'ung Ta-lin, *The Basis of the Great Development of Agricultural Cooperativization [Nung-yeh ho-tso-hua ta fa-chan ti ken-chu]* (Peking: Jen-min ch'u-pan-she, 1956).

22. This was the view not only of urban Party workers. There are many reports of cadres sent to lead the work in newly liberated rural areas coming to depressing conclusions about the impenetrable backwardness and conservatism of the peasants they were trying to mobilize.

23. The earliest statements on this problem came in opposition to the 'deviation' of "peaceful land reform." See the classic statement of Tu Jun-sheng on this matter in "Some Problems in Leading Land Reform at Present," *Hupeh Jih Pao,* 4 December 1950.

24. "The Deviation of Peacefully Dividing Up the Land Emerges in Wu-ch'ang Experimental Land Reform Work," *Hupeh Jih Pao,* 27 November 1950; "Sum Up the Lessons of Experience; Gradually Overcome the Bad Workstyle of Doing Every-

thing Oneself," *Ch'ang-chiang Jih Pao,* 20 April 1951; and "Educating Peasants to Strengthen Political Work Is a Serious Problem" *Ch'ang-chiang Jih Pao,* 8 November 1951.

25. For elaboration of this problem, see my paper for the JCCC workshop on the Pursuit of Political Interest in the PRC (August 1977) entitled "Personal Power and Village Politics: Hunan Peasants During Land Reform."

26. I am referring here primarily to stories, reports, and editorials on rural affairs in the central and provincial presses of the period, such as those cited throughout this chapter. Since they are all at best fragmentary bits of evidence in the construction of a possible CCP theory of cultural change processes, it would not be helpful now to select and cite just a few as if they were conclusive. For more evidence that this is the way the Party conceived of the process of cultural change in which it was involved, and for many more references to the relevant literature, see my longer study *Peasant China in Transition-The Dynamics of Development Toward Socialism, 1949-1956,* University of California Press, forthcoming.

27. As everyone knows, cultures, especially the cultures of great civilizations such as the Chinese, are very complex. They seem to contain what can only be considered opposed values, alternative modes of behavior, various expressed yearnings and exemplary stories or models that are in tension with each other and, when pressed to their extremes, are probably incompatible.

Thus we often say of traditional Chinese culture that it required the individual to define his or her existence largely in terms of accepted social relationships, and through the ritual and actual conduct of these relationships to discover the chief satisfactions of a human life. Yet this same Chinese culture reserved a place of reverence and respect for the isolated poet-hermit, the principled official who disengages himself from the corruption of politics at the appropriate moment, and the family-abandoning seeker who tries for a personal oneness with the universe transcending the pedestrian clamorings for proper social relations that drove him from the city to his mountain retreat. In the cultural heritage of the Chinese people there are many other values in tension such as these.

This complexity is what has fueled many a long debate about whether what we witness at times of apparent cultural upheaval might best be regarded as instances of cultural change or cultural continuity. Even the most revolutionary-sounding propositions, it has been argued, may not represent attempts at cultural change at all, but only shifts in emphasis to other sets of themes which had been there in the cultural underbrush all along.

The argument is not an idle one since it is true that revolutionary movements linking themselves to the cultural past, by deliberate resonance with alternative traditions there, will probably find a more ready and positive response among the masses. But, it should be remembered that what is aimed at, where whole societies are concerned, need not be brand new fabrications or importations from alien cultures in order for the reorientations in human values that are finally produced to be significant ones. A cyclical theory of human culture is as unsatisfying as are the cyclical theories of human history. We would do better to think in terms of minor course corrections along routes of cultural development that may make for potentially cosmic differences in the final trajectory of a people. From this standpoint we can better judge the possible contributions of revolutionary movements to the cultural transformations they often seek.

28. Here again it is useful to refer to Fagen's observations in *The Transformation of Political Culture in Cuba*. See note 12 above.

29. This formula can be contrasted therefore with the "shock therapy" approach to changing attitudes explored in Lowell Dittmer's chapter in this volume.

30. Vivienne Shue, "Reorganizing Rural Trade: Unified Purchase and Socialist Transformation," *Modern China* 2, no. 1 (January 1976):104–134. For many more examples, see also my longer study cited above, *Peasant China in Transition.*

31. For examples of some of these types of incentives, see "Central South Gives Out Ten Thousand Hundred Million Yuan in Agricultural Loans," *Ch'ang-chiang Jih Pao*, 22 June 1952; and on the expectations of peasants that they would receive loans after joining co-ops, see "Economize from Beginning to End to Solve Capital Difficulties," *Hunan Ch'un-chung Pao*, 1 April 1956; "Advance Purchase of Agricultural and Sideline Products Can Promote Rural Mutual Aid and Cooperation," *Hsin Hunan Pao*, 15 May 1954; and "Agricultural and Pastoral Products Will Be Purchased through Advance Purchase Contracts," *Jen Min Jih Pao*, 28 March 1954.

32. See Ko Lin, *Rural Finance Work [Nung-ts'un chin-jung kung-tso]* (Shanghai: Chung-hua shu-chu, 1953), pp. 102–103; and also "Open the Door to Free Borrowing and Lending,"*Ch'ang-chiang Jih Pao*, 24 May 1951.

33. On the decline in private rural commercial activity, see, e.g., Ch'u Ch'ing et al., *Reorganization of China's Rural Market [Wo-kuo nung-ts'un shih-ch'ang ti kai-tsu]* (Peking: Ts'ai-cheng ching-chi ch'u-pan-she, 1957), esp. p. 21.

34. See, e.g., "Provisional Regulations for the 1952 Agricultural Tax in Land Reform Areas of the Central South," in *Handbook for 1952 Agricultural Tax Work in the Central South [Chung-nan ch'u 1952-nien nung-yeh-shui-shou kung-tso shou-ts'e]* (Canton: Hua-nan jen-min ch'u-pan-she, 1952), pp. 2–11. And also *Thirty Questions and Answers on Agricultural Tax Policy [Nung-yeh-shui cheng-ts'e wen-ta san-shih t'iao]* (Hankow: Chung-nan jen-min ch'u-pan-she, 1952).

35. See "Rural Finance over the Last Three Years,"*Chung-kuo Chin-jung* 1, no. 12 (December 1951):7–8; also "Central South Gives Out Ten Thousand Hundred Million Yuan in Agricultural Loans," cited above. Of course, sometimes the deliberate preferential treatment of teams in making loans could backfire at the peasants' expense; see, e.g., "Overcome Subjectivism in Agricultural Loan Work," *Ta Kung Pao*, 23 May 1953; and "Various Places Study State Council Directive on Agricultural Loans . . . " *Chung-kuo Chin-jung* (20 December 1953):17. Another revealing report touching on this question is "Questions and Answers on the Timely Collection of Agricultural Debts," *Hsin Hunan Pao*, 16 August 1955.

36. There was an enormous amount of reporting and propaganda on workpoint systems in production groups at this time. For mutual aid teams, two of the more comprehensive pieces are "Fundamental Systems of Agricultural Production Mutual Aid Teams in Yao-shui County [Hupeh]," in *Reference Material on Agricultural Production Mutual Aid Teams*, pp. 66–74; and "Some Problems in Opening the Labor Mutual Aid Movement in Huang-kang Special District [Hupeh]," *Ch'ang-chiang Jih Pao*, 14 April 1952. On APCs, some comparable reports are "Getting Onto the Right Track of Collective Operations," *Jen Min Jih Pao*, 19 March 1955; "How Several Huang-kang Special District APCs Are Improving Labor Organization and Labor Calculation," *Jen Min Jih Pao*, 4 April 1955; "East Is Red Co-op Thinks of Ways to Guarantee the Quality of Work,"*Hsiang Nan*

Nung Min, 13 May 1956; and *Happy and Prosperous Advanced Agricultural Production Cooperatives [Hsing-fu ti kao-chi nung-yeh sheng-ch'an ho-tso-she]*
(Hankow: Hu-pei jen-min ch'u-pan-she, 1956).

37. *Mutual Aid and Cooperation in China's Agricultural Production,* p. 4.

38. "Thoroughly Implement the Policy of Mutual Benefit," *Jen Min Jih Pao,* 23
October 1955; and "Income of the Great Majority of Co-op Members Rises," *Jen
Min Jih Pao,* 18 September 1955.

39. For detailed information on loans and repayments in one province, see *Hunan
Agriculture [Hu-nan Nung-yeh]* (Peking: Kao-teng chiao-yu ch'u-pan-she, 1959),
pp. 109–110. See also William R. Corson, "An Examination of Banking, Monetary,
and Credit Practices in Communist China, 1949–1957," Ph.D. dissertation, American University, 1969, p. 114; and John Wong, *Land Reform in the People's Republic of China* (New York: Praeger, 1973), p. 314.

40. Li Ch'eng-jui, *Outline History of Agricultural Taxation in the People's Republic of China [Chung-hua jen-min kung-ho-kuo nung-yeh-shui shih-kao]* (Peking:
Ts'ai-cheng ch'u-pan-she, 1959), pp. 138–141. See also the Central South tax regulations cited above.

41. Dwight H. Perkins, *Market Control and Planning in Communist China*
(Cambridge: Harvard University Press, 1966), p. 34. See also *Hunan Agriculture,* p.
220.

42. "The Function of the Contract System in Organizing the Marketing of Rural
Sideline Products and Some Problems Needing Attention," *Chung-kuo Nung Pao*
1, no. 6:103–111.

43. "Central South Gives Out . . . " and "Credit Co-ops Organized in Yao-shui
County [Hupeh] Help Peasants Solve Difficulties in Production and Livelihood,"
Jen Min Jih Pao, 6 September 1953.

44. See, e.g., *Hunan Agriculture,* pp. 106–107.

45. See "Overcome Subjectivism . . . " on the well-digging issue. On cotton output, see "Strive for Completion of Collection of 1952 Agricultural Tax," *Survey of
the China Mainland Press,* no. 359 (20 June 1952), and also Perkins, *Market Control and Planning,* p. 37.

46. For two reports on collapses, see "Some Problems in Opening the Labor
Mutual Aid Movement in Huang-kang Special District" and "The Work for a Rich
Harvest and the Mutual Aid Movement in Hunan's Villages," *Ch'ang-chiang Jih
Pao,* 19 May 1952. Reports reflecting bickering within co-ops concerning work and
property are legion. Two good examples are "Do a Good Job of Rearing All Co-op
Draught Animals," *Jen Min Jih Pao* editorial, 17 May 1956; and "Will Middle
Peasants Who Invest in Co-ops Suffer Losses?" *Jen Min Jih Pao,* 19 April 1955.

47. See "Summarize Production Work; Augment Mutual Aid and Cooperation
Organization," *Hsin Hunan Pao,* 17 May 1954; and "The General Line Illuminated
My Vision," *Ta Kung Pao,* 27 December 1953.

48. "Doing a Good Job of Distribution and of Summing Up Is a Key to the Consolidation of Co-ops," *Jen Min Jih Pao,* 25 January 1955.

49. This issue is discussed at length in the collection *Discussion of the Problem of
Combining the Interest of the Individual Worker with the Public Interest [Kuan-yu
lao-tung-che ti ko-jen li-i ho she-hui kung-kung li-i chieh-ho wen-t'i ti t'ao-lun]*
(Peking: Hsueh-hsi tsa-chih she, 1956).

50. This is the thrust of many of the accounts in the important collection *The*

High Tide of Socialism in China's Villages [Chung-kuo nung-ts'un ti she-hui chu-i kao-ch'ao] (Peking: Jen-min ch'u-pan-she, 1956).

51. Quoted in "The Economist" by Christopher Howe and Kenneth Walker, in *Mao Tse-tung in the Scales of History,* ed. Dick Wilson (London: Cambridge University Press, 1977), p. 206.

52. "Do a Good Job of Propaganda to Eliminate Peasants' Anxieties," *Ch'ang-chiang Jih Pao,* 9 January 1951; and "Thoroughly Propagandize the Land Reform Law," *Ch'ang-chiang Jih Pao,* 15 October 1950.

53. "Flower Bridge Village in Ch'ang-sha County Peacefully Divides Up the Land," *Hsin Hunan Pao,* 18 December 1950; "Problems of Raising Up Cadres and Opposing Sabotage in Land Reform," *Hsin Hunan Pao,* 20 December 1950; and "Vice Chairman Teng [Hsiao-p'ing] Points Out the Policy Line for Land Reform During a Regular Administrative Meeting of the MAC," *Ch'ang-chiang Jih Pao,* 8 January 1951.

54. "Correct Feelings of Indifference and Self-Satisfaction Among Cadres; Arduously and Deeply Mobilize the Peasant Masses," *Ch'ang-chiang Jih Pao,* 17 January 1951.

55. See, e.g., "Once Land Reform Is Completed, Immediately Investigate and Summarize," *Ch'ang-chiang Jih Pao,* 12 February 1951; and "In Areas of Ch'ang-sha Special District Where Land Reform Is Completed, Review of Land Reform Is Carried Out and Victory is Consolidated," *Ch'ang-chiang Jih Pao,* 4 March 1951.

56. Thomas P. Bernstein has examined this phenomenon at some length in "Keeping the Revolution Going: Problems of Village Leadership after Land Reform," in *Party Leadership and Revolutionary Power in China,* ed. John Wilson Lewis (Cambridge: Cambridge University Press, 1970), pp. 239–267. See also "Village Cadres Cannot Become Proud or Relax," *Ch'ang-chiang Jih Pao,* 2 August 1951; and "Some Problems in Changing Over from Land Reform to Production," *Ch'ang-chiang Jih Pao,* 27 May 1951.

57. Ch'en K'o-chien and Kan Min-chung, *The Objective Basis of the Rapid Attainment of Advanced Agricultural Cooperativization in China [Wo-kuo hsun-su shih-hsien kao-chi hsing-shih nung-yeh ho-tso-hua ti k'o-kuan i-chu]* (Shanghai: Shang-hai jen-min ch'u-pan-she, 1956), pp. 6–16.

58. Edward Friedman, *Backward Toward Revolution* (Berkeley: University of California Press, 1974); and Mark Selden, *The Yenan Way in Revolutionary China* (Cambridge: Harvard University Press, 1971).

14

Communication and Value Change in the Chinese Program of Sending Urban Youths to the Countryside

Thomas P. Bernstein

The Program and Media Coverage

"Up to the mountains and down to the villages" *(shang-shan hsia-hsiang)* is a program under which young urbanites, born and raised in cities and towns, and for the most part graduates of junior or senior middle schools, are sent to rural areas. This program should be distinguished from other urban-to-rural flows, such as the *hsia-fang* (transfer downward) of cadres or of trained specialists such as physicians. It should also be distinguished from the policy of returning young peasants to their home villages following attendance at secondary or higher schools (they are called *hui-hsiang chih-shih ch'ing-nien,* returned educated youths, while their urban counterparts are termed *hsia-hsiang chih-shih ch'ing nien,* sent-down educated youths). In principle, urban youths are sent to the countryside for life. Actually, about one third of those sent have eventually been reassigned to the urban sector, especially to factory work in state-run enterprises, and to a lesser extent to study in higher schools.[1] The open-ended nature of the transfer, the requirement that the young urbanites not only "temper" themselves in the rural areas but also "take root" there *(cha-ken),* is the most dramatically radical aspect of the program and distinguishes it from service programs of the Peace Corps type. It is this aspect also that raises the issue of value change, the source of difficulties which have beset the program.

The long-term nature of the transfer points to the first and probably most important reason it was adopted, namely, to cope with urban unemployment. Since at least 1957, with the exception of the Great Leap Forward, it has not been possible in the People's Republic to assign jobs to all young urbanites coming of working age;

with the concurrent expansion of secondary education, the problem became one of finding employment for secondary school graduates. Resettlement in the rural areas was one of the answers. The second reason makes a virtue of the first: the program aims at contributing to rural and frontier development. In principle, sent-down youths contribute both their labor and their modernizing skills to the advancement of the rural area to which they are sent. In practice, their contributions vary enormously but in the aggregate they have lagged behind expectations. Third, the program was undertaken for ideological reasons. In the broadest sense, it has been and continues to be regarded as one way in which the Maoist revolution can be preserved and advanced. More specifically, the program seeks to contribute to the reduction of the "three great differences"—between mental and manual labor, worker and peasant, town and country. Still more specifically, the program aims at the rearing of "revolutionary successors." Those coming under its purview are expected to undergo a process of resocialization, exchanging the bourgeois values which to a greater or lesser extent are said to contaminate them in the cities for pure revolutionary "proletarian" ones in the villages.[2]

The transfer program began on a modest scale before the Great Leap Forward, gathered momentum in the years 1962-1966, but grew to major size only in the wake of the Cultural Revolution. According to a statistic published in December 1975, 1.2 million educated youths were sent to the countryside between 1956 and 1966, and 12 million between 1968 and 1975.[3] The flow to the rural areas has not been uniform but has varied considerably in the years since the Cultural Revolution.

Like all other mass movements in China, the youth transfer program is heavily dependent on communication strategies. To what extent is intensity of flow reflected, for example, in media coverage? Both the central dailies and the provincial broadcasting stations have devoted a great deal of attention to the transfer program; hence, it is possible to juxtapose data on the annual rates of transfer with media coverage (Table 1). Coverage in the *People's Daily* seems to reflect the size of the flow. For example, the largest number of articles appear in 1969, when the largest number of youths were sent. But other considerations than simply size also play a part in determining coverage. The disproportionately large number of articles in 1973 reflects the fact that a decision was made

TABLE 1

Annual Transfer Rates and People's Daily *Coverage*

Year	Number Sent	Number of *People's Daily* Articles on the Program
1968	1,725,000	99
1969	2,700,000	195
1970	1,067,000	105
1971	738,000	51
1972	646,000	87
1973	1,123,000	161
1974	2,000,000	112
1975	2,000,000	150
1976	⎱ 4,000,000	89
1977	⎰	16

SOURCES: The transfer statistics for the years 1968–1975 are taken from T. P. Bernstein, *Up to the Mountains and Down to the Villages: The Transfer of Youth from Urban to Rural China* (New Haven: Yale University Press, 1977), p. 32. The statistics for 1976 and 1977 are derived from data in an article in *People's Daily,* January 25, 1978, which states that 16 million youths were sent in the preceding ten years, thus implying a rate of transfer of 4 million for these two years.

in that year to accelerate the rate of transfer again and to maintain it at a high level in future years, even though the actual number sent in 1973 was not all that great. What about 1977? Despite the drastic curtailment in *People's Daily* coverage, the program has been maintained since the death of Chairman Mao Tse-tung, certainly in 1977, and very possibly in 1978 as well.[4]

Why then the sharp 1977 cutback in publicity for the transfer in the *People's Daily,* a cutback mirrored, though to a somewhat lesser extent, by reduced coverage in provincial broadcasts?[5] One reason may be that not all policymakers agree on the desirability of the program. The new chairman, Hua Kuo-feng, made a commitment to maintenance shortly after his accession, one that he has reaffirmed in various contexts since then, including his speech to the eleventh Party Congress.[6] Judging by accusations levied against him, however, Teng Hsiao-p'ing has been skeptical about the program. During the Cultural Revolution, he was charged with opposing a large-scale transfer; allegedly, he wanted to assign jobs in the emerging cooperative street industries to school leavers rather than to housewives.[7] In 1975, Teng was charged with favoring a rotation system (that is, permit return to the urban sector after two years in the villages), which would take the sting out of the program but which also raises the question of where to find jobs for the returnees.[8] Moreover, Teng objected to the requirement, in force since the Cultural Revolution, that middle school graduates first spend several years in production, either in a factory, a farm, or the People's Liberation Army, before becoming eligible to enter higher schools. This requirement, when combined with small university enrollments and admissions policies that downgraded academic achievement, had led to the long-term resettlement in the countryside of many bright youths, thereby doing severe damage to China's modern sector. In October 1977 a major change in policy was put into effect, which permits the most talented middle school students to proceed directly to college.[9] The reduction in publicity accorded to the transfer program may thus reflect the new developmental priorities of the post-Mao leadership. The reduction in attention mirrors a shift in priorities away from mass-oriented policies such as transfer to elitist policies of rehabilitating and strengthening advanced studies. The latter policy is now symbolized by press articles that extol high achievers, who devote themselves to bringing China's science and technology up to world standards.[10] Continued low-key coverage of the transfer program as well as of other mass-oriented development policies such as village "scientific experiment" suggests that a shift in balance is taking place, not an abandonment of mass-oriented programs.

Still another reason for reduction in media attention has to do with the purge of the Gang of Four. Although the transfer program originated before the appearance of Chiang Ch'ing and her colleagues—a point made since the purge is that Chou En-lai played a key role in its inception—as a major program the transfer can in fact be regarded as one of the "newborn things" of the Cultural Revolution associated with the rise of the radical left.[11] Radical influence over the media undoubtedly helps account for the extent of the publicity accorded the program. In the view of other leaders, including those in favor of the program, the publicity probably was excessive, hence warranting a cutback. Moreover, judging by postpurge charges, the Gang utilized the transfer program to build a base of support and patronage among young people, whom they incited against the older generation. The Gang not only allegedly incited groups of sent-down youths to struggle against established authorities during the succession crisis, they also recruited and coopted urban youths into their factional network. Several prominent sent-down youths, now labeled "black models," have been purged, as we will see later in this chapter. Undoubtedly, some housecleaning is going on among urban youths in the countryside who have attained positions of responsibility but are suspected of affiliation with the Gang. The embarrassing connection between the program and the machinations of the Gang helps account for reduced media attention.

This brief discussion of media coverage suggests that communication in the People's Republic of China is influenced by multiple purposes. This is a point to be kept in mind as we proceed to look at the question of the impact of communication on value change.

The Issue of Value Change among Sent-down Youth

The Chinese political system has devoted intensive efforts to changing the values of those affected by the transfer program. It has utilized the various channels of communication at its disposal, such as the mass media, for this purpose. It has also mobilized the mass organizations, the schools, the residential groups, and the organizations for sent-down youths established in the countryside to aim value-changing messages at their respective audiences. Intensive efforts have been made not simply to communicate messages but to involve people in discussing them, utilizing the small groups into which most larger units are divided. Models of successful value change are studied, such as Chin Hsün-hua, a Shanghai youth who settled in Heilungkiang in 1968 and sacrificed his life protecting public property in 1969, fortuitously leaving a devotional diary reminiscent of that of Lei Feng.[12] School children study the conduct of such models and pledge to emulate them. At the same time, discussion is not thought adequate to attain value change; practice is required. Thus, school children are not simply told that the educated should value manual labor; they also regularly participate in physical labor. Young urbanites are not simply taught about the worth of peasants; they are sent to the countryside to experience rural life.

At the core of the values to which young urbanites settling in the countryside are asked to subscribe is an ethic of service. As a broadcast made in 1977 suggests:

> . . . our educated youths going to the countryside must carry forward the spirit of wholeheartedly serving the people, modestly receive reeducation by the poor and lower-middle peasants under the leader-

ship of party organizations at all levels, and establish roots in the countryside to make revolution. They must persist in Chairman Mao's basic principles of "three dos and three don'ts," make strict demands on themselves in accordance with the five requirements for successors to the proletarian revolutionary cause, strive to remold their world outlook, wholeheartedly serve the poor and lower-middle peasants and contribute their flaming young years to building the new socialist countryside.[13]

The idea of subordinating oneself to a larger collective is probably not very new. It could be argued that Chinese have always been taught to subordinate individual interests to those of a larger entity, be it the extended family in traditional times or, more recently, the nation. What is new and radical about the service ethic associated with the transfer program is that it demands the unselfish acceptance of personal disadvantage, including the subordination or even abandonment of aspirations held by young educated urbanites and their families.

What are these aspirations? They are simply upward mobility and the belief that education ought to lead to high-status jobs. Thus, in the 1950s, the press freely acknowledged that secondary school students had a hierarchy of preferences: at the top came continued education, preferably including university study; if that could not be attained, a white-collar job followed; after that, a blue-collar job in urban industry; and, last of all, work in agriculture. These preferences had been taught in the family and in the schools. In the family, traditional concepts converged with aspirations generated by the revolution. Parents took pride in the educational achievements of their children in line with the traditional expectation that academic success brings prestige and benefit to the entire family. Those parents who themselves had been unable to get an education in the old society now wanted such opportunities for their children in the new society. Families who held such attitudes found them reinforced in society at large; it was acknowledged that "public opinion" *(yü-lun)* put a low valuation on manual labor, especially in the agricultural sector.[14]

In the early 1950s, the meaning of the ethic of service to socialist construction was more or less congruent with these aspirations. One could serve party and state by going to a university and becoming a high-status scientist or engineer, or at least by remaining within the urban sector. But from about 1957 on, urban opportunities contracted, including university enrollments in relation to applicants. Gradually, the idea of service came to be redefined in ways widely perceived as amounting to downward mobility. Urbanites were asked not only to serve the peasants, but actually to become peasants (*hsin nung-min,* "new peasants").[15] As one editorial put it, as early as 1957, an opportunity to become an engineer, a scientist, or a cadre is regarded as opening up a "big future"; having to become a peasant is regarded as opening up a "small future."[16] The time dimension is very important here: urban youths are asked not only to contribute their "flaming young years" to the countryside, but to "take root" there as well. It is one thing to ask young people to defer satisfaction of their aspirations for a few years; it is quite another to ask them to abandon them for the long term.

The disadvantage associated with the transfer program is rooted in the realities of rural-urban inequalities. As T'an Chen-lin, a high official purged during the Cultural Revolution but since rehabilitated, put it in remarks divulged during that upheaval:

> The existing mode of production being what it is, who is willing to be in the rural district? All want to go to the cities. One who sweeps the ground in a city can earn 30–40 yüan a month, while in the rural district one can earn no more than 200–300 yüan a year. Among those present, who is willing to be a peasant? Even if one raises his hand expressing the wish to be a peasant, he can only do so reluctantly. This is a fundamental question.[17]

T'an believed that only after the countryside had advanced to the level of the cities, only after the disappearance of rural-urban disparities, would urbanites be willing to accept life in the countryside:

> Many people are unwilling to work in rural areas and want to return to the cities. They will be ready to stay in the countryside in the future when rural construction will be completed because of clean air in the rural areas and the possibility of having electric lighting, asphalt-paved roads, and foreign-style buildings.[18]

Even if it is true that urban-rural differences have narrowed since the 1960s, undoubtedly they remain very substantial. Not only must the young people sent to the countryside put up with the material hardships of rural life, they must also cope with a reduction in status implied by the term "reeducation by the poor and lower-middle peasants." The transfer program seeks to change the old values that education sets men apart and that the educated are entitled to special status. Participation in the transfer program seeks to reshape attitudes of the educated toward the laboring masses, which Liu Shao-ch'i reportedly described as follows in 1964: "And what about the students from fulltime school? The general rule is that those graduated from a junior middle school despise the peasant, and those graduated from senior high despise workers, and those graduated from a university despise all of them."[19] "Reeducation" puts peasants in charge of educated youth; by laboring under their nurturing tutelage, the urban students will presumably deflate their intellectual arrogance. (It is worth adding that reeducation has other meanings as well: it suggests that sent-down youths are not regarded as change agents sent to the villages to spread modern urban ideas and practices. Only when they have adapted to rural life, when they have been reeducated, are they supposed to contribute what modernizing skills they have but on terms set and defined by ruralites.)

Have the revolutionary values associated with the transfer program—unselfish service to the common good even at the price of long-term personal disadvantage—been internalized by the young urbanites? Obviously, this is not a question that can easily be answered in the absence of adequate access to the population in question. Sent-down youths who have escaped to Hong Kong have by definition not internalized the new values. Talking with young people in China also does not help much, since the new values form the language of public discourse in China, and it is therefore not easy to distinguish those who have actually internalized the new values from those who only pretend to have done so.

Pretense aside, evidence about adaptation to rural life suggests that some sent-down youths, probably a minority, have come to terms with their situation; they are *an-hsin,* at peace. Yet we do not know whether this adaptation is due to conversion to revolutionary values of unselfish service to the peasants or to the fact that their conventional personal aspirations have at least to some extent been satisfied in the countryside. The deprivations associated with rural life are of course variables: it is easier to adapt in a prosperous sub-urban commune with ready access to city and family life than in a distant, poor commune. Sent-down youths marry, probably at increasing rates, and some attain positions of responsibility within the rural political and collective structures—that is, there is upward mobility among the sent-down urban youths.[20] Undoubtedly, some value change is involved as young urbanites come to terms with rural life, but it need not be the radical commitment to self-abnegating service implied by the revolutionary ideal. And finally, we are dealing with adolescents, who by nature of their age, their susceptibility to peer pressures, and their relative freedom from adult commitments can be seized by intense self-sacrificing idealism.[21] Hence, a test of commitment to the new values would not be adequate if it merely examined commitment at one particular time, such as at the time of volunteering to go to the countryside, without reexamining commitment, say, five years later.

Skepticism is in order when evaluating claims that the transfer program is giving rise to the new Maoist man. This skepticism is reinforced by evidence of substantial dissatisfaction with the program, especially when it turns out in fact to be long-term. This dissatisfaction has been amply reported in the press, though usually in the context of showing how "wavering" *(tung-yao)* was overcome by means of political education. Escapes to Hong Kong and illegal return to the cities also are evidence of dissatisfaction. Even when there is no outward manifestation of unhappiness with rural life, it appears that a great many sent-down youths conduct themselves well *(piao-hsien hao)* in the hope of winning an eventual reassignment to the urban sector.[22] Thus, it is probably fair to conclude that the revolutionary value of self-sacrificing service to the people plays only a minor, intermittent role in the operation of the program.

If the revolutionary values have not by and large been internalized, what role has communication played? Is it in principle possible that those in charge of China's communication strategies could have used the various instrumentalities at their disposal to secure drastic value change? Whether a communication system can attain such a result is an intriguing theoretical question but one that need not be considered here. The reason is that the Chinese case does not permit an adequate test of such a hypothesis. For one, it is difficult to isolate the effect of communication from other influences, such as coercion. A youth who goes to the countryside because his parents' job security has been threatened has not only been communicated with; he has been coerced. But a test is also not possible because of the communication messages themselves. That is, following Martin Whyte's reasoning, if communication messages are to have the effect of changing values, they must at a minimum "sing the same tune."[23] If they do not, then the power of the message is weakened. A major feature of communication policies pertaining to the transfer program is that they have not all been carrying the same value-changing message. Let us explore this point in detail.

Official Communication and the Transfer Program

Official communication programs are those that emanate from party and state, and from their instrumentalities and agents. Before the Cultural Revolution, when the vision of China as a full-fledged totalitarian system held sway, it was thought that the only communication flows that could be found in China were official ones, since organization had replaced society and "comradeship" had replaced "friendship," to quote the title of a famous article. Since then, outsiders have become more cognizant of the continued existence of unofficial "societal" communication. With regard to the transfer program, both press and Hong Kong informants suggest that a good deal of communication at variance with the official values has been taking place in the cities within families, among relatives, and among friends; and in the countryside among sent-down youths, as well as between them and the peasants. The content of such informal interchanges points to the persistence of more conventional values than the radical ones espoused by long-term rural resettlement.[24] Delineating unofficial societal communication, however, is not the topic of this study. It can be shown that official communication programs have not only disseminated the new revolutionary values, but have also, intentionally or not, sent messages more or less congruent with fairly conventional conceptions of personal interest. In making this point, we do not simply have in mind communication by lower-level officials—for instance, a teacher in an urban middle school who tries to get graduating students to sign up for rural service by stressing return opportunities, or a rural cadre trying to cope with poor morale by telling an urban youth that if he behaves, he will be allowed to go back to the city. Communication messages that play in some way or other on calculations of self-interest have permeated the transfer program much more thoroughly than these examples of deviating local cadres imply.

Official messages that reinforce a calculative orientation in urban youths and their families are sent in part simply because the program is not just a social movement but a complex administrative enterprise. To be sure, the transfer program can be depicted in its value-changing dimension as a mass movement, in which young people, inspired by revolutionary ideals, "rush" to the villages to integrate with the peasants. This image of enthusiasm generated in the course of a mobilization campaign has some truth to it, but it is not the whole story. The transfer program poses problems that cannot be solved simply by mobilizing the masses; these problems require the "departments concerned"—and there is, in fact, a complex bureaucracy from the State Council down which administers the program—to work out policies, rules, and regulations. For instance, each year's graduating urban middle school class must be allocated to employment in the urban or the rural sector or to the People's Liberation Army (and now to the universities). Rules and regulations must be drawn up to define eligibilities and exemptions, such as the kinds of physical handicaps that entitle one to stay in the city, or the kinds of family situations that require an offspring to be retained (for example, to care for aging or sick parents, lest they become public burdens). For those going to the countryside, policies are needed to define to what rural institutions youths should be sent—that is, people's communes, state farms, or to farms operated by the army's Production and Construction Corps. And for communes, decisions must be made about just what the form of integration should be, and what the size of initial support payments should be. Further rules and regulations are needed to govern return assignments of sent-down youths to state factories or to higher educational institutions.

For the most part, the details of the policies, rules, and regulations that govern the transfer system are not communicated in the mass media available to foreigners, although their existence is not infrequently confirmed by the media. They are transmitted to the relevant Chinese public through the internal communication system hidden from outsiders—through the study groups, through meetings in relevant units, such as enterprises where parents of sent-down youths work, or through meetings of sent-down youths convened by commune or county authorities. In the mass media, rules and regulations are often referred to in the context of revolutionary heroes who disregard the advantages that policies confer. For instance, in November 1977, the *People's Daily* ran a story about the new chairman, Hua Kuo-feng, who, *"according to policy"* could have retained "by his side" his youngest daughter, but nonetheless chose to send her to the countryside.[25] Or, a story is broadcast of a sent-down youth from Shenyang, who, after having settled in a village, joined the army. Upon demobilization, he chose to return to the village, even though, *"according to regulations,* I could return to Shenyang and get a job there."[26] Sometimes the press simply tells of the existence of a particular category of young people. For instance, in a bout of frankness, the *People's Daily* in October 1977 carried the gist of the new regulations governing university entrance examinations. Among those eligible to take the test are "educated youths who have gone up to the mountains and down to the countryside . . . (including those who, *according to policy,* have been retained in the city but have not been assigned work)."[27] "Policies" and "regulations" that define categories and eligibilities provide opportunities for those inclined to take a self-interested view of the program to calculate their options: Do I qualify under this or that rule to stay in the city or to come back? How can I best take advantage of existing rules and regulations to get the best possible deal? Unquestionably, a good many of the "clients" of the program have in fact taken their cues from such implementational communications rather than from value-changing appeals, even if they pay lip service to the latter.

The administrative need for rules and regulations has thus had the unanticipated consequence of facilitating calculative involvement with the program. In addition, however, policy makers and administrators have relied deliberately on various kinds of personal interest–oriented incentives in order to make the program work. From their point of view, they must deal with people as they are, not simply as they might be. Theirs is the problem of securing compliance, of seeing to it that x percent of this year's graduating middle class departs for the rural areas and also that it stays there. To be sure, transfer administrators do utilize normative power. They appeal to revolutionary values because it is the appropriate and expected thing to do, because it helps create a climate of enthusiasm and dedication for mobilization, and because some young people unquestionably respond to such messages. In addition, in the context of the struggle between the two lines, public announcements calling for commitment to revolutionary goals have coercive overtones, particularly when transmitted through the medium of organized group study. Those in charge of the transfer have not been content, however, to rely only on a mix of normative and coercive incentives (there are limits to the amount of coercion that can be used, since the program is aimed not at class enemies, or even only at young people with bad class backgrounds, but at urban youth in general). Instead, they have tried to make the program palatable by adopting policies that reduce as far as possible the gap between personal preferences and the settlement. Nor has this appeal to personal interests always been considered illegitimate. Although at times it has been, particularly during the Cultural Revolution, at other times Mao Tse-tung himself has given his imprimatur to such appeals.

One example concerns destinations. It is easier to secure compliance if urban youths are sent to destinations close to their homes. As already noted, conditions are likely to be better in such locations and it is possible to maintain close contact with the family and with urban life generally. Consequently, judging by local regulations in such cities as Canton, transfer administrators, by permitting volunteers to choose from several destinations, have long utilized this circumstance to encourage early compliance.[28] In addition, there is evidence that a national-level effort has been made to make the program more acceptable by settling youths to the extent possible, in areas close to home. Thus, in 1974, national publicity was given to a new model for settlement, namely, the city of Chuchou, Hunan, which drew up a long-term plan for the settlement of its graduates in the surrounding county, rather than dispersing them throughout the province. This model was hailed by the *People's Daily* as combining "rather well the long-run with the immediate interests of the masses."[29]

Officials have also stimulated the desire for advancement in the rural sector as a way of linking personal interest with the program. This practice, however, came under sharp fire during the Cultural Revolution. Liu Shao-ch'i was accused of tempting young people to comply with the program by offering opportunities to rise to positions of importance.[30] Since Liu's fall, other purged leaders have been accused of doing the same thing. In Liaoning, "the manager of the sworn follower [of the Gang] . . . took the mean measure of using Lin Piao's 'inducements'—official posts, emoluments and favors—to win people's hearts. He told the youths that after 20 years they would occupy leading posts at all levels and that they should therefore begin to pay attention to the questions of whether or not to carry out revolution and which road to take at present."[31] Despite these indictments, recruitment of sent-down youths to local positions has been and continues to be a way of rewarding adaptive behavior, a point that has long been signaled to the urban youths by the media. Indeed, it is difficult not to do so, since recruitment to significant positions is one of the ways of enabling sent-down youths to contribute to rural advancement, a basic purpose of the program.

To facilitate adaptation to rural life, policy makers have also relied not only on the communication of political messages (though political education has always been strongly emphasized) but on keeping lines of communication open to solve some of the real problems involved. When a Fukien father of a sent-down youth succeeded in telling Mao Tse-tung about the hardships his son was experiencing (the father, a primary school teacher, had the letter dropped into the mail in Peking by a relative lest it be intercepted by local authorities—a revealing sidelight on problems of communicating with the powerful), the Chairman responded in 1973 by initiating a campaign to ameliorate settlement conditions, premised on the notion that "the young people must first enjoy peace physically before they can have peace of mind."[32] For a time, media articles celebrating the endurance of hardship as a way of building selfless revolutionary heroes were supplemented by very realistic articles dealing with the concrete material problems of the settlement.[33]

Perhaps the most effective way of securing at least temporary adaptation to rural life is to communicate to the sent-down youths that their resettlement is not permanent. Official guarantees of return, reportedly issued by Kwangtung's T'ao Chu in the early 1960s, were repudiated and criticized bitterly during the Cultural Revolution as corrupting the young people. They were also counterproductive: they were not honored (presumably because of lack of urban jobs) and the disappointed youths in question made the issue a focal point for protest during the Cultural Revolution.[34] Since then, as far as is known, guarantees of return have not been issued, but there is good evidence that officials have manipulated the return opportunities that have existed in order to elicit good behavior.[35] One informant interviewed in 1972, for instance, reported that a talk by Chang Ch'un-ch'iao had been disseminated within

China in which Chang held out the possibility of reassignment for those showing good conduct. In recent years, in fact, new settlement approaches have been devised with the apparent intent to give some structure and predictability to return opportunities. The main approach has been to link up urban industrial enterprises with particular rural places of settlement of sent-down youths. Visitors to the Tractor Plant in Loyang, Honan, for instance, were told in 1977 that the offspring of the workers of the enterprise were being sent to two communes and that, as vacancies arose, they would be filled by calling the youths back.[36] Ties between urban units and rural settlements were a prominent feature of the nationally publicized model of Chuchou, Hunan, mentioned earlier, and while the press did not say so, return there has probably been handled in ways like those of the Loyang Tractor Plant. Other cities, including Canton, have reported similar linkages.[37] Such arrangements would seem to obviate the need for radical value change.

The continuing interest on the part of sent-down youths in return to the urban sector testifies to the hold of conventional preferences. This raises the question of the role of the state: it is, after all, state-run institutions such as industrial enterprises or universities that attract the young people sent to the countryside. The very existence of such institutions complicates the problem of value change. The new values not only demand that the young person commit himself to the ideal of self-abnegating service in the countryside but that he do so in the realization that others, including some of his classmates, are much better off as workers in a state-run enterprise or as students in a higher school. From the point of view of the new value system, this advantage enjoyed by others does not matter: a properly motivated person will serve socialist construction in whatever capacity he or she is called upon to fill, "whether in a factory or on a farm."[38] Yet this ostensibly egalitarian service ethic rationalizes quite unequal personal fates, leading no doubt to feelings of relative deprivation.

There are presumably good reasons why the attractiveness of state enterprises cannot be greatly reduced in comparison to agricultural labor. In the case of higher education, however, because of the radicalization of Chinese politics in the Cultural Revolution, a genuine effort was in fact made to reduce its comparative attractiveness. Before the Cultural Revolution, decisions on university entrance and transfer to the countryside were made at more or less the same time, with the predictable result that those who failed to get into the higher schools and were asked to go to the rural areas felt keenly disappointed, despite the propagation of revolutionary values that rural service was just as glorious. During and after the Cultural Revolution, sustained assaults sought to reduce the prestige and status of higher education, university graduates, and intellectuals in general. Admissions decisions were separated from the last year of middle school with virtually every graduate being asked to engage first in some kind of manual labor. Efforts were made to reduce the comparative advantage of university students by emphasizing return of graduates to the production units from which they had come. In 1975 an attempt was made to deny state cadre status to graduates; they were asked to serve as ordinary workers or peasants, earning work points in the latter instance.[39] Remarkably enough, however, it appears that these efforts to reduce the status of higher education, though costly in developmental terms, apparently did not reduce the attractiveness of higher education to young people as routes to higher status. This is shown by the "back door" *(tsou hou-men)* phenomenon: high-ranking cadres used their power and influence to secure the enrollment of their offspring in higher educational institutions. Ironically, the absence of a proper objective entrance examination made it easier to do this.[40] The continuing attractiveness of higher education is also indicated by charges made against the radical leaders that they held out university study as rewards for their supporters.

Since the death of Chairman Mao, the central importance of the universities in the nation's modernization effort has been restored. To a striking degree, it seems that the pre–Cultural Revolution message that to be sent to the countryside is to come out second best is being sent out again. In the fall of 1977 the Chinese government introduced a major reform in university admissions, including restoration of direct transition from middle to higher school, the goal being to select "outstanding young people":

> The work of enrolling students for institutions of higher learning is directly related to the quality of high-level specialists being trained, affects middle and primary school education and concerns all trades and professions and all families and households. It is, therefore, a matter of prime importance.[41]

In unambiguous tones, the articles stress that it is essential to make up for lost time in the training of advanced specialists, that the quality of education must be raised, and that the best and the brightest must make "greater contributions" to national construction. The result has been that literally millions of candidates are presenting themselves to take the entrance examinations. According to the official account, 5.7 million young people competed for 278,000 first-year slots.[42] These remarkable numbers attest to the strength of the conventional value system, which sees in university study the road to upward mobility, or the road to a more satisfactory form of service to socialist construction than labor down on the farm. The desire for higher education is clear, but so is the fact that the vast majority will inevitably be disappointed. As an editorial note in the *People's Daily* observed: " . . . the absolute majority of educated youths must continue to remain at their original posts or go up to the mountains and down to the countryside." The paper pointed out that it would be necessary to

> educate the vast number of youth in the correct ideological line in order to enable everyone taking the college entrance examinations to "prepare for two possibilities with one red heart" *[i-k'e hung-hsin, liang-chung chun-pei].* Those who are admitted into universities should try hard to study. Those who fail to be admitted . . . should cheerfully go back to their original posts and continue to display enthusiasm for work and study. . . . Young people who fail their college entrance examinations should not feel disappointed or depressed. It is false to think they have no future after failing such tests.[43]

The press stresses that those in the countryside will also have a chance to study part time (for example, in local "May Seventh universities" or in correspondence schools) and that they too can contribute their knowledge to modernization.[44] Above all, it is trying to convince young people that "entering higher school or remaining in the village both accord with the needs of the party" (to quote a headline), that is, both are equally worthy ways of serving the people.[45] Yet many young people clearly think otherwise, and moreover the regime, by rebuilding the prestige and status of higher education, has effectively reinforced the conventional values.

What we are seeing, then, is a dual communication pattern. On one hand, a revolutionary value system is being intensively communicated to young people, one that aims at creating the selfless Maoist man who serves the people regardless of personal disadvantage. On the other hand, messages emanate from party and government that in effect tell young people that it isn't all that necessary to subscribe to such a new value system. To some extent, this is clearly due to developmental constraints. But to a greater extent, it may be due to circularity: official communications cannot all sing the same tune of unselfish service because conventional values haven't changed that much, but one reason they haven't changed is that official communications do not all sing the same tune. This dual communication pattern may also be seen as reflecting the utopian and the pragmatic or realistic strains in Chinese communism. On one hand is the ascetic ideal of the renunciation of self-interest, propagated particularly intensively during the Cultural Revolution. On the other hand is the realistic understanding that individual interest does have a legitimate claim in the socialist system, even if it must take third place behind the interests of the state and the collective. Perhaps it can be argued that the existence of interest-oriented communication messages increases popular support for the political system by demonstrating the party's "solicitude" and "concern" for popular welfare. Conversely, if interest-oriented communications arouse unfulfillable expectations, they can also lead to increased dissatisfaction and social tensions.

To conclude, let us raise the question of the impact of the co-existence of idealistic and realistic communications. One possibility is that radical, value-changing messages become an empty ritual, to be changed at the appropriate occasions. Another is that the co-existence of the two sets of messages raises distrust for those who claim to be fully committed to the first set. The idealistic messages are public; the interest-oriented messages are most probably, though not completely, hidden from public view. This circumstance would seem to reinforce a sense of suspicion for the pure revolutionary: What is in it for him? Where is the hidden angle, the hidden advantage?[46]

A major point is that the vagaries of the Chinese political process have probably reinforced this suspiciousness. From the time of the Cultural Revolution, it has been one of the stocks-in-trade of political discourse that avowals of revolutionary purity cannot necessarily be taken at face value. The assumption has been that things are not necessarily what they seem to be. Some people, revisionists, capitalist roaders, ultra-leftists, have ulterior motives. They wave the red flag in order to fight the red flag. As major leaders such as

Lin Piao or the Gang of Four, who outwardly claimed to be the most committed to the revolutionary values sought by the program, were purged, it was charged that they too had played on self- interested motivations to enlist young people in their goal of seizing power:

> The despicable adviser of the "gang of four," Chang Ch'un-ch'iao, employed another method to undermine the revolutionary movement of the rustication of intellectual youth. He said to a group of such youth who were about to go to the farms to make revolution: "You will go to the lower level first. Later on the universities will go to the farms where you are staying to enroll students." He thus peddled the theory of going to the countryside to glorify oneself. It was precisely this person, who shouted at the top of his voice about restricting bourgeois rights, that thrust into the university his children who should have gone to the countryside.[47]

Elsewhere, "flaunting the banner of supporting newborn things," the radicals would talk at a conference about "taking root in the countryside, stress the importance of combatting the restorationist forces and oppose pulling up roots." But "outside the conference," they would advise the sent-down youths to stay in their brigades and honestly serve as party secretaries for a few years, whereupon they would see to it that suitable rewards followed.[48]

As a result of the purge of the radicals, a series of model revolutionary heroes of the transfer movement has been discredited. One such is Chu K'o-chia, a Shanghainese who settled in Yünnan in 1969 and did extremely well as a teacher and innovator in minority villages. Chu was publicized as an embodiment of the new values because he not only selflessly served the peasants but turned down a chance to study in a university. Now he has been charged with having become one of the ringleaders of the Gang's "factional setup" in Yünnan.[49] Another hero was Liaoning's Chai Ch'un-tse, publicized as a "model in breaking with old ideas" by refusing offers to return to the city. Before the purge of the Gang, it is not implausible that some people in China already doubted whether commitment to revolutionary values was the only motivation, seeing that Chu became a Yünnan party secretary and an alternate member of the tenth Central Committee, while Chai's refusals to return were accompanied by promotion to brigade party secretary.[50] But now, with the exposure of the "sinister models and sinister experiences,"[51] the doubting Thomases have been confirmed: things were in fact not what they seemed to be.

It need not be concluded that the entire idea of commitment to selfless service to the collective has been discredited. After all, the movement to send youths "up to the mountains and down to the villages" has been going on for such a long time, and there are other models that can still be emulated—such as Chin Hsün-hua, mentioned earlier, whose self-sacrificing death is obvious testimony to his revolutionary purity. Or is it? Maybe there was a hidden angle in his case, too. It would be remarkable if popular belief in the models of self-denying commitment to the new values has not been significantly impaired by the political shakeups of recent times, since the revelations would seem to confirm suspicions that are likely to be aroused by the very existence of the dual communication pattern. Thus, the revolution devours its models; will it not also devour the values it has so zealously propagated?

NOTES

1. *Jenmin Jihpao* [People's Daily], January 25, 1978, reports that of sixteen million youths sent down in ten years, "nearly ten million" were still serving in agriculture. This chapter includes post-Mao changes in the program to early 1978.

2. For an elaboration of these points, see Thomas P. Bernstein, *Up to the Mountains and Down to the Countryside: The Transfer of Youth from Urban to Rural China* (New Haven, Conn.: Yale University Press, 1977).

3. "Twelve Million School Graduates Settle in the Countryside," *Peking Review* 19, no. 2 (January 8, 1976):11–13.

4. "Ch'en Yung-kuei t'an chih-ch'ing chuang-k'uang" [Ch'en Yung-kuei talks about the situation of educated youths], *Hsing-tao Jihpao* [Sintao Daily], October 13, 1977 (New York edition). See also *People's Daily,* November 19, 1977, for a report on the transfer in Tientsin and Kiangsu, and especially *People's Daily,* January 25, 1978, for a major and authoritative article on the topic.

5. In 1977, about half of China's provincial radio stations carried reports indicating continued transfer activities. For some examples, see Radio Hofei, May 4, 1977, *Foreign Broadcast Information Service* no. 94, May 17, 1977, for a report on Anhwei; Radio Shenyang, August 5, 1977, *Foreign Broadcast Information Service* no. 159, August 17, 1977, for a report on Liaoning; and Radio Nanchang, March 17, 1978, *Foreign Broadcast Information Service* no. 58, March 24, 1978, for a report on Kiangsi.

6. See *People's Daily,* November 23, 1976; *People's Daily,* December 28, 1976; and Hua's political report to the eleventh Congress, in *Peking Review* 20, no. 35 (August 26, 1977):56.

7. See Bernstein, *Up to the Mountains,* p. 39.

8. Ibid., pp. 74–75.

9. See *People's Daily,* October 22, 1977, October 23, 1977, and October 26, 1977. The last article argues that Chou En-lai ordered direct transition already in the early 1970s, reportedly on Mao's instruction, but the Gang sabotaged his efforts.

10. See, e.g., *Ta Kung Report* (Hong Kong), November 7, 1977.

11. "In Commemoration of the First Anniversary of the Passing of Our Esteemed and Beloved Premier Chou En-lai," *Peking Review* 20, no. 3 (January 14, 1977):8.

12. "A Model for Revolutionary Youth," *Hung-ch'i* [Red Flag] no. 12, November 29, 1969, in *Selections from China Mainland Magazines* no. 669, December 29, 1969. See "The Use of Models," in Donald Munro, *The Concept of Man in Contemporary China* (Ann Arbor: University of Michigan Press, 1977), pp. 135–137, for an analysis of the significance of models in China.

13. Radio Hofei, March 19, 1977, *Foreign Broadcast Information Service* no. 58, March 25, 1977.

14. For sources, see Bernstein, *Up to the Mountains,* p. 49.

15. The formulation of becoming a new peasant is still used, e.g., in the *People's Daily,* June 17, 1977, story about a female sent-down youth who married a peasant.

16. See note 14.

17. "T'an Chen-lin's Speeches on Resettlement Work," *Chih-nung Hung-ch'i* no. 7, January 1968, in *Selections of China Mainland Press* no. 4123, February 21, 1968.

18. Ibid.

19. "Selected Edition of Liu Shao-ch'i's Counterrevolutionary Crimes," Nankai University, April 1967, in *Selections from China Mainland Magazines* no. 653 (May 5, 1969):22.

20. For a recent article on marriage, see *People's Daily,* June 17, 1977, and also *Up to the Mountains,* pp. 161–166. For recent materials on recruitment, see Radio Changchun, May 18, 1977, *Foreign Broadcast Information Service* no. 100, May 24, 1977; Radio Changsha, May 4, 1977, *Foreign Broadcast Information Service* no. 88, May 6, 1977; and New China News Agency, Peking, May 5, 1977, in *Foreign Broadcast Information Service* no. 96, May 18, 1977 (J-3). Cf. *Up to the Mountains,* chap. 5.

21. This point is stressed in Richard Madsen, "Social Causes and Consequences of Radicalism in a South China Village," paper prepared for Workshop on the Pursuit of Political Interest in the People's Republic of China, Ann Arbor, Michigan, August 10–17, 1977.

22. See *Up to the Mountains,* chap. 6.

23. See Martin Whyte, "Small Groups and Communications in China: Ideal Forms and Imperfect Realities," in this volume.

24. See *Up to the Mountains,* esp. pp. 96–103.

25. *People's Daily,* November 23, 1976.

26. Radio Shenyang, April 6, 1976, *Foreign Broadcast Information Service* no. 67, April 7, 1975.

27. *People's Daily,* October 22, 1977.

28. Based on data obtained from informants in Hong Kong, 1972–1973.

29. "I-ke hen hao-ti tien-hsin" [A very good model], *People's Daily,* June 12, 1974.

30. *Nung-ts'un Ch'ing-nien* [Rural Youth] no. 20, October 25, 1967, in *Selections from China Mainland Magazines* no. 612, January 29, 1968.

31. Radio Shenyang, June 15, 1977, *Foreign Broadcast Information Service* no. 120, June 20, 1977.

32. See *Up to the Mountains,* p. 82. Informants interviewed in Hong Kong are the source for the details of mailing the letter.

33. See, e.g., *People's Daily,* July 5, 1973.

34. See *Up to the Mountains,* chap. 6.

35. Ibid.

36. Information supplied by K. Lieberthal, Swarthmore College.

37. See *People's Daily,* February 13, 1975, for a story about the links between Canton's "textile system" *(fang-chih hsi-t'ung)* and rural settlement units.

38. *Red Flag,* no. 8 (August 1, 1972):67.

39. See *Up to the Mountains,* pp. 243–245.

40. Ibid., pp. 109–111 and 252–256.

41. Radio Peking, October 20, 1977, *Foreign Broadcast Information Service* no. 204, October 21, 1977.

42. Radio Peking, May 11, 1978, *Foreign Broadcast Information Service* no. 96, May 17, 1978.

43. *People's Daily,* November 16, 1977; the quote is from the translation in *Foreign Broadcast Information Service* no. 224.

44. Ibid.; see also *People's Daily,* November 27, 1977.

45. "Sheng-hsüeh huo liu-tsai nung-ts'un tou shih tang ti hsü-yao" [Entering Higher School or Remaining in the Village Both Accord with the Needs of the Party], *People's Daily,* November 16, 1977.

46. In this connection, cf. Lucian Pye's chapter, "Communication and Political Culture," in this volume.

47. Radio Nanchang, January 10, 1977, *Foreign Broadcast Information Service* no. 100, May 24, 1977.

48. Radio Changchun, May 18, 1977, *Foreign Broadcast Information Service* no. 100, May 24, 1977.

49. On Chu's career, see *Up to the Mountains,* p. 176, and also Radio Kunming, June 26, 1977, *Foreign Broadcast Information Service* no. 124, June 28, 1977.

50. On Chai, see *Up to the Mountains,* p. 257, and Radio Shenyang, *Foreign Broadcast Information Service* no. 120, June 22, 1977.

51. Radio Peking, June 23, 1977, *Foreign Broadcast Information Service* no. 144, June 28, 1977.

15

Communication and Changing Rural Life

William L. Parish

China has experienced massive changes in rural economic organization, with the countryside rapidly proceeding through land reform
and then reorganization into progressively larger economic units in
the mid-1950s. Though the reasons for this rapid change remain
elusive, its depth and extent are not in question. What remains less
easy to define is the impact this change has had on other areas of
village social life and, in turn, the extent to which changes in all
aspects of social life have responded to commands from Peking.
We shall tackle one aspect of the latter problem in this chapter, asking how the Chinese countryside has responded to appeals from Peking for ever more radical social change and how these responses
have depended on communication networks reaching ever more
deeply into villages.

Methods

This chapter is based on a larger study done in collaboration with
Martin K. Whyte.[1] It relies primarily on interviews conducted in
Hong Kong during 1973–1974 with informants from a total of
sixty-three villages. With the exception of one village in neighboring Fukien Province, all the villages are in Kwangtung Province,
which abuts, and historically included, Hong Kong. In most of the
discussion presented here, the unit of analysis is the production
team, the lowest unit for production and income sharing in the
Chinese countryside, which typically includes thirty or forty households living in a single small village or in the neighborhood of a
larger village. We will at times also refer to the brigade, the administrative unit just above the team, which includes an average of
some 400 households living in a large village or in several small villages that have been combined into one administrative unit.

Interviews with refugees justifiably raise questions about representativeness and bias. We have tried to use our interviewees not as *respondents,* as in a sociological survey, but rather as *informants,* as in an anthropological study. Though we use data on the informants' age, sex, class origins, and political errors to check on potential biases, we are less concerned with their personal experiences and opinions than with the information they can supply on their home production team and neighbors. Checks on the validity of the information supplied include (1) an emphasis on concrete details of everyday life, for which there is usually less motivation to distort and greater difficulty in constructing a coherent distortion, (2) statistical controls by the personal backgrounds of the informants, and (3) comparisons of interview results with official media reports for Kwangtung.

Statistical controls by informant backgrounds indicate that a history of political error, negative class origins, and the like have no consistent effect on our results. Comparisons to official figures show virtually identical results in six areas: grain yields, school enrollments, barefoot doctors, cooperative medicine, land per person, private plot size, household size, and number of laborers per household. Given these checks, the general validity of our results seems relatively well established.[2] In addition, since the emphasis in this chapter is not so much on descriptive statistics as on interrelationships between communication facilities and village behavior, it is less critical that our results be completely representative than that they include sufficient variability in both independent and dependent measures so as to detect covariation. As the information on the measures that follow indicates, that variability is present.

Communication Measures

We have six measures of differential exposure to communication among production teams. These range from the number of newspapers in a village to the number of intellectual youth from cities.

Newspapers. Very few peasants receive a newspaper in their home, but newspapers are frequently available in the team office. The team may subscribe to the *People's Daily* or to the *Southern Daily* or to other national and regional newspapers, each usually being six pages in length and in full newspaper format. In addition, some counties have a biweekly compendium of local production figures and other local news in four- to eight-page tabloid or mimeograph sheet form, which is mailed to production teams. Just over half the teams in our sample subscribed to two or more national and regional newspapers, and we have coded newspaper availability as: 1 = no or only one national or regional newspaper in the team office, 2 = two or more newspapers available. With rural school enrollments being near 90 percent of all school-age youngsters, peasants are increasingly able to read written materials.[3] By 1973, about 83 percent of all adult males and 61 percent of all adult females were literate in rural Kwangtung, which places Kwangtung in almost the same league with other highly literate Asian societies such as Taiwan, Thailand, Sri Lanka, and the Philippines.[4] Nevertheless, newspapers at the team office are only sporadically read by most peasants. Other more visual and oral channels have a much wider audience, and we must investigate these other channels to tap the full range of communication media in villages.

Movie teams. Most brigades and some isolated teams are visited at least once every few months by a film team showing newsreels and movies of revolutionary operas.[5] Our measure is dichotomized with: 1 = film team visits no more than once every three months, and 2 = more often.

Wired broadcasts. Over the years, wired broadcasting networks have spread ever more widely. Some networks are wired into a commune central station whereby commune leaders can communicate directly with villages. Other networks originate in the brigade. Among the forty-five villages for which we have information, thirty-nine had a broadcast network of some sort or other. Most of these networks had speakers atop posts or buildings in the street. A few broadcast through speakers in each peasant's home.[6] Through these networks, local cadres awakened the peasants early in the morning with martial music, announcements about the day's work, and, occasionally, morning political lessons. Some localities broadcast farm bulletins and revolutionary music intermittently thoughout the day. Our measure of type of broadcast network is coded: 1 = none, 2 = wired street speakers, 3 = wired speakers in homes.

Private radios. Peasants are not limited completely to what the local broadcasters have to offer. Some peasants also buy their own radio sets and tune to provincial radio broadcasts—broadcasts which are given both in the regional and national dialects. In some villages almost no households had radios. In other, more affluent villages, as many as 80 percent of all households had private radios. The average was around 15 percent of all households with radios.

Our measure is: 1 = less than 10 percent of all households with radios, and 2 = 10 percent or more of all households with radios.

Total communication. Any impact that messages have on a village is likely to be cumulative rather than discrete. Accordingly, besides the four individual measures already noted, we have prepared a "total communication scale" which sums the four. The new scale is then coded: 1 = low, 2 = medium, 3 = high, depending on whether a village scores high on no more than one, two, or several of the previous four communication measures.

Political study meetings. Though widely touted following the Cultural Revolution, team meetings for political study were rare in Kwangtung at the time of our study. Only about one fourth of our villages had regular study meetings. It simply proved too difficult to make the directives and documents coming down from above relevant and interesting to peasants, and sent-down urban youth who had served as study directors often reported great exasperation at trying to make political study materials comprehensible to peasants. In most villages, enthusiasm and discussion among peasants was reserved for production planning sessions and workpoint meetings, where new values about sharing and cooperation might well be learned but only through very applied questions. Given the infrequency of regular political study, we will want to note whether those villages with political study were specially socialist in character and more likely to implement government policies and ideals. Our coding of this measure is simply: 1 = regular political study absent, and 2 = regular political study meetings present.

Urban youth. Another way central values may sift down to villages is through educated urban youth. Starting in the early 1960s but increasing in tempo after 1968, graduates of urban lower middle and upper middle schools have been sent to live in villages. The difficulties of adjusting to reduced living standards and inhospitality by some peasants, who cannot tolerate "lazy urban manners," have been severe. Many urban youths have slipped back to Canton or even to Hong Kong. Nevertheless, in villages some youth have assumed positions as primary school teachers, political study leaders, cultural performers, workpoint recorders, pig breeders, and occasionally barefoot doctors. Gradually, technical roles for educated youth are emerging, and books about pig breeding, seed selection, and other kinds of agricultural technology written explicitly for educated youth are pouring off the presses. In remote areas that previously had little urban contact, urban youth may have great cultural impact.[7] Averaging just under 3 percent of village populations, our measure of urban youth presence is dichotomized with: 1 = less than 3 percent, 2 = 3 percent or more of the village population being sent-down urban youth.

There is one other channel of government communication which has not been subjected to systematic analysis in this paper, but which can be described. Spare-time propaganda teams, run by brigade or county, were much less common in 1973 than immediately after the Cultural Revolution—they appeared with any frequency in only about a third of the villages for which we have information. Where they continued to exist, the spare-time propaganda teams consisted of village youth who practiced in the evening after fieldwork and then traveled about neighboring villages performing short skits, arias from revolutionary operas, or other pieces of music.

Communication and Village Altruism

The effect of communication upon village life can be examined by noting whether villages high in communication were also the ones most likely to have adopted practices favored by the government in Peking. Results of such an examination can be summarized for several areas of village life, but let us start with a detailed examination of measures of village cooperation and sharing, or of what we call *village altruism*. We have measures of village altruism in four major areas: distribution systems, education, medical care, and conflict (see Table 1).

Production teams must decide on their own how to distribute workpoints and grain. Workpoints may be distributed completely on what the Chinese see as a more egalitarian time rate basis. Or they may be distributed completely according to task rates, which emphasize individual effort and large differential rewards for different jobs. Or they may be distributed with some combination of these two rates. Our coding is arranged accordingly, with 1 = task rates alone, 2 = combination of rates, 3 = time rates alone. The Tachai workpoint system, adopted widely throughout China between 1968 and 1971, is a variant of time rates that postpones decisions about one's rate of pay until one's work is already completed. This system emphasizes political attitude along with work effort as well as collective discussion and approval of one's point rate. The sys-

TABLE 1
Collective Altruism by Mode of Communication (Gamma Values)

Collective Altruism	News-papers	Movie Teams	Wired Broad-casts	Private Radios	Total Communi-cation	Political Study	Urban Youth
Distribution Systems							
Time rate	.12	.36	-.09	.00	.21	.49[a]	-.28
Tachai system abandoned late	.46[a]	-.36	-.41	.80[a]	.35	.29	.20
Per capita grain distribution	.70[a]	-.41	.25	.14	.01	.42	.54[a]
Collective Education							
Nursery/kindergarten	.68[a]	.30	-.15	.60[a]	.41	.30	-.47[a]
Lower-middle school	.42	.36	-.56[a]	.26	.21	-.20	-.19
Medical System							
Doctor-patient ratio	.54[a]	.43	-.27	-.09	.41	.00	-.11
Early cooperative medicine	.54[a]	-.11	.32	-.28	.06	.12	-.13
Extensive coverage	-.24	.14	.00	-.20	.17	.68[a]	.64[a]
Low annual medical fee	-.47[a]	.33	.08	-.38	.02	.30	-.22
Low medical visit fee	.61[a]	.60[a]	.53[a]	.00	.55[a]	.33	-.33
Conflict							
Absence of conflict	.11	-.17	.07	.11	.09	-.04	-.28
Average of the Above Values	.32[b]	.13	-.02	.09	.23[b]	.24[b]	-.06[b]

[a]Probability of a value this large occurring by chance alone is less than one in ten in a chi square test of significance.
[b]Probability of the observed number of plus or minus values in this column occurring by chance alone less than one in ten in a sign test pitting number of positive against number of negative gammas.

tem tended to lead to drawn-out meetings and rancorous conflict in some villages and was rapidly rejected after central permission to do so in late 1971. Our coding is: 1 = Tachai system abandoned before 1972, and 2 = abandoned in 1972 or later, with the assumption that those who abandoned the system later were more attached to the extreme socialist principles in force in the late 1960s.

Sooner or later, virtually all grain has to be paid for by the family that consumes it. Nevertheless, there are more and less egalitarian grain distribution systems. Some villages in our study distributed grain primarily on a per capita basis (called "basic grain"), which tends to guarantee that a family can eat regardless of whether it can pay for its staples immediately. Other villages distributed grain more on a workpoint basis, which means that a family can consume only in proportion to its number of able-bodied laborers and their days of work. Families with few laborers and few work points had to find other sources of income and grain or go without. Our coding of local grain distribution practices is: 1 = 100 percent workpoint distribution, 2 = mixed distribution, 3 = 100 percent per capita distribution.

The first three rows of Table 1 show the relationships between these distribution measures and different modes of communication. The index of association is Goodman and Kruskal's gamma which varies between −1.00 and 1.00. A value of 1.00 indicates that two measures are perfectly correlated—for example, if all villages that had several newspapers had also abandoned the Tachai system late, the association between these two measures would be 1.00. A value of −1.00 indicates just the inverse situation—using the previous example, if all villages with several newspapers had abandoned the Tachai system early, gamma would be −1.00. A value of zero indicates no relationship—if villages with several newspapers were no more likely to have kept the Tachai system than those without, then gamma would be zero. As an added check on these relationships, we have applied tests of significance, signified by *a* and *b*, which indicate whether the observed relationships would often have occurred by the chances of sampling error alone. Generally, given the relatively small sample sizes, we will assume that relationships greater than +.60 are moderately strong, relationships greater than +.40 are modest, and relationships of lesser magnitude are inconsequential.

With the partial exception of newspapers and political study, intense communication fails to create the more egalitarian distribution systems desired by Peking in the later 1960s and early 1970s. Most of the relationships between distribution and individual modes of communication are inconsequential, contradictory, or the inverse of what one would expect if communication had a strong impact on village practices (see Table 1, top three rows). In tabulations with additional village characteristics, not shown here, we find that the major determinants of distribution practices are things other than communication. Time rates were most likely to be used in large villages (gamma = .49) with little land (gamma = .56). Large villages with many laborers find it difficult to keep accounting and work assignments straight when task rates are used. So as to relieve the already overburdened accountant and workpoint recorders, large villages tend to switch to the more easily recorded time rates. Instead of keeping detailed daily accounts of who has done what job worth a certain number of points, they just record who shows up for work each day of the month.

Consideration of local production problems also causes villages with little land to switch to time rates. Where task rates are used, peasants work hard in order to reap larger incomes, but at the same time they tend to be less careful in seeing that every row is planted absolutely straight or in getting every last grain from the fields at harvest. Villages without much land cannot afford this kind of sloppy work nor do they have enough work to go around once a few eager workers hog the better, high-paying jobs. Therefore, villages with little land rely mostly on time rates.

Local structural conditions also have had a major influence on whether the Tachai system was abandoned late. Large (gamma = .43) and affluent (gamma = .55) villages tend to have held onto the contention-generating Tachai system until after 1972. Large teams liked the time rate aspect of the Tachai system, while affluent teams seem to have been able to afford better than others the lengthy meetings and occasional disputes that went along with that system. Similarly, the grain distribution system in villages is determined primarily by the affluence of a team (gamma = .84). Wealthier teams with better crops can afford to be more generous.

The close relationship between affluence and collective sharing sheds additional light on some other relationships in the top part of Table 1. Affluent villages can afford more newspapers and radios. Part of the apparent relationships among newspapers, radios, and

egalitarian distribution, then, is an artifact of the affluence relationship.[8] Affluent villages are able both to be more generous in
their distribution and to purchase more goods, including newspapers and radios. With the possible exceptions of political study,
then, there is no consistently positive relationship between communication and distribution. The influence of communication on
village distribution systems takes a distant second place to more
concrete local influences such as village size, affluence, and amount
of land. In this realm, peasants respond less to appeals from afar
than to their immediate local needs and resources.

A similar pattern is found with the remaining measures of collective altruism. The measures of collective education are simply
whether nurseries or kindergartens and brigade-run lower middle
schools are present. Additional tabulations show that lower middle
schools are most common in large brigades (gamma = .58). Nurseries and kindergartens, usually run by teams, are most common in
large, affluent teams located in the delta regions of Kwangtung
—the relevant gamma values are .88, .75, and .87. Large villages
with more children generate more demand for local education while
more affluent villages can more easily support new preschool
facilities. Again, part of the apparent ties between newspapers,
radios, and collective education in Table 1 is an artifact of village
affluence. Affluence supports both more purchases and more
schools. Eliminating the effect of affluence in our tabulation leaves
very little relationship between communication and collective education.[9] Whether a village supports collective education depends
less on messages from Peking than on its own local interests, particularly as defined by village size and affluence.

Greater communication might be expected to support the government's program for more widespread and more equal medical
care. Five measures of the quantity and equality of medical care are
available: (1) the ratio of doctors to population, (2) whether cooperative medical insurance was begun before 1970, (3) whether the
insurance covers all drug and surgical fees, (4) whether the annual
insurance fee per individual is below 3.60 *yüan,* and (5) whether the
fee per visit is below 0.10 *yüan.* The first four modes of communication as well as the presence of urban youth are inconsistently
related to medical care, if related at all. Most relationships are quite
weak, and some of the stronger relationships are not positive but
negative. Only a combination of communication modes (indexed

by the total communication scale) and political study consistently support cooperative medical care, and even that support is often very weak.

Finally, closer contact with messages from the center might be seen as promoting more cooperation among villages and the absence of conflict among these same units. Production units, both teams and brigades, come into competition over land, water, and animal rights, and in some places this competition has flared into verbal arguments and occasional physical attacks. The degree of conflict among villages between 1967 and 1973 was indexed by whether informants reported physical fights, major arguments, minor disagreements, or absolutely no disagreements between their own and neighboring teams and villages between 1967 and 1973. The results in Table 1 show no relationship between communication and conflict. Again, at best, communication has had a minimal impact on village altruism.

We can summarize the full variety of results just given by computing average gamma scores for all our measures of village altruism (still respecting positive or negative signs) and by noting whether most of the scores were positive or negative (see the last row of Table 1). In this summary, which pulls together the results for eleven altruism measures under each mode of communication, somewhat smaller gamma values (generally +.20 or greater) are worthy of note. The summary gamma values show that the presence of many urban youth and wired broadcasts in villages are unrelated to village altruism, or even slightly negatively related. Though the relationships are weak, there is actually a preponderance of negative relationships in the urban youth column. Though positively related overall, the average relationships of movie teams and private radios with altruism are so weak as to be considered essentially zero. The only communication measures that have a predominantly positive and moderately great effect on village practices of sharing and cooperation on the average, then, are newspapers, total communication, and political study. As already suggested, the relationship with newspapers is inflated by affluent villages being more able both to share and to buy newspapers. The reported relationship should then be discounted somewhat. And to an extent the total communication scale, being influenced by newspapers as a constituent element, should also be discounted somewhat.[10] Yet the overall positive relationship (even if weak) between total communi-

cation and altruism should not be denied and political study stands
on its own as a modestly consistent, if weak, correlate of altruism.

Change in Other Realms of Village Life

Besides change in the realm of village altruism, it is possible to measure change in five other dimensions of collective life plus changes
in family life and ceremonial life. We measured change in five additional aspects of collective life, thirteen aspects of family life, and
thirteen aspects of ceremonial life. Only summary results are presented here. The remaining aspects of collective life include active
male cadre campaigning and severe collective sanctions in support
of birth control, ample female representation in village cadre posts,
and active collective celebration of new national holidays. Measures of change in family life include popular acceptance of birth
control; late marriage ages; an absence of parental dominance in
marriage; an absence of introduction in marriage; low bride prices;
husbands helping with domestic work; less sexual division of labor,
as indicated by women taking a role in private plot work, marketing, and management of the family purse; and closer attachment
between husband and wife, as indicated by husbands siding with
their wives in disputes involving a man's mother and use of the
term "beloved" *(ai-jen)* when talking about one's spouse. Measures of change in ceremonial life include those connected with
both life cycle and annual ceremonies. Life cycle practices judged
in line with government ideals include free choice of a child's name
by parents or grandparents without reference to generational
names or a fortune teller; wedding costs under 1000 *yüan;* wedding
feasts with less than ten tables of invited guests; no worship at the
groom's home as part of the wedding; some or many cases of traveling marriages, which tend to be more spartan and economical,
few or no old age birthday feasts; no use of ancestral tablets; and
no geomancers in a village. Annual ritual practices judged in line
with government ideals as expressed in the official media include no
or simplified *Ch'ing-ming* festival activities; less than six days off
granted for the lunar new year holiday; holidays granted for only
one festival during the year; and summary scales indexing the
reduced elaborateness of traditional festivals throughout the year.

The summary relationships for all sixteen measures of collective
life (including the eleven measures of altruism already presented)
and all thirteen measures of family life and of ceremonial life are

shown in Table 2. These are the same type of summary gamma values as shown in Table 1. Again, ample movie teams, wired broadcasts, private radios, and urban youth have no influence on a village, regardless of the realm of village life. The positive relationship between newspapers, total communication, political study, and altruism is repeated for the full sixteen measures of collective life. But when one moves away from collective life into the more private realms of family and ceremonial life, these means of communication have no effect. Decisions about family and ceremonial practices are made independently of the number of newspapers in a team, of total communication effort, and of what goes on in study groups. In sum, most modes of communication are unrelated to village behavior, except that newspapers, total communication, and political study are modestly related to collective life. How then are we to explain this pattern?

Discussion

Among several possible explanations of the observed pattern of relationships between communication and villages change, one is that the content disseminated in each mode of communication is simply not what one would at first think. Something besides the content of *People's Daily* and provincial radio broadcasts is being transmitted at the village level. There is some support for this sort of interpretation. Though movie teams show newsreels and movies of model operas, peasants often appreciate these for their entertainment value as much as for any political message they might carry. Broadcast networks are as concerned with announcing production plans and playing entertaining music as with presenting a political message that would influence villagers' lives. Newspapers and political study groups have far more to do with national issues and economic issues than with issues of family reform and ceremonial change. The differential emphasis in each mode of communication and the relative inattention to family and ceremonial matters, then, may explain part of the pattern of change.

Similarly, the absence of any impact of sent-down urban youth on villages may be explained by the types of areas to which youth are sent and their peculiar position in villages. In our interviews there are several anecdotes of villagers who were initially shocked by the dress, mannerisms, and consumption standards of youths from Canton but eventually adopted some of these same patterns

TABLE 2

Rural Change by Mode of Communication (Summary Gamma Values)

Arena of Change	News-papers	Movie Teams	Wired Broad-casts	Private Radios	Total Communi-cation	Political Study	Urban Youth	No. of Values[a]
Collective life	.26[b]	.13	-.03	-.01	.17[b]	.29[b]	-.02	(16)
Family life	.08	-.07	-.11	-.06	-.08	-.06	-.05	(13)
Ceremonial life	.01	-.03	-.11	.09	.02	.00	.03	(13)

[a]Total number of gamma values which are averaged to produce the summary gamma value.
[b]Probability of the observed number of plus values among the total values occurring by chance alone less than one in ten in a sign test.

of behavior, buying new kinds of clothes, allowing freer talk among youths of different sex, and the like. Most of these stories, however, come from remote villages, whereas sent-down youth are sent disproportionately to delta villages near Canton, where they are less likely to be extremely different from their receiving villagers. Regardless of where they go, because they have averaged less than 3 percent of a village's population they tend not to be a major social group in a village. And what voice they might have is attenuated by the inability of many urban youth to match the labor output, or earn the esteem, of the leading native laborers who dominate formal and informal leadership positions in most villages. With increasing mechanization and rural industrialization and the spread of scientific farming, new roles requiring less physical ability may give the sent-down youth more esteem and a greater voice in village affairs, but whether even these roles will lead to their having a significant impact on peasant family and ceremonial behavior remains to be seen.

What are we to conclude from the foregoing? Is it possible that despite multiple communication channels, the government's message about its ideals is simply not getting through to peasants? We think not. Though we have no consistent information on this question, the impression emerging from the interviews is that most peasants had a good idea of the general outlines of most government programs. From radio broadcasts, public meetings, occasional special campaigns, and other sources, some of them repeating the same message over and over again for over twenty years, most peasants had learned well the central government's ideals.

An example of this is provided by a study of the populace's knowledge of the government's birth planning program. Birth planning began to be urged on peasants in earnest after 1963, when birth planning commissions were established in each province. In 1965 Robert Worth interviewed recently arrived refugees in the Portuguese colony of Macao.[11] Of 125 refugee women aged eighteen through forty-four, 95 percent unequivocally approved the idea of birth planning. Sixty percent knew about the IUD, and almost all were interested in learning about additional methods. Sixty percent knew that the government wanted family size to be limited, and they themselves wanted a smaller number of children than did a comparable sample of rural Hong Kong women who Worth also interviewed. (They wanted fewer, our interviews suggest, because having to work in the fields during the day and having to take care of housework by themselves at night, they found a large number of children just too great a burden.) Despite all this, about as many of the Kwangtung women as of their Hong Kong counterparts were pregnant (15 percent), only 6 percent had spoken with their husband about limiting births, and only 2 percent reported that they knew friends and fellow villagers who used birth control. And by asking women to report on births in their villages in the past several months, Worth estimated a very high annual birthrate of between 33 and 46 per thousand population. Despite the preliminary desire for birth control and despite the reception of government communication on the necessity of birth control, no action had been taken. The clinics for giving advice and inserting intrauterine devices were too far away for most village women to visit, and most women remained ignorant of precise methods for controlling births. Some rural incentives also continued to favor a moderate number of male births. Sons continued to support their parents in old age and each new child continued to bring in more rations. It was only with the spread of rural clinics and new birth control techniques and with the changing of rationing incentives in some villages that the knowledge of birth control goals in the 1960s could be carried into action in the 1970s. Communication of goals without the facilities and incentives for implementing these goals, in short, leads to no action at all.

If change today is so erratic and often out of line with centrally communicated goals, how is it that massive changes in line with central goals were possible in the 1950s? Our analysis can only be tentative, but we suggest that much of the Party's analysis of class interests must be given credence, at least for the 1940s and 1950s. Major groups of poor peasants were thirsty for land, and in addition many other aggrieved groups such as women could be relied on to support the Communist cause.[12] These groups were identified by class analysis and by the instructions of organizers to go out and seek out the most oppressed elements in the rural community. Though women as an active interest group were restrained by administrative decree after 1953, many of the same poor peasants who had supported land reform could also be mobilized to form collectives. The deep desire for a better standard of living generated in the land reform campaign could not begin to be slaked by the small parcels of land handed out, and even these parcels were in danger of being lost in poor harvest years. The poor peasants of land reform remained an active interest group which could be mobilized to support the efforts to collectivize agriculture in the mid-1950s.

Once collectivization was completed, however, and income came to depend not on individual property holdings but on the wealth of one's team and the labor power of one's household, there was no longer any easily mobilizable interest group that could be used to carry out new government initiatives for social change. Or, to be more precise, there were no interest groups which the government found acceptable. Women could have been encouraged to pursue their interests, as they were in some places in the early 1950s before local Party leaders complained of the havoc caused by the marriage law campaign.[13] Poor teams could have been turned against rich teams, and in the 1970s discontent sent-down youth could have been encouraged to pursue their interests. Any of these courses of action would have led to social change and some disorder, but all were judged improper. Instead, the government continued to use routine class analysis in trying to identify those who would favor government-sponsored programs of change. With no easily identifiable group to appeal to, the pace of change was becalmed in the 1960s and 1970s and even reversed in the retrenchment for the 1958–1961 Great Leap Forward.

The pace of change was further becalmed because the rural structures created in the mid-1950s helped sustain village and family solidarity, a solidarity which supported some government goals while opposing others. Though loyalty to the state and collective ideally should supersede loyalty to the family and many of its traditional practices, collective structures continue to rely on the family for many economic activities. Income is distributed by family and individual economic well-being depends on the degree of cooperation and hard work among fellow family members. The aged depend on their sons for support, and with strict migration laws and little chance of migration out to urban jobs, most parents can look forward to their sons living nearby for their whole lifetime. The loss of family control over most private property and the complete loss of lineage control over property has meant a weakening of parental authority. Child-bride marriages arranged by parents and concubinage are no more. Though parents typically initiate marriage negotiations, children have veto power over the spouse eventually selected and some children initiate their own marriage negotiations. Mother-in-law–daughter-in-law conflict has been reduced somewhat, aided in part by early division of the married son's family finances. Once they retire from field labor, aged parents have considerably less control over family finances. Nevertheless, the family remains a central institution, as reflected in the continuing importance of family rituals such as marriage feasts, full-month birth celebrations, and funerals even while community and lineage rituals have declined in significance.

Some of the changes instituted in the 1950s have even promoted changes in opposition to government policy. In Kwangtung, women have increasingly gone to work in the fields. While in the 1930s only about 29 percent of agricultural labor was done by women in Kwangtung, today as much as 40 percent of all agricultural labor is performed by women.[14] Instead of making women more powerful, however, these changes simply have made women more valuable, so that a groom's family is willing to pay as much as ever in bride price for a new bride while the bride's family no longer needs to contribute anything of substance in the way of a dowry. Instead of an approximately equal set of exchanges for the average peasant family, most monetary exchanges at marriage have shifted in favor of the bride's family, a pattern common in many societies where women do a large share of field labor. The pattern of change in Chinese villages, then, has responded less to messages being communicated from Peking and less to the political consciousness or socialist character of each village than to the mixed structure of incentives created by new collective structures established in the 1950s. Contrary to what one might assume, many of those structures continue to support old, and even promote new, practices which run counter to government ideals.

Thus, the impression gained from talking with informants from Kwangtung is that most peasants today know fairly well what the government ideals in all areas of life are, but in everyday action they respond much more readily to the constraints and incentives of their immediate local situation and to the mixed collective structures that were created in the 1950s. How is it that they have the freedom to act so independently? The answer to this question, we feel, is the key both to the relative success of Chinese collective farming (in contrast, say, to Russian collective farming) and to the difficulty of getting full compliance with many of Peking's more idealistic programs. First, Chinese collective production units were created around small, preexisting natural units. The basic production and income-sharing unit consists not of specialized units spread over a wide area but of a production team of thirty or forty households in a single small village or a neighborhood of some larger village. Peasants thus work and share income with people who are their close neighbors and often their close kinsmen as well —in our Kwangtung sample, three fourths of all teams included people from only a single lineage. Besides incorporating old loyalties, these production units have generated new loyalties over the previous twenty years, a loyalty that is illustrated in statistics on intervillage and interunit conflict. Except for the large single-lineage brigades, multilineage teams are just as likely to come into conflict with their neighbors over rights to land, water, and animals as single-lineage teams are. Being split by old lineage loyalties does not inhibit a team's ability to come together to protect its own interests against outsiders. The new collective identities have become strong for all teams.

These identities and the relative autonomy of Chinese collective units are further supported by the nature of village leaders. In contrast to the Soviet collective farms, Chinese village leaders at the level of the brigade and the production team are virtually all natives of the villages they lead. They are not on a state salary but exist instead off the same workpoints as their fellow brigade and team members, and suffer the same ups and downs in income depending on fluctuations in the annual harvest as other peasants. Though brigade-level Party officers are nominated from above and elected only by Party members in a brigade, all depend heavily on persuasion and good will to run their village well. With a loss of good will, overt and covert public criticism quickly appears and most officers suffering added burdens and no extra rewards from office soon resign, creating a high rate of turnover in most offices other than that of brigade Party secretary. Similarly, with little hope of being promoted within the bureaucracy, and understanding that they may soon step down to spend the rest of their lives as ordinary peasants in their village, local cadres keep their primary social ties and loyalties within their village rather than in the bureaucracy outside. They may want to please higher authorities, but if a given policy is one they know is unpopular with their neighbors, they may enforce it reluctantly or not at all. Even refusal to participate in wedding feasts and to pay bride prices may jeopardize their relations with, and authority over, local peasants. This reliance on local leaders and policy enforcers who are "not very different" is both a great strength and a weakness of the Chinese system of collectivized agriculture. Kwangtung peasants no doubt work more cooperatively and diligently under individuals they know and trust than they would under outsiders, and the problems of nepotism and local recalcitrance are kept in check by the nesting of teams and brigades under commune and county levels, whose leaders, many of them outsiders, must review and approve lower level decisions. But locally bred leaders are constrained by their ties with other villagers, and cannot be depended upon to enforce every new policy vigorously. China's leaders are clearly aware of this problem, and at times when they want to induce particularly rapid rural change, they send in outside work teams to take command temporarily from local leaders. This strategy has its own costs, however, particularly since by displacing and perhaps disgracing local cadres it may later be difficult to get peasants to assume these posts. The Chinese Communists have built a rural system that works fairly effectively, but one that constrains their ability to introduce further changes on all fronts at once.

In sum, the Chinese have built a workable compromise system that achieves many of their major goals, particularly in the economic realm. They are able to communicate many of their other goals respecting family and community change to peasants, but the system they have created has sufficiently mixed incentives and allows sufficient autonomy for families and small collective units that the response by peasants to official goals is highly variable. Indeed, peasants live their life much of the time with little attention to appeals from Peking, paying much more attention to the local needs of their own family, production team, and, to a lesser extent, their brigade. Decisions about how to distribute grain or workpoints, for example, have more to do with the relative size, prosperity, and land pressure of their family and collective units than with policies emanating from Peking.[15] There are exceptions to this, of course, such as in campaign periods when outside work teams are sent into a village, or when so much administrative pressure is put on local cadres that they have to enforce unpopular policies. (The latter situation occurred in 1968-1971, when the unpopular Tachai workpoint system was almost universally enforced.)

Yet the backlash, seen in mass resignations of local officers, is so severe that Peking usually chooses to relax the pressure, allowing local units again to make decisions in these areas on their own. Central policies, such as increased birth control, more widespread medical care, and more local schooling, are readily adopted and have staying power only because these programs resonate with locally defined needs. This leads to an imperfect system that falls short of many ideals defined in Peking, but it is a workable system with which most central leaders as well as peasants seem willing to live.

NOTES

1. William L. Parish and Martin K. Whyte, *Village and Family in Contemporary China* (Chicago: University of Chicago Press, 1978).

2. For a more detailed discussion of checks on selectivity and bias, see ibid., appendix 1.

3. According to radio reports, 92 percent of Kwangtung primary school-age children were enrolled in 1973 and 95 percent in 1974. (These figures include urban areas. Rural figures alone would be 2 to 4 percentage points lower.) *Summary of World Broadcasts,* FE/4369/B11/6, August 10, 1973, and *Foreign Broadcast Information Service,* May 10, 1974, p. H9. Our interviews agree with these figures.

4. Our statistic on Kwangtung literacy is based on a census of the closest neighbors of each informant.

5. A Chinese source states that in 1974 the average peasant in Kwangtung attended more than ten film shows. See *Peking Review* 17, no. 45(1975):30.

6. These wired broadcasting networks continue to develop rapidly. A recent source claims that in 1975, 92.7 percent of the production teams in the entire country were reached by wired broadcasting, and 70 percent of rural households had loudspeakers within the home. See *Peking Review* 18, no. 39(1975):30.

7. One of our informants, a sent-down youth, provided the following example: "The women there do not wear short-sleeved clothes—they feel that wearing short sleeves is for ghosts and not for people. Women also do not wear colored clothing. The only thing they have is black clothing. In the last two years, these women have received influence from us sent-down girls, and they have started to wear westernized clothes, and two or three young women are wearing short-sleeved clothing. Some young males are wearing watches" (Interview TeCl, p. 4). For a more detailed analysis, see the chapter by Thomas Bernstein in this volume.

8. When controlled for collective affluence, the relationship of newspapers with time rate changes to a negative .53, while the relationship with Tachai system declines to .21 and grain distribution to .41.

9. Controlling by affluence reduces the relationship between newspapers and nurseries from a positive .68 to a negative .40.

10. When controlled for affluence, the average gamma value for newspapers declines from .32 to .18 (with the total number of plus values no longer being signifi-

cant), while the average value for total communication declines from .23 to .19 (with ten of the eleven constituent values remaining on the plus side—a significant number).

11. Robert M. Worth, "Recent Demographic Patterns in Kwangtung Province Villages," unpublished paper, n.d.

12. On women as revolutionary agitators, see, for example, Jack Belden, *China Shakes the World* (New York: Monthly Review Press, 1970), pp. 275–307.

13. See M. J. Meijer, *Marriage Law and Policy in the Chinese People's Republic* (Hong Kong University Press, 1971).

14. John L. Buck, *Land Utilization in China: Statistics Volume* (Nanking: University of Nanking Press, 1937), pp. 292–293. The Kwangtung percentages are higher than those for most provinces around 1930 because it includes a sizable Hakka ethnic group in which women have traditionally done much of the fieldwork.

15. In part, our findings for Chinese villages replicate findings in Western communications research of the 1950s. That research emphasized in study after study how communication flows not directly from communicator to receiver but tortuously, often haltingly, through social networks. A person's immediate kin, friends, and neighbors are among the most important determinants of whether a person will respond to, or even hear, a mass communication appeal to vote Dewey for president, buy Maxwell House coffee, and so on. See, for example, Elihu Katz, "The Two-Step Flow of Communication: An Up-to-Date Report on an Hypothesis," *Public Opinion Quarterly* 21 (1957):61–78. The Chinese system intensified this process by encapsulating peasants in relatively autonomous production teams.

V

CONCLUSIONS

In this section, A. Doak Barnett, a senior fellow at the Brookings Institution, takes an overall look at China's communication system and discusses various features relevant to its impact on behavioral modification and value change. Barnett points out several areas in which fruitful research could be undertaken to advance our knowledge of communication processes in China.

What do we know about cultural change in China and the role of communication in that change process? Francis L. K. Hsu and Godwin C. Chu attempt to answer this question. Drawing on data from this volume, they discuss the changes in self-material relations, self-other relations, and self-ideas relations, and consider the possible impact of communication on cultural change. A theoretical perspective is offered to explain both the changes and the continuity in Chinese culture.

16

The Communication System in China: Some Generalizations, Hypotheses, and Questions for Research

A. Doak Barnett

The revolution in communications in China since 1949 has played a major role in the broader processes of political, economic, and cultural change that have altered profoundly the nature of Chinese society in the past quarter century. Valuable research has already been done on aspects of China's new system of communication. But there is clearly a need for more.

On the basis of what is now known, what are some of the basic characteristics of this new communication system that need further examination? What are some of the major questions about it that now need to be investigated? Can one formulate hypotheses about the system, its operation, and its effects—in practice as well as in theory—that point to areas for research that should be given priority in the period ahead?

One of the most striking characteristics of the communication system in China today is its pervasiveness, penetration, and intensity, with *minimum technology*. In relation to its size, China still has only limited communications technology. It is true that the Communists have done a good deal to develop modern media. If one compares the situation of today with that of twenty-five years ago (to say nothing of that in traditional China), the technology of communication has advanced considerably. Yet if one compares China with societies that are more highly developed technologically and scientifically, such as Japan, it is clear that the Chinese are still operating with minimum technological facilities for communication. For example, even though the Chinese press has developed substantially, its distribution is still relatively small for the size of its population. The written word obviously has a crucial importance in China today, but its direct impact is greatest on elite groups and those in the bureaucratic structure of power. Television is in its infancy. Of the modern means of mass communication, radio—including the wired rediffusion system that has spread widely throughout the country—probably now has the greatest mass impact. But even in radio communication, if one compares China and Japan there is no doubt that China's technological capabilities are still limited.

In examining communication media in China, one must look, therefore, at things other than the modern media. A notable characteristic of the present communication system in China is that it incorporates almost every conceivable means of communication, including many traditional ones, such as storytelling, old-style "comic books," and popular drama. Nevertheless, even taking these into account, the Chinese system appears to be far more pervasive, penetrating, and intense than one would expect simply from an analysis of the media. Why?

One answer is that there is an intimate and crucial link between communication and organization in contemporary China. The Chinese Communists see communication as a means to create new political and social organizations, and they see all political and social organizations as important channels of communication. This makes the system fundamentally different from that in any modern pluralistic society, such as in the United States or Japan, where there is a great outpouring of communications, through many channels, that reaches millions of individuals. But no disciplined organizational structure exists to reinforce them, nor is one desired. In China, a direct link exists between organization and communication. Great stress is placed on face-to-face, oral communication, through organizations. In analyzing how communications are diffused throughout China, it is misleading, therefore, to look simply at what is transmitted via the identifiable media. Even more important are the messages communicated down through the regime's major organizational hierarchies, then out from these hierarchies through organizational channels, and ultimately to the mass of the population.

The following key elements exist in the organizational apparatus in this dual system of communication and organization: at the top, the disciplined Party, state, and military hierarchies are of key importance, as are the organizations for mass campaigns; finally, and perhaps most important, at the bottom levels, Chinese society is organized in a unique way into *hsiao-tzu* (small groups) of many sorts, including *hsüeh-hsi hsiao-tzu* (study groups). The organization of the entire population into small overlapping groups is distinctive. Through these groups, intense social pressures of many sorts are exerted on virtually all individuals in Chinese society.

The dividing lines between organization and communication or, more broadly, between state and society are blurred; it is often hard, in fact, to define that line in China. Some scholars argue that this has always been true in Chinese society, at least to some extent: that traditionally the state and society were much more intimately linked than in pluralistic Western societies. Perhaps so, but this is even more true now. Since 1949, the state and the society in China have at times seemed to be virtually merged (although in periods when central control has been weakened, as during the Cultural Revolution, it has been evident that the merger is by no means complete).

What are the characteristics of the small groups that play such important roles in the political, social, and communication systems in China today? To start with, normally they are directly linked to higher authorities, which makes them very different from most citizens' groups in pluralistic societies. There is almost always a politically directed hierarchy to which a group is connected. Someone within the group is usually in close touch with the hierarchy, or at least with some group within the leadership sector. Instructions, information, and the definition of acceptable values come from above; they are sent down to these groups by higher authorities. The prime functions of local groups are to mobilize peer pressure and, through propaganda, indoctrination, and "criticism and self-criticism," to achieve acceptance, compliance, commitment, and action—based on the impulses coming from above. At times, the local groups also express their own interests, but this is not their primary function (in fact, it is generally not viewed as a legitimate function).

The intensity with which the system affects different types of people in China clearly varies. The pressure to submit and conform is greatest with respect to deviants—for example, those in reform-through-labor institutions. However, the pressure is also great both on all those who work within the bureaucratic hierarchies of the regime and on intellectuals and students. "Ordinary people," that is, rank-and-file workers and peasants, feel the effects of this system, but with less intensity. There are also obvious differences between urban and rural areas; people in cities are clearly more affected than peasants in the countryside. How great the differences are is a question that deserves further research.

The communication system in China today is a highly centralized and national system that communicates with speed, as well as intensity, throughout most of the country. This is very different from what existed in the past. Traditional China had an effective, but slow, system of communication. Over the decades, and even centuries, the diffusion of cultural values and social practices through this system was impressive. But it was the result of a very gradual filtering-down process. Education was of key importance, and various kinds of social pressures reinforced particular values. But not only was the process extremely slow; there was also a great deal of regional variation and localism. Today, once the impulses are sent by the center, they are transmitted very rapidly throughout the entire country.

In order to understand China's present national communication system, it is necessary to analyze the interrelationships of several elements, some public, some not. The regime has an elaborate internal structure of bureaucratic communication (which we have learned something about in recent years from documents that have filtered out of China) that obviously is a key element in this system. Its messages are highly differentiated; they are contained in many types of directives, with different levels of authoritativeness and with different degrees of classification. However, since most of these messages are classified, we know much less about them than we would like. Ordinary Chinese do not know much about them, either.

What we do have easy access to is the open system of public mass communication. Several interesting studies have been made of the mass media in China, and there is beginning to be a significant literature dealing with them. But much can still be done to increase our understanding of the media. Finally, a better understanding is needed of the social dynamics of how small groups operate in China, that is, how social pressure is exerted through them. There have been a few interesting studies of such groups, but much more needs to be done.

In China—in contrast with countries such as Japan or the United States—the content of communications emanating from the center, and disseminated through the Party-controlled system, tends to be highly focused, not diffuse. At any particular time, the top leadership usually focuses attention on a few priority objectives, and the communication system concentrates on trying to deal with these. This too makes the system very different from those in pluralistic societies.

The communication system in China today is highly purposeful. Its function is not primarily to inform; rather, it is to stimulate action, to mobilize people, to change values and beliefs, and to change behavior. The Chinese Communists see an intimate link between beliefs and behavior.

By concentrating on a few objectives, Chinese leaders can achieve visible results. But such concentration also has obvious liabilities. The leaders often neglect certain problems while concentrating on priority tasks; the costs of this deserve careful analysis.

Above all, the communication system in China today puts an extraordinary emphasis on normative goals, on values. The leadership stresses what the Chinese call "thought reform," *ssu hsiang kai tsao.* Because their goal is to create a new "culture," they spend a great deal of time on basic ideological education. This is true in most small groups as well as in the mass media. Great effort is spent on communicating, through repetition, fundamental ideology—simplified, with values usually defined in black and white terms—good and bad. The distinctive scale of values of the late Chairman Mao Tse-tung put enormous stress on the need for ideological transformation, often giving it higher priority than increased production or structural social change, although these are obviously linked. His assumption was that if the mass of people could be induced to accept a new culture, a new set of values, this would automatically set a new framework for thinking and behavior. It would set boundaries on what people could think and do, and make "right thinking" and compliance close to being automatic. The assumption has been that if the people know what the new ground rules of the society are, they will know what patterns of behavior are required and will conform to them.

In China today, language per se is an enormously important transmitter of values. Every revolution introduces a new language, and the Chinese revolution is no exception. The Communists' new terminology carries tremendous freight, introducing new norms and political and social ideas. Language is a tool for change, and the regime's new slogans, symbols, and models have powerful effects. The use of historical analogy and allusion, as well as of "esoteric communication" (using ideological "code words") requires that members of the society (and outside observers) learn entirely new ways of communicating.

One of the basic functions of the communication system in China today is to control, limit, and restrict information, as well as to diffuse new ideas and values. In certain respects, of course, the system is very effective in transmitting information that the regime wants to spread. One example is the dissemination of simple agricultural information through the regime's extension system, which may well be more effective in China than in any other developing society. The other side of the coin, however, is that the information diffused in China is extremely restricted. The average Chinese today has little knowledge of many aspects of his or her own society, and even less about the rest of the world. These people must spend a great amount of time and effort trying to learn what in another type of society would be in public domain. This raises important questions that deserve further analysis: What information is disseminated, and what is *not,* in China? What is the level of knowledge, or *lack* of knowledge, about key questions among different groups of Chinese?

Finally, it is important to recognize that the present Chinese system is based on a complex mix of persuasion and coercion. Many observers, including myself, have stressed the importance of political persuasion in China. The Chinese put an enormous stress on "voluntarism." Yet much of the persuasion in China is clearly "coercive persuasion." Coercion—sometimes subtle, sometimes not; usually in the background, but at times in the foreground—is essential for the system to work as it does. In the early days of the regime (especially during land reform and the campaign against counterrevolutionaries), there were periods of open violence that demonstrated to everyone the capacity of the regime to deal harshly with its opponents, or deviants, and people did not forget this. Today, everyone is aware of the sanctions that are built into the system to discourage and punish nonconformists. These include extreme penal sanctions, reform through labor, and less severe surveillance.

Let me conclude with a few broad judgments, questions, and hypotheses about the strengths and weaknesses of the communication system in China today. Most observers are impressed, rightly, by many of its strengths. I, however, believe that it is most clearly effective in achieving control, compliance, conformity, and submission. How effective it is in achieving basic value change, in bringing about "conversions," and in eliciting real "commitment" is harder to judge. This is not meant to imply that there have not been important changes in values; there obviously have been, although the amount of change doubtless varies, depending on the groups one considers and at what time. For the nation as a whole, however, the changes may be less far-reaching than is sometimes assumed.

It is a reasonable hypothesis, in my opinion, that there is a considerable amount of dissimulation and role playing by large numbers of people in China. Many probably simply do what they feel they must do to get along under the system. Doubtless, many differences exist between public postures and private beliefs. There is unquestionably a great deal of ritualism in political behavior. Clearly, many old values persist, sometimes in new form. But more research is needed if we are to have a better basis for judging both the extent to which the Chinese today accept new values, or old ones, or some complicated mix, and the extent to which their loyalties focus on old social institutions or on the new political groups. At present, we really do not know.

It would also be illuminating to have more research on how much "cognitive dissonance" may exist in China today; that is, how much are people disturbed by the roles they have to play in relation to the realities they see? Perhaps it is easier in Chinese culture than in some others to cope with the diffences between the private views that people hold and the public roles that they must play. In any case, more research should be done on this question.

Further research is needed on the evolution of the mobilization system in China. This system has been impressively effective in many respects, but there is some evidence that its effectiveness has declined, in part because of a tendency toward routinization. Is this in fact the trend? This area too deserves systematic investigation.

Much more research needs to be done on the ways in which traditional forms of communication persist, sub rosa, outside the official system, transmitting values different from those officially propagated in the Party-controlled system. How and to what extent are information and values differing from those contained in the official media disseminated informally through friends, families, factions, cliques, local groups, and the rumor network? There is evidence that a great deal of communication of this sort persists in China, totally outside the official system. But more study is needed on how much there is, on how important it is, and on the extent to which it transmits values that seriously compete with those propagated in the Party's system.

Further research is also needed on other questions concerning possible limitations and costs inherent in China's present communication system, which may counterbalance some of its more obvious advantages. How much does the deliberate restriction of the information disseminated create problems for the regime, retard the development of an efficient economy and social system, and work against real integration of the society? There is little question that it does create problems, but how serious are they? What costs, in terms of utilization of talent, does the system involve? One can argue that in many respects it effectively mobilizes new talent; to a notable degree, it stresses the potentialities of ordinary people and encourages local initiative, creativity, and problem solving, thereby fostering local innovation and change. It is probably true, however, that the system, by demanding conformity and perpetuating learning by rote, wastes much talent. It clearly has inhibited the creativity of many of the country's ablest intellectuals. How should one weigh these pluses and minuses?

Still another question deserves careful examination. Although, in theory, the "mass line" demands effective two-way communication both up and down the regime's hierarchies, in practice does it operate this way? Considerable evidence indicates that, although communication downward is usually very effective, there are many inhibitions that make communication upward less effective. The channels for communication upward do exist, but the deep sense of hierarchy and awe of authority held by the Chinese appear to create major obstacles to having effective communication upward to the leadership. It also appears that generally there is relatively little effective lateral communication in Chinese society today. Communication channels focus on the center, and the center seems to discourage lateral communication among different groups and regions. If all this is true, these are obviously flaws in the system. How serious are they?

Further research also needs to be done on the role of communication in China today as it affects conflict resolution. There is considerable evidence that in some respects the system inhibits social conflicts; it clearly provides controlled outlets for aggressive impulses. However, it is also clear that in some respects the system fosters tensions and conflicts. By stressing contradictions among different groups and classes, the leadership under Mao tried to maintain a state of constant dynamic tension in society. Without doubt, there were many overt as well as latent tensions in the society. Periodically, they have come to the fore, either when the leadership has deliberately highlighted them or when the system has temporarily broken down.

The system appeared to operate most effectively during the regime's first few years. Because China's leadership was unified at that time, the regime's propaganda and mass mobilization campaigns generally reflected a consensus at the center, were articulated in a planned way, and were systematically implemented throughout the country, down to the bottom levels of society. The leadership was doubtless genuinely shocked by the evidence of latent dissidence and tension in Chinese society during the Hundred Flowers period. In the early 1960s, during the post–Great Leap depression, the entire political control system loosened and the intensity and effectiveness of communication from the center temporarily declined, in part because of the adverse impact of economic conditions on the entire political and social system. Then, during the Cultural Revolution, when Mao and his closest followers deliberately attacked the bureaucracies, the system temporarily broke down. As a result, communications from the center no longer originated from a single authoritative source; they emanated from many competitive factional groups. At the end of the Cultural Revolution, steps were taken to restore a centralized system but in the ongoing struggle among Chinese leaders, conflict was more notable than consensus up until the death of Mao. Without a unified leadership to set clear goals and define values, competing groups argued fiercely over priorities and policies. Different bureaucratic and interest groups in the top elite actually debated against one another in the media. A crucial question now is whether, with Mao gone and the radicals purged, China's leadership will be able to restore a more unified system, as they are obviously trying to do.

Many of the observations and judgments made here are tentative hypotheses. All of them are debatable. They all raise questions that deserve further research. More, and better, research needs to be done both on the system in its ideal form and on its strengths and weaknesses in practice.

Much can be done by expanding the kinds of research already completed on the communication system in China, applying old approaches to new questions. However, a need for new approaches also exists. In particular, there needs to be a wider use of two techniques. One is sophisticated content analysis of media output. To date, much of the research done on Chinese media has focused on how the communication system is organized. There should now be more extensive and more sophisticated content analysis to determine the values and information communicated by the system.

Second, in order to understand how the system actually works in practice, a greater effort should be made to combine media research with interviewing. One cannot know how the Chinese system really works, and what effects it has, simply by reading the press or listening to the radio. There needs to be deeper analysis of the actual impact of the system through direct observation through intensive interviewing of people who have lived under it. More systematic efforts can be made to interview both refugees from China and visitors of many kinds who have gone to China—especially overseas Chinese who have returned home, many of whom have had a kind of experience quite different from that of most other visitors. Recently, greater opportunities for interviewing people within China itself have begun to open up.

A great many of the most interesting and important questions that now need to be explored require research that combines indepth interviewing with sophisticated content analysis. Research of this kind is needed to provide greater understanding not just of the surface appearance of China's new communication system but also of its strengths and weaknesses in operation. And it is this kind of understanding of the system that is required to improve our knowledge of the broad political, economic, social, and cultural changes that have occurred, and are still occurring, in the world's most revolutionary and most populous nation.

17

Changes in Chinese Culture: What Do We Really Know?

Francis L. K. Hsu
Godwin C. Chu

In old China, an herbal physician faced an interesting dilemma when he had to attend to an unmarried female patient. Because such a young woman was not supposed to be seen or touched by a strange male, all the physician could do was to have a string tied to her wrist and "take the pulse" at the other end of the string outside the curtained bed.

This is how modern scholars feel when they attempt to measure the dimensions of cultural change in China today, and the role of communication in that process. The evidence is, in a word, secondhand. Much valuable data have been collected by scholars who have been studying China in a multidisciplinary perspective, but the physical restrictions on data sources have been severe.[1] Official publications—the *People's Daily, Red Flag,* short stories, picture storybooks—are readily available, but they usually present limited perspectives. Provincial radio broadcasts, which can add local color, are also part of the official network. Since 1972, many visitors, including those of Chinese ancestry, have been admitted into China, and they have brought back accounts of their personal experiences. The representativeness of their experiences, however, interesting as they are, is as yet unascertained. Refugees and former residents sometimes provide useful information and occasional insight on those aspects of the Chinese system that are unrelated to their decision to leave. Asking refugees for their opinions and attitudes, however, calls to mind the pitfalls of relying on army deserters for an assessment of military life. It is, in effect, like asking Martin Luther to evaluate the Catholic church.

Because of these difficulties, as well as the enormous scope of the issues involved, students of modern China are in reality more like the traditional physician taking a pulse by remote control than social scientists analyzing systematic, empirical evidence. The discussion that follows should be viewed in this light.

As editors, we shall not attempt to sum up the findings. The papers in this book speak for themselves and contribute to a whole. Nor do we presume to speak for the contributors. The diverse observations expressed in this volume will be best appreciated in their original tenor. In this chapter, we merely note some of the salient points that we learned from the conference. We shall discuss them within the framework of four related questions:

1. What aspects of Chinese culture have shown visible signs of change?
2. What aspects of Chinese culture have manifested a trend of continuity with the past?
3. What are the roles of communication in facilitating the process of cultural change and, conversely, in contributing to cultural continuity?
4. What core attributes in traditional Chinese culture can increase our understanding of the dynamics of cultural change in contemporary China?

Self-Material Relations

Of the three components in the framework of cultural change proposed in the Introduction to this volume, we shall first discuss the relations between the individual and his material environment. This is an aspect about which we have somewhat more knowledge from other sources, and for this reason the chapters in this volume have not dwelt upon these relations. It is also, however, the aspect of Chinese culture that appears to have changed more substantially than any other during the last three decades.

The most profound change has been in the ownership of and access to means of production. The small minority of people who previously owned most of China's available resources no longer enjoy that privilege. Arable land, the basis of subsistence for the rural population, has been transferred initially from the landlords to the peasants and later to the cooperatives and the communes. Factories, mines, and business establishments have been nationalized since the late 1950s, and are now operated by the state.[2]

The new relations between the individual and material resources have varied, mostly along the rural-urban dimension. In the rural sector, the majority of the peasants, except those who are excluded from full-fledged commune membership *(she-yüan)* because of their class background, have acquired a voice in the management of resources and distribution of rewards to an extent unknown in the past. They now participate in drawing up local production plans and have more or less equitable shares of the crops.[3] In the urban sector, however, something similar to the former owner-employee relations remains, except that the new owners are the state. Demands for wage adjustments were raised as early as the 1950s, but it was not until recently, in the aftermath of the Gang of Four episode, that some moderate scales of wage increments were approved.

For centuries, Chinese peasants had lived at a subsistence level, partly due to inefficient technology and partly due to inadequate access to resources. Their response to the economic environment had been one of adaptation and almost resignation. To traditional Chinese peasants, efforts to improve material well-being were of marginal usefulness, if not entirely futile. Now, with the changes in the economic structure at the grassroots level, Chinese peasants seem to be responding to development programs with renewed energy. The Tachai experience, because it was a model, may not be typical. Nevertheless, it signifies a gradual change of orientation from resignation and adjustment toward manipulation and even control of the material environment.

One aspect of self-material relations in traditional Chinese culture, however, has shown subtle continuity. This concerns the pursuit of material gains. The Chinese, like any other people, have sought to fulfill their material needs. The pursuit of material gains as a primary if not ultimate goal of life, however, appears to have been alien to most Chinese under the Confucian influence. This is not to say that the Chinese did not enjoy material comfort. But there was usually something else, either of an affiliative nature (such as family togetherness), or of a symbolic nature (such as loyalty to someone of superior status, or dedication to a principle), that was more important to Chinese people of different backgrounds.

The new government in China has not only reaffirmed the low priority of material pursuits, but has even gone a step further by denouncing individual material gains as undesirable. An intriguing manifestation of this trend is the recurring debates on the use of material incentive versus symbolic reward as a stimulant for performance and production.[4] Taken at face value, these debates may give the misleading impression that some members in the Party leadership are putting material pursuits above other objectives. The real issue, however, is not whether the emphasis should be placed on material incentive per se or on symbolic rewards such as medals, banners, or hero status. Even those leaders in the Party who have advocated a policy known as "material stimulation" *(wu-chih tz'u-chi)* are only proposing minor material rewards—piece-rate wages and small year-end bonuses, for example. They are by no means espousing the unrestrained pursuit of material gains by the individuals. The deemphasis of individual material gains is indisputable. By and large, our impression is that the Chinese are no more (and possibly less) concerned about individual material pursuit now than in the past.[5]

Self-Other Relations

Regarding self-other relations in Chinese culture, a complex picture of varying degrees of change and continuity emerges. Let us first discuss kinship and family relations, the very basis of the traditional Chinese sociocultural fabric. The pervasive influence of the kinship groups that once dominated social, economic, and political life has indeed been greatly weakened. Most of the people who held high-status positions by virtue of their kinship links, especially at the local level, have been removed. The Party, instead of kinship groups, is the most powerful organization in China.

The change of status occupants, however, does not necessarily mean that kinship-oriented patterns of social relations have been abandoned. The findings of Thomas Bernstein, S. K. Lau, William Parish, Martin Whyte, and Francis Hsu all suggest the persistence of social relations among local cadres and peasants that are still oriented toward kinship patterns. When vacancies are available in factories, for instance, they are reserved for children of the factories' own workers, so that they can be brought back from the "sent-down" villages. In the production brigades and teams, cadres have a tendency to protect their kinsmen and to rely on them for support at times of political criticism. Informants in Hong Kong to whom Godwin Chu talked in 1977 suggested that this trend has become more apparent in southern China since the Cultural Revolution, which weakened the local cadres' dependence on the Party apparatus. During the upheavals of 1966–1968, local cadres in Kwangtung often had to turn to their kinsmen for help when they were being attacked by the various factions within the Party.

Kinship ties existing at the grassroots level apparently compete with the small *hsiao-tsu* groups that Martin Whyte examines. Although the kinship structure no longer controls the economic life of the Chinese, as it did prior to 1949, it nevertheless provides a residual but sufficiently important network for communication among the people.

The Chinese family has remained intact, as far as we know, despite occasional reports to the contrary. Parents still have a voice, sometimes a major one, in the spouse selection of their children.[6] In the villages, married children are likely to stay with their parents, partly because of government policy to discourage outward mobility to the cities. Rural family members are most likely to work at the family private plots together. Grandparents play an important role in caring for the young. In the urban areas, the national program of sending students to the country has in some cases even heightened the children's dependence on their parents for supplies and financial subsidy. The traditional attitude that "parents can never be wrong" seems to be no longer universally endorsed. On the other hand, children who are eager to criticize their parents for not following the teachings of Chairman Mao Tse-tung are probably not in the majority, despite the publicity of such cases during the Cultural Revolution. The impression of visitors of Chinese origin suggests on the whole a degree of warmth and respect in the Chinese family today that is similar to what prevailed in the past.

Chinese women have undoubtedly improved their status, inside the family as well as outside. In most cases, the wife contributes to the family income by gainful work. If she and her husband happen to live in different locations, an urban situation which is not uncommon, then she has almost complete independence from her spouse. Many Chinese women have apparently attained positions of considerable responsibility at the local level, although the top national leadership is still primarily male. It is difficult to say whether and to what extent the husband still plays the dominant role within the family. The new marriage law was promulgated in the early 1950s. In general, we know that the man and the woman enter into a marriage as equal partners. We also know that when both the husband and wife work, they share the housework. Both in protrayals of real life and in revolutionary short stories, as analyzed by Ai-li Chin, the model wife is often shown as someone who does not hesitate to correct her husband's error, either in ideology or in official role behavior. This she does in a good-natured, half-reproving manner. Is this a predominant new behavioral mode? Or does the Chinese wife still retain the traditional deference to her husband in important family decisions and in official business? We have no clear answer. We suspect, however, that models like Li Shuang-shuang are probably still the exceptions, not the rule. The very fact that these models need publicizing would imply that they are not quite universal. Then, even though many Chinese women now hold professional positions, Chinese society is still a man's world as far as major decisions are concerned. Men tend to have better political connections than do women.

We have observed in the Introduction that role relations were to a great extent subordinate to affect relations in traditional Chinese society. How far has the importance of the five *t'ung* relations, which traditionally provided an affect-based network in which various types of obligations and duties were transacted, been modified? Our impression is that there has been some change, but not nearly as much as what is officially expected. An important sign of the persistence of the old *t'ung* relations is the practice of *tsou hou men,* that is, "enter through the back door." A letter sent to the *People's Daily* by two Party members in March 1977 further confirms the prevalence of the *t'ung* relations:

> In recent years, due to the interference and destruction wrought by the Gang of Four, some comrades do not pay attention to keeping the classified information of the Party. Others rather carelessly disseminate internal materials that should not be disseminated. There are still others who would pass on important instructions from their superior, without authorization, to their "old *t'ung shih*" [former colleagues], "old *pu-hsia*" [former subordinates], "dear ones," and "close friends," whether or not they are Party members. . . .[7]

Both from visitors to China and from refugees in Hong Kong, we gain the impression that such personal connections are still important. In fact, the Cultural Revolution was launched in part to correct this condition. There are even indications that the purges and mass criticisms of 1966 and 1967 may have given some impetus to the importance of these personal connections. Since accusations during the purges were often not directed at verifiable individual wrongdoing but were instead predicated on distinguishing those who belonged to the established bureaucracy from those who wanted to destroy the old bureaucracy, some hard-pressed targets of attack often found old personal bonds more reliable than new official connections. And after the downfall of the Gang of Four, the official media revealed detailed accounts of how members of the Gang, particularly Wang Hung-wen, developed a powerful network of personal followers in his Shanghai base whom he tried to place in key positions in various provinces and in the central government. On the other side of the fence, Teng Hsiao-p'ing also seems to have gathered around him an influential group of allies consisting mostly of old comrades from the Long March days. It is primarily old affect, rather than official role, that binds the opposing camps. Though clad in new garb, *t'ung* relations seem to be very much alive.

Hierarchy was a fact of life in traditional Chinese society. Those in authority did not have to apologize for exercising their authority and those in lower positions felt no embarrassment in complying with it. What, then, is the situation today? China under communism is not an egalitarian society—indeed, no society can ever be. By and large, however, the People's Republic of China is more egalitarian than before in a variety of ways. Income differences are probably fewer than in most other societies. While accounts of luxuries and waste surfaced during the initial campaign against the Gang of Four, nobody has ever been accused of amassing huge personal wealth. High-level cadres live in relative comfort compared to the average citizen, but their privileges are not automatically transferable to their offspring. (This is not to say, however, that children of high-level cadres enjoy no advantages; better access to higher education apparently is one.)

Compliance behavior underwent some significant changes during the Cultural Revolution, as Lowell Dittmer has illustrated. The mass criticism campaigns during that period of struggle and disorder emboldened the common people to speak out against their immediate superiors, something a majority of Chinese would not have attempted in the past. This spirit has apparently been retained since the Cultural Revolution, as illustrated by two events. During the campaign against Lin Piao and Confucius in 1974 and 1975, people in several major cities took advantage of the movement to criticize the Party in several *tatzupao* in public places. For example, the severity and sharpness of the criticism in Li I-che's *tatzupao* in

Canton would match, if not pale, the harshest complaints by intellectuals of the previous generation during the Hundred Flowers movement of 1957.[8] Dittmer's informant told him that, but for the Cultural Revolution in which the Chinese were encouraged to fight the established bureaucracy, the Tienanmen Square riots would not have occurred.

How far this trend will continue remains unclear. Within the last year, institutions of higher learning have become more fully attended, and some of the latest (1978) visitors to China have related how students seem again to be as attentive to their teachers as before the Cultural Revolution.

A very important traditional attribute in self-other relations in traditional China was interpersonal harmony. Confrontations were generally avoided as much as possible. Cooperation within the kinship and local network was far more valued than individual competition. When material resources were scarce, the culturally endorsed Chinese response was to withdraw from competing rather than to fight for them. A widely known Chinese story was that of K'ung Yung, who in adult life became a noted Han Dynasty statesman. One day his father brought home a few pears. When young K'ung Yung realized that there were not enough pears for him and his elder brothers, he declined his share. This exemplary behavior was praised as a virtue in every grade school book prior to 1949.

Another culturally encouraged trait in old China that contributed to interpersonal harmony was moderation. Since many disputes in daily life concern allocation of material gain or status, striving for moderation by reducing one's desires, so the philosophy went, can minimize them. When a conflict did develop to a point where legitimate interests were infringed upon, Chinese culture still encouraged tolerance for losses. As a popular saying went: "A present loss may be an eventual gain" *(Ch'ih k'uei chiu shih p'ien yi)*.

This attitude is in marked contrast to the stated new ideals of struggle, conflict, and "daring to challenge the tide." But to what extent has the traditional emphasis on harmony in interpersonal relations been altered in real life? Only one thing is certain: harmony is no longer an officially endorsed virtue; struggle is. During the many campaigns since 1949, the Chinese have participated in mass criticisms, confrontations, and struggles of varying intensity, culminating in the Cultural Revolution. There is much portrayal of violent retaliation by the Chinese people against the imperialists, the Kuomintang, and other class enemies in picture storybooks for children, as Parris Chang has shown. A dual standard seems to be rising—love your class brothers and hate your class enemies. The current campaign against the Gang of Four provides another illustration of what the Chinese are supposed to do to their enemies, once the latter have been identified.

Does all this mean that Chinese culture is being transformed into one which endorses the principle of an eye for an eye and a tooth for a tooth? We think not. We are not suggesting that the traditional virtue of interpersonal harmony is being followed to the same extent as it was in the past; we simply do not know. But we suggest that the manifest behavior of struggle and criticism contains a large degree of dissimulation,[9] or "ritualized" role playing, as Martin Whyte has phrased it. There is no denying that during the initial period of the Cultural Revolution, many young rebels went about the struggle and criticism with genuine enthusiasm. But the seasoned cadres, and the adult population in general, have seen the way the "tide" has changed back and forth, and have learned that one way to survive in the see-saw battle between the radical faction and the so-called rightist faction is not to make premature and unalterable commitment. This mode of behavior must be troublesome to the Party leadership.[10]

A final thought: since harmony is no longer an official virtue, we would not expect the Chinese to seek distinction and social recognition by exemplary harmonious behavior. There is little doubt that messages regarding pro-social violence were initally received with enthusiasm among the younger generation. Whether the present younger generation will continue this trend as they gain more experience remains to be seen.

Self-Ideas Relations

Man's relations with the social and economic environments are permeated with ideological undertones. Indeed, from the self-material and self-other relations in a society, we can extract some of the predominant values and beliefs that provide the cognitive and affective foundation for the system. We have already alluded to changes in interpersonal relations and material incentives that bear upon values and beliefs. We shall now examine the traditional Chinese ideology that the Party leadership has been seeking to change through the use of communication.

The first predominant value is fatalism. Fatalism refers to a set of cause and effect perceptions that are considered to be beyond human control. It leads not only to adaptation to, rather than conquest of, nature, but also to acceptance of or resignation to the larger social and economic system. The individual may attempt to do something to improve his or her position in the system, but the existence of such a system is seen as final.

We think that this traditional belief in fatalism is on the wane. The Chinese are being told that if they work together, nothing is impossible. In this effort, China's new leaders are assisted by certain dormant elements in tradition. Furthermore, the Chinese government has demonstrated the new spirit by actual, phsyical achievements such as the Tachai Brigade, the Tach'ing Oilfield, the giant bridges across the Yangtze River, and the new railroads linking Szechwan with Kueichow. The peasants can see with their own eyes what happens as a result of their own efforts.

Thus, although for ages the Chinese have had a saying that "human determination can overcome heaven's will" *(jen ting shen t'ien),* not until now have they been able to put this concept to an empirical test.

Related to fatalism is another traditional belief, the power of the gods. Belief in the supernatural is pan-human.[11] It is man's attempt to make sense of what he cannot understand and reflects his hope that gods can change what he considers unalterable by man. Belief in the supernatural apparently still exists in China today, as Lau Siu-kai shows in his chapter. We do not know how extensive such beliefs are in Kwangtung, where Lau collected his data, nor whether his findings from Kwangtung are representative of other regions of China. There are logical reasons for us to think that, as technology for the control of agricultural and health conditions becomes more widely available, belief in the supernatural will diminish. The problem, however, may not be so simple in reality.[12]

A major new value which the Chinese are being encouraged to adopt is altruism—selfless service. Mao's essays "Serve the People" and "In Memory of Dr. Norman Bethune" espouse this new value. Many of the heroes that have been posthumously praised as models for national emulation, whether they were Party cadres or members of the People's Liberation Army, exemplify the spirit of selfless service. This is the value that millions of sent-down students are asked to embrace in the villages and remote areas of resettlements.

Selfless service as a value is not completely new in China. Sons have always been praised for sacrificing themselves for the comfort, pleasure, health, and safety of their parents. That was the core of filial piety. The Chinese even had a motto, "restrain oneself for the benefit of others" *(k'o-chi wei-jen)*.

The difference, however, is that whereas filial piety was formerly centered in the kinship group, the selfless service now being promoted applies to society at large. Also, whereas in the past the emphasis was on "restraining" oneself so that other people could receive a bigger share of scarce resources, the accent today is on exerting oneself largely so that the total resource pie will be bigger for the benefit of other people and, presumably, for oneself as well. The ultimate limit of this self-exertion is to sacrifice one's own life, which many of the new national heroes did not hesitate to do. Therefore, we might say that the new value of self-exertion is simply a modification of the old one of self-negation.

Once again, it is extremely difficult even to speculate as to what extent the new value of altruistic, selfless service has been adopted. Because of the subtle cultural continuity noted, this new value may be more readily acceptable to the Chinese than to people raised in other cultures where the focus is on self-gratification. William Parish, for instance, found some relations between the presence of communication media and altruistic practices at the village level. Evidence also exists, however, that many young Chinese found their "sent-down" experience frustrating, as Thomas Bernstein has shown. Some of these youths learned that what the administrative cadres at the middle and lower levels did was inconsistent with what the Party said in the mass media, thus creating a situation of conflicting messages.

Another new value is loyalty to the collectivity. Once again we can trace a linkage with the past, in terms of the Chinese patterns of kinship allegiance. To the Chinese, kinship composed both a permanent group and a reference group as well; it served as a framework in which to measure achievement and social standing. Community decisions and local disputes were usually settled along kinship lines. The core of this loyalty was filial piety, which radiated from one's relationship to parents toward a wider network. The existence of this traditional group orientation has probably helped rural Chinese readjust their lifestyle to the new social organization built on the basis of the commune. Both official statements and accounts by refugees in Hong Kong seem to bear out the fact that Chinese peasants have developed a new loyalty to their local groups, primarily the production teams, which in most cases are the same as the villages. They have a tendency to protect the collective welfare of their team as a way of securing their own material well-being, but their concern for the collective interest seems to wane as the scope widens to include the production brigade and the commune.

During the decade before the death of Chairman Mao, the radical group now identified as the Gang of Four made various attempts to move the basis of collective loyalty away from the production team to the brigade, the commune, and even the entire proletariat. The revolutionary opera *Song of the Dragon River (Lung Chiang Sung),* for instance, strongly espouses this theme. The opera shows how the Lung Chiang Brigade chose to sacrifice its own land in order to divert a flood, thus eventually saving many more acres in the larger collectivity. Merle Goldman's chapter pinpoints a hidden agenda of the campaign for the dictatorship of the proletariat, namely, the transfer of loyalty from the local collective to the proletariat at large. Our impression, however, is that such a change is not likely to take place unless and until further alterations of the economic structure occur at the grassroots level. There are few indications that the current leadership under Chairman Hua Kuo-feng and Vice Premier Teng Hsiao-p'ing is ready for such a structural change.

Effects of Communication

The Chinese leadership in the last three decades has initiated numerous communication campaigns to change the traditional Chinese culture. To what extent have these campaigns been successful? To answer this question, we shall consider the nature of the communication system in China, the messages produced by the system, the sociocultural environment in which the messages are received, the initial response of the audience, and, finally, the secondary effects of these messages.

We recognize that China is not a homogeneous society. The Chinese population consists of various categories: cadres, intellectuals, urban dwellers, rural peasants, soldiers, and so on. And there are those, a relatively small minority, who have been classified as undesirable remnants of the old society. As Doak Barnett has pointed out, the intensity with which the Chinese experience the impact of official communications varies considerably. The following discussion presents a general perspective only, and needs to be further qualified if applied to any specific group.

Since the 1950s, the People's Republic of China has developed perhaps the world's best-coordinated communication system, as Frederick Yu has demonstrated in his chapter. Even without the use of highly efficient technology, the Chinese leaders have been able to reach large segments of the population with various kinds of messages. This objective is being achieved by the ingenious use of many media, some modern and some traditional, supported by an extensive network of small groups, the various features of which have been summarized by Barnett.

Will this communication system be able to influence the perceptual input of the audience to such an extent that their overt behavior and internal values can be changed in the direction desired by the Party?

To answer this question, we shall also consider the audience that receives the messages. In the literature on the effects of communication, there is an implicit assumption that regards the audience as the "recipients" of the messages, who are either affected or not affected. This view inadvertently treats the audience as a passive receptacle. The audience may be seen occasionally as sending feedback to the communicator, but the feedback is viewed largely from the perspective of the communicator, who can have the benefit of readjusting his message to improve effectiveness. In reality, the individual in an audience is actively surveying his environment for information in order to evaluate his alternatives. He *responds* to the communication; he does not merely receive it. The behavioral or attitudinal modifications he makes are what *he* considers to be appropriate and rewarding under the circumstances, based on his active perceiving and evaluating, whether or not they are consistent with the intended outcome of the communicator.

Two basic questions need to be asked about the effects of communication on values and attitudes: What determines the people's perception? What is the role of messages in the people's perception? The messages they receive are undoubtedly an important input, sometimes the only input. But people also rely on their direct experience. As a contemporary Communist theoretician, Mao apparently recognized these two factors when he emphasized the importance of "correct recognition" to ideological reform. Following the various measures of social and economic change, the Chinese now live in an environment that represents a set of life experiences different from that of the past, and have made adjustments accordingly. A loosely Marxist interpretation would suggest that new values and beliefs will develop from the new experience, particularly from its economic aspect. Mao, however, has gone a step further. He wanted to use communication campaigns to make sure that the new experience was perceived and interpreted in a way that would lead to the desired ideological change. We shall refer to this as the specific *content* effects of communication.

In China, we have seen that messages reaching the people come from multiple sources. There are the official media, of course, but even here disagreements are sometimes expressed and are apparently detectable, as Merle Goldman has analyzed. Wilbur Schramm has referred to such disagreements as "incongruence of messages."[13] Many unofficial channels contribute to a further incongruence. The "alley news," or *hsiao-tao hsiao-hsi* which Thomas Bernstein discussed, transmits in face-to-face contacts information and interpretation that can be at variance with official views. The Party is apparently aware of the prevalence of *hsiao-tao hsiao-hsi,* as indicated by the letter in the *People's Daily* we referred to earlier: "There are those comrades who like to play the role of the 'well informed.' They are particularly interested in *hsiao-tao hsiao-hsi.* They probe around, and gossip. . . ."[14]

Another incongruence that may have hindered the effects of communication is what Martin Whyte refers to as messages "not singing the same tune." This is clearly illustrated by Bernstein in his analysis of the rustication *(hsia-hsiang)* movement. While the official media under the direction of the central leadership was extolling the virtue of selfless service and altruistic spirit, the lower-level cadres, under the administrative pressure of getting enough students to go to the villages, were resorting to various kinds of nonaltruistic appeals.

The incongruence of messages is probably a major factor that interferes with the "correct" perception of the new experience by the Chinese. When competing or conflicting messages reach the audience from the official and grapevine channels, or when the official messages are inconsistent with one's direct experience, the effectiveness of the former is likely to be reduced.

Research in persuasive communication suggests that the credibility of the source of the message is another important factor for effectiveness.[15] From Lynn White's chapter, we get the impression that the official media in the 1950s were not all accorded undisputed credibility by the people. The accusations recently directed at the Gang of Four suggest that this credibility had not improved during the several years before 1976. The possibility that some of the models and heroes in that period were perceived to be less than realistic is suggested by the editorial in the *Liberation Army Daily,* cited earlier by Godwin Chu.

A further finding from research in mass communication points out the importance of group influence in shaping the response of the audience.[16] The group one belongs to can apply pressure to enforce behavioral conformity and at the same time provide the desirable social context to induce genuine conversion. China uses small groups for these purposes much more extensively than do other Communist countries. From Martin Whyte's chapter, however, we get the impression that these small groups are not as effective, or even as extensive, as accounts in the official media suggest. It seems that a significant amount of private communication still exists and probably weakens the "correct recognition" of objective reality as defined by the Party.

Another factor relevant to communication effects is the predisposition of the audience. In terms of cultural change, this is reflected in the existing sociocultural environment, which mediates the effects of communication. Both direct experience and verbal messages, whether official or not, are evaluated in the light of this environment. In the communication campaigns of the early 1950s, as analyzed by Vivienne Shue, this evaluation was consistent with some of the basic values and desires of the peasants. Such campaigns were therefore successful in arousing the peasants' emotional resentment against the landlord class and in cultivating a new normative basis for the peasants' participation in the purge of the landlords. In other campaigns—the youth rustication movement, for instance—this congruence with the sociocultural environment was not so apparent, and the result has been less than a success.

Other than this type of effect, which is attributable to the specific communication content, we have noted a secondary effect in China that is the result of the audience's initial response to official messages. The Red Guards may be used as an illustration. First, there were the revolutionary messages about destroying the old and establishing the new. The Red Guards responded by joining the movement; they engaged in new behavior, some of which might or might not have been intended by the official messages. But because of their new experience in the movement, certain changes took place in their attitudes and subsequent behavior, as illustrated by Lowell Dittmer. Thus, the source of effect was the *experience* the Red Guards had in responding to the original messages, rather than the message content itself. The secondary, *experiential* effect seems to be quite noticeable in China, and deserves closer analysis.

Apparently the nature of the experiential effect varies with people's different encounters. As Dittmer has observed, the Red Guards and those individuals who were the targets of struggle had entirely different experiences. It is interesting to ask, however, whether these two groups, despite their divergent initial exposures, came away from the Cultural Revolution with some common residual modifications in their values that are long lasting.

These two types of effects, whether due to the content or the secondary experience, are by and large traceable to some identifiable messages. They are either behavioral, manifested in modification of conduct, or evaluative, seen in change of attitudes and values. A third type of effect is cognitive; that is, the cumulation of messages changes the general perception of the social-political context in which the Chinese function. According to some informants Parish and Whyte talked to, for instance, most peasants in Kwangtung had a good idea of the general outlines of government programs.[17] By and large, the Chinese are aware of the new political culture, as described by Lucian Pye, and understand its varying degrees of importance to them depending on their class status, residential locale, and position. We shall call this *contextual* effect.[18]

While the general socialist context has remained the same in China since 1949, an important feature of the Chinese political culture, particularly in the last two decades, has been its many twists and turns, some more subtle than others. The Chinese people must recognize them in order to function effectively in their various roles. The campaign for the dictatorship of the proletariat and the *Water Margin* campaign, analyzed by Merle Goldman, are appropriate examples. The official media play an essential role in providing the appropriate social-political context.

Finally, there is the *dissemination* effect, which refers to the extent to which agricultural technology and scientific information are distributed to the final users. This kind of effect seems to depend as much on the capacity of the communication channels as it does on the acceptability of the messages. The channel capacity, particularly for disseminating agricultural technology to the communes, as shown by Lau Siu-kai, appears to be rather impressive.

Consider the following as a general hypothesis for further investigation. As far as the impact of communication on cultural change in China is concerned, the effects attributable to specific content do not seem to be pronounced, for two reasons: first, the incongruence of the messages themselves; and second, the divergence between the messages and the prevailing sociocultural environment. Because of these two factors, the diverse communication input reaching the people from both the official media and grapevine sources seems to have contributed as much to continuity as to change in the Chinese culture.

The experiential effects have on occasion been dramatic, as in the Cultural Revolution. Such effects seem to have left some lasting impact on the youth who took part in the Cultural Revolution. The cumulative, contextual effects do not show themselves in any remarkable fashion, but they have important consequences for the people as well as for the Party leadership. It is through these contextual effects of communication that the people and the leadership adjust to each other's expectations and wishes as changes gradually evolve in the Communist Chinese social system as well as in its participants. What eventually may assume great importance to China's development and change are the dissemination effects, particularly for agricultural technology and scientific information. Quite possibly, the new leadership in the post-Mao era will place more emphasis on dissemination effects rather than on specific content effects for cultural change. That, however, remains to be seen.

Psychosocial Homeostasis: A Possible Answer

Mao wanted to build a new socialist China on the basis of the new socialist man. The Party has taken measures to change economic and social relations in China. Over the years, the Party has been using communication campaigns to lay a new ideological foundation for the proletarian social system. The success has been partial. Why?

Our ordinary misconception is that China is traditional and

America, for instance, is very new. The reality is that every society has continuity with the past. China today is founded on the cultural heritage of the past, one that came down to the individual through the channeling of the Chinese social organizaton. So is the United States. Its cultural heritage dates back to Greece and Rome, and in fact even earlier.

Once this is understood we can see that American society is as "traditional" as its Chinese counterpart. The basic difference between them is that while the Chinese cultural heritage and social organization have consistently promoted continuity with the past, the American cultural heritage and social organization have forever been claiming discontinuity from the past. Therefore, the United States differs from China in one important respect. China has a tradition of continuity of continuity (or stability), while the United States has a tradition of continuity of discontinuity (or change).[19]

The tradition of discontinuity and that of continuity with the past led to different consequences for the two societies. The point is: the two general patterns are equally difficult to change. And it might be further hypothesized that, contrary to popular belief, a society such as the United States is not really future oriented and prone to change, but rather present oriented and resistant to change.

All this takes us once more to the important distinction and link between role and affect in human behavior. Social scientists have yet to appreciate and deal squarely with the primacy of affect in culture. The American commitment to the continuity of discontinuity is buttressed by their particular cultural heritage no less than the Chinese commitment to the continuity of continuity was buttressed by theirs. In their commitment to continuity, the Chinese anchored their view of the world and their place in it on man's relations with fellow men. In their commitment to discontinuity, the Americans anchored their view of the world and their place in it on man's relations with things. Neither of these commitments, along with their consequences, can be easily altered by persuasive messages, any more than the Protestants and Catholics in Northern Ireland, or the Israelis and Arabs in the Middle East, can be convinced to end their hostility by rational arguments.

Herein lies the key to understanding the variable effects of communication campaigns in inducing cultural change in China. The reason that the effects are below the official expectation is partly due to the incongruence of messages which we have discussed earlier, but primarily due to the basic nature of the affect-dominated Chinese culture.

All human beings need to receive and give affect. Their most preferred universal source and object of affect is firstly parents and siblings and then other fellow human beings. Only when human affect is not readily available in a particular cultural setting is there a tendency to seek substitutive sources, such as things or gods. This is the core of what Francis Hsu has called psychosocial homeostasis.[20] In traditional Chinese culture, the affect was earnestly sought and steadily provided in the context of kinship and kinship-oriented wider social relations. It was on the basis of these social relations that economic transactions took place. These same social relations were in turn supported by the traditional Chinese ideology.

This particular Chinese pattern of psychosocial homeostasis, in which the pull of kinship and kinship-oriented wider social relations is stronger than that of other sources of affect, was the substance that held the Chinese society together. In the past, messages reaching the Chinese were acted out through these kinship-oriented social networks, usually resulting in maintaining the traditional culture.[21] Today, these same social networks, permeated with a persistent element of personal affect and buttressed by the residuals of traditional values, form a web of tentacles, as it were, through which the revolutionary messages have to pass and become twisted, thus losing much of their original appeal.

China's situation is quite unlike that of the United States. Because the American psychosocial homeostasis is based on self-material relations, the American people more readily alter their human relations to suit their technological superiority. In China, because the psychosocial homeostasis is primarily based on self-other relations, the Chinese have shown less readiness to bend their human relations in the face of technological change.

It is the enormous strength of the Chinese cultural bond, based as it is on thick affective ties in human relations, that has not only resisted the impact of technological innovation but proven to be difficult for the communication campaigns to penetrate within the span of one generation. Over the years not only the Chinese people seem to have found their way around these campaigns—by moving along with the tide rather than going against it—the local cadres have also developed support networks of their own along kinship-simulated lines. Indeed, even the top leaders, who are the source of ideological inspiration and the impetus for change, have at times not been immune to the influence of traditional Chinese culture, perhaps unknowingly, as reflected in their power alliances.

Chairman Mao, with his insightful understanding of Chinese culture, saw the need to change it at its foundation by an ideological approach. He liked to talk about *The Foolish Old Man Who Moved the Mountain,* a task so awesome in its dimensions that it necessitates the energy and patience of many generations to come. Is it possible that Mao was aware that the cultural bond that held the Chinese together for more than twenty centuries was so strong that it could not be dissolved within his lifetime?

NOTES

1. Oksenberg has identified five primary sources of data: (1) mainland Chinese press and monitored radio broadcasts; (2) former residents of the People's Republic; (3) visitors' accounts; (4) novels and short stories published by the People's Republic; and (5) secret Chinese Communist documents. See Michel Oksenberg, "Sources and Methodological Problems in the Study of Contemporary China," in *Chinese Communist Politics in Action,* ed. A. Doak Barnett (Seattle: University of Washington Press, 1969), pp. 577–606. One more source can be mentioned, now that the door to China is ajar: on-the-scene interviews and observations in China. This is what Lau Siu-kai did for his study in this volume.

2. For an analysis of the nationalization movement in the 1950s, see Godwin C. Chu, "Communication, Social Structural Change, and Capital Formation in People's Republic of China," East-West Communication Institute paper no. 9, East-West Center, Honolulu, Hawaii, 1974. The extent to which the state dominates the economic life of the Chinese was revealed in an article by Chang Ch'un-ch'iao, then vice premier, "On Total Dictatorship against the Capitalist Class," in *Hung Ch'i* [Red Flag] 4 (1975):3–12. In industries, state-operated industries account for 97 percent of all assets, 63 percent of industrial workers, and 86 percent of all industrial productions. Industries operated at the commune level constitute 3 percent of assets, 36.2 percent of industrial workers, and 14 percent of industrial productions. Only 0.8 percent of industrial workers engage in individually operated handicrafts.

3. For a description of China's commune system see William L. Parish, Jr., "Communist Agricultural Organization: China—Team, Brigade, or Commune?" in *Problems of Communism* 25 (March–April, 1976):51–65. Individuals who are offspring of former landlords or former rich peasants perform manual labor in the commune's production teams and earn workpoints, but they do not have the same rights as full-fledged members *(she-yuan)* to vote in local elections or to participate in public meetings.

4. For a discussion of the alternating trend on the use of material incentive versus symbolic incentive, see "Competition and Cooperation: Processes of Task-Oriented

Communication," in Godwin C. Chu, *Radical Change through Communication in Mao's China* (Honolulu: The University Press of Hawaii, 1977), pp. 88–134.

5. The flurry of "Americanization" signs after Vice Premier Teng's visit to the United States was short-lived.

6. See Martin K. Whyte, "Rural Marriage Customs," *Problems of Communism* 26 (July–August, 1977):41–55.

7. Lo Ming-shou and Chang Hsüeh-fa, Communist Party members, "Pay Close Attention to Classified Materials of the Party," *Jenmin Jihpao* [People's Daily], March 28, 1977.

8. The *tatzupao,* signed by Li I-che, was posted in a street in Canton in November 1974 and addressed to Chairman Mao Tse-tung and the fourth National People's Congress. The Canton authorities did not remove it immediately, apparently because they were not sure whether it was part of a power struggle between two contending factions. For a brief summary of the criticisms, see "Lee's Tatzupao: To Mao with Dissent," *The Asian Messenger* (Spring, 1976):27.

9. It may be interesting to speculate on the psychological effects of dissimulation. Let us assume that a person is making a confession in front of his *hsiao-tzu* group without really meaning what he says. Let us further assume that he is doing so in an atmosphere that is supposed to be voluntary. According to the theory of cognitive dissonance of Leon Festinger, that person faces two cognitions that are dissonant with one another: he holds one kind of belief, and yet he is saying something to the contrary with an air of conviction. One way of resolving his dissonance is to change his belief. Dissimulation, however, does not imply the persistence of dissonance if the person realizes that the discrepancy between his own belief and his confession is simply necessary for survival. For a detailed discussion of cognitive dissonance, see Leon Festinger, *A Theory of Cognitive Dissonance* (Stanford, Ca.: Stanford University Press, 1957). For examples of dissimulation and the concern about this problem the Party revealed in the 1950s, see Godwin C. Chu, "Revolutionary Language and Chinese Cognitive Processes," in A. Doak Barnett and Godwin C. Chu, "Communication in China: Perspectives and Hypotheses," East-West Communication Institute paper no. 16, East-West Center, Honolulu, Hawaii, March 1978, pp. 19–20.

10. In the aftermath of the Gang of Four episode, there has been criticism in the official Chinese media about a trend known as *feng p'ai* among the Party cadres. *Feng* (literally, "wind") refers to the vacillating tendency among some of the Party cadres to go with the prevailing tide.

11. In his study, Lau has used the conventional term "superstition" to describe such beliefs. "Superstition," however, carries a negative connotation. The editors prefer the term "belief in the supernatural," which includes religious beliefs.

12. See Francis L. K. Hsu, *Religion, Science, and Human Crisis* (London: Routledge and Keagan Paul, 1952).

13. Remarks made by Wilbur Schramm at the conference.

14. Lo Ming-shou and Chang Hsüeh-fa, "Pay Close Attention to Classified Materials."

15. See C. I. Hovland and W. Weiss, "The Influence of Source Credibility on Communication Effectiveness," *Public Opinion Quarterly* 15 (1951–1952):635–650. Also, C. I. Hovland, I. L. Janis, and H. H. Kelly, *Communication and Persuasion* (New Haven, Conn.: Yale University Press, 1953).

16. See Paul Lazarsfeld and Herbert Menzel, "Mass Media and Personal In-

fluence," in *The Science of Human Communication,* ed. Wilbur Schramm (New York: Basic Books, 1963), pp. 94–115; and Elihu Katz and Paul Lazarsfeld, *Personal Influence: The Part Played by People in the Flow of Mass Communication* (Glencoe, Ill.: The Free Press, 1955). Also Kurt Lewin, "Group Decision and Social Change," in *Readings in Social Psychology,* ed. Eleanor E. Maccoby, Theodore M. Newcomb, and Eugene L. Hartley (New York: Holt, Rinehart and Winston, 1958), pp. 183–211.

17. That the Chinese people, particularly the peasants, may not take the official messages very seriously is suggested by the experience described by Stephen Uhalley at the conference. During his visit to a peasant home in northern China shortly after Nixon's official journey, Uhalley was impressed by the display of a copy of the *People's Daily* that carried a picture of Nixon. Uhalley made a remark to the peasant to compliment his political consciousness. The Chinese peasant seemed puzzled. As it turned out, he had simply used the newspaper to cover up a hole in the wall so that his home would be more presentable to the foreign visitor.

18. A special case of contextual effects is what McCombs and Shaw call the agenda-setting function of mass media. That is, the mass media may not tell us what to think, but they can tell us what to think about. The media, by focusing on certain public issues, set the agenda for the audience, so to speak. See Maxwell McCombs and Donald Shaw, "The Agenda-Setting Function of Mass Media," *Public Opinion Quarterly* 36 (1972):176–187.

19. When we scrutinize the areas where Americans claim change, however, we find that they are rather limited in scope. For the American commitment to change applies only to those areas where change is, by American tradition, acceptable; but not to other areas where change is, again by American tradition, not acceptable. For example, the changes greatly valued in America pertain to production of goods, fashion, housing, means of transportation and communication, fads in childrearing, formation of new clubs (but not their organizational patterns), more efficient weapons, and new worlds to conquer. These are sought and sought after eagerly. But changes, for instance, in rules governing interpersonal privacy, in systems of weight and measurement, in speed limits, in conservation efforts—these and many others are not generally welcome. As to religion, not only can we not change sections of the Bible but even the change from Latin to English in Catholic liturgy is strongly resisted. The difficulties encountered by American women in suffrage, and in trying to join medical and bar associations, are too well known to need documentation. We now have had gay rights demonstrations and affirmative programs for women and minorities, but the ERA has yet to be passed in the required number of states.

20. For a fuller explication of this hypothesis, see Francis Hsu, "Psychosocial Homeostasis and *Jen:* Conceptual Tools for Advancing Psychological Anthropology," *American Anthropologist* 73 (February 1971):23–44.

21. The American emphasis on change is a result of the American pattern of psychosocial homeostasis. The latter is what makes Westerners in general and Americans in particular adhere to their tradition of continuity of discontinuity.

Appendix A
Some Observations
on Confucian Ideology

Fred C. Hung

Over the past two thousand years, Confucianism in China has gone through varied changes. It was influenced by the teachings of several schools, including Legalism, Taoism, the Yin-Yang school, and Buddhism. It was subject to interpretations and reinterpretations, and was often manipulated by China's imperial courts to justify their absolute power. As a result, what was generally accepted as Confucianism in imperial China up to the beginning of the twentieth century was quite different from the ideology originally taught by Confucius himself and by Mencius, one of his chief disciples.

A basic teaching of Confucius is "reciprocity" or "mutual benevolence." In defining the five relationships, that is, the relationships between king and subordinates, father and son, husband and wife, elder brother and younger brother, and between friends, Confucius stresses the importance of self-discipline and mutual benevolence. While the subordinates must obey the king, the latter must be righteous and kind to his subjects. It is also the duty of the king's ministers to let him know of his mistakes and suggest alternative actions. The same general principle applies to the other four types of relationship. Each party must play his or her role correctly if he or she expects the other party to do the same. It is Confucius' belief that only when the principle of mutual benevolence is observed can people live in harmony. Mencius goes even further in saying that when a king misbehaves and treats his subjects without justice, he loses his mandate of heaven and becomes a "mere fellow." Then when he is exiled or killed in a revolution, it is only the mere fellow, not the king, who is exiled or killed. To Mencius, the people are the most precious possession of a nation, the government comes second, and the king is the least important of all. It is because of his "rebellious" ideas that Mencius was not allowed a place in the Temple of Confucius during the reign of the first emperor of the Ming Dynasty.

Absolute despotism was incorporated into Confucianism under the influence of the Legalists and to the delight of China's imperial rulers. Unconditional obedience on the part of the subordinates was demanded while the emperor, under the aura of the "son of heaven," could do no wrong. The mandate of heaven was mystified, with the help of the Yin-Yang school's interpretation of the order of heaven, and was removed several steps from the will of the people. Even if the people were badly treated, it had to be the fault of those evil few who surrounded and misled the emperor. Sooner or later, the emperor would see through their deceptions and purge them. Then order would return. In the meantime, the people were supposed to pledge their complete loyalty to the emperor and unconditionally obey government orders. Such a position was carried to the extreme when it was preached in imperial China that a subordinate must die, and willingly do so, if for whatever reason the emperor ordered him to die. We can easily see that absolute despotism runs counter to the principle of mutual benevolence and became an integral part of Confucianism in imperial China only through a twist of the original teachings of Confucius.

Chinese history is replete with usurpations of the throne. Oftentimes, a minister or general was able to usurp power by pretending allegiance to the emperor and then taking over the throne through a military or political coup. Thus, absolute despotism became a convenient excuse for ambitious and "evil-minded" high officials to participate in court intrigues and gain power. It was always easy to declare a change in the mandate of heaven after the throne was captured and a new dynasty initiated.

Second, later developments and practice of an ideology may be excessive and go far beyond the original intentions of its founders. Confucianism has often been criticized for its elaborate and wasteful rites and its oppression of women. Although Confucius advocates the proper observation of rites in government and private ceremonies, including the worship of heaven and of the ancestors, he believes that it is better to be frugal than to be lavish on such occasions. Most of the elaborate and wasteful rites observed in imperial China or among overseas Chinese today are additions from later centuries.

On several occasions Confucius condemned women who seduced kings into wrongdoings that resulted in the downfall of dynasties in the past. In one particular instance, he spoke of women and the "small people" *(hsiao-jen)* together and condemned them both.

But it was not until near the end of the former Han Dynasty that the concept of the "Three Followings and Four Virtues" *(san-ts'ung ssu-te),* which tend to restrict the conduct of women, was formulated. Bound feet and monuments for chastity were even later inventions.

Third, Confucius has been criticized for his advocacy of "rule of men" rather than "rule by law." Distinction between the two, however, is unnecessary if the rulers are righteous and the laws are just. After all, administration of laws depends primarily on their right interpretation.

According to Confucius, a learned man, through constant self-criticism and self-improvement, will reach the pure state of mind and become a righteous person. He will extend his love and concern for the immediate members of his family to the rest of his clan, and then to other members of society and of the nation as well. He respects and cares for other people's elders because he respects and cares for his own elders. He loves and cares for other people's children because he loves and cares for his own children. When the state is governed only by righteous persons, then justice and peace will prevail in a state of "Grand Harmony" *(ta-tung).*

When disputes and crimes arise among the people, righteous rulers will govern with justice. In the ideal situation, when everybody in the nation follows the example set by righteous rulers and practices the Golden Rule of "do not unto others as you would not wish done unto yourself," disputes and crimes will not arise and laws and punishments will be abandoned. Confucius believes that persuasion and education are far more important than punishment and imprisonment in dealing with crimes. His ideas are thus quite compatible with modern thinking.

The Golden Rule just mentioned is another expression of the principle of mutual benevolence. It is sagaciously stated in the negative. When a Christian missionary insists that others must receive the Gospel and believe what he himself believes in, he may not realize that he has violated the Golden Rule of Confucius by forcing his own belief on others. If he does not want a Buddhist, for instance, to convert him to Buddhism, then he should not insist on converting the Buddhist to Christianity.

Fourth, Confucianism is usually considered to be anti-utilitarian and therefore nonconducive to economic development. It is true that Confucius disapproves of learned men striving for personal wealth and therefore ignoring their responsibility to the nation and to the people. He is against concentration of wealth among the rulers and a privileged few. He advises specifically against the government's overtaxing the people and competing with the people in the accumulation of wealth. He believes that the government, which derives its revenues from the people, can never be poor if its people are rich. On the other hand, if the people are poor, its government cannot be rich in the long run even if it has accumulated a great deal of wealth for the time being.

It must be kept in mind that at the time of Confucius, the government was basically a consumer, and the rulers were lavish in their expenditures. His anti-utilitarianism is directed at the government, the rulers, and the intellectual elite. It is only appropriate that the ruling class should be encouraged not to take advantage of their positions, to exploit the people, or to accumulate wealth for wasteful personal consumption. Confucius never denies the acquisitive instinct of the "small people." He argues for more equitable distribution of wealth and condones the selfish motive of the small people in acquiring it. When a man is learned, however, he should be concerned with the welfare of others rather than only with his personal gain. He should therefore not follow the practices and selfish motives of the small people. Yet if his honest intention is to improve the living conditions and welfare of the people through either governmental or private endeavors to promote agriculture or industry, he would certainly meet with Confucius' approval even if the end result is that the government or he himself also gets rich. Viewed in this perspective, we may conclude that even though Confucius may be idealistic in denying material incentives as a motivating force, he is not against economic development as such.

Fifth, Confucius has been blamed for his recognition of social classes—the division into a ruling class, that is, the learned men, and the ruled, that is, the small people, who are further divided into the farmers, the craftsmen, and the merchants, with the last class accorded the least respect. Actually, Confucius is one of the more liberal among ancient philosophers. He believes that through education and self-improvement, a person can climb the social ladder, become a learned man, and then join the ruling class. He has low esteem for the merchants only because of their selfish motives. His concern is more with the actual conduct of a person than with his class origin.

If we realize that Confucius expects much more from learned

men, in proper conduct and selflessness, than from the other classes of society, then most objections to his exaltation of learned men as a class can be viewed as groundless. In the real world, a "learned man" may be as selfish and corrupted as, or even more so than, a farmer, a craftsman, or a merchant. But by Confucius' definition, he can hardly be called a learned man.

The final observation I would like to make is that cultural change does not occur overnight. As time and the needs of people change, changes in values and attitudes evolve. Government and spiritual leaders may succeed in conditioning the people and influencing their minds to some extent, but it requires time for cultural change to take root. In general, the less drastic the proposed changes are and the more compatible they are with the existing culture, the more likely they will be accepted by the people and the more long lasting the changes are likely to be. This explains why there is always a certain degree of continuity with the past in cultural change.

For three decades, the Chinese Communist leaders have tried to eradicate the influence of Confucius on the Chinese mainland. For several years there was a major campaign against Confucianism. But if we look carefully at the teachings of Mao Tse-tung and the Chinese government's policies, we can detect a trace of continuity of the "Confucian" culture. For example, the exaltation of Mao as the supreme ideologist and the paramount leader reminds us of the "son of heaven" in imperial China. The "selfless" cadre reminds us of the "learned man." And an "egalitarian society" is similar to the Confucian ideal of "Grand Harmony." Self-criticism and self-improvement, so important in Confucianism, are practiced now in the mass meetings. And the downplaying of material incentives as well has its counterpart in Confucian ideology.

Of course, there have also been changes in Chinese culture under Communism. Some of them may take root, some may not. It should be kept in mind, however, that a discrepancy usually exists between what is professed and proclaimed by government decrees, and what the people are doing in practice and really believe in. How successful the Chinese Communist leaders have been in molding the minds of the Chinese people and in changing their practices cannot be determined from short-term studies. How long lasting the changes are, only time can tell.

Appendix B
Programs of Peking Television Stations

Channel 2

August 8, 1977 (Monday)
    19:00   TV news
    19:20   Gate No. 6 (Tientsin Opera Group)

August 9, 1977 (Tuesday)
  First broadcast (morning)
    10:00   Children's program
             Science: Sea Horse
             Children's poem: My Grandpa
    10:30   Feature film: Lei Feng
  Second broadcast (evening)
    19:00   TV news
    19:20   International news
    19:30   Health and hygiene: How to Prevent Encephalitis
    19:45   Feature film: Air Force Heroes

August 10, 1977 (Wednesday)
    19:00   TV news
    19:20   Science and technology
    19:35   Songs and dances

August 11, 1977 (Thursday)
  First broadcast (morning)
    10:00   Special: The Glorious August 1 Day
    10:20   Children's songs and dances
    10:45   Color art films:
             Little Fishermen
             Red Army Bridge
    11:25   TV feature: Norman Bethune
  Second broadcast (evening)
    19:00   TV news
    19:20   International news
    19:30   Children's program: Serial pictures
             A Magpie's Dream
             An IQ Test

19:45 TV feature: Sino-Rumanian Friendship—The Visit to Rumania by the Delegation from the Chinese People's Congress

20:10 Movie: Railroad Guerrillas

August 12, 1977 (Friday)

19:00 TV news

19:20 TV feature: New China News Agency Delegation Visits Korea

19:35 Cultural life: Songs of Unity in Combat—A Few Songs Lenin Liked

20:05 Color cartoon film: Little Sisters Are Heroines on the Prairie

20:45 Opera: Horses on the Move (Tientsin Opera Group)

August 13, 1977 (Saturday)

19:00 TV news

19:20 International news

19:30 Art exhibition

19:50 Color film: Battle of Yenan River

August 14, 1977 (Sunday)

First broadcast (morning)

10:00 TV news

10:20 Children's program: Little Red Soldiers
       A Meaningful Activity
       Military Drills

10:50 Movie: Under the Yen-hung Ridge

Second broadcast (evening)

19:00 TV news

19:20 International news

19:30 Opera: Butterfly Loves Flowers (China Opera Group)

Channel 8

August 8, 1977 (Monday)

19:00 TV news

19:20 TV feature: Armored Units on the March

19:30 Hsiang Sheng (Traditional Chinese comic duet): Learn from the Iron Man

19:45 TV documentary: Pioneers at Sea

20:00 Documentary movie: Tung Ch'un-jui

August 9, 1977 (Tuesday)

19:00 TV news

19:20 International news

19:30 Health and hygiene: Children's Diarrhea

19:40 Variety Show: Wuhan Variety Troupe

August 10, 1977 (Wednesday)

19:00 TV news

19:20 TV feature: Manpower Surpasses Heaven

19:35 Movie: Go Up Kan Ridge

August 11, 1977 (Thursday)
  19:00   TV news
  19:20   International news
  19:30   Folk dances from Yugoslavia
  20:00   Color movie: Linden Tree Village
August 12, 1977 (Friday)
  19:00   TV news
  19:20   TV documentary: Industry in Changchou Continues to Advance
  19:35   Science and technology: How to Use Chemical Fertilizers
  19:45   TV documentary: Journey to Linfeng
  19:55   Color movie: Great Wall in South Sea
August 13, 1977 (Saturday)
  19:00   TV news
  19:20   International news
  19:30   Children's program: To Catch a Mouse (Drama)
  19:50   TV documentary: People's Liberation Army Delegation Visits
          Korea
  20:15   Movie: Spring Comes to Withered Trees
August 14, 1977 (Sunday)
  First broadcast (morning)
  9:00   TV news
  9:20   Color paper-cutting film: An Arrow that Sings
  9:50   Movie: The Twelfth Train
  Second broadcast (evening)
  19:00   TV news
  19:20   International news
  19:30   TV documentary: A Peasants' Art Propaganda Team
  19:45   Opera film: Ch'aoyang Village

Bibliography

Almond, Gabriel, and G. Bingham Powell, Jr. *Comparative Politics.* Boston: Little, Brown, 1966.

An, Chan. "Comment on Sung Chiang, the Capitulationist." *Red Flag,* October 1, 1975. *Selections from People's Republic of China Magazines,* no. 844–845, p. 50.

Apter, David. *The Politics of Modernization.* Chicago: University of Chicago Press, 1965.

Bales, Robert F. "Task Roles and Social Roles in Problem-Solving Groups." In Eleanor E. Maccoby, Theodore M. Newcomb, and Eugene L. Hartley, eds. *Readings in Social Psychology.* New York: Holt, Rinehart and Winston, 1958.

Bandura, A. *Psychological Modeling.* Chicago: Aldine-Atherton, 1971.

Banton, Michael. *Roles: An Introduction to the Study of Social Relations.* London: Tavistock Publications, 1965.

Barcata, Louis. *China in the Throes of the Cultural Revolution.* New York: Hart Publication Co., 1968.

Barnett, A. Doak (with a contribution by Ezra Vogel). *Cadres, Bureaucracy, and Political Power in Communist China.* New York: Columbia University Press, 1967.

———, ed. *Chinese Communist Politics in Action.* Seattle: University of Washington Press, 1969.

Barnett, H. G. *Innovation: The Basis of Cultural Change.* New York: McGraw-Hill, 1953.

Belden, Jack. *China Shakes the World.* New York: Monthly Review Press, 1970.

Bennett, Gordon A., and Ronald N. Montaperto. *Red Guard: The Political Diary of Dai Hsiao-ai.* Garden City, N.Y.: Doubleday and Co., 1971.

Berkowitz, Leonard. "The Self, Selfishness and Altruism." In J. Macaulay and L. Berkowitz, eds. *Altruism and Helping Behavior: Social Psychological Studies of Some Antecedents and Consequences.* New York: Academic Press, 1970.

Bernstein, Thomas P. "Keeping the Revolution Going: Problems of Village Leadership after Land Reform." In John Wilson Lewis, ed., *Party Leadership and Revolutionary Power in China*. Cambridge: Cambridge University Press, 1970.

———. *Up to the Mountains and Down to the Countryside: The Transfer of Youth from Urban to Rural China*. New Haven, Conn.: Yale University Press, 1977.

Blumenthal, Eileen Polley. "Models in Chinese Moral Education: Perspectives from Children's Books." Ph.D. thesis, University of Michigan, 1976.

Bolnick, Bruce. "Toward a Behavioral Theory of Philanthropic Activity." In Edmund S. Phelps, ed. *Altruism, Morality, and Economic Theory*. New York: Russell Sage Foundation, 1975.

Bowers, John Z., and Elizabeth F. Purcell. *Medicine and Society in China*. New York: Josiah Macy, Jrs. Foundation, 1974.

Broman, Barry M. " *Tatzepao:* Medium of Conflict in China's Cultural Revolution." *Journalism Quarterly* 46 (Spring 1969):100–104, 127.

Bryson, Lyman, ed. *The Communication of Ideas*. New York: Institute for Religious and Social Studies, 1948.

Buck, John L. *Land Utilization in China: Statistics Volume*. Nanking: University of Nanking Press, 1937.

Canetti, Elias. *Crowds and Power*. Translated by Carol Stewart. New York: Viking Press, 1962.

Chang, Kuo-hsin. "World News Read Only by China's Selected Few."*IPI* [International Press Institute] *Report* 25 (February 1976):1–2.

Chang, Kuo-tao. *Autobiography*. Vol. 1, *The Rise of the Chinese Communist Party, 1921–1927*. Lawrence, Kansas: The University of Kansas Press, 1971.

Chen, A. S. [Ai-li Chin]. "The Ideal Local Party Secretary and the Model Man." *China Quarterly* (January–March, 1964):220–240.

Chin, Ai-li S. "Family Relations in Modern Chinese Fiction." In Maurice Freedman, ed. *Family and Kinship in Chinese Society*. Stanford, Calif.: Stanford University Press, 1970.

Chin, Ai-li S., and Nien-ling Liu. "Short Stories in China—Theory and Practice, 1973–1975." In Godwin C. Chu, ed. *Popular Media in China: Shaping New Cultural Patterns*. Honolulu: The University Press of Hawaii, 1978.

Chin, Robert, and Ai-li Chin. *Psychological Research in Communist China: 1949–1966*. Cambridge, Mass.: M.I.T. Press, 1969.

Chu, Godwin C. "Communication and Group Transformation in the People's Republic of China: The Mutual Aid Teams." In Godwin C. Chu et al., eds. *Communication for Group Transformation in Development*. Honolulu: East-West Center, East-West Communication Institute, 1976.

————. "Communication, Social Structural Change, and Capital Formation in People's Republic of China." Paper no. 9, East-West Communication Institute, East-West Center, Honolulu, Hawaii, 1974.

————. "Group Communication and Development in Mainland China: The Functions of Social Pressure." In Wilbur Schramm and Daniel Lerner, eds. *Communication and Change: The Last Ten Years—and the Next.* Honolulu: The University Press of Hawaii, 1976.

————, ed. *Popular Media in China: Shaping New Cultural Patterns.* Honolulu: The University Press of Hawaii, 1978.

————. *Radical Change through Communication in Mao's China.* Honolulu: The University Press of Hawaii, 1977.

Chu, Godwin C., Philip H. Cheng, and Leonard Chu. *The Roles of Tatzepao in the Cultural Revolution.* Carbondale, Ill.: Southern Illinois University, 1972.

Chu, Leonard. "Television Broadcasting in China." *Ming Pao,* April 26, 1977.

Chuang, H. C. *The Great Proletarian Cultural Revolution: A Terminological Study.* Berkeley, Ca.: Institute for International Studies, University of California, August 1967.

Corson, William R. "An Examination of Banking, Monetary, and Credit Practices in Communist China, 1949–57." Ph.D. thesis, American University, 1969.

Dedmon, Emmett. *China Journal.* Chicago: Rand McNally, 1973.

Deutsch, Karl W. "Social Mobilization and Political Development." *American Political Science Review* 55 (1961):493–514.

Dieny, Jean-Pierre. *Le Monde est à vous: La Chine et les livres pour enfants.* Paris: Gallimard, 1971.

Dittmer, Lowell. *Liu Shao-chi and the Chinese Cultural Revolution.* Berkeley: University of California Press, 1974.

————. "Revolution and Reconstruction in Contemporary Chinese Bureaucracy." *Journal of Comparative Administration* (February 1974): 443–487.

Djilas, Milovan. *The New Class: An Analysis of the Communist System.* New York: Praeger, 1962.

Dudman, Richard. "Headlines and Deadlines: Chinese Style." *Nieman Reports* (Spring and Summer 1977):19–21.

Easton, David, and Jack Dennis. *Children in the Political System.* New York: McGraw-Hill, 1969.

Elston, Wilbur E. "In China, Newspapers Serve the Party." In *China Today.* Detroit: Detroit News, 1972.

Elvin, Mark. *The Patterns of the Chinese Past.* Stanford, Ca.: Stanford University Press, 1973.

Etzioni, Amitai, ed. *A Sociological Reader on Complex Organizations.* 2nd ed. New York: Holt, Rinehart and Winston, 1969.

Fenichel, Otto. "The Counterphobic Attitude." In *Collected Papers*. London: Routledge and Keagan Paul, 1955.

Firth, Raymond. *Elements of Social Organization*. London: C. A. Watts, 1951.

Freedman, Maurice, ed. *Family and Kinship in Chinese Society*. Stanford, Ca.: Stanford University Press, 1970.

Freud, Sigmund. *Group Psychology and the Analysis of the Ego*. Translated by James Strachey. New York: Liveright, 1949.

Friedman, Edward. *Backward toward Revolution*. Berkeley: University of California Press, 1974.

Giles, Herbert. *Strange Stories from a Chinese Studio*. Cambridge: Cambridge University Press, 1908.

Goldman, Merle. *Literary Dissent in Communist China*. Cambridge, Mass.: Harvard University Press, 1967.

_____. "The Fall of Chou Yang." *China Quarterly* 27 (July–September 1966):132–148.

Gray, Jack, and Patrick Cavendish. *Chinese Communism in Crisis*. New York: Praeger, 1968.

Gruson, Sidney. "On the Resolution of Contradictions among the People." *New York Times,* June 13, 1957, pp. 1, 8.

Hage, Jerald, and Michael Aiken. *Social Change in Complex Organizations*. New York: Random House, 1970.

Harper, Francis. "A Journalist and His Paper." In Francis Harper, ed. *Out of China: A Collection of Interviews with Refugees from China*. Hong Kong: Dragonfly Books, 1964.

Homans, George. *The Human Group*. New York: Harcourt, Brace & Co., 1950.

Houn, Franklin W. *A Short History of Chinese Communism*. Englewood Cliffs, N.J.: Prentice-Hall, 1967.

_____. *To Change a Nation*. New York: The Free Press of Glencoe, 1961.

Howe, Christopher, and Kenneth Walker. "The Economist." In Dick Wilson, ed. *Mao Tse-tung in the Scales of History*. London: Cambridge University Press, 1977.

Hsia, C. T. *A History of Modern Chinese Fiction, 1917–1957*. New Haven, Conn.: Yale University Press, 1961.

Hsia, T. A. "Twenty Years after the Yenan Forum." *China Quarterly* (January–March 1963):226–253.

Hsiao, Kung-chuan. *Rural China: Imperial Control in the Nineteenth Century*. Seattle: University of Washington Press, 1960.

Hsu, Francis L. K. *Americans and Chinese: Reflections on Two Cultures and Their People*. 2nd ed. New York: Doubleday, 1970.

_____. "Eros, Affect and *Pao*." In Francis L. K. Hsu, ed. *Kinship and Culture*. Chicago: Aldine, 1971.

_____. *Psychological Anthropology*. Cambridge, Mass.: Schenkman, 1972.

———. "Psychosocial Homeostasis and *Jen:* Conceptual Tools for Advancing Psychological Anthropology." *American Anthropologist* 73, no. 1 (1971):23–44.

———. *Religion, Science, and Human Crisis.* London: Routledge and Keagan Paul, 1952.

———. *Under the Ancestors' Shadow.* Stanford, Ca.: Stanford University Press, 1971.

Hsu, Kai-yu. *The Chinese Literary Scene—A Writer's Visit to the People's Republic.* New York: Vintage, 1975.

Hsu-Balzer, Eileen, Richard Balzer, and Francis L. K. Hsu. *China Day by Day.* New Haven, Conn.: Yale University Press, 1974.

Hsueh, Mu-chiao et al. *The Socialist Transformation of the National Economy in China.* Peking: Foreign Languages Press, 1960.

Huai, Yu. "Television Broadcasting in Communist China." In *Studies of Chinese Communism* 11 (March 15, 1977):73–78.

Huang, Joe. *Heroes and Villains in Communist China.* New York: PICA Press, 1973.

Hunter, Neale. *Shanghai Journal.* New York: Praeger, 1969.

Huntington, Samuel. *Political Order in Changing Societies.* New Haven, Conn.: Yale University Press, 1968.

Inkeles, Alex. "Social Change and Social Character: The Role of Parental Mediation." *Journal of Social Issues* 2 (1955):12–23.

Isaacs, Harold, ed. *Straw Sandals—Chinese Short Stories, 1918–1933.* Cambridge, Mass.: M.I.T. Press, 1974.

King, Vincent. *Propaganda Campaigns in Communist China.* Cambridge, Mass.: M.I.T. Press, 1966.

Kluckhohn, Clyde. *Mirror for Man.* New York: McGraw-Hill, 1949.

Kroeber, A. K., and Clyde Kluckhohn. *Culture, A Critical Review of Concepts and Definitions.* New York: Vintage Books, 1963.

Lamott, Kenneth. "The Maoist Solution to the Energy Crisis." *Human Behavior* 6, no. 8 (1977).

Langer, Susanne K. *Philosophy in a New Key: A Study in the Symbolism of Reason, Rite, and Art.* New York: Penguin, 1942.

Lasswell, Harold D. "The Structure and Function of Communication in Society." In Lyman Bryson, ed. *The Communication of Ideas.* New York: Institute for Religious and Social Studies, 1948.

Lau, Siu-kai. "Monism, Pluralism, and Segmental Coordination: Toward an Alternative Theory of Elite, Power and Social Stability." *Journal of the Chinese University of Hong Kong* 3 (December 1975): 187–206.

Lee. "Lee's *Tatzepao:* To Mao with Dissent." *The Asian Messenger.* (Spring 1976):27.

Lee, Hong Yung. "The Politics of Cadre Rehabilitation since the Cultural Revolution." Unpublished manuscript, 1977.

Lersch, Philipp. *Zur Psychologie der Indoktrination.* Munich: Beck, 1969.

Lewis, John Wilson, ed. *Party Leadership and Revolutionary Power in China.* Cambridge: Cambridge University Press, 1970.

————, ed. *The City in Communist China.* Stanford, Ca.: Stanford University Press, 1971.

Lifton, Robert Jay. *Thought Reform and the Psychology of Totalism: A Study of "Brainwashing" in China.* New York: Norton, 1963.

Liu, Alan P. L. *Communications and National Integration in Communist China.* New enl. ed. Berkeley, Ca.: University of California Press, 1975.

————. *Political Culture and Group Conflict in Communist China.* Santa Barbara: Clio Books, 1976.

————. *The Use of Traditional Media for Modernization in Communist China.* Cambridge, Mass.: Massachusetts Institute of Technology, 1965.

Macaulay, J., and L. Berkowitz, eds. *Altruism and Helping Behavior: Social Psychological Studies of Some Antecedents and Consequences.* New York: Academic Press, 1970.

Maccoby, Eleanor E., Theodore M. Newcomb, and Eugene L. Hartley, eds. *Readings in Social Psychology.* New York: Holt, Rinehart and Winston, 1958.

MacFarquhar, Roderick. *The Hundred Flowers Campaign and the Chinese Intellectuals.* New York: Praeger, 1960.

Madsen, Richard. "Social Causes and Consequences of Radicalism in a South China Village." Paper prepared for Workshop on the Pursuit of Political Interest in the People's Republic of China, Ann Arbor, Michigan, August 10–17, 1977.

Malinowski, Bronislaw. "Culture." In *Encyclopedia of the Social Sciences.* Vol. 4, pp. 621–646. New York: Macmillan, 1931.

Mao Tse-tung. *Selected Works of Mao Tse-tung.* Vols. 1–5. Peking: Foreign Languages Press, 1977.

————. *The Poems of Mao Tse-tung.* Translated by Willis Barnstone. New York: Harper & Row, 1972.

Marwell, Gerald, and David R. Schmitt. *Cooperation: An Experimental Analysis.* New York: Academic Press, 1975.

McKean, Roland N. "Economics of Trust, Altruism and Corporate Responsibility." In Edmund S. Phelps, ed. *Altruism, Morality, and Economic Theory.* New York: Russell Sage Foundation, 1975.

McKenna, Richard. *The Sand Pebbles.* New York: Harper & Row, 1962.

Meijer, M. J. *Marriage Law and Policy in the Chinese People's Republic.* Hong Kong: Hong Kong University Press, 1971.

Moravia, Alberto. *The Red Book and the Great Wall.* New York: Farrar, Strauss & Giroux, 1968.

Morgan, Edmund S. *Puritan Family: Religion and Domestic Relations in Seventeenth Century New England.* Boston: Trustees of the Public Library, 1944. New rev. ed. New York: Harper & Row, 1966.

Mu Fu Sheng. *The Wilting of the Hundred Flowers.* New York: Praeger, 1963.

Munro, Donald J. *The Concept of Man in Contemporary China.* Ann Arbor: University of Michigan Press, 1977.

Murray, J. Edward. "How China's Press Handles News." In *4000 Miles Across China.* Detroit: Detroit Free Press, 1972.

Nebiolo, Gino. *The People's Comic Book.* Garden City, N.Y.: Doubleday, 1973.

Needham, Joseph. *Chinese Science.* London: Pilot Press, 1945.

———. *Chinese Science: Exploration of an Ancient Tradition.* Edited by Shigeru Nakayama and Nathan Sivin. Cambridge, Mass.: M.I.T. Press, 1973.

Nettl, J. P. *Political Mobilization: A Sociological Analysis of Methods and Concepts.* London: Faber and Faber, 1967.

Oksenberg, Michel C. "China's Politics and the Public Health Issue." In John Z. Bowers and Elizabeth F. Purcell, eds. *Medicine and Society in China.* New York: Josiah Macy, Jrs. Foundation, 1974.

———. "Sources and Methodological Problems in the Study of Contemporary China." In A. Doak Barnett, ed. *Chinese Communist Politics in Action.* Seattle: University of Washington Press, 1969.

Pan, Stephen C. Y., and the Rev. Raymond J. de Jaegher. *Peking's Red Guard.* New York: Twin Circle Publishing Co., Inc., 1968.

Parish, William L., Jr. "Communist Agricultural Organization: China—Team, Brigade, or Commune?" In *Problems of Communism* 25 (March–April 1976):51–65.

Parish, William L., Jr., and Martin King Whyte. *Village and Family in Contemporary China.* Chicago: University of Chicago Press, 1978.

Parsons, Talcott. *The Social System.* New York: The Free Press, 1951.

Pennell, Wilfred V. *A Life Time with the Chinese.* Hong Kong: South China Morning Post, 1974.

Perkins, Dwight H. *Market Control and Planning in Communist China.* Cambridge, Mass.: Harvard University Press, 1966.

Phelps, Edmund S., ed. *Altruism, Morality, and Economic Theory.* New York: Russell Sage Foundation, 1975.

Poon, David Jim-tat. " *Tatzepao:* Its History and Significance as a Communication Medium." In Godwin C. Chu, ed. *Popular Media in China: Shaping New Cultural Patterns.* Honolulu: The University Press of Hawaii, 1978.

Portisch, Hugo. *Red China Today.* Chicago: Quadrangle Books, 1966.

Pye, Lucian W. *Aspects of Political Development.* Boston: Little, Brown, 1966.

———. *Politics, Personality and Nation Building.* New Haven, Conn.: Yale University Press, 1962.

———. *The Spirit of Chinese Politics.* Cambridge, Mass.: M.I.T. Press, 1968.

Raddock, David. *Political Behavior of Adolescents in China.* Tucson: University of Arizona Press, 1977.

Rescher, Nicholas. *Unselfishness: The Role of the Vicarious Affects in Moral Philosophy and Social Theory.* Pittsburgh, Pa.: University of Pittsburgh Press, 1975.

Ridley, Charles P., Paul H. B. Godwin, and Dennis J. Doolin. *The Making of a Model Citizen in Communist China.* Stanford, Ca.: Hoover Institution, 1971.

Rogers, Everett M. "Change Agents, Clients, and Change." In *Modernization Among Peasants: The Impact of Communication.* New York: Holt, Rinehart and Winston, 1969.

Rohter, I. S. "A Social Learning Approach to Political Socialization." In D. C. Schwartz and S. K. Schwartz, eds. *New Directions in Political Socialization.* New York: The Free Press, 1975.

Salisbury, Harrison E. *To Peking—And Beyond.* New York: Quadrangle/ New York Times Books Co., 1973.

Sapir, Edward. "Communication." In *Encyclopedia of the Social Sciences.* Vol. 4. New York: Macmillan, 1931.

———. *Selected Writings of Edward Sapir in Language, Culture, and Personality.* Edited by D. G. Mandelbaum. Berkeley: University of California Press, 1949.

Schein, Edgar H. *Coercive Persuasion.* New York: Norton, 1961.

Schram, Stuart. *The Political Thought of Mao Tse-tung.* New York: Praeger, 1963.

Schramm, Wilbur, ed. *Mass Communications.* Urbana: University of Illinois Press, 1960.

Schramm, Wilbur, and Daniel Lerner, eds. *Communication and Change: The Last Ten Years—and the Next.* Honolulu: The University Press of Hawaii, 1976.

Schurmann, Franz. *Ideology and Organization in Communist China.* 2nd ed. Berkeley: University of California Press, 1968.

Schwartz, D. C., and S. K. Schwartz, eds. *New Directions in Political Socialization.* New York: The Free Press, 1975.

Selden, Mark. *The Yenan Way in Revolutionary China.* Cambridge, Mass.: Harvard University Press, 1971.

Shue, Vivienne. "Personal Power and Village Politics: Hunan Peasants During Land Reform." Paper for the Joint Committee on Contemporary China Workshop on the Pursuit of Political Interest in the People's Republic of China, August, 1977.

———. "Reorganizing Rural Trade: Unified Purchase and Socialist Transformation." *Modern China* 2 (January 1976):104–134.

Skinner, B. F. *Beyond Freedom and Dignity.* New York: Alfred A. Knopf, 1971.

———. *Science and Human Behavior.* New York: Macmillan, 1953.

Skinner, G. William, and Edwin A. Winckler. "Compliance Succession in Rural Communist China: A Cyclical Theory." In Amitai Etzioni, ed. *A Sociological Reader on Complex Organizations.* 2nd ed. New York: Holt, Rinehart and Winston, 1969.

Solomon, Richard H. *Mao's Revolution and the Chinese Political Culture.* Berkeley: University of California Press, 1971.

Spencer, Herbert. *Principles of Sociology.* London: Williams and Norgate, 1876.

Terrill, Ross. *800,000,000—The Real China.* New York: Dell, 1971.

Townsend, James. *Political Participation in Communist China.* Berkeley: University of California Press, 1969.

Trumbull, Robert, ed. *This is Communist China.* New York: David McKay, 1968.

Tuchman, Barbara W. *Notes from China.* New York: Collier Books, 1972.

Tung, Chi-ping, and Humphrey Evans. *The Thought Revolution.* New York: Coward-McCann, Inc., 1966.

Vogel, Ezra F. *Canton under Communism: Programs and Politics in a Provincial Capital, 1949–1968.* Cambridge, Mass.: Harvard University Press, 1969.

Vuylsteke, Richard. "Tung Chung-shu: A Philosophical Case for Rights in Chinese Philosophy." In Richard Vuylsteke, ed. *Law and Society.* Honolulu: East-West Culture Learning Institute, East-West Center, 1977.

Wallace, Anthony F. C. *Culture and Personality.* New York: Random House, 1961.

White, Lynn T. (III) "Shanghai's Polity in Cultural Revolution." In John W. Lewis, ed. *The City in Communist China.* Stanford, Ca.: Stanford University Press, 1971.

Whyte, Martin King. "Change and Continuity in China: The Case of Rural Marriage." *Problems of Communism* 26, no. 4 (1977):41–55.

_____. *Small Groups and Political Rituals in China.* Berkeley: University of California Press, 1974.

Wilson, Dick, ed. *Mao Tse-tung in the Scales of History.* London: Cambridge University Press, 1977.

Witke, Roxane. *Comrade Chiang Ch'ing.* Boston: Little, Brown and Co., 1977.

Wolf, Margery, and Roxane Witke, eds. *Women in Chinese Society.* Stanford, Ca.: Stanford University Press, 1975.

Wong, John. *Land Reform in the People's Republic of China.* New York: Praeger, 1973.

Worsley, Peter. *The Trumpet Shall Sound: A Study of "Cargo" Cults in Melanesia.* London: MacGibbon & Kee, 1957.

Worth, Robert M. "Recent Demographic Patterns in Kwangtung Province Villages." Unpublished paper, n.d.

Yu, Frederick T. C. *Mass Persuasion in Communist China.* New York: Praeger, 1964.

Zaltman, Gerald et al. *Innovations and Organizations.* New York: John Wiley & Sons, 1973.

Contributors

A. DOAK BARNETT, born in China, received his doctorate from Franklin and Marshall College. A leading scholar in China studies, Dr. Barnett was professor of political science at Columbia University before he joined the Brookings Institution, where he is now a Senior Fellow. He has published numerous books on China, including *Communist China in Perspective; Cadres, Bureaucracy, and Political Power in Communist China; Uncertain Passage: China's Transition to the Post-Mao Era;* and, most recently, *China and the Major Powers in East-Asia.* He was a Senior Fellow at the East-West Center in 1976–1977.

THOMAS P. BERNSTEIN is an associate professor of political science at Columbia University and an associate of its East Asian Institute. He is the author of *Up to the Mountains and Down to the Villages: The Transfer of Youth from Urban to Rural China,* and has written articles on rural Chinese politics and on Soviet and Chinese collectivation of agriculture. He is currently studying rural change in China and Russia. Professor Bernstein received his Ph.D. from Columbia University.

PARRIS H. CHANG is a professor of political science at The Pennsylvania State University. The author of *Radicals and Radical Ideology in China's Cultural Revolution, Power and Policy in China,* and numerous scholarly articles, Professor Chang was president of the Mid-Atlantic Region, Association for Asian Studies, in 1976–1977. He received his doctorate in political science from Columbia University.

AI-LI S. CHIN, born in China, received her Ph.D. in sociology from Harvard University. She is the coauthor of *Psychological Research in Communist China, 1949–1966* and a contributor to academic journals and volumes on China and Chinese-Americans. Her main research interests are roles and values in modern Chinese society and Chinese-American identity and community affairs.

GODWIN C. CHU is a research associate at the East-West Communication Institute of the East-West Center in Honolulu. Born in Peking, Dr. Chu received his Ph.D. in communication research from Stanford University and has done extensive work in the field of communication and social change. He is the author of *Radical Change through Communication in Mao's China,* editor of *Popular Media in China,* senior author of *The Role of Tatzepao in the Cultural Revolution—A Structural-Functional Analysis,* and coeditor of two other books on communication theory.

LOWELL DITTMER is an associate professor of political science and vice chairman of the Center for Chinese Studies at the University of California at Berkeley. He taught previously at the University of Michigan and the State University of New York at Buffalo. The author of *Liu Shao-chi and the Chinese Cultural Revolution* and numerous scholarly articles, Dr. Dittmer is currently engaged in an analysis of Chinese political culture. He received his Ph.D. in political science from the University of Chicago.

MERLE GOLDMAN, who received her Ph.D. in history and Far Eastern languages from Harvard University, is an associate professor of history at Boston University and a research associate at the John Fairbank Center for East Asian Research at Harvard University. She is the author of *Literary Dissent in Communist China* and editor of *Modern Chinese Literature in the May Fourth Era.*

FRANCIS L. K. HSU, born in China, earned his B.A. at the University of Shanghai in 1933 and completed his Ph.D. in cultural anthropology at London University in 1940. President of the American Anthropological Association in 1977–1978, Dr. Hsu is professor of anthropology and director of the Center for Cultural Studies in Education at the University of San Francisco. His works include *Under the Ancestors' Shadow, Americans and Chinese, China Day by Day,* and *Iemoto, the Heart of Japan.*

FRED C. HUNG, born in China, is a professor of economics and chairman of East Asian Studies at the University of Hawaii. Professor Hung earned his doctorate in economics at the University of Washington and has published in numerous journals in the field of economics. He is the coauthor of *The Economic Potential of Communist China* and *Communist China's Trade Patterns and Economic Capability.*

LAU SIU-KAI, who received his Ph.D. in sociology from the University of Minnesota, is a lecturer in sociology at the Chinese University of Hong Kong and the associate director of its Social Research Centre. Dr. Lau has done research in the diffusion of technological innovations in Chinese agriculture and the sociocultural basis of politics in Hong Kong.

WILLIAM L. PARISH is an associate professor of sociology at the University of Chicago. He is the coauthor of *Village and Family in Contemporary*

China, and a contributor to several scholarly journals in China studies. He received his Ph.D. in sociology from Cornell University.

LUCIAN W. PYE, born in China, is a professor of political science at the Massachusetts Institute of Technology, and a senior researcher at its Center for International Studies. He is the author of *Politics, Personality, and Nation Building; The Spirit of Chinese Politics; China: An Introduction; Mao Tse-tung: the Man in the Leader; Warlord Politics; Guerilla Communism in Malaya;* and *Aspects of Political Development.* He is coauthor of *The Politics of the Developing Areas, The Emerging Nations,* and *Crises and Sequences in Political Development;* editor of *Communications and Political Development* and *Political Science and Area Studies;* and coeditor of *Political Power and Communications in Indonesia* and *The Citizen and Politics: A Comparative Perspective.*

VIVIENNE SHUE is an assistant professor of political science at Yale University. She did her graduate work at Oxford and Harvard, from which she received her Ph.D., and has been a senior research associate at the Center for Chinese Studies at the University of California at Berkeley. Professor Shue has contributed articles to *Modern China* and *Peasant Studies,* and is the author of a forthcoming book on the transition to socialism in rural China.

LYNN T. WHITE III is an assistant professor in the Woodrow Wilson School, the Politics Department, and the East Asian Studies Department at Princeton University. The author of *Careers in Shanghai,* Professor White has published in the *American Political Science Review, Journal of Asian Studies, China Quarterly,* and other journals. He received his Ph.D. in political science from the University of California at Berkeley.

MARTIN K. WHYTE, who received his Ph.D. in sociology from Harvard University, is an associate professor of sociology at the University of Michigan and an associate of its Center for Chinese Studies. He is the author of *Small Groups and Political Rituals in China* and *The Status of Women in Pre-industrial Societies,* and coauthor of *Village and Family in Contemporary China.* He was formerly director of Universities Service Centre in Hong Kong.

FREDERICK T. C. YU, born in China, is a professor of journalism at Columbia University. He is the author of *Mass Persuasion in Communist China* and coeditor of *Mass Communication Research—Major Issues and Future Directions.* He received his doctorate from the State University of Iowa.

Index

Agenda-setting function, 417n
Agricultural Research, Bureau of (Nung-k'o Pu), 128
Agricultural Research Institute (Nung-k'o So), 128–129
Agricultural Science Institute, 147n
Ai Ssu-ch'i, 37, 44
Alley news *(hsiao-tao hsiao-hsi),* 409
Altruism, 367–373, 405–406
Anti-Confucian/Anti–Lin Piao campaign, 180, 181, 203, 224, 227, 228, 276
Anti-Rightist movement, 18, 47, 58, 65, 78, 84, 103. *See also* Hundred Flowers movement
Audience predisposition, 410

Bales, Robert, 8
Barnett, A. Doak, 386–395, 407–408, 416n
Barnett, H. G., 22n
Bernstein, Thomas P., 341–362, 399, 409
Big character posters *(tatzupao),* 27, 47–48, 64–66, 73–74n, 154–155, 164, 402–403, 416n
Birth control, communication of, 373, 376–377
Blackboard newspapers *(hei-pan pao),* 97–99
Blumenthal, Eileen Polley, 255n, 256n
Boxer Rebellion, 14
Broman, Barry M., 73n
Buddhism, 419

Canton Daily, 72n, 93, 103
Canton Evening Post, 93
Central Broadcasting Bureau, 38, 67, 68, 223
Central People's Broadcasting Station, 44, 66–67

Chai Ch'un-tse, 359
Chang Ch'un-ch'iao, 52–53, 181, 186–189, 191, 229, 285, 354–355, 359, 415n
Chang Kuo-hsing, 111n
Chang Kuo-t'ao, 28, 31
Chang, Parris H., 237–256
Chao Kai, 192, 197, 198
Chaos *(luan),* 169
Cheng Feng campaign, 33–34
Chen Shao-yü (Wang Ming), 31
Ch'en Tu-hsiu, 28, 29
Chesneax, Jean, 238
Chiang Ch'ing, 41, 45, 52, 53, 59, 66, 71, 174, 179–180, 224, 227, 276, 285, 290; revolutionary operas by, 224–225, 250
Chiang Kai-shek, 30, 47
Chiang Tse-lung, 292–293
Chieh Fang Chün Pao. See Liberation Army Daily
Chieh-fang Jihpao. See Liberation Daily
Chin, Ai-li, 24n, 280–304, 400
Ch'in Dynasty, 13, 17
Chinese Communist Party, 23n, 60, 237; birth of, 28; class interest analysis by, 377–378; cultural change policies of, 14–16, 17–18, 20, 337n; media control by, 60, 77, 78–88, 153–154, 179–180, 202–204, 244; membership of, 35; promoter of new peasant culture, 14–15, 309–334; propaganda policies of, 28–53; small groups leadership, 114, 116, 121–122
Chinese Soviet Republic, 31
Ch'ing Dynasty, 16, 244
Ching-kan-shan, 282
Chin Hsün-hua, 345, 360
Ch'in Pang-hsien (Po Ku), 31, 36–37

Chin Sheng-t'an, 192
Chi Yen, 189–190
Chou En-lai, 38, 58, 66, 83, 109n, 159, 167, 223, 224, 235n, 285, 289, 344; media campaigns, role in, 180, 181, 191, 192, 194, 196, 198, 201–202
Chou Jung-hsin, 181, 202
Chou Ssu, 182, 183
Chou Yang, 45–46, 53
Chu Ch'iu-pai, 31
Chu Fang-ming, 194
Chu, Godwin, 2–24, 57–75, 396–417
Chu Teh, 255n
Comics, 243. *See also* Picture storybooks
Communes, 118–119, 271, 351, 397–398; characteristics of, 125–127, 145–146n, 146n; communication system in, 68, 79, 127–128, 134, 137–138, 140, 142, 143–145; four-tiered network, 128–131, 149n; role integration in, 138–142, three-tiered network, 128, 131–134, 139, 144; vs. traditional villages, 135–137
Communication system, 27, 141, 156–157, 349–350, 393–395; centralized organization of, 386–391; and communes, 127–128, 134, 137–138, 143–145; criticism strategy in, 15, 30, 33, 61–62, 81–83, 113–114, 119, 210, 213, 216–219, 229–230; and cultural change, 2–8, 12–21, 76–78, 104–105, 111–112, 407–415; history of, 27–55; language in, 390–391; measures of, 364–382; and peasant culture, 364–373, 373–382, 383n; value dualism in, 350–360; and youth transfer program, 350–360. *See also* Mass media and individual listings
Compliance behavior, 402–403
Confucianism, 2, 17, 24n, 33, 157, 159, 202, 238, 244, 269; Golden Rule of, 421; history of, 419–423
Confucius, 17, 21n, 240, 246, 286–287, 419
Contextual effect, 411
County and commune bulletins *(t'ung-hsün),* 78
Cultural change, 4, 12, 14, 16, 23–24n, 397–404; Chinese ideology in, 15–16, 17, 18, 23–24n; communication system in, 18, 20–21, 76–78, 104–105, 111–112, 404–412, 423;

Cultural Revolution, 231–232; definition of, 4, 303–309, 316–319, 337n; Maoist theory of, 205–215; mathematical annex of, 111–112; process of, 2–4, 6, 11, 17–21, 332, 334, 337n; self in, 4–8, 19, 20, 21–22n; technological development in, 7–8, 10, 11, 13–14, 23n. *See also* Chinese Communist Party, promoter of new peasant culture
Cultural Revolution, 18, 30, 41, 48, 49, 50, 51, 58, 66, 88, 103–104, 154, 158, 163, 179–180, 190; communication strategies of, 216–218, 225–227; institutionalization efforts of, 218–225, 227–232; Maoist theory of, 205–215; *tatzupao* development in, 65–66; and youth transfer program, 231, 342, 344, 353, 354, 355–356, 358

Deutsch, Karl W., 145n
Dictatorship of the Proletariat campaign, 180–191, 199, 200, 203
Dissemination effect, 411–412
Dittmer, Lowell, 207–236, 411
Double work force *(shuang chih kung),* 272
Dream of the Red Chamber, 50, 193

Education, 344, 345, 346–348, 351, 352–353, 366, 368, 371; changing university status in, 355–357
Elvin, Mark, 23n
Experiential effect, 411

Fang La, 192, 195
Fatalism, 405
Female Street Cleaners, 250
feng p'ai trend, 416n
Festinger, Leon, 416n
Fiery Years, 249
Filial piety, 406
Firth, Raymond, 21–22n
Five-Anti *(Wu-fan)* campaign, 15, 18, 89
Five Barbarian Dynasties, 16
Five Sovereigns *(Wu Ti),* 173
Foolish Old Man Who Moved the Mountain, The, 158, 248, 278, 415

Gang of Four, 35, 41, 51, 52, 70, 71, 154, 158, 160, 170, 174, 176, 177–

178n, 294–295, 344–345, 359, 402, 404, 407
Geomancy, 136
Golden Lotus (Chin P'ing), 262
Goldman, Merle, 179–206, 407, 409, 411
Great Leap Forward, 58, 84, 93, 103, 180, 187, 378
Group loyalty, 406–407

Hai Jui, 199, 200
Hai Jui, Dismissal of, 158
Han Dynasty, 78, 421
Hard-Boned Sixth Company, 177–178n
Homans, George, 8
Honan Masses, 89
Hong Kong, 349, 362, 366
Hsiang River Review (Hsiang-chiang P'ing-lun), 29
Hsiao Kui, 73n
Hsiao-tsu. See Small groups
Hsinhua. *See* New China News Agency
Hsin Hui Agricultural Machinery Factory, 147n
Hsin Min Study Group, 29
Hsüeh-hsi. See Study groups
Hsu, Francis, 8, 22n, 23n, 259–279, 396–417, 413
Hua Kuo-feng, 59, 71, 165–166, 201, 202, 232, 289, 294, 343, 351–352
Huan Ch'eng commune, 128, 129
Huan T'ai County, 132–133, 134, 139
Hundred Flowers movement, 47, 58, 65, 83, 101, 102, 213, 394
Hung Ch'i. See Red Flag
Hung, Fred C., 419–423
Hung Wei orchard, 133, 139, 146n
Hu Shih, 333

Ideological remolding *(ssu-hsiang kai-tsao),* 30, 33–35, 210
Ideological struggle *(ssu-hsiang tou-cheng),* 30, 33, 35
Internal notices *(nei-pu t'ung-pao),* 96
Interpersonal harmony, 403–404

Jenmin Jihpao. See People's Daily
Jenmin Wen-hsueh. See People's Literature
Jesus, 21n

Kao Ch'iu, 192, 194
Kinship system, 119, 399–400; characteristic patterns in, 260–262,

274–278; courtship in, 262–267; marital life in, 270–274; work ethic in, 267–270
Kluckhohn, Clyde, 21n, 21–22n
Kluckhohn, Florence, 22n
Korean War, 322
Kroeber, A. K., 21n, 21–22n
Kuangchow Daily, 61
Kung fu, 14
Kwantung Province, 118, 362, 365, 405

Land reform, 14, 18, 29, 322, 377–378, 397
Lau, Siu-kai, 125–149, 399, 405, 412
Legalism, 17, 203, 419, 420
Lei Feng, 166, 167, 240, 345
Liang Ch'i-ch'ao, 333
Liang Hsiao, 51, 70, 75n, 182, 184–185, 194, 197. *See also* Gang of Four
Liberation Army Daily (Chieh Fang Chun Pao), 44, 50–51, 286
Liberation Daily (Chieh-fang Jihpao), 36–37, 79, 82, 87
Li I-che, 66, 73–74n, 416n
Li K'uei, 199
Li Li-san, 31
Lin Piao, 160, 166, 170, 216, 218, 223, 229, 240, 277, 286–287
Li Ta, 28
Little Coast Guards, The, 249
Little Red Book, 278
Liu Shao-ch'i, 33, 41, 51, 103, 160, 163, 168, 170, 174, 210, 348, 353
Lo Jui-ch'ing, 191
Long March, The, 31–32, 193, 201
Lo Ssu-ting, 183
Lu Chün-i, 196, 202
Lu Hsün, 196
Lu Ting-i, 33–34

McCombs, Maxwell, 417n
McFarquhar, Roderick, 92
Magazines, 29, 33, 43–44, 86, 180, 223, 281, 286. *See also People's Literature*
Malinowski, Bronislaw, 21n
Mandarin, 67, 112
Maoism, 49. *See also* Mao Tse-tung, thought of
Mao Tse-tung, 14, 31, 102, 103, 104, 159, 168, 353, 354, 390, 394, 415,

423; poetry of, 209, 282, 286; propaganda policies of, 29–52, 157,
159, 173; vs. radicals, 184, 185, 188,
189, 193, 196, 198
Mao Tse-tung, Quotations of, 50
Mao Tse-tung, Selected Works of, 49,
50
Mao Tse-tung, thought of, 48–51, 71,
207, 211, 212–213, 214, 405; on art
and literature, 33, 39–40; on
children, 237; on Chinese goals, 277;
on communication, 57; on the
Cultural Revolution, 220–221; on
the dictatorship of the proletariat,
181–182; on ideological remolding,
34–35, 210; on mass line, 35–36; on
newspapers, 57; on peasants, 325;
on propaganda, 29; on the Red Army, 209; on *Reference Information,*
46–47; on revisionism, 207–209, 210;
on revolution, 278; on the Long
March, 32; on *tatzupao,* 47–48, 164;
on work, 269
Mao Tse-tung, writings of, 49. *See
also* Mao Tse-tung, thought of
Mao Tun, 281
Marxism-Leninism, 32–34, 49–50, 168,
192, 224, 280
Marx, Karl, 15–16
Masses Daily (Ta-chung Jihpao),
85–86
Mass line policy, 35–36, 393
Mass media, 27; function of, 57–72,
174–176; ideological campaigns of,
179–204; linguistic techniques of,
153–167, 172–174; political charac-
teristics, 167–176. *See also* Big char-
acter posters, Magazines, Movies,
newspapers, radio, television, wired
broadcasts
Material incentive, 398–399, 415–416
Mencius, 17, 419
Ming Dynasty, 192, 419
Mo Ti, 17
Movies, 374
Muddy *(tu)* correspondents, 63–64
Murray, Edward, 61

Nan Fang Daily, 61–62, 72n
Nationalization movement, 415n
Needham, Joseph, 23n
Nettl, J. P., 145n
*New China Daily News (Hsin-hua
Jihpao),* 38

New China News Agency (Hsinhua),
31–32, 59, 61, 80, 82, 84, 98
News Front (Hsin-wen Chan-hsien)
magazine, 86
Newspapers, 28–53 passim, 76, 105n,
154, 223, 364–365, 370–371, 372,
374; communal and provincial,
61–62, 63–64; content regulation of,
79–86; distribution system of, 88–94;
journalists on, 81, 82, 83–84, 85–86;
political functions of 57–61, 96, 180;
publishers of, 78; readership of, 60,
94–100; reform of, 71–72, 86–88,
101–104
New Youth (Hsin Ching-nien)
magazine, 29
Northern Kingdoms, 16
Northern Sung Dynasty, 192

Oksenberg, Michel, 415n
Old Chinese sayings, 11, 163, 279n,
406
On Contradiction, 49
On the Docks (Hai Kang), 250
Ouyang, Hai, 240

Pan Tzu-nien, 38
Parental visits *(sheng ch'in),* 276
Parish, William L., 363–383, 399, 406,
415n
Parsons, Talcott, 8, 10
Peasant culture, 14–15, 118–119, 410;
changing values, 335n, 373–382; col-
lectivization of, 319–321, 323–325,
330–331, 367–373, 378–382,
405–407; entrepreneurship of,
321–322, 325–326, 331; politicization
of, 322–323, 326–330, 331; and
small groups, 118–119; traditional
characteristics of, 309–316. *See also*
Chinese Communist Party, promoter
of new peasant culture
Peking opera, 52, 224–225, 250, 407
Peking Television Station, 68, 69, 74–
75n
P'eng Chen, 191, 200
P'eng Shu-shih, 28
Pennell, Wilfred V., 279n
People's Art Publishing House, 243
People's Daily (Jenmin Jihpao), 77,
78, 80, 92, 101, 223, 286, 364;
coverage of youth transfer program,
342–345; operation of, 28–29, 37,
44, 50–52, 53, 59, 60–61, 71, 84, 102

People's Liberation Army, 49–50, 216, 218, 240, 264, 282, 344, 351
People's Literature (Jenmin Wen-hsueh), 281–282, 285–299; new themes in, 298–310
Perception of message, 20–21, 408–409
Picture storybooks, 237–254; function of, 238–241; major themes in, 243–251; political socialization of, 244, 251–254
Poetry (Shih K'an) magazine, 3, 281, 286
Political culture, 159, 167–170, 172, 174–176, 411; consensus and conflict in, 169–170, 172, 174–175; elitism in, 170–172, 176
Post offices, 77, 88–94, 111
Propaganda, Department of, 28, 41, 44–45, 51, 59, 60, 67, 79
Puritan ethic, misconception of, 267–270
Pye, Lucian W., 153–178, 411

Radicals. *See* Gang of Four and Shanghai group
Radio, 59, 64, 154, 223; development of, 38, 66–68, 111, 387; peasant owners of, 365–366, 368, 370–371, 374, 375
Red Army, 32, 88, 114. *See also* People's Liberation Army
Red China (Hung-se Chung-hua), 31
Red Flag (Hung Ch'i), 44, 50–51, 223, 286
Red Guards, 51, 104, 163, 220, 284, 410–411
Red Star (Hung Hsin), 31
Reference Information (Ts'an-k'ao Hsiao-hsi), 46–47, 62–63, 73n, 80, 92, 105–106n, 109n
Reference Material (Ts'an-k'ao Tzu-liao), 80
Returned educated youths *(hui-hsiang chih-shih ch'ing-nien)*, 341
Ridley, Charles P., 255n
Romance of the Three Kingdoms, 50
Rustication movement. *See* Youth transfer movement *(shang-shan hsia-hsiang)*

Sand Pebbles, The, 270
San kang relations, 12, 24n
San-yuan-li, 249
Sapir, Edward, 21n

Schramm, Wilbur, 409
Schwartz, Henry G., 106n
Sent-down educated youths *(hsia-hsiang chih-shih ch'ing nien),* 341
Shanghai group, 172, 179–204 passim, 285–286. *See also* Gang of Four
Shanghai Publishing House, 290
Shang-shan hsia-hsiang. See Youth transfer program
Shih Huang Ti, Emperor, 17
Short stories, 280–304; changing values in, 303; enduring values in, 301–302; ideological struggle in, 285–286; revolutionary themes of, 282–285. *See also People's Literature*
Shue, Vivienne, 305–340, 410
Skinner, B. F., 120, 124n
Skinner, William G., 22–23n
Small groups *(hsiao-tsu),* 20–21, 85, 124n, 130, 323, 386–388, 400, 410; function of, 113–114; effective communication of, 114–116, 123; ineffective communication of, 116–123
Snow, Edgar, 212
Social relations, 6, 7, 8, 178n; affect concept in, 8, 9, 10, 259–260, 274–278, 413, 414; psychosocial homeostasis, 412–415, 417n; role concept in, 8, 10, 259–260, 274–278, 413, 414; *san kang* in, 12, 24n; self in, 4–6, 19; *t'ung* concept in, 9–11, 12, 22n. *See also* Kinship system
Solomon, Richard H., 255n
Song of the Dragon River (Lung Chiang Sung), 247, 250, 407
Source credibility, 410
Southern Daily, 79, 80, 86, 88, 89–90, 364
Soviet Union, 114
Spencer, Herbert, 3
Study groups *(hsüeh-hsi),* 27, 49, 210–211, 372, 374, 375, 387–388; development of, 33, 42–44, 366. *See also* Small groups
Study (Hsüeh Hsi) magazine, 43–44
Study Primer (Hsüeh Hsi Ch'u-chi-pan), 43
Sung Chiang, 159, 192, 195, 196, 197, 198, 202, 241
Sun Yat-sen, 333, 334
Superstition, 137, 405

Tachai workpoint system, 367–374, 375, 381, 382n, 398

Takung Report (Takung Pao), 70
Ta Li commune, 130
T'an Chen-lin, 347
Taoism, 419
Tatzupao. See Big character posters
Teacher's Report, 85, 86
Technological development, 7–8, 10,
    11, 13–14, 23n, 111, 124, 386;
    agritechnology, 134, 137–138,
    143–145, 147n, 147–148n, 412
Television, 59, 68–69, 74n, 223,
    386–387, 424–426
Teng Hsiao-p'ing, 59, 66, 159,
    160–161, 224–225, 226, 285,
    289–290, 291, 343–344, 402; media
    campaigns, role in, 180, 181, 191,
    192, 194, 196, 197, 198, 200, 201,
    202, 286
Thought reform *(ssu hsiang kai tsao)*,
    13, 390
Three-Anti *(San-fan)* campaign, 15, 18
Three breakthroughs literary principle
    (san-tu-ch'u), 296
Three-in-one groups *(san-chieh-ho)*
    140–141, 142, 290
Three-in-one leadership principle,
    289–290
Tien Lu brigade, 129–130
Ti Pao, 78
Transfer downward movement *(hsia-
    fang)*, 271, 341
*Ts'an k'ao Hsiao-hsi. See Reference
    Information*
*Ts'an k'ao Tzu-liao. See Reference
    Material*
Tso Yeh, 83, 84
Tuchman, Barbara, 267, 269
Tung Chung-shu, 17, 24n
T'ung relations 9–11, 12, 22n, 401, 402

Uhalley, Stephen, 417n
Union Research Institute, 78, 105n

Wang Chieh, 240
Wang Hung-wen, 52–53, 402
War bulletin *(chan pao)*, 63
Washing the Party *(hsi-tang)*, 30. *See
    also* Ideological remolding
Water Margin, 159, 238, 241, 286
Water Margin campaign, 180,
    191–202, 203, 226, 276
*We Are Chairman Mao's Red Guards
    (Wo-men shih Mao Chu-hsi ti
    Hung-weiping)*, 284
Weber, Max, 261
Wen Hui Report (Wen Hui Pao), 64,
    83, 84, 103–104
White, Lynn, T., III, 76–112, 410
Whyte, Martin King, 23–24n, 113–124,
    124n, 399–400, 404, 409, 410
Wilder, George, 158
Winckler, Edwin A., 22–23n
Wired broadcasts, 67, 365, 372, 387
Women, changing status of, 249, 250,
    255n, 262–265, 274, 377, 378, 379,
    382n, 400–401, 420–421
Wu, Emperor, 17
Wu Han, 158

Yang Chu, 17
Yao Pang-tse, 53
Yao Wen-yüan, 41, 45–46, 53, 158,
    183–184, 191, 195, 229
Yin-Yang school, 17, 24n, 419–420
Youth transfer program *(shang-shan
    hsia-hsiang)*, 18, 341–360, 366–367,
    409, 410; function of, 341–345;
    urban-rural inequalities, 347–348;
    value change in, 345–349, 350–361
Yüan Dynasty, 16, 192
Yu, Frederick T. C., 27–56, 54–55n,
    408
Yu Hui-yung, 181, 285

Zaltman, Gerald, 146n

⛩ Production Notes

This book was designed by Roger J. Eggers and typeset on the Unified Composing System by the design and production staff of The University Press of Hawaii.

The text typeface is Compugraphic Times Roman and the display typeface is Univers.

Offset presswork and binding were done by Halliday Lithograph. Text paper is Glatfelter P & S Offset, basis 55.